COMMON LISP

THE LANGUAGE

Would it be wonderful if, under the pressure of all these difficulties, the Convention should have been forced into some deviations from that artificial structure and regular symmetry which an abstract view of the subject might lead an ingenious theorist to bestow on a constitution planned in his closet or in his imagination?

—*James Madison, The Federalist No. 37, January 11, 1788*

COMMON LISP

THE LANGUAGE

GUY L. STEELE JR.
Thinking Machines Corporation

with contributions by

SCOTT E. FAHLMAN
Carnegie-Mellon University

RICHARD P. GABRIEL
Stanford University
Lawrence Livermore National Laboratory

DAVID A. MOON
Symbolics, Inc.

DANIEL L. WEINREB
Symbolics, Inc.

Digital Press

9 8 7 6 5

Printed in the United States of America.

Designed by David Ford. Automatically typeset from magnetic tape by Waldman Graphics, Pennsauken, New Jersey. Printed and bound by Halliday Lithographers, Hanover, Massachusetts.

Order number EY-00031-DP

Library of Congress Cataloging in Publication Data

Steele, Guy.
    Common LISP: The Language.

    Includes bibliographical references and index.
    1. LISP (Computer program language) I. Title.
II. Title: Common LISP: The Language.
QA76.73.L23S73 1984   001.64'24   84-7681
ISBN 0-932376-41-X

Contents

Acknowledgments

COMMON LISP was designed by a diverse group of people affiliated with many institutions. Contributors to the design and implementation of COMMON LISP and to the polishing of this manual are hereby gratefully acknowledged:

Paul Anagnostopoulos	Digital Equipment Corporation
Dan Aronson	Carnegie-Mellon University
Alan Bawden	Massachusetts Institute of Technology
Eric Benson	University of Utah, Stanford University, and Symbolics, Incorporated
Jon Bentley	Carnegie-Mellon University and Bell Laboratories
Jerry Boetje	Digital Equipment Corporation
Gary Brooks	Texas Instruments
Rodney A. Brooks	Stanford University
Gary L. Brown	Digital Equipment Corporation
Richard L. Bryan	Symbolics, Incorporated
Glenn S. Burke	Massachusetts Institute of Technology
Howard I. Cannon	Symbolics, Incorporated
George J. Carrette	Massachusetts Institute of Technology
Robert Cassels	Symbolics, Incorporated
Monica Cellio	Carnegie-Mellon University
David Dill	Carnegie-Mellon University
Scott E. Fahlman	Carnegie-Mellon University
Richard J. Fateman	University of California, Berkeley
Neal Feinberg	Carnegie-Mellon University
Ron Fischer	Rutgers University
John Foderaro	University of California, Berkeley
Steve Ford	Texas Instruments

Richard P. Gabriel	Stanford University and Lawrence Livermore National Laboratory
Joseph Ginder	Carnegie-Mellon University and Perq Systems Corp.
Bernard S. Greenberg	Symbolics, Incorporated
Richard Greenblatt	Lisp Machines Incorporated (LMI)
Martin L. Griss	University of Utah and Hewlett-Packard Incorporated
Steven Handerson	Carnegie-Mellon University
Charles L. Hedrick	Rutgers University
Gail Kaiser	Carnegie-Mellon University
Earl A. Killian	Lawrence Livermore National Laboratory
Steve Krueger	Texas Instruments
John L. Kulp	Symbolics, Incorporated
Jim Large	Carnegie-Mellon University
Rob Maclachlan	Carnegie-Mellon University
William Maddox	Carnegie-Mellon University
Larry M. Masinter	Xerox Corporation, Palo Alto Research Center
John McCarthy	Stanford University
Michael E. McMahon	Symbolics, Incorporated
Brian Milnes	Carnegie-Mellon University
David A. Moon	Symbolics, Incorporated
Beryl Morrison	Digital Equipment Corporation
Don Morrison	University of Utah
Dan Pierson	Digital Equipment Corporation
Kent M. Pitman	Massachusetts Institute of Technology
Jonathan Rees	Yale University
Walter van Roggen	Digital Equipment Corporation
Susan Rosenbaum	Texas Instruments
William L. Scherlis	Carnegie-Mellon University
Lee Schumacher	Carnegie-Mellon University
Richard M. Stallman	Massachusetts Institute of Technology
Barbara K. Steele	Carnegie-Mellon University
Guy L. Steele Jr.	Carnegie-Mellon University and Tartan Laboratories Incorporated
Peter Szolovits	Massachusetts Institute of Technology
William vanMelle	Xerox Corporation, Palo Alto Research Center
Ellen Waldrum	Texas Instruments
Allan C. Wechsler	Symbolics, Incorporated
Daniel L. Weinreb	Symbolics, Incorporated
Jon L. White	Xerox Corporation, Palo Alto Research Center
Skef Wholey	Carnegie-Mellon University

| Richard Zippel | Massachusetts Institute of Technology |
| Leonard Zubkoff | Carnegie-Mellon University and Tartan Laboratories Incorporated |

Some contributions were relatively small; others involved enormous expenditures of effort and great dedication. A few of the contributors served more as worthy adversaries than as benefactors (and do not necessarily endorse the final design reported here), but their pointed criticisms were just as important to the polishing of COMMON LISP as all the positively phrased suggestions. All of the people named above were helpful in one way or another, and I am grateful for the interest and spirit of cooperation that allowed most decisions to be made by consensus after due discussion.

Considerable encouragement and moral support were also provided by:

Norma Abel	Digital Equipment Corporation
Roger Bate	Texas Instruments
Harvey Cragon	Texas Instruments
Dennis Duncan	Digital Equipment Corporation
Sam Fuller	Digital Equipment Corporation
A. Nico Habermann	Carnegie-Mellon University
Berthold K. P. Horn	Massachusetts Institute of Technology
Gene Kromer	Texas Instruments
Gene Matthews	Texas Instruments
Allan Newell	Carnegie-Mellon University
Dana Scott	Carnegie-Mellon University
Harry Tennant	Texas Instruments
Patrick H. Winston	Massachusetts Institute of Technology
Lowell Wood	Lawrence Livermore National Laboratory
William A. Wulf	Carnegie-Mellon University and Tartan Laboratories Incorporated

I am very grateful to each of them.

Jan Zubkoff of Carnegie-Mellon University provided a great deal of organization, secretarial support, and unfailing good cheer in the face of adversity.

The development of COMMON LISP would most probably not have been possible without the electronic message system provided by the ARPANET. Design decisions were made on several hundred distinct points, for the most part by consensus, and by simple majority vote when necessary. Except for two one-day face-to-face meetings, all of the language design and discussion was done through the ARPANET message system, which permitted effortless dissemination of messages to dozens of people, and several interchanges per day. The message system also provided automatic archiving of the entire discussion, which has proved invaluable in the preparation of this reference manual. Over the course of thirty months, approximately 3000 messages were sent (an average of three per day), ranging in length from one line to twenty pages. Assuming 5000 characters per printed page of text, the entire discussion totaled about 1100 pages. It would have been substantially more difficult to have conducted this discussion by any other means, and would have required much more time.

The ideas in COMMON LISP have come from many sources and been polished by much discussion. I am responsible for the form of this manual, and for any errors or inconsistencies that may remain; but the credit for the design and support of COMMON LISP lies with the individuals named above, each of whom has made significant contributions.

The organization and content of this manual were inspired in large part by the *MacLISP Reference Manual* by David A. Moon and others[12], and by the *LISP Machine Manual* (fourth edition) by Daniel Weinreb and David Moon[21], which in turn acknowledges the efforts of Richard Stallman, Mike McMahon, Alan Bawden, Glenn Burke, and "many people too numerous to list."

I thank Phyllis Keenan, Chase Duffy, Virginia Anderson, John Osborn, and Jonathan Baker of Digital Press for their help in preparing this book for publication. Jane Blake did an admirable job of copy-editing. James Gibson and Katherine Downs of Waldman Graphics were most cooperative in typesetting this book from my on-line manuscript files.

I am grateful to Carnegie-Mellon University and to Tartan Laboratories Incorporated for supporting me in the writing of this manual over the last three years.

Part of the work on this book was done in conjunction with the Carnegie-Mellon University Spice Project, an effort to construct an advanced scientific software development environment for personal computers. The Spice Project is supported by the Defense Advanced Research Projects Agency, Department of Defense, ARPA Order 3597, monitored by the Air Force Avionics Laboratory under contract F33615-78-C-1551. The views and conclusions contained in this book are those of the author and should not be interpreted as representing the official policies, either expressed or implied, of the Defense Advanced Research Projects Agency or the U.S. Government.

Most of the writing of this book took place between midnight and 5 A.M. I am grateful to Barbara, Julia, and Peter for putting up with it, and for their love.

Guy L. Steele Jr.
Pittsburgh, Pennsylvania
March 1984

1

Introduction

COMMON LISP is a new dialect of LISP, a successor to MACLISP [12, 15], influenced strongly by ZETALISP [21, 13] and also to some extent by SCHEME [18] and INTERLISP [20].

1.1. Purpose

COMMON LISP is intended to meet these goals:

Commonality

COMMON LISP originated in an attempt to focus the work of several implementation groups, each of which was constructing successor implementations of MACLISP for different computers. These implementations had begun to diverge because of the differences in the implementation environments: microcoded personal computers (ZETALISP, SPICE LISP), commercial timeshared computers (NIL), and supercomputers (S-1 LISP). While the differences among the several implementation environments of necessity will continue to force certain incompatibilities among the implementations, COMMON LISP serves as a common dialect to which each implementation makes any necessary extensions.

Portability

COMMON LISP intentionally excludes features that cannot be implemented easily on a broad class of machines. On the one hand, features that are difficult or expensive to implement on hardware without special microcode are avoided or provided in a more abstract and efficiently implementable form. (Examples of this are the invisible forwarding pointers and locatives of ZETALISP. Some of the problems that they solve are addressed in different ways in COMMON LISP.) On the other hand, features that are useful only on certain "ordinary" or "commercial" processors are avoided or made optional. (An example of this is the type declaration facility, which is useful in some implementations and completely ignored in others. Type declarations are completely optional and for correct programs affect only efficiency, not semantics.) COMMON LISP is designed to make it easy to write programs that depend as little as possible on machine-specific characteristics, such as word length, while allowing some variety of implementation techniques.

Consistency

Most LISP implementations are internally inconsistent in that by default the interpreter and compiler may assign different semantics to correct programs. This semantic difference stems primarily from the fact that the interpreter assumes all variables to be dynamically scoped, whereas the compiler assumes all variables to be local unless explicitly directed otherwise. This difference has been the usual practice in LISP for the sake of convenience and efficiency, but can lead to very subtle bugs. The definition of COMMON LISP avoids such anomalies by explicitly requiring the interpreter and compiler to impose identical semantics on correct programs so far as possible.

Expressiveness

COMMON LISP culls what experience has shown to be the most useful and understandable constructs from not only MACLISP, but also INTERLISP, other LISP dialects, and other programming languages. Constructs judged to be awkward or less useful have been excluded. (An example is the store construct of MACLISP.)

Compatibility

Unless there is a good reason to the contrary, COMMON LISP strives to be compatible with ZETALISP, MACLISP, and INTERLISP, roughly in that order.

Efficiency

COMMON LISP has a number of features designed to facilitate the production of high-quality compiled code in those implementations whose developers care to invest effort in an optimizing compiler. One implementation of COMMON LISP, namely S-1 LISP, already has a compiler that produces code for numerical computations that is competitive in execution speed with that produced by a FORTRAN compiler [3]. The S-1 LISP compiler extends the work done in MACLISP to produce extremely efficient numerical code [7].

Power

COMMON LISP is a descendant of MACLISP, which has traditionally placed emphasis on providing system-building tools. Such tools may in turn be used to build the user-level packages such as INTERLISP provides; these packages are not, however, part of the COMMON LISP core specification. It is expected such packages will be built on top of the COMMON LISP core.

Stability

It is intended that COMMON LISP will change only slowly and with due deliberation. The various dialects that are supersets of COMMON LISP may serve as laboratories within which to test language extensions, but such extensions will be added to COMMON LISP only after careful examination and experimentation.

The goals of COMMON LISP are thus very close to those of STANDARD LISP [11] and PORTABLE STANDARD LISP [16]. COMMON LISP differs from STANDARD LISP primarily in incorporating more features, including a richer and more complicated set of data types and more complex control structures.

This book is intended to be a language specification rather than an implementation specification (although implementation notes are scattered throughout the text). It defines a set of standard language concepts and constructs that may be used for communication of data structures and algorithms in the COMMON LISP dialect. This set of concepts and constructs is sometimes referred to as the "core COMMON LISP language" because it contains conceptually necessary or important features. It is not necessarily implementationally minimal. While many features could be defined in terms of others by writing LISP code, and indeed may be implemented that way, it was felt that these features should be conceptually primitive so that there might be agreement among all users as to their usage. (For example, bignums and rational numbers could be implemented as LISP code given operations on fixnums. However, it is important to the conceptual integrity of the language that they be regarded by the user as primitive, and they are useful enough to warrant a standard definition.)

For the most part, this book defines a programming language, not a programming environment. A few interfaces are defined for invoking such standard programming tools as a compiler, an editor, a program trace facility, and a debugger, but very little is said about their nature or operation. It is expected that one or more extensive programming environments will be built using COMMON LISP as a foundation, and will be documented separately.

1.2. Notational Conventions

A number of special notational conventions are used throughout this book.

1.2.1. Decimal Numbers

All numbers in this book are in decimal notation unless there is an explicit indication to the contrary. (Decimal notation is normally taken for granted, of course. Unfortunately, for certain other dialects of LISP, MACLISP in particular, the default notation for numbers is octal (base 8) rather than decimal, and so the use of decimal notation for describing COMMON LISP is, taken in its historical context, a bit unusual!)

1.2.2. Nil, False, and the Empty List

In COMMON LISP, as in most LISP dialects, the symbol nil is used to represent both the empty list and the "false" value for Boolean tests. An empty list may, of course, also be written (); this normally denotes the same object as nil. (It is possible, by extremely perverse manipulation of the package system, to cause the sequence of letters nil to be recognized not as the symbol that represents the empty list but as another symbol with the same name. This obscure possibility will be ignored in this manual.) These two notations may be used interchangeably as far as the LISP system is concerned. However, as a matter of style, this manual uses the notation () when it is desirable to emphasize the use of an empty list, and uses the notation nil when it is desirable to emphasize the use of the Boolean "false." The notation 'nil (note the explicit quotation mark) is used to emphasize the use of a symbol. For example:

```
(defun three () 3)          ;Emphasize empty parameter list.
(append '() '()) ⇒ ()       ;Emphasize use of empty lists
(not nil) ⇒ t               ;Emphasize use as Boolean "false"
(get 'nil 'color)           ;Emphasize use as a symbol
```

Any data object other than nil is construed to be Boolean "not false," that is, "true." The symbol t is conventionally used to mean "true" when no other value is more appropriate. When a function is said to "return *false*" or to "be *false*" in some circumstance, this means that it returns nil. However, when a function is said to "return *true*" or to "be *true*" in some circumstance, this means that it returns some value other than nil, but not necessarily t.

1.2.3. Evaluation, Expansion, and Equivalence

Execution of code in LISP is called *evaluation* because executing a piece of code normally results in a data object called the *value* produced by the code. The symbol ⇒ is used in examples to indicate evaluation. For example,

```
(+ 4 5) ⇒ 9
```

means "the result of evaluating the code `(+ 4 5)` is (or would be, or would have been) `9`."

The symbol → is used in examples to indicate macro expansion. For example,

```
(push x v) → (setf v (cons x v))
```

means "the result of expanding the macro-call form `(push x v)` is `(setf v (cons x v))`." This implies that the two pieces of code do the same thing; the second piece of code is the definition of what the first does.

The symbol ≡ is used in examples to indicate code equivalence. For example,

```
(gcd x (gcd y z)) ≡ (gcd (gcd x y) z)
```

means "the value and effects of evaluating the form `(gcd x (gcd y z))` are always the same as the value and effects of `(gcd (gcd x y) z)` for any values of the variables x, y, and z." This implies that the two pieces of code do the same thing; however, neither directly defines the other in the way macro expansion does.

1.2.4. Errors

When this manual specifies that it "is an error" for some situation to occur, this means that:

- No valid COMMON LISP program should cause this situation to occur.
- If this situation occurs, the effects and results are completely undefined as far as adherence to the COMMON LISP specification is concerned.
- No COMMON LISP implementation is required to detect such an error. Of course, implementors are encouraged to provide for detection of such errors wherever reasonable.

This is not to say that some particular implementation might not define the effects and results for such a situation; the point is that no program conforming to the COMMON LISP specification may correctly depend on such effects or results.

On the other hand, if it is specified in this manual that in some situation "an error is *signalled*," this means that:

- If this situation occurs, an error will be signalled (see `error` and `cerror`).
- Valid COMMON LISP programs may rely on the fact that an error will be signalled.
- Every COMMON LISP implementation is required to detect such an error.

Table 1-1: Sample Function Description

sample-function *arg1* *arg2* &optional *arg3* *arg4* [*Function*]

The function sample-function adds together *arg1* and *arg2*, and then multiplies the result by *arg3*. If *arg3* is not provided or is nil, the multiplication isn't done. sample-function then returns a list whose first element is this result and whose second element is *arg4* (which defaults to the symbol foo). For example:

```
(sample-function 3 4) ⇒ (7 foo)
(sample-function 1 2 2 'bar) ⇒ (6 bar)
```

In general, (sample-function *x* *y*) ≡ (list (+ *x* *y*) 'foo).

Table 1-2: Sample Variable Description

sample-variable [*Variable*]

The variable *sample-variable* specifies how many times the special form sample-special-form should iterate. The value should always be a non-negative integer or nil (which means iterate indefinitely many times). The initial value is 0.

Table 1-3: Sample Constant Description

sample-constant [*Constant*]

The named constant sample-constant has as its value the height of the terminal screen in furlongs times the base-2 logarithm of the implementation's total disk capacity in bytes, as a floating-point number.

In places where it is stated that so-and-so "must" or "must not" or "may not" be the case, then it "is an error" if the stated requirement is not met. For example, if an argument "must be a symbol," then it "is an error" if the argument is not a symbol. In all cases where an error is to be *signalled*, the word "signalled" is always used explicitly in this manual.

1.2.5. Descriptions of Functions and Other Entities

Functions, variables, named constants, special forms, and macros are described using a distinctive typographical format. Definition 1-1 illustrates the manner in which COMMON LISP functions are documented. The first line specifies the name of the function, the manner in which it accepts arguments, and the fact that it is a function. If the function takes many arguments, then the names of the arguments

Table 1-4: Sample Special Form Description

sample-special-form [*name*] ({*var*}*) {*form*}$^+$ [*Special form*]

This evaluates each form in sequence as an implicit progn, and does this as many times as specified by the global variable ∗sample-variable∗. Each variable *var* is bound and initialized to 43 before the first iteration, and unbound after the last iteration. The name *name*, if supplied, may be used in a return-from form to exit from the loop prematurely. If the loop ends normally, sample-special-form returns nil. For example:

```
(setq *sample-variable* 3)
(sample-special-form () form1 form2)
```

This evaluates *form1*, *form2*, *form1*, *form2*, *form1*, *form2* in that order.

Table 1-5: Sample Macro Description

sample-macro *var* {*tag* | *statement*}*   [*Macro*]

This evaluates the statements as a prog body, with the variable *var* bound to 43.

```
(sample-macro x (return (+ x x))) ⇒ 86
(sample-macro var . body) → (prog ((var 43)) . body)
```

---

may spill across two or three lines. The paragraphs following this standard header explain the definition and uses of the function and often present examples or related functions.

Sometimes two or more related functions are explained in a single combined description. In this situation the headers for all the functions appear together, followed by the combined description.

In general, actual code (including actual names of functions) appears in this typeface: (cons a b). Names that stand for pieces of code (metavariables) are written in *italics*. In a function description, the names of the parameters appear in italics for expository purposes. The word &optional in the list of parameters indicates that all arguments past that point are optional; the default values for the parameters are described in the text. Parameter lists may also contain &rest, indicating that an indefinite number of arguments may appear, or &key, indicating that keyword arguments are accepted. (The &optional/&rest/&key syntax is actually used in COMMON LISP function definitions for these purposes.)

Definition 1-2 illustrates the manner in which a global variable is documented. The first line specifies the name of the variable and the fact that it is a variable.

Purely as a matter of convention, all global variables used by COMMON LISP have names beginning and ending with an asterisk.

Definition 1-3 illustrates the manner in which a named constant is documented. The first line specifies the name of the constant and the fact that it is a constant. (A constant is just like a global variable, except that it is an error ever to alter its value or to bind it to a new value.)

Definitions 1-4 and 1-5 illustrate the documentation of special forms and macros, which are closely related in purpose. These are very different from functions. Functions are called according to a single, specific, consistent syntax; the &optional/&rest/&key syntax specifies how the function uses its arguments internally, but does not affect the syntax of a call. In contrast, each special form or macro can have its own idiosyncratic syntax. It is by special forms and macros that the syntax of COMMON LISP is defined and extended.

In the description of a special form or macro, an italicized word names a corresponding part of the form that invokes the special form or macro. Parentheses stand for themselves, and should be written as such when invoking the special form or macro. Brackets, braces, stars, plus signs, and vertical bars are metasyntactic marks. Brackets, [and], indicate that what they enclose is optional (may appear zero times or one time in that place); the square brackets should not be written in code. Braces, { and }, simply parenthesize what they enclose, but may be followed by a star, *, or a plus sign, +; a star indicates that what the braces enclose may appear any number of times (including zero, that is, not at all), whereas a plus sign indicates that what the braces enclose may appear any non-zero number of times (that is, must appear at least once). Within braces or brackets, a vertical bar, |, separates mutually exclusive choices. In summary, the notation $\{x\}*$ means zero or more occurrences of x, the notation $\{x\}^+$ means one or more occurrences of x, and the notation $[x]$ means zero or one occurrence of x. These notations are also used for syntactic descriptions expressed as BNF-like productions, as in Table 22-2.

In the last example in Definition 1-5, notice the use of dot notation. The dot appearing in the expression (sample-macro *var* . *body*) means that the name *body* stands for a list of forms, not just a single form, at the end of a list. This notation is often used in examples.

1.2.6. The Lisp Reader

The term "LISP reader" refers not to you, the reader of this manual, nor to some person reading LISP code, but specifically to a LISP procedure, namely the function read, that reads characters from an input stream and interprets them by parsing as representations of LISP objects.

1.2.7. Overview of Syntax

Certain characters are used in special ways in the syntax of COMMON LISP. The complete syntax is explained in detail in chapter 22, but a quick summary here may be useful:

(A left parenthesis begins a list of items. The list may contain any number of items, including zero. Lists may be nested. For example, `(cons (car x) (cdr y))` is a list of three things, of which the last two are themselves lists.

)   A right parenthesis ends a list of items.

'   An acute accent (also called single quote or apostrophe) followed by an expression *form* is an abbreviation for `(quote form)`. Thus `'foo` means `(quote foo)` and `'(cons 'a 'b)` means `(quote (cons (quote a) (quote b)))`.

;   Semicolon is the comment character. It and all characters up to the end of the line are discarded.

"   Double quotes surround character strings: `"This is a thirty-nine character string."`

\   Backslash is an escape character. It causes the next character to be treated as a letter rather than for its usual syntactic purpose. For example, `A\( B` denotes a symbol whose name is consists of the three characters `A`, `(`, and `B`. Similarly, `"\""` denotes a character string containing one character, a double quote, because the first and third double quotes serve to delimit the string, and the second double quote serves as the contents of the string. The backslash causes the second double quote to be taken literally, and prevents it from being interpreted as the terminating delimiter of the string.

| Vertical bars are used in pairs to surround the name (or part of the name) of a symbol that has many special characters in it. It is roughly equivalent to putting a backslash in front of every character so surrounded. For example, `|A(B)|`, `A|(|B|)|`, and `A\(B\)` all mean the symbol whose name consists of the four characters `A`, `(`, `B`, and `)`.

The number sign signals the beginning of a complicated syntactic structure. The next character designates the precise syntax to follow. For example, `#o105` means 105_8 (105 in octal notation); `#x105` means 105_{16} (105 in hexadecimal notation); `#b1011` means 1011_2 (1011 in binary notation); `#\L` denotes a character object for the character `L`; and `#(a b c)` denotes a vector of three elements a, b, and c. A particularly important case is that `#'fn` means `(function fn)`, in a manner analogous to `'form` meaning `(quote form)`.

`   Grave accent (''backquote'') signals that the next expression is a template that may contain commas. The backquote syntax represents a program that will construct a data structure according to the template.

Commas are used within the backquote syntax.

Colon is used to indicate which package a symbol belongs to. For example, `network:reset` denotes the symbol named `reset` in the package named `network`. A leading colon indicates a *keyword*, a symbol that always evaluates to itself. The colon character is not actually part of the print name of the symbol. This is all explained in chapter 11; until you read that, just keep in mind that a symbol notated with a leading colon is in effect a constant that evaluates to itself.

Brackets, braces, question mark, and exclamation point (that is, [,], {, }, ?, and !) are not used for any purpose in standard COMMON LISP syntax. These characters are explicitly reserved to the user, primarily for use as *macro characters* for user-defined lexical syntax extensions. See section 22.1.3.

All code in this manual is written using lowercase letters. COMMON LISP is generally insensitive to the case in which code is written. Internally, names of symbols are ordinarily converted to and stored in uppercase form. There are ways to force case conversion on output if desired; see *print-case*. In this manual, wherever an interactive exchange between a user and the LISP system is shown, the input is exhibited with lowercase letters and the output with uppercase letters.

2

Data Types

COMMON LISP provides a variety of types of data objects. It is important to note that in LISP it is data objects that are typed, not variables. Any variable can have any LISP object as its value. (It is possible to make an explicit declaration that a variable will in fact take on one of only a limited set of values. However, such a declaration may always be omitted, and the program will still run correctly. Such a declaration merely constitutes advice from the user that may be useful in gaining efficiency. See `declare`.)

In COMMON LISP, a data type is a (possibly infinite) set of LISP objects. Many LISP objects belong to more than one such set, and so it doesn't always make sense to ask what *the* type of an object is; instead, one usually asks only whether an object belongs to a given type. The predicate `typep` may be used to ask whether an object belongs to a given type, and the function `type-of` returns *a* type to which a given object belongs.

The data types defined in COMMON LISP are arranged into a hierarchy (actually a partial order) defined by the subset relationship. Certain sets of objects, such as the set of numbers or the set of strings, are interesting enough to deserve labels. Symbols are used for most such labels (here, and throughout this book, the word "symbol" refers to atomic symbols, one kind of LISP object, elsewhere known as literal atoms). See chapter 4 for a complete description of type specifiers.

The set of all objects is specified by the symbol `t`. The empty data type, which contains no objects, is denoted by `nil`. A type called `common` encompasses all the data objects required by the COMMON LISP language. A COMMON LISP implementation is free to provide other data types that are not subtypes of `common`.

The following categories of COMMON LISP objects are of particular interest: numbers, characters, symbols, lists, arrays, structures, and functions. There are others as well. Some of these categories have many subdivisions. There are also standard types defined to be the union of two or more of these categories. The categories listed above, while they are data types, are neither more nor less "real" than other data types; they simply constitute a particularly useful slice across the type hierarchy for expository purposes.

Here are brief descriptions of various COMMON LISP data types. The remaining sections of this chapter go into more detail, and also describe notations for objects of each type. Descriptions of LISP functions that operate on data objects of each type appear in later chapters.

- *Numbers* are provided in various forms and representations. COMMON LISP provides a true integer data type: any integer, positive or negative, has in principle a representation as a COMMON LISP data object, subject only to total memory limitations (rather than machine word width). A true rational data type is provided: the quotient of two integers, if not an integer, is a ratio. Floating-point numbers of various ranges and precisions are also provided, as well as Cartesian complex numbers.

- *Characters* represent printed glyphs such as letters or text formatting operations. Strings are one-dimensional arrays of characters. COMMON LISP provides for a rich character set, including ways to represent characters of various type styles.

- *Symbols* (sometimes called *atomic symbols* for emphasis or clarity) are named data objects. LISP provides machinery for locating a symbol object, given its name (in the form of a string). Symbols have *property lists*, which in effect allow symbols to be treated as record structures with an extensible set of named components, each of which may be any LISP object. Symbols also serve to name functions and variables within programs.

- *Lists* are sequences represented in the form of linked cells called *conses*. There is a special object (the symbol `nil`) that is the empty list. All other lists are built recursively by adding a new element to the front of an existing list. This is done by creating a new *cons*, which is an object having two components called the *car* and the *cdr*. The *car* may hold anything, and the *cdr* is made to point to the previously existing list. (Conses may actually be used completely generally as two-element record structures, but their most important use is to represent lists.)

- *Arrays* are dimensioned collections of objects. An array can have any non-negative number of dimensions and is indexed by a sequence of integers. A general array can have any LISP object as a component; other types of arrays are specialized for efficiency and can hold only certain types of LISP objects. It is possible for two arrays, possibly with differing dimension information, to share the same set of elements (such that modifying one array modifies the other also) by causing one to be *displaced* to the other. One-dimensional arrays of any kind are called *vectors*. One-dimensional arrays of characters are called *strings*. One-dimensional arrays of bits (that is, of integers whose values are 0 or 1) are called *bit-vectors*.

- *Hash tables* provide an efficient way of mapping any LISP object (a *key*) to an associated object.

- *Readtables* are used to control the built-in expression parser `read`.

- *Packages* are collections of symbols that serve as name spaces. The parser recognizes symbols by looking up character sequences in the current package.

- *Pathnames* represent names of files in a fairly implementation-independent manner. They are used to interface to the external file system.

- *Streams* represent sources or sinks of data, typically characters or bytes. They are used to perform I/O, as well as for internal purposes such as parsing strings.

- *Random-states* are data structures used to encapsulate the state of the built-in random-number generator.

- *Structures* are user-defined record structures, objects that have named components. The `defstruct` facility is used to define new structure types. Some COMMON LISP implementations may choose to implement certain system-supplied data types, such as *bignums*, *readtables*, *streams*, *hash tables*, and *pathnames*, as structures, but this fact will be invisible to the user.

- *Functions* are objects that can be invoked as procedures; these may take arguments and return values. (All LISP procedures can be construed to return values and therefore every procedure is a function.) Such objects include *compiled-functions* (compiled code objects). Some functions are represented as a list whose *car* is a particular symbol such as `lambda`. Symbols may also be used as functions.

These categories are not always mutually exclusive. The required relationships among the various data types are explained in more detail in section 2.15.

2.1. Numbers

Several kinds of numbers are defined in COMMON LISP. They are divided into *integers*; *ratios*; *floating-point numbers*, with names provided for up to four different floating-point representations; and *complex numbers*.

2.1.1. Integers

The `integer` data type is intended to represent mathematical integers. Unlike most programming languages, COMMON LISP in principle imposes no limit on the magnitude of an integer; storage is automatically allocated as necessary to represent large integers.

In every COMMON LISP implementation there is a range of integers that are represented more efficiently than others; each such integer is called a *fixnum*, and an integer that is not a fixnum is called a *bignum*. COMMON LISP is designed to hide this distinction as much as possible; the distinction between fixnums and bignums is visible to the user in only a few places where the efficiency of representation is important. Exactly which integers are fixnums is implementation-dependent; typically they will be those integers in the range -2^n to $2^n - 1$, inclusive, for some n not less than 15. See `most-positive-fixnum` and `most-negative-fixnum`.

Integers are ordinarily written in decimal notation, as a sequence of decimal digits, optionally preceded by a sign and optionally followed by a decimal point. For example:

0	;Zero
-0	;This *always* means the same as 0
+6	;The first perfect number
28	;The second perfect number
1024.	;Two to the tenth power
-1	;$e^{\pi i}$
15511210043330985984000000.	;25 factorial (25!), probably a bignum

---

Compatibility note: MACLISP and ZETALISP normally assume that integers are written in octal (radix-8) notation unless a decimal point is present. INTERLISP assumes integers are written in decimal notation and uses a trailing Q to indicate octal radix; however, a decimal point, even in trailing position, *always* indicates a floating-point number. This is of course consistent with FORTRAN. ADA does not permit trailing decimal points, but instead requires them to be embedded. In COMMON LISP, integers written as described above are always construed to be in decimal notation, whether or not the decimal point is present; allowing the decimal point to be present permits compatibility with MACLISP.

Integers may be notated in radices other than ten. The notation

*#nn*r*ddddd*   or   *#nn*R*ddddd*

means the integer in radix-*nn* notation denoted by the digits *ddddd*. More precisely, one may write *#*, a non-empty sequence of decimal digits representing an unsigned decimal integer *n*, r (or R), an optional sign, and a sequence of radix-*n* digits, to indicate an integer written in radix *n* (which must be between 2 and 36, inclusive). Only legal digits for the specified radix may be used; for example, an octal number may contain only the digits 0 through 7. For digits above 9, letters of the alphabet of either case may be used in order. Binary, octal, and hexadecimal radices are useful enough to warrant the special abbreviations #b for #2r, #o for #8r, and #x for #16r. For example:

#2r11010101	;Another way of writing 213 decimal
#b11010101	;Ditto
#b+11010101	;Ditto
#o325	;Ditto, in octal radix
#xD5	;Ditto, in hexadecimal radix
#16r+D5	;Ditto
#o-300	;Decimal -192, written in base 8
#3r-21010	;Same thing in base 3
#25R-7H	;Same thing in base 25
#xACCEDED	;181202413, in hexadecimal radix

2.1.2. Ratios

A ratio is a number representing the mathematical ratio of two integers. Integers and ratios collectively constitute the type rational. The canonical representation of a rational number is as an integer if its value is integral, and otherwise as the ratio of two integers, the *numerator* and *denominator*, whose greatest common divisor is one, and of which the denominator is positive (and in fact greater than 1, or else the value would be integral). A ratio is notated with / as a separator, thus: 3/5. It is possible to notate ratios in non-canonical (unreduced) forms, such as 4/6, but the LISP function print always prints the canonical form for a ratio.

If any computation produces a result that is a ratio of two integers such that the denominator evenly divides the numerator, then the result is immediately converted to the equivalent integer. This is called the rule of *rational canonicalization*.

Rational numbers may be written as the possibly signed quotient of decimal numerals: an optional sign followed by two non-empty sequences of digits separated by a /. This syntax may be described as follows:

ratio ::= [*sign*] {*digit*}⁺ / {*digit*}⁺

The second sequence may not consist entirely of zeros. For example:

2/3	;This is in canonical form
4/6	;A non-canonical form for the same number
-17/23	;A not very interesting ratio
-30517578125/32768	;This is $(-5/2)^{15}$
10/5	;The canonical form for this is 2

To notate rational numbers in radices other than ten, one uses the same radix specifiers (one of #*nn*R, #O, #B, or #X) as for integers. For example:

#o-101/75	;Octal notation for -65/61
#3r120/21	;Ternary notation for 15/7
#Xbc/ad	;Hexadecimal notation for 188/173
#xFADED/FACADE	;Hexadecimal notation for 1027565/16435934

2.1.3. Floating-Point Numbers

COMMON LISP allows an implementation to provide one or more kinds of floating-point number, which collectively make up the type float. A floating-point number is a (mathematical) rational number of the form $s \cdot f \cdot b^{e-p}$, where s is $+1$ or -1, the *sign*; b is an integer greater than 1, the *base* or *radix* of the representation; p is a positive integer, the *precision* (in base-b digits) of the floating-point number; f is a positive integer between b^{p-1} and $b^p - 1$ (inclusive), the *significand*; and e is an integer, the *exponent*. The value of p and the range of e depends on the implementation and on the type of floating-point number within that implementation. In addition, there is a floating-point zero; depending on the implementation, there may also be a "minus zero." If there is no minus zero, then 0.0 and -0.0 are both interpreted as simply a floating-point zero.

Implementation note: The form of the above description should not be construed to require the internal representation to be in sign-magnitude form. Two's-complement and other representations are also acceptable. Note that the radix of the internal representation may be other than 2, as on the IBM 360 and 370, which use radix 16; see float-radix.

Floating-point numbers may be provided in a variety of precisions and sizes, depending on the implementation. High-quality floating-point software tends to depend critically on the precise nature of the floating-point arithmetic, and so may not always be completely portable. To aid in writing programs that are moderately portable, however, certain definitions are made here:

- A *short* floating-point number (type short-float) is of the representation of smallest fixed precision provided by an implementation.

- A *long* floating-point number (type long-float) is of the representation of the largest fixed precision provided by an implementation.

- Intermediate between short and long formats are two others, arbitrarily called *single* and *double* (types single-float and double-float).

Table 2-1: Recommended Minimum Floating-Point Precision and Exponent Size

Format	Minimum Precision	Minimum Exponent Size
Short	13 bits	5 bits
Single	24 bits	8 bits
Double	50 bits	8 bits
Long	50 bits	8 bits

The precise definition of these categories is implementation-dependent. However, the rough intent is that short floating-point numbers be precise to at least four decimal places or so (but also have a space-efficient representation); single floating-point numbers, to at least seven decimal places; and double floating-point numbers, to at least fourteen decimal places. It is suggested that the precision (measured in "bits," computed as $p \log_2 b$) and the exponent size (also measured in "bits," computed as the base-2 logarithm of one plus the maximum exponent value) be at least as great as the values in Table 2-1.

Floating-point numbers are written in either decimal fraction or computerized scientific notation: an optional sign, then a non-empty sequence of digits with an embedded decimal point, then an optional decimal exponent specification. If there is no exponent specifier, then the decimal point is required, and there must be digits after it. The exponent specifier consists of an exponent marker, an optional sign, and a non-empty sequence of digits. For preciseness, here is a modified-BNF description of floating-point notation.

floating-point-number ::= [*sign*] {*digit*}* *decimal-point* {*digit*}$^+$ [*exponent*]
             | [*sign*] {*digit*}$^+$ [*decimal-point* {*digit*}*] *exponent*
sign ::= + | -
decimal-point ::= .
digit ::= 0 | 1 | 2 | 3 | 4 | 5 | 6 | 7 | 8 | 9
exponent ::= *exponent-marker* [*sign*] {*digit*}$^+$
exponent-marker ::= e | s | f | d | l | E | S | F | D | L

If no exponent specifier is present, or if the exponent marker e (or E) is used, then the precise format to be used is not specified. When such a representation is read and converted to an internal floating-point data object, the format specified by the variable *read-default-float-format* is used; the initial value of this variable is single-float.

The letters s, f, d, and l (or their respective uppercase equivalents) explicitly specify the use of *short*, *single*, *double*, and *long* format, respectively.

Examples of floating-point numbers:

0.0	;Floating-point zero in default format
0E0	;Also floating-point zero in default format
-.0	;This may be a zero or a minus zero,
	; depending on the implementation
0.	;The *integer* zero, not a floating-point zero!
0.0s0	;A floating-point zero in *short* format
0s0	;Also a floating-point zero in *short* format
3.14159265358979323846d0	;A *double*-format approximation to π
6.02E+23	;Avogadro's number, in default format
602E+21	;Also Avogadro's number, in default format
3.1010299957f-1	;$\log_{10}$ 2, in *single* format
-0.000000001s9	;$e^{\pi i}$ in *short* format, the hard way

The internal format used for an external representation depends only on the exponent marker, and not on the number of decimal digits in the external representation.

While COMMON LISP provides terminology and notation sufficient to accommodate four distinct floating-point formats, not all implementations will have the means to support that many distinct formats. An implementation is therefore permitted to provide fewer than four distinct internal floating-point formats, in which case at least one of them will be "shared" by more than one of the external format names *short*, *single*, *double*, and *long* according to the following rules:

- If one internal format is provided, then it is considered to be *single*, but serves also as *short*, *double*, and *long*. The data types short-float, single-float, double-float, and long-float are considered to be identical. An expression such as (eql 1.0s0 1.0d0) will be true in such an implementation because the two numbers 1.0s0 and 1.0d0 will be converted into the same internal format and therefore be considered to have the same data type, despite the differing external syntax. Similarly, (typep 1.0L0 'short-float) will be true in such an implementation. For output purposes all floating-point numbers are assumed to be of *single* format, and so will print using the exponent letter E or F.

- If two internal formats are provided, then either of two correspondences may be used, depending on which is the more appropriate:

  - One format is *short*; the other is *single* and serves also as *double* and *long*. The data types single-float, double-float, and long-float are considered to be identical, but short-float is distinct. An expression such as (eql 1.0s0 1.0d0) will be false, but (eql 1.0f0 1.0d0) will be true. Similarly, (typep 1.0L0 'short-float) will be false, but (typep 1.0L0 'single-float) will be true. For output purposes all floating-point numbers are assumed to be of *short* or *single* format.

- One format is *single* and serves also as *short*; the other is *double* and serves also as *long*. The data types short-float and single-float are considered to be identical, and the data types double-float and long-float are considered to be identical. An expression such as (eql 1.0s0 1.0d0) will be false, as will (eql 1.0f0 1.0d0); but (eql 1.0d0 1.0L0) will be true. Similarly, (typep 1.0L0 'short-float) will be false, but (typep 1.0L0 'double-float) will be true. For output purposes all floating-point numbers are assumed to be of *single* or *double* format.

- If three internal formats are provided, then either of two correspondences may be used, depending on which is the more appropriate:

  - One format is *short*; another format is *single*; and the third format is *double* and serves also as *long*. Similar constraints apply.

  - One format is *single* and serves also as *short*; another is *double*; and the third format is *long*.

Implementation note: It is recommended that an implementation provide as many distinct floating-point formats as feasible, given Table 2-1 as a guideline. Ideally, short-format floating-point numbers should have an "immediate" representation that does not require heap allocation; single-format floating-point numbers should approximate IEEE proposed standard single-format floating-point numbers; and double-format floating-point numbers should approximate IEEE proposed standard double-format floating-point numbers [9, 5, 6].

2.1.4. Complex Numbers

Complex numbers (type complex) are represented in Cartesian form, with a real part and an imaginary part each of which is a non-complex number (integer, ratio, or floating-point number). It should be emphasized that the parts of a complex number are not necessarily floating-point numbers; in this, COMMON LISP is like PL/I and differs from FORTRAN. However, both parts must be of the same type: either both are rational, or both are of the same floating-point format.

Complex numbers may be notated by writing the characters #c followed by a list of the real and imaginary parts. If the two parts as notated are not of the same type, then they are converted according to the rules of floating-point contagion as described in chapter 12. (Indeed, *#c(a b)* is equivalent to *#.(complex a b)*; see the description of the function `complex`.) For example:

```
#C(3.0s1 2.0s-1)
#C(5 -3)            ;A Gaussian integer
#C(5/3 7.0)         ;Will be converted internally to #C(1.66666 7.0)
#C(0 1)             ;The imaginary unit, that is, i
```

The type of a specific complex number is indicated by a list of the word `complex` and the type of the components; for example, a specialized representation for complex numbers with short floating-point parts would be of type (complex short-float). The type `complex` encompasses all complex representations.

A complex number of type (complex rational), that is, one whose components are rational, can never have a zero imaginary part. If the result of any computation would be a complex rational with a zero imaginary part, the result is immediately converted to a non-complex rational number by taking the real part. This is called the rule of *complex canonicalization*. This rule does not apply to complex numbers whose parts are floating-point numbers; #C(5.0 0.0) and 5.0 are different.

2.2. Characters

Characters are represented as data objects of type `character`. There are two subtypes of interest, called `standard-char` and `string-char`.

A character object can be notated by writing *#* followed by the character itself. For example, *#\g* means the character object for a lowercase g. This works well enough for printing characters. Non-printing characters have names, and can be notated by writing *#* and then the name; for example, *#\Space* (or *#\SPACE* or *#\space* or *#\sPaCE*) means the space character. The syntax for character names after *#* is the same as that for symbols. However, only character names that are known to the particular implementation may be used.

2.2.1. Standard Characters

COMMON LISP defines a "standard character set" (subtype `standard-char`) for two purposes. COMMON LISP programs that are *written in* the standard character set can be read by any COMMON LISP implementation; and COMMON LISP programs that *use* only standard characters as data objects are most likely to be portable. The COMMON LISP character set consists of a space character *#\Space*, a newline character *#\Newline*, and the following ninety-four non-blank printing characters or their equivalents:

```
!  "  #  $  %  &  '  (  )  *  +  ,  -  .  /  0  1  2  3  4  5  6  7  8  9  :  ;  <  =  >  ?
@  A  B  C  D  E  F  G  H  I  J  K  L  M  N  O  P  Q  R  S  T  U  V  W  X  Y  Z  [  \  ]  ^  _
`  a  b  c  d  e  f  g  h  i  j  k  l  m  n  o  p  q  r  s  t  u  v  w  x  y  z  {  |  }  ~
```

The COMMON LISP standard character set is apparently equivalent to the ninety-five standard ASCII printing characters plus a newline character. Nevertheless, COMMON LISP is designed to be relatively independent of the ASCII character encoding. For example, the collating sequence is not specified except to say that digits must be properly ordered, the uppercase letters must be properly ordered, and the lowercase letters must be properly ordered (see char< for a precise specification). Other character encodings, particularly EBCDIC, should be easily accommodated (with a suitable mapping of printing characters).

Of the ninety-four non-blank printing characters, the following are used in only limited ways in the syntax of COMMON LISP programs:

```
[  ]  {  }  ?  !  ^  _  ~  $  %
```

All of these characters except ! and _ are used within format strings as formatting directives. Except for this, [,], {, }, ?, and ! are not used in COMMON LISP and are reserved to the user for syntactic extensions; ^ and _ are not yet used in COMMON LISP, but are part of the syntax of reserved tokens, and are reserved to implementors; ~ is not yet used in COMMON LISP, and is reserved to implementors; and $ and % are normally regarded as alphabetic characters, but are not used in the names of any standard COMMON LISP functions, variables, or other entities.

The following characters are called *semi-standard*:

```
#\Backspace   #\Tab   #\Linefeed   #\Page   #\Return   #\Rubout
```

Not all implementations of COMMON LISP need to support them; but those implementations that use the standard ASCII character set should support them, treating them as corresponding respectively to the ASCII characters BS (octal code 010), HT (011), LF (012), FF (014), CR (015), and DEL (177). These characters are not members of the subtype standard-char unless synonymous with one of the standard characters specified above. For example, in a given implementation it might be sensible for the implementor to define #\Linefeed or #\Return to be synonymous with #\Newline, or #\Tab to be synonymous with #\Space.

2.2.2. Line Divisions

The treatment of line divisions is one of the most difficult issues in designing portable software, simply because there is so little agreement among operating systems. Some use a single character to delimit lines; the recommended ASCII character for this purpose is the line feed character LF (also called the new line character, NL), but some systems use the carriage return character CR. Much more common is the two-character sequence CR followed by LF. Frequently line divisions have no representation as a character but are implicit in the structuring of a file into records, each record containing a line of text. A deck of punched cards has this structure, for example.

COMMON LISP provides an abstract interface by requiring that there be a single character, #\Newline, that within the language serves as a line delimiter. (The language C has a similar requirement.) An implementation of COMMON LISP must translate between this internal single-character representation and whatever external representation(s) may be used.

Implementation note: How the character called #\Newline is represented internally is not specified here, but it is strongly suggested that the ASCII LF character be used in COMMON LISP implementations that use the ASCII character encoding. The ASCII CR character is a workable, but in most cases inferior, alternative.

The requirement that a line division be represented as a single character has certain consequences. A character string written in the middle of a program in such a way as to span more than one line must contain exactly one character to represent each line division. Consider this code fragment:

```
(setq a-string "This string
contains
forty-two characters.")
```

Between g and c there must be exactly one character, #\Newline; a two-character sequence, such as #\Return and then #\Newline, is not acceptable, nor is the absence of a character. The same is true between s and f.

When the character #\Newline is written to an output file, the COMMON LISP implementation must take the appropriate action to produce a line division. This might involve writing out a record or translating #\Newline to a CR/LF sequence.

Implementation note: If an implementation uses the ASCII character encoding, uses the CR/LF sequence externally to delimit lines, uses LF to represent #\Newline internally, and supports #\Return as a data object corresponding to the ASCII character CR, the question arises as to what action to take when the program writes out #\Return followed by #\Newline. It should first be noted that #\Return is not a standard COMMON LISP character, and the action to be taken when #\Return is written out is therefore not defined by the COMMON LISP language. A plausible approach is to buffer the #\Return character, and suppress it if and only if the next character is #\Newline (the net effect is to generate a CR/LF sequence). Another plausible approach is simply to ignore the difficulty and declare that writing #\Return and then #\Newline results in the sequence CR/CR/LF in the output.

2.2.3. Non-standard Characters

Any implementation may provide additional characters, whether printing characters or named characters. Some plausible examples:

#\π   #\α   #\Break   #\Home-Up   #\Escape

The use of such characters may render COMMON LISP programs non-portable.

2.2.4 Character Attributes

Every object of type `character` has three attributes: *code*, *bits*, and *font*. The code attribute is intended to distinguish among the printed glyphs and formatting functions for characters; it is a numerical encoding of the character proper. The bits attribute allows extra flags to be associated with a character. The font attribute permits a specification of the style of the glyphs (such as italics). Each of these attributes may be understood to be a non-negative integer.

The font attribute may be notated in unsigned decimal notation between the #
and the \. For example, #3\a means the letter a in font 3. This might mean the same thing as #\α if font 3 were used to represent Greek letters. Note that not all COMMON LISP implementations provide for non-zero font attributes; see `char-font-limit`.

The bits attribute may be notated by preceding the name of the character by the names or initials of the bits, separated by hyphens. The character itself may be written instead of the name, preceded if necessary by \. For example:

#\Control-Meta-Return	#\Meta-Control-Q
#\Hyper-Space	#\Meta-\a
#\Control-A	#\Meta-Hyper-\:
#\C-M-Return	#\Hyper-\π

Note that not all COMMON LISP implementations provide for non-zero bits attributes; see `char-bits-limit`.

2.2.5. String Characters

Any character whose bits and font attributes are zero may be contained in strings. All such characters together constitute a subtype of the characters; this subtype is called `string-char`.

2.3. Symbols

Symbols are LISP data objects that serve several purposes and have several interesting characteristics. Every object of type `symbol` has a name, called its *print name*.

Given a symbol, one can obtain its name in the form of a string. Conversely, given the name of a symbol as a string one can obtain the symbol itself. (More precisely, symbols are organized into *packages*, and all the symbols in a package are uniquely identified by name. See chapter 11.)

Symbols have a component called the *property list*, or *plist*. By convention this is always a list whose even-numbered components (calling the first component zero) are symbols, here functioning as property names, and whose odd-numbered components are associated property values. Functions are provided for manipulating this property list; in effect, these allow a symbol to be treated as an extensible record structure.

Symbols are also used to represent certain kinds of variables in LISP programs, and there are functions for dealing with the values associated with symbols in this role.

A symbol can be notated simply by writing its name. If its name is not empty, and if the name consists only of uppercase alphabetic, numeric, or certain "pseudo-alphabetic" special characters (but not delimiter characters such as parentheses or space), and if the name of the symbol cannot be mistaken for a number, then the symbol can be notated by the sequence of characters in its name. Any uppercase letters that appear in the (internal) name may be written in either case in the external notation (more on this below). For example:

`FROBBOZ`	;The symbol whose name is `FROBBOZ`
`frobboz`	;Another way to notate the same symbol
`fRObBoz`	;Yet another way to notate it
`unwind-protect`	;A symbol with a - in its name
`+$`	;The symbol named `+$`
`1+`	;The symbol named `1+`
`+1`	;This is the integer 1, not a symbol.
`pascal_style`	;This symbol has an underscore in its name.
`b^2-4*a*c`	;This is a single symbol!
	; It has several special characters in its name.
`file.rel.43`	;This symbol has periods in its name.
`/usr/games/zork`	;This symbol has slashes in its name.

In addition to letters and numbers, the following characters are normally considered to be "alphabetic" for the purposes of notating symbols:

```
+ - * / @ $ % ^ & _ \ < > ~ .
```

Some of these characters have conventional purposes for naming things; for example, symbols that name special variables generally have names beginning and ending with *. The last character listed above, the period, is considered alphabetic *provided* that a token does not consist entirely of periods. A single period standing by itself is used in the notation of conses and dotted lists; a token consisting of two or more periods is syntactically illegal. (The period also serves as the decimal point in the notation of numbers.)

The following characters are also alphabetic by default, but are explicitly reserved to the user for definition as reader macro characters (see section 22.1.3) or any other desired purpose, and therefore should not be used routinely in names of symbols:

```
?  !  [  ]  {  }
```

A symbol may have uppercase letters, lowercase letters, or both in its print name. However, the LISP reader normally converts lowercase letters to the corresponding uppercase letters when reading symbols. The net effect is that most of the time case makes no difference when *notating* symbols. Case *does* make a difference internally and when printing a symbol. Internally the symbols that name all standard COMMON LISP functions, variables, and keywords have uppercase names; their names appear in lower case in this manual for readability. Typing such names with lowercase letters works because the function read will convert lowercase letters to the equivalent uppercase letters.

If a symbol cannot be simply notated by the characters of its name because the (internal) name contains special characters or lowercase letters, then there are two "escape" conventions for notating them. Writing a \ character before any character causes the character to be treated itself as an ordinary character for use in a symbol name; in particular, it suppresses internal conversion of lowercase letters to their uppercase equivalents. If any character in a notation is preceded by \, then that notation can never be interpreted as a number. For example:

```
\(                      ;The symbol whose name is (
\+1                     ;The symbol whose name is +1
+\1                     ;Also the symbol whose name is +1
\frobboz                ;The symbol whose name is fROBBOZ
3.14159265\s0           ;The symbol whose name is 3.14159265s0
3.14159265\S0           ;A different symbol, whose name is 3.14159265S0
3.14159265s0            ;A short-format floating-point approximation to π
APL\\360                ;The symbol whose name is APL\360
apl\\360                ;Also the symbol whose name is APL\360
\(b^2\)\ -\ 4*a*c       ;The name is (B^2) - 4*A*C.
                        ;    It has parentheses and two spaces in it.
\(\b^2\)\ -\ 4*\a*\c    ;The name is (b^2) - 4*a*c.
                        ;    The letters are explicitly lowercase.
```

It may be tedious to insert a \ before *every* delimiter character in the name of a symbol if there are many of them. An alternative convention is to surround the name of a symbol with vertical bars; these cause every character between them to be taken as part of the symbol's name, as if \ had been written before each one, excepting only ¦ itself and \, which must nevertheless be preceded by \. For example:

```
¦"¦                      ;The same as writing \"
¦(b^2) - 4*a*c¦          ;The name is (b^2) - 4*a*c
¦frobboz¦                ;The name is frobboz, not FROBBOZ
¦APL\360¦                ;The name is APL360, because
                         ;   the \ quotes the 3
¦APL\\360¦               ;The name is APL\360
¦apl\\360¦               ;The name is apl\360
¦\¦\¦¦                    ;Same as \¦\¦: the name is ¦¦
¦(B^2) - 4*A*C¦          ;The name is (B^2) - 4*A*C.
                         ;   It has parentheses and two spaces in it.
¦(b^2) - 4*a*c¦          ;The name is (b^2) - 4*a*c.
```

2.4. Lists and Conses

A cons is a record structure containing two components called the *car* and the *cdr*. Conses are used primarily to represent lists.

A *list* is recursively defined to be either the empty list or a cons whose *cdr* component is a list. A list is therefore a chain of conses linked by their *cdr* components and terminated by nil, the empty list. The *car* components of the conses are called the *elements* of the list. For each element of the list there is a cons. The empty list has no elements at all.

A list is notated by writing the elements of the list in order, separated by blank space (space, tab, or return characters), and surrounded by parentheses. For example:

```
(a b c)                  ;A list of three symbols
(2.0s0 (a 1) #\*)        ;A list of three things: a short floating-point
                         ;   number, another list, and a character object
```

The empty list nil therefore can be written as (), because it is a list with no elements.

A *dotted list* is one whose last cons does not have nil for its *cdr*, rather some other data object (which is also not a cons, or the first-mentioned cons would not be the last cons of the list). Such a list is called "dotted" because of the special

notation used for it: the elements of the list are written between parentheses as
before, but after the last element and before the right parenthesis are written a dot
(surrounded by blank space) and then the *cdr* of the last cons. As a special case,
a single cons is notated by writing the *car* and the *cdr* between parentheses and
separated by a space-surrounded dot. For example:

```
(a . 4)                    ;A cons whose car is a symbol
                           ;   and whose cdr is an integer
(a b c . d)                ;A dotted list with three elements whose last cons
                           ;   has the symbol d in its cdr
```

Compatibility note: In MacLisp, the dot in dotted-list notation need not be surrounded by
white space or other delimiters. The dot is required to be delimited in Common Lisp, as in
ZetaLisp.

It is legitimate to write something like (a b . (c d)); this means the same as
(a b c d). The standard Lisp output routines will never print a list in the first
form, however; they will avoid dot notation wherever possible.

Often the term *list* is used to refer either to true lists or to dotted lists. When
the distinction is important, the term "true list" will be used to refer to a list
terminated by nil. Most functions advertised to operate on lists expect to be given
true lists. Throughout this manual, unless otherwise specified, it is an error to pass
a dotted list to a function that is specified to require a list as an argument.

Implementation note: Implementors are encouraged to use the equivalent of the predicate
endp wherever it is necessary to test for the end of a list. Whenever feasible, this test should
explicitly signal an error if a list is found to be terminated by a non-nil atom. However,
such an explicit error signal is not required, because some such tests occur in important
loops where efficiency is important. In such cases, the predicate atom may be used to test
for the end of the list, quietly treating any non-nil list-terminating atom as if it were nil.

Sometimes the term *tree* is used to refer to some cons and all the other conses
transitively accessible to it through *car* and *cdr* links until non-conses are reached;
these non-conses are called the *leaves* of the tree.

Lists, dotted lists, and trees are not mutually exclusive data types; they are simply
useful points of view about structures of conses. There are yet other terms, such
as *association list*. None of these are true Lisp data types. Conses are a data type,
and nil is the sole object of type null. The Lisp data type list is taken to mean
the union of the cons and null data types, and therefore encompasses both true
lists and dotted lists.

2.5. Arrays

An `array` is an object with components arranged according to a Cartesian coordinate system. In general, these components may be any LISP data objects.

The number of dimensions of an array is called its *rank* (this terminology is borrowed from APL); the rank is a non-negative integer. Likewise, each dimension is itself a non-negative integer. The total number of elements in the array is the product of all the dimensions.

An implementation of COMMON LISP may impose a limit on the rank of an array, but this limit may not be smaller than 7. Therefore, any COMMON LISP program may assume the use of arrays of rank 7 or less. (A program may determine the actual limit on array ranks for a given implementation by examining the constant `array-rank-limit`.)

It is permissible for a dimension to be zero. In this case, the array has no elements, and any attempt to access an element is in error. However, other properties of the array, such as the dimensions themselves, may be used. If the rank is zero, then there are no dimensions, and the product of the dimensions is then by definition 1. A zero-rank array therefore has a single element.

An array element is specified by a sequence of indices. The length of the sequence must equal the rank of the array. Each index must be a non-negative integer strictly less than the corresponding array dimension. Array indexing is therefore zero-origin, not one-origin as in (the default case of) FORTRAN.

As an example, suppose that the variable `foo` names a 3-by-5 array. Then the first index may be 0, 1, or 2, and the second index may be 0, 1, 2, 3, or 4. One may refer to array elements using the function `aref`; for example, `(aref foo 2 1)` refers to element (2, 1) of the array. Note that `aref` takes a variable number of arguments: an array, and as many indices as the array has dimensions. A zero-rank array has no dimensions, and therefore `aref` would take such an array and no indices, and return the sole element of the array.

In general, arrays can be multidimensional, can share their contents with other array objects, and can have their size altered dynamically (either enlarging or shrinking) after creation. A one-dimensional array may also have a *fill pointer*.

Multidimensional arrays store their components in row-major order; that is, internally a multidimensional array is stored as a one-dimensional array, with the multidimensional index sets ordered lexicographically, last index varying fastest. This is important in two situations: (1) when arrays with different dimensions share their contents, and (2) when accessing very large arrays in a virtual-memory implementation. (The first situation is a matter of semantics; the second, a matter of efficiency.)

An array that is not displaced to another array, has no fill pointer, and is not to have its size adjusted dynamically after creation is called a *simple* array. The user may provide declarations that certain arrays will be simple. Some implementations can handle simple arrays in an especially efficient manner; for example, simple arrays may have a more compact representation than non-simple arrays.

2.5.1. Vectors

One-dimensional arrays are called *vectors* in COMMON LISP and constitute the type vector (which is therefore a subtype of array). Vectors and lists are collectively considered to be *sequences*. They differ in that any component of a one-dimensional array can be accessed in constant time, whereas the average component access time for a list is linear in the length of the list; on the other hand, adding a new element to the front of a list takes constant time, whereas the same operation on an array takes time linear in the length of the array.

A general vector (a one-dimensional array that can have any data object as an element, but has no additional paraphernalia) can be notated by notating the components in order, separated by whitespace and surrounded by #(and). For example:

```
#(a  b  c)              ;A vector of length 3
#(2  3  5  7  11  13  17  19  23  29  31  37  41  43  47)
                        ;A vector containing the primes below 50
#()                     ;An empty vector
```

Note that when the function read parses this syntax, it always constructs a *simple general vector*.

Rationale: Many people have suggested that brackets be used to notate vectors, as [a b c] instead of #(a b c). This notation would be shorter, perhaps more readable, and certainly in accord with cultural conventions in other parts of computer science and mathematics. However, to preserve the usefulness of the user-definable macro-character feature of the function read, it is necessary to leave some characters to the user for this purpose. Experience in MACLISP has shown that users, especially implementors of languages for use in artificial intelligence research, often want to define special kinds of brackets. Therefore COMMON LISP avoids using brackets and braces for any syntactic purpose.

Implementations may provide certain specialized representations of arrays for efficiency in the case where all the components are of the same specialized (typically numeric) type. All implementations provide specialized arrays for the cases when the components are characters (or rather, a special subset of the characters); the one-dimensional instances of this specialization are called *strings*. All implementations are also required to provide specialized arrays of bits, that is, arrays of type (array bit); the one-dimensional instances of this specialization are called *bit-vectors*.

2.5.2. Strings

A string is simply a vector of characters. More precisely, a string is a specialized vector whose elements are of type `string-char`. The type `string` is therefore a subtype of the type `vector`. A string can be written as the sequence of characters contained in the string, preceded and followed by a " (double quote) character. Any " or \ character in the sequence must additionally have a \ character before it. For example:

`"Foo"`	; A string with three characters in it
`""`	; An empty string
`"\"APL\\360?\" he cried."`	; A string with twenty characters
`"|x| = |-x|"`	; A ten-character string

Notice that any vertical bar | in a string need not be preceded by a \. Similarly, any double quote in the name of a symbol written using vertical-bar notation need not be preceded by a \. The double-quote and vertical-bar notations are similar but distinct: double quotes indicate a character string containing the sequence of characters, whereas vertical bars indicate a symbol whose name is the contained sequence of characters.

The characters contained by the double quotes, taken from left to right, occupy locations within the string with increasing indices. The leftmost character is string element number 0, the next one is element number 1, and so on.

Note that the function `prin1` will print any character vector (not just a simple one) using this syntax, but the function `read` will always construct a simple string when it reads this syntax.

2.5.3 Bit-Vectors

A bit-vector can be written as the sequence of bits contained in the string, preceded by `#*`; any delimiter character, such as whitespace, will terminate the bit-vector syntax. For example:

`#*10110`	; A five-bit bit-vector; bit 0 is a 1
`#*`	; An empty bit-vector

The bits notated following the `#*`, taken from left to right, occupy locations within the bit-vector with increasing indices. The leftmost notated bit is bit-vector element number 0, the next one is element number 1, and so on.

The function `prin1` will print any bit-vector (not just a simple one) using this syntax, but the function `read` will always construct a simple bit-vector when it reads this syntax.

2.6. Hash Tables

Hash tables provide an efficient way of mapping any LISP object (a *key*) to an associated object. They are provided as primitives of COMMON LISP because some implementations may need to use internal storage management strategies that would make it very difficult for the user to implement hash tables himself in a portable fashion. Hash tables are described in chapter 16.

2.7. Readtables

A readtable is a data structure that maps characters into syntax types for the LISP expression parser. In particular, a readtable indicates for each character with syntax *macro character* what its macro definition is. This is a mechanism by which the user may reprogram the parser to a limited but useful extent. See section 22.1.5.

2.8. Packages

Packages are collections of symbols that serve as name spaces. The parser recognizes symbols by looking up character sequences in the current package. Packages can be used to hide names internal to a module from other code. Mechanisms are provided for exporting symbols from a given package to the primary "user" package. See chapter 11.

2.9. Pathnames

Pathnames are the means by which a COMMON LISP program can interface to an external file system in a reasonably implementation-independent manner. See section 23.1.1.

2.10. Streams

A stream is a source or sink of data, typically characters or bytes. Nearly all functions that perform I/O do so with respect to a specified stream. The function `open` takes a pathname and returns a stream connected to the file specified by the pathname. There are a number of standard streams that are used by default for various purposes. See chapter 21.

2.11. Random-States

An object of type `random-state` is used to encapsulate state information used by the pseudo-random number generator. For more information about `random-state` objects, see section 12.9.

2.12. Structures

Structures are instances of user-defined data types that have a fixed number of named components. They are analogous to records in PASCAL. Structures are declared using the defstruct construct; defstruct automatically defines access and constructor functions for the new data type.

Different structures may print out in different ways; the definition of a structure type may specify a print procedure to use for objects of that type (see the :print-function option to defstruct). The default notation for structures is:

#S(*structure-name*
          slot-name-1 slot-value-1
          slot-name-2 slot-value-2
                    . . .)

where #S indicates structure syntax, *structure-name* is the name (a symbol) of the structure type, each *slot-name* is the name (also a symbol) of a component, and each corresponding *slot-value* is the representation of the LISP object in that slot.

2.13. Functions

A *function* is anything that may be correctly given to the funcall or apply function, and is to be executed as code when arguments are supplied.

A *compiled-function* is a compiled code object.

A lambda-expression (a list whose *car* is the symbol lambda) may serve as a function. Depending on the implementation, it may be possible for other lists to serve as functions. For example, an implementation might choose to represent a "lexical closure" as a list whose *car* contains some special marker.

A symbol may serve as a function; an attempt to invoke a symbol as a function causes the contents of the symbol's function cell to be used. See symbol-function and defun.

The result of evaluating a function special form will always be a function.

2.14. Unreadable Data Objects

Some objects may print in implementation-dependent ways. Such objects cannot necessarily be reliably reconstructed from a printed representation, and so they are usually printed in a format informative to the user but not acceptable to the read function:

#<*useful information*>

The LISP reader will signal an error on encountering `#<`.

As a hypothetical example, an implementation might print

```
#<stack-pointer si:rename-within-new-definition-maybe #o311037552>
```

for an implementation-specific "internal stack pointer" data type whose printed representation includes the name of the type, some information about the stack slot pointed to, and the machine address (in octal) of the stack slot.

2.15. Overlap, Inclusion, and Disjointness of Types

The COMMON LISP data type hierarchy is tangled and purposely left somewhat open-ended so that implementors may experiment with new data types as extensions to the language. This section explicitly states all the defined relationships between types, including subtype/supertype relationships, disjointness, and exhaustive partitioning. The user of COMMON LISP should not depend on any relationships not explicitly stated here. For example, it is not valid to assume that because a number is not complex and not rational that it must be a `float`, because implementations are permitted to provide yet other kinds of numbers.

First we need some terminology. If x is a supertype of y, then any object of type y is also of type x, and y is said to be a subtype of x. If types x and y are disjoint, then no object (in any implementation) may be both of type x and of type y. Types a_1 through a_n are an *exhaustive union* of type x if each a_j is a subtype of x, and any object of type x is necessarily of at least one of the types a_j; a_1 through a_n are furthermore an *exhaustive partition* if they are also pairwise disjoint.

- The type `t` is a supertype of every type whatsoever. Every object belongs to type `t`.
- The type `nil` is a subtype of every type whatsoever. No object belongs to type `nil`.
- The types `cons`, `symbol`, `array`, `number`, and `character` are pairwise disjoint.
- The types `rational`, `float`, and `complex` are pairwise disjoint subtypes of `number`.
- The types `integer` and `ratio` are disjoint subtypes of `rational`.

Rationale: It might be thought that `integer` and `ratio` should form an exhaustive partition of the type `rational`. This is purposely avoided here in order to permit compatible experimentation with extensions to the COMMON LISP rational number system.

- The types `fixnum` and `bignum` are disjoint subtypes of `integer`.

Rationale: It might be thought that `fixnum` and `bignum` should form an exhaustive partition of the type `integer`. This is purposely avoided here in order to permit compatible experimentation with extensions to the COMMON LISP integer number system, such as the idea of adding explicit representations of infinity or of positive and negative infinity.

- The types `short-float`, `single-float`, `double-float`, and `long-float` are subtypes of `float`. Any two of them must be either disjoint or identical; if identical, then any other types between them in the above ordering must also be identical to them (for example, if `single-float` and `long-float` are identical types, then `double-float` must be identical to them also).
- The type `null` is a subtype of `symbol`; the only object of type `null` is `nil`.
- The types `cons` and `null` form an exhaustive partition of the type `list`.
- The type `standard-char` is a subtype of `string-char`; `string-char` is a subtype of `character`.
- The type `string` is a subtype of `vector`, for `string` means (`vector string-char`).
- The type `bit-vector` is a subtype of `vector`, for `bit-vector` means (`vector bit`).
- The types (`vector t`), `string`, and `bit-vector` are disjoint.
- The type `vector` is a subtype of `array`; for all types x, the type (`vector` x) is the same as the type (`array` x (`*`)).
- The type `simple-array` is a subtype of `array`.
- The types `simple-vector`, `simple-string`, and `simple-bit-vector` are disjoint subtypes of `simple-array`, for they respectively mean (`simple- array t` (`*`)), (`simple-array string-char` (`*`)), and (`simple- array bit` (`*`)).
- The type `simple-vector` is a subtype of `vector`, and indeed is a subtype of (`vector t`).
- The type `simple-string` is a subtype of `string`. (Note that although `string` is a subtype of `vector`, `simple-string` is not a subtype of `simple-vector`.)

Rationale: The type `simple-vector` might better have been designated `simple-general-vector`, but in this instance euphony and user convenience were deemed more important to the design of COMMON LISP than a rigid symmetry.

- The type `simple-bit-vector` is a subtype of `bit-vector`. (Note that although `bit-vector` is a subtype of `vector`, `simple-bit-vector` is not a subtype of `simple-vector`.)

- The types `vector` and `list` are disjoint subtypes of `sequence`.

- The types `hash-table`, `readtable`, `package`, `pathname`, `stream`, and `random-state` are pairwise disjoint.

- Any two types created by `defstruct` are disjoint unless one is a supertype of the other by virtue of the `:include` option.

- An exhaustive union for the type `common` is formed by the types `cons`, `symbol`, (`array` x) where x is either `t` or a subtype of `common`, `string`, `fixnum`, `bignum`, `ratio`, `short-float`, `single-float`, `double-float`, `long-float`, (`complex` x) where x is a subtype of `common`, `standard-char`, `hash-table`, `readtable`, `package`, `pathname`, `stream`, `random-state`, and all types created by the user via `defstruct`. An implementation may not unilaterally add subtypes to `common`; however, future revisions to the COMMON LISP standard may extend the definition of the `common` data type.

Note that a type such as `number` or `array` may or may not be a subtype of `common`, depending on whether or not the given implementation has extended the set of objects of that type.

3

Scope and Extent

In describing various features of the COMMON LISP language, the notions of *scope* and *extent* are frequently useful. These notions arise when some object or construct must be referred to from some distant part of a program. *Scope* refers to the spatial or textual region of the program within which references may occur. *Extent* refers to the interval of time during which references may occur.

As a simple example, consider this program:

```
(defun copy-cell (x) (cons (car x) (cdr x)))
```

The scope of the parameter named x is the body of the defun form. There is no way to refer to this parameter from any other place but within the body of the defun. Similarly, the extent of the parameter x (for any particular call to copy-cell) is the interval from the time the function is invoked to the time it is exited. (In the general case, the extent of a parameter may last beyond the time of function exit, but that cannot occur in this simple case.)

Within COMMON LISP, a referenceable entity is *established* by the execution of some language construct, and the scope and extent of the entity are described relative to the construct and the time (during execution of the construct) at which the entity is established. For the purposes of this discussion, the term "entity" refers not only to COMMON LISP data objects, such as symbols and conses, but also to variable bindings (both ordinary and special), catchers, and go targets. It is important to distinguish between an entity and a name for the entity. In a function definition such as

```
(defun foo (x y) (* x (+ y 1)))
```

there is a single name, x, used to refer to the first parameter of the procedure whenever it is invoked; however, a new binding is established on every invocation. A *binding* is a particular parameter instance. The value of a reference to the name x depends not only on the scope within which it occurs (the one in the body of foo in the example occurs in the scope of the function definition's parameters) but also on the particular binding or instance involved. (In this case, it depends on the invocation during which the reference is made). More complicated examples appear at the end of this chapter.

There are a few kinds of scope and extent that are particularly useful in describing COMMON LISP:

- *Lexical scope*. Here references to the established entity can occur only within certain program portions that are lexically (that is, textually) contained within the establishing construct. Typically the construct will have a part designated the *body*, and the scope of all entities established will be (or include) the body.

  Example: the names of parameters to a function normally are lexically scoped.

- *Indefinite scope*. References may occur anywhere, in any program.

- *Dynamic extent*. References may occur at any time in the interval between establishment of the entity and the explicit disestablishment of the entity. As a rule, the entity is disestablished when execution of the establishing construct completes or is otherwise terminated. Therefore entities with dynamic extent obey a stack-like discipline, paralleling the nested executions of their establishing constructs.

  Example: the with-open-file construct opens a connection to a file and creates a stream object to represent the connection. The stream object has indefinite extent, but the connection to the open file has dynamic extent: when control exits the with-open-file construct, either normally or abnormally, the stream is automatically closed.

  Example: the binding of a "special" variable has dynamic extent.

- *Indefinite extent*. The entity continues to exist so long as the possibility of reference remains. (An implementation is free to destroy the entity if it can prove that reference to it is no longer possible. Garbage collection strategies implicitly employ such proofs.)

  Example: most COMMON LISP data objects have indefinite extent.

  Example: the bindings of lexically scoped parameters of a function have indefinite extent. (By contrast, in ALGOL the bindings of lexically scoped parameters of a procedure have dynamic extent.) The function definition

```
(defun compose (f g)
  #'(lambda (x) (funcall f (funcall g x))))
```

when given two arguments, immediately returns a function as its value. The parameter bindings for f and g do not disappear because the returned function, when called, could still refer to those bindings. Therefore

```
(funcall (compose #'sqrt #'abs) -9.0)
```

produces the value 3.0. (An analogous procedure would not necessarily work correctly in typical ALGOL implementations, or, for that matter, in most LISP dialects.)

In addition to the above terms, it is convenient to define *dynamic scope* to mean *indefinite scope and dynamic extent*. Thus we speak of "special" variables as having dynamic scope, or being dynamically scoped, because they have indefinite scope and dynamic extent: a special variable can be referred to anywhere as long as its binding is currently in effect.

The above definitions do not take into account the possibility of *shadowing*. Remote reference of entities is accomplished by using *names* of one kind or another. If two entities have the same name, then the second may shadow the first, in which case an occurrence of the name will refer to the second and cannot refer to the first.

In the case of lexical scope, if two constructs that establish entities with the same name are textually nested, then references within the inner construct refer to the entity established by the inner one; the inner one shadows the outer one. Outside the inner construct but inside the outer one, references refer to the entity established by the outer construct. For example:

```
(defun test (x z)
  (let ((z (* x z))) (print z))
  z)
```

The binding of the variable z by the `let` construct shadows the parameter binding for the function `test`. The reference to the variable z in the `print` form refers to the `let` binding. The reference to z at the end of the function refers to the parameter named z.

In the case of dynamic extent, if the time intervals of two entities overlap, then one interval will necessarily be nested within the other one. This is a property of the design of COMMON LISP.

Implementation note: Behind the assertion that dynamic extents nest properly is the assumption that there is only a single program or process. COMMON LISP does not address the problems of multiprogramming (timesharing) or multiprocessing (more than one active processor) within a single LISP environment. The documentation for implementations that extend COMMON LISP for multiprogramming or multiprocessing should be very clear on what modifications are induced by such extensions to the rules of extent and scope. Implementors should note that COMMON LISP has been carefully designed to allow special variables to be implemented using either the "deep binding" technique or the "shallow binding" technique, but the two techniques have different semantic and performance implications for multiprogramming and multiprocessing.

A reference by name to an entity with dynamic extent will always refer to the entity of that name that has been most recently established that has not yet been disestablished. For example:

```
(defun fun1 (x)
  (catch 'trap (+ 3 (fun2 x))))
(defun fun2 (y)
  (catch 'trap (* 5 (fun3 y))))
(defun fun3 (z)
  (throw 'trap z))
```

Consider the call (fun1 7). The result will be 10. At the time the throw is executed, there are two outstanding catchers with the name trap: one established within procedure fun1, and the other within procedure fun2. The latter is the more recent, and so the value 7 is returned from the catch form in fun2. Viewed from within fun3, the catch in fun2 shadows the one in fun1. Had fun2 been defined as

```
(defun fun2 (y)
  (catch 'snare (* 5 (fun3 y))))
```

then the two catchers would have different names, and therefore the one in fun1 would not be shadowed. The result would then have been 7.

As a rule this manual simply speaks of the scope or extent of an entity; the possibility of shadowing is left implicit.

The important scope and extent rules in COMMON LISP follow:

- Variable bindings normally have lexical scope and indefinite extent.

- Variable bindings that are declared to be special have dynamic scope (indefinite scope and dynamic extent).

- A catcher established by a catch or unwind-protect special form has dynamic scope.

- An exit point established by a block construct has lexical scope and dynamic extent. (Such exit points are also established by do, prog, and other iteration constructs.)

- The go targets established by a tagbody, named by the tags in the tagbody, and referred to by go have lexical scope and dynamic extent. (Such go targets may also appear as tags in the bodies of do, prog, and other iteration constructs.)

- Named constants such as nil and pi have indefinite scope and indefinite extent.

The rules of lexical scoping imply that lambda-expressions appearing in the function construct will, in general, result in "closures" over those non-special variables visible to the lambda-expression. That is, the function represented by a lambda-expression may refer to any lexically apparent non-special variable and get the correct value, even if the construct that established the binding has been exited in the course of execution. The compose example shown earlier in this chapter provides one illustration of this. The rules also imply that special variable bindings are not "closed over" as they may be in certain other dialects of LISP.

Constructs that use lexical scope effectively generate a new name for each established entity on each execution. Therefore dynamic shadowing cannot occur (though lexical shadowing may). This is of particular importance when dynamic extent is involved. For example:

```
(defun contorted-example (f g x)
  (if (= x 0)
      (funcall f)
      (block here
        (+ 5 (contorted-example g
                                #'(lambda ()
                                    (return-from here 4))
                                (- x 1)))))))
```

Consider the call (contorted-example nil nil 2). This produces the result 4. During the course of execution, there are three calls on contorted-example, interleaved with two establishments of blocks:

```
(contorted-example nil nil 2)

  (block here₁ ...)

    (contorted-example nil
                       #'(lambda () (return-from here₁ 4))
                       1)

      (block here₂ ...)

        (contorted-example #'(lambda () (return-from here₁ 4))
                           #'(lambda () (return-from here₂ 4))
                           0)
          (funcall f)
                where f ⇒ #'(lambda () (return-from here₁ 4))

            (return-from here₁ 4)
```

At the time the `funcall` is executed there are two `block` exit points outstanding, each apparently named `here`. In the trace above, these exit points are distinguished for expository purposes by subscripts. The `return-from` form executed as a result of the `funcall` operation refers to the *outer* outstanding exit point ($here_1$), not the inner one ($here_2$). This is a consequence of the rules of lexical scoping: it refers to that exit point textually visible at the point of execution of the `function` construct (here abbreviated by the `#'` syntax) that resulted in creation of the function object actually invoked by the `funcall`.

If, in this example, one were to change the form `(funcall f)` to `(funcall g)`, then the value of the call `(contorted-example nil nil 2)` would be ٩. The value would change because the `funcall` would cause the execution of `(return-from` $here_2$ `4)`, thereby causing a return from the inner exit point ($here_2$). When that occurs, the value 4 is returned from the middle invocation of `contorted-example`, 5 is added to that to get ٩, and that value is returned from the outer block and the outermost call to `contorted-example`. The point is that the choice of exit point returned from has nothing to do with its being innermost or outermost; rather, it depends on the lexical scoping information that is effectively packaged up with a lambda-expression when the `function` construct is executed.

This function `contorted-example` works only because the function named by `f` is invoked during the extent of the exit point. Block exit points are like non-special variable bindings in having lexical scope, but differ in having dynamic extent rather than indefinite extent. Once the flow of execution has left the block construct, the exit point is disestablished. For example:

```
(defun illegal-example ()
  (let ((y (block here #'(lambda (z) (return-from here z)))))
    (if (numberp y) y (funcall y 5))))
```

One might expect the call `(illegal-example)` to produce 5 by the following incorrect reasoning: the `let` statement binds the variable `y` to the value of the `block` construct; this value is a function resulting from the lambda-expression. Because `y` is not a number, it is invoked on the value 5. The `return-from` should then return this value from the exit point named `here`, thereby exiting from the block *again* and giving `y` the value 5 which, being a number, is then returned as the value of the call to `illegal-example`.

The argument fails only because exit points are defined in COMMON LISP to have dynamic extent. The argument is correct up to the execution of the `return-from`. The execution of the `return-from` is an error, however, *not* because it cannot refer to the exit point, but because it does correctly refer to an exit point *and* that exit point has been disestablished.

4

Type Specifiers

In COMMON LISP, types are named by LISP objects, specifically symbols and lists, called *type specifiers*. Symbols name predefined classes of objects, whereas lists usually indicate combinations or specializations of simpler types. Symbols or lists may also be abbreviations for types that could be specified in other ways.

4.1. Type Specifier Symbols

The type symbols defined by the system include those shown in Table 4-1. In addition, when a structure type is defined using `defstruct`, the name of the structure type becomes a valid type symbol.

4.2. Type Specifier Lists

If a type specifier is a list, the *car* of the list is a symbol, and the rest of the list is subsidiary type information. In many cases a subsidiary item may be *unspecified*. The unspecified subsidiary item is indicated by writing *. For example, to completely specify a vector type, one must mention the type of the elements and the length of the vector, as for example

```
(vector double-float 100)
```

To leave the length unspecified, one would write

```
(vector double-float *)
```

To leave the element type unspecified, one would write

```
(vector * 100)
```

Suppose that two type specifiers are the same except that the first has a * where

Table 4-1: Standard Type Specifier Symbols

array	fixnum	package	simple-vector
atom	float	pathname	single-float
bignum	function	random-state	standard-char
bit	hash-table	ratio	stream
bit-vector	integer	rational	string
character	keyword	readtable	string-char
common	list	sequence	symbol
compiled-function	long-float	short-float	t
complex	nil	simple-array	vector
cons	null	simple-bit-vector	
double-float	number	simple-string	

the second has a more explicit specification. Then the second denotes a subtype of the type denoted by the first.

As a convenience, if a list has one or more unspecified items at the end, such items may simply be dropped rather than writing an explicit * for each one. If dropping all occurrences of * results in a singleton list, then the parentheses may be dropped as well (the list may be replaced by the symbol in its *car*). For example, (vector double-float *) may be abbreviated to (vector double-float), and (vector * *) may be abbreviated to (vector) and then to simply vector.

4.3. Predicating Type Specifiers

A type specifier list (satisfies *predicate-name*) denotes the set of all objects that satisfy the predicate named by *predicate-name*, which must be a symbol whose global function definition is a one-argument predicate. (A name is required; lambda-expressions are disallowed in order to avoid scoping problems.) For example, the type (satisfies numberp) is the same as the type number. The call (typep x '(satisfies p)) results in applying p to x and returning t if the result is true and nil if the result is false.

As an example, the type string-char could be defined as

```
(deftype string-char ()
  '(and character (satisfies string-char-p)))
```

See deftype.

It is not a good idea for a predicate appearing in a `satisfies` type specifier to cause any side effects when invoked.

4.4. Type Specifiers That Combine

The following type specifier lists define a data type in terms of other types or objects.

(`member` *object1 object2 . . .*)

This denotes the set containing precisely those objects named. An object is of this type if and only if it is `eql` to one of the specified objects.

Compatibility note: This is approximately equivalent to what the INTERLISP DECL package calls `memq`.

(`not` *type*)

This denotes the set of all those objects that are *not* of the specified type.

(`and` *type1 type2 . . .*)

This denotes the intersection of the specified types.

Compatibility note: This is roughly equivalent to what the INTERLISP DECL package calls `allof`.

When `typep` processes an `and` type specifier, it always tests each of the component types in order from left to right and stops processing as soon as one component of the intersection has been found to which the object in question does not belong. In this respect an `and` type specifier is similar to an executable `and` form. The purpose of this similarity is to allow a `satisfies` type specifier to depend on filtering by previous type specifiers. For example, suppose there were a function `primep` that takes an integer and says whether it is prime. Suppose also that it is an error to give any object other than an integer to `primep`. Then the type specifier

(`and integer` (`satisfies primep`))

is guaranteed never to result in an error because the function `primep` will not be invoked unless the object in question has already been determined to be an integer.

(or *type1 type2* ...)

This denotes the union of the specified types. For example, the type list by definition is the same as (or null cons). Also, the value returned by the function position is always of type (or null (integer 0 *)) (either nil or a non-negative integer).

Compatibility note: This is roughly equivalent to what the INTERLISP DECL package calls oneof.

As for and, when typep processes an or type specifier, it always tests each of the component types in order from left to right and stops processing as soon as one component of the union has been found to which the object in question belongs.

4.5. Type Specifiers That Specialize

Some type specifier lists denote *specializations* of data types named by symbols. These specializations may be reflected by more efficient representations in the underlying implementation. As an example, consider the type (array short-float). Implementation A may choose to provide a specialized representation for arrays of short floating-point numbers, and implementation B may choose not to.

If you should want to create an array for the express purpose of holding only short-float objects, you may optionally specify to make-array the element type short-float. This does not *require* make-array to create an object of type (array short-float); it merely *permits* it. The request is construed to mean, "Produce the most specialized array representation capable of holding short-floats that the implementation can provide." Implementation A will then produce a specialized array of type (array short-float), and implementation B will produce an ordinary array of type (array t).

If one were then to ask whether the array were actually of type (array-short-float), implementation A would say "yes," but implementation B would say "no." This is a property of make-array and similar functions: what you ask for is not necessarily what you get.

Types can therefore be used for two different purposes: *declaration* and *discrimination*. Declaring to make-array that elements will always be of type short-float permits optimization. Similarly, declaring that a variable takes on values of type (array short-float) amounts to saying that the variable will take on values that might be produced by specifying element type short-float to make-array. On the other hand, if the predicate typep is used to test whether an object is of type (array short-float), only objects actually of that specialized type can satisfy the test; in implementation B no object can pass that test.

The valid list-format names for data types are as follows:

(array *element-type dimensions*)

This denotes the set of specialized arrays whose elements are all members of the type *element-type* and whose dimensions match *dimensions*. For declaration purposes, this type encompasses those arrays that can result by specifying *element-type* as the element type to the function make-array; this may be different from what the type means for discrimination purposes. *element-type* must be a valid type specifier or unspecified. *dimensions* may be a non-negative integer, which is the number of dimensions, or it may be a list of non-negative integers representing the length of each dimension (any dimension may be unspecified instead), or it may be unspecified. For example:

```
(array integer 3)          ;Three-dimensional arrays of integers
(array integer (* * *))    ;Three-dimensional arrays of integers
(array * (4 5 6))          ;4-by-5-by-6 arrays
(array character (3 *))    ;Two-dimensional arrays of characters
                           ;   that have exactly three rows
(array short-float ())     ;Zero-rank arrays of short-format
                           ;   floating-point numbers
```

Note that (array t) is a proper subset of (array *). The reason is that (array t) is the set of arrays that can hold any COMMON LISP object (the elements are of type t, which includes all objects). On the other hand, (array *) is the set of all arrays whatsoever, including for example arrays that can hold only characters. Now (array character) is not a subset of (array t); the two sets are in fact disjoint because (array character) is not the set of all arrays that can hold characters, but rather the set of arrays that are specialized to hold precisely characters and no other objects. To test whether an array foo can hold a character, one should not use

(typep foo '(array character))

but rather

(subtypep 'character (array-element-type foo))

See array-element-type.

(simple-array *element-type dimensions*)

This is equivalent to (array *element-type dimensions*) except that it additionally specifies that objects of the type are *simple* arrays. (See section 2.5.)

(vector *element-type size*)

This denotes the set of specialized one-dimensional arrays whose elements are all of type *element-type* and whose lengths match *size*. This is entirely equivalent to (array *element-type* (*size*)). For example:

(vector double-float)	;Vectors of double-format
	; floating-point numbers
(vector * 5)	;Vectors of length 5
(vector t 5)	;General vectors of length 5
(vector (mod 32) *)	;Vectors of integers between 0 and 31

The specialized types (vector string-char) and (vector bit) are so useful that they have the special names string and bit-vector. Every implementation of COMMON LISP must provide distinct representations for these as distinct specialized data types.

(simple-vector *size*)

This is the same as (vector t *size*) except that it additionally specifies that its elements are *simple* general vectors.

(complex *type*)

Every element of this type is a complex number whose real part and imaginary part are each of type *type*. For declaration purposes, this type encompasses those complex numbers that can result by giving numbers of the specified type to the function complex; this may be different from what the type means for discrimination purposes. As an example, Gaussian integers might be described as (complex integer), even in implementations where giving two integers to the function complex results in an object of type (complex rational).

(function (*arg1-type arg2-type* ...) *value-type*)

This type may be used only for declaration and not for discrimination; typep will signal an error if it encounters a specifier of this form. Every element of this type is a function that accepts arguments at *least* of the types specified by the *argj-type* forms and returns a value that is a member of the types specified by the *value-type* form. The &optional, &rest, and &key markers may appear in the list of argument types. The *value-type* may be a values type specifier in order to indicate the types of multiple values.

As an example, the function cons is of type (function (t t) cons), because it can accept any two arguments and always returns a cons. The function `cons` is also of type (`function (float string) list`), because it can certainly accept a floating-point number and a string (among other things), and its result is always of type `list` (in fact a `cons` is never `null`, but that does not matter for this type declaration). The function `truncate` is of type (`function (number number) (values number number)`), as well as of type (`function (integer (mod 8)) integer`).

(`values` *value1-type value2-type* ...)

This type specifer is extremely restricted: it may be used *only* as the *value-type* in a `function` type specifier or in a `the` special form. It is used to specify individual types when multiple values are involved. The `&optional`, `&rest`, and `&key` markers may appear in the *value-type* list; they thereby indicate the parameter list of a function that, when given to `multiple-value-call` along with the values, would be suitable for receiving those values.

4.6. Type Specifiers That Abbreviate

The following type specifiers are, for the most part, abbreviations for other type specifiers that would be far too verbose to write out explicitly (using, for example, `member`).

(`integer` *low high*)

Denotes the integers between *low* and *high*. The limits *low* and *high* must each be an integer, a list of an integer, or unspecified. An integer is an inclusive limit, a list of an integer is an exclusive limit, and `*` means that a limit does not exist and so effectively denotes minus or plus infinity, respectively. The type `fixnum` is simply a name for (`integer` *smallest largest*) for implementation-dependent values of *smallest* and *largest* (see `most-negative-fixnum` and `most-positive-fixnum`). The type (`integer 0 1`) is so useful that it has the special name `bit`.

(`mod` *n*)

Denotes the set of non-negative integers less than *n*. This is equivalent to (`integer` 0 $n-1$) or to (`integer 0 (n)`).

(`signed-byte` *s*)

Denotes the set of integers that can be represented in two's-complement form in a byte of *s* bits. This is equivalent to (`integer` -2^{s-1} $2^{s-1}-1$). Simply `signed-byte` or (`signed-byte *`) is the same as `integer`.

(unsigned-byte *s*)

Denotes the set of non-negative integers that can be represented in a byte of *s* bits. This is equivalent to (mod 2^s), that is, (integer 0 2^s − 1). Simply unsigned-byte or (unsigned-byte *) is the same as (integer 0 *), the set of non-negative integers.

(rational *low high*)

Denotes the rationals between *low* and *high*. The limits *low* and *high* must each be a rational, a list of a rational, or unspecified. A rational is an inclusive limit, a list of a rational is an exclusive limit, and * means that a limit does not exist and so effectively denotes minus or plus infinity, respectively.

(float *low high*)

Denotes the set of floating-point numbers between *low* and *high*. The limits *low* and *high* must each be a floating-point number, a list of a floating-point number, or unspecified; a floating-point number is an inclusive limit, a list of a floating-point number is an exclusive limit, and * means that a limit does not exist and so effectively denotes minus or plus infinity, respectively.

In a similar manner, one may use:

(short-float *low high*)
(single-float *low high*)
(double-float *low high*)
(long-float *low high*)

In this case, if a limit is a floating-point number (or a list of one), it must be one of the appropriate format.

(string *size*)

Means the same as (array string-char (*size*)): the set of strings of the indicated size.

(simple-string *size*)

Means the same as (simple-array string-char (*size*)): the set of simple strings of the indicated size.

(bit-vector *size*)

Means the same as (array bit (*size*)): the set of bit-vectors of the indicated size.

```
(simple-bit-vector size)
```

This means the same as (simple-array bit (size)): the set of bit-vectors of the indicated size.

4.7. Defining New Type Specifiers

New type specifiers can come into existence in two ways. First, defining a new structure type with defstruct automatically causes the name of the structure to be a new type specifier symbol. Second, the deftype special form can be used to define new type-specifier abbreviations.

deftype *name lambda-list {declaration | doc-string}* {form}** [*Macro*]

This is very similar to a defmacro form: *name* is the symbol that identifies the type specifier being defined, *lambda-list* is a lambda-list (and may contain &optional and &rest markers), and the *forms* constitute the body of the expander function. If we view a type specifier list as a list containing the type specifier name and some argument forms, the argument forms (unevaluated) are bound to the corresponding parameters in *lambda-list*. Then the body forms are evaluated as an implicit progn, and the value of the last form is interpreted as a new type specifier for which the original specifier was an abbreviation. The *name* is returned as the value of the deftype form.

deftype differs from defmacro in that if no *initform* is specified for an &optional parameter, the default value is *, not nil.

If the optional documentation string *doc-string* is present, then it is attached to the *name* as a documentation string of type type; see documentation.

Here are some examples of the use of deftype:

```
(deftype mod (n) '(integer 0 (,n)))

(deftype list () '(or null cons))

(deftype square-matrix (&optional type size)
  "SQUARE-MATRIX includes all square two-dimensional arrays."
  '(array ,type (,size ,size)))

(square-matrix short-float 7) means (array short-float (7 7))

(square-matrix bit) means (array bit (* *))
```

If the type name defined by deftype is used simply as a type specifier symbol, it is interpreted as a type specifier list with no argument forms. Thus, in the example above, square-matrix would mean (array * (* *)), the set of two-dimensional arrays. This would unfortunately fail to convey the constraint that the two dimensions be the same; (square-matrix bit) has the same problem. A better definition is:

```
(defun equidimensional (a)
  (or (< (array-rank a) 2)
      (apply #'= (array-dimensions a))))

(deftype square-matrix (&optional type size)
  '(and (array ,type (,size ,size))
        (satisfies equidimensional)))
```

4.8. Type Conversion Function

The following function may be used to convert an object to an equivalent object of another type.

coerce *object result-type*   [*Function*]

The *result-type* must be a type specifier; the *object* is converted to an "equivalent" object of the specified type. If the coercion cannot be performed, then an error is signalled. In particular, (coerce x 'nil) always signals an error. If *object* is already of the specified type, as determined by typep, then it is simply returned. It is not generally possible to convert any object to be of any type whatsoever; only certain conversions are permitted:

- Any sequence type may be converted to any other sequence type, provided the new sequence can contain all actual elements of the old sequence (it is an error if it cannot). If the *result-type* is specified as simply array, for example, then (array t) is assumed. A specialized type such as string or (vector (complex short-float)) may be specified; of course, the result may be of either that type or some more general type, as determined by the implementation. Elements of the new sequence will be eql to corresponding elements of the old sequence. If the *sequence* is already of the specified type, it may be returned without copying it; in this, (coerce *sequence type*) differs from (concatenate *type sequence*), for the latter is required to copy the argument *sequence*. In particular, if one specifies sequence, then the argument may simply be returned if it already is a sequence.

  (coerce '(a b c) 'vector) ⇒ #(a b c)

- Some strings, symbols, and integers may be converted to characters. If *object* is a string of length 1, then the sole element of the string is returned. If *object* is a symbol whose print name is of length 1, then the sole element of the print name is returned. If *object* is an integer *n*, then (int-char *n*) is returned. See character.

```
(coerce "a" 'character) ⇒ #\a
```

- Any non-complex number can be converted to a short-float, single-float, double-float, or long-float. If simply float is specified, and *object* is not already a float of some kind, then the object is converted to a single-float.

```
(coerce 0 'short-float) ⇒ 0.0S0
(coerce 3.5L0 'float) ⇒ 3.5L0
(coerce 7/2 'float) ⇒ 3.5
```

- Any number can be converted to a complex number. If the number is not already complex, then a zero imaginary part is provided by coercing the integer zero to the type of the given real part. (If the given real part is rational, however, then the rule of canonical representation for complex rationals will result in the immediate re-conversion of the result from type complex back to type rational.)

```
(coerce 4.5s0 'complex) ⇒ #C(4.5S0 0.0S0)
(coerce 7/2 'complex) ⇒ 7/2
(coerce #C(7/2 0) '(complex double-float))
    ⇒ #C(3.5D0 0.0D0)
```

- Any object may be coerced to type t.

```
(coerce x 't) ≡ (identity x) ≡ x
```

Coercions from floating-point numbers to rationals and from ratios to integers are purposely *not* provided because of rounding problems. The functions rational, rationalize, floor, ceiling, truncate, and round may be used for such purposes. Similarly, coercions from characters to integers are purposely not provided; char-code or char-int may be used explicitly to perform such conversions.

4.9. Determining the Type of an Object

The following function may be used to obtain a type specifier describing the type of a given object.

type-of *object*   [*Function*]

(type-of *object*) returns an implementation-dependent result: some *type* of which the *object* is a member. Implementors are encouraged to arrange for type-of to return the most specific type that can be conveniently computed and is likely to be useful to the user. If the argument is a user-defined named structure created by defstruct, then type-of will return the type name of that structure. Because the result is implementation-dependent, it is usually better to use type-of primarily for debugging purposes; however, in a few situations portable code requires the use of type-of, such as when the result is to be given to the coerce or map function. On the other hand, often the typep function or the typecase construct is more appropriate than type-of.

Compatibility note: In MACLISP the function type-of is called typep, and anomalously so, for it is not a predicate.

5

Program
Structure

In chapter 2 the syntax was sketched for notating data objects in COMMON LISP. The same syntax is used for notating programs because all COMMON LISP programs have a representation as COMMON LISP data objects.

LISP programs are organized as forms and functions. Forms are *evaluated* (relative to some context) to produce values and side effects. Functions are invoked by *applying* them to arguments. The most important kind of form performs a function call; conversely, a function performs computation by evaluating forms.

In this chapter forms are discussed first, and then functions. Finally, certain "top level" special forms are discussed; the most important of these is defun, whose purpose is to define a named function.

5.1. Forms

The standard unit of interaction with a COMMON LISP implementation is the *form*, which is simply a data object meant to be *evaluated* as a program to produce one or more *values* (which are also data objects). One may request evaluation of *any* data object, but only certain ones are meaningful. For instance, symbols and lists are meaningful forms, while arrays normally are not. Examples of meaningful forms are 3, whose value is 3, and (+ 3 4), whose value is 7. We write 3 ⇒ 3 and (+ 3 4) ⇒ 7 to indicate these facts. (⇒ means "evaluates to.")

Meaningful forms may be divided into three categories: self-evaluating forms, such as numbers; symbols, which stand for variables; and lists. The lists in turn may be divided into three categories: special forms, macro calls, and function calls.

Any COMMON LISP data object not explicitly defined here to be a valid form is not a valid form. It is an error to evaluate anything but a valid form.

Implementation note: An implementation is free to make implementation-dependent extensions to the evaluator, but is strongly encouraged to signal an error on any attempt to evaluate anything but a valid form or an object for which a meaningful evaluation extension has been purposely defined.

5.1.1. Self-Evaluating Forms

All numbers, characters, strings, and bit-vectors are *self-evaluating* forms. When such an object is evaluated, that object (or possibly a copy in the case of numbers or characters) is returned as the value of the form. The empty list `()`, which is also the false value `nil`, is also a self-evaluating form: the value of `nil` is `nil`. Keywords (symbols written with a leading colon) also evaluate to themselves: the value of `:start` is `:start`.

5.1.2. Variables

Symbols are used as names of variables in COMMON LISP programs. When a symbol is evaluated as a form, the value of the variable it names is produced. For example, after doing `(setq items 3)`, which assigns the value `3` to the variable named `items`, then `items ⇒ 3`. Variables can be *assigned* to, as by `setq`, or *bound*, as by `let`. Any program construct that binds a variable effectively saves the old value of the variable and causes it to have a new value, and on exit from the construct the old value is reinstated.

There are actually two kinds of variables in COMMON LISP, called *lexical* (or *static*) variables and *special* (or *dynamic*) variables. At any given time either or both kinds of variable with the same name may have a current value. Which of the two kinds of variable is referred to when a symbol is evaluated depends on the context of the evaluation. The general rule is that if the symbol occurs textually within a program construct that creates a *binding* for a variable of the same name, then the reference is to the variable specified by the binding; if no such program construct textually contains the reference, then it is taken to refer to the special variable of that name.

The distinction between the two kinds of variable is one of scope and extent. A lexically bound variable can be referred to *only* by forms occurring at any *place* textually within the program construct that binds the variable. A dynamically bound (special) variable can be referred to at any *time* from the time the binding is made until the time evaluation of the construct that binds the variable terminates. Therefore lexical binding of variables imposes a spatial limitation on occurrences of references (but no temporal limitation, for the binding continues to exist as long as the possibility of reference remains). Conversely, dynamic binding of variables imposes a temporal limitation on occurrences of references (but no spatial limitation). For more information on scope and extent, see chapter 3.

The value a special variable has when there are currently no bindings of that variable is called the *global* value of the (special) variable. A global value can be given to a variable only by assignment, because a value given by binding is by definition not global.

It is possible for a special variable to have no value at all, in which case it is said to be *unbound*. By default, every global variable is unbound unless and until explicitly assigned a value, except for those global variables defined in this manual or by the implementation already to have values when the LISP system is first started. It is also possible to establish a binding of a special variable and then cause that binding to be valueless by using the function makunbound. In this situation the variable is also said to be "unbound," although this is a misnomer; precisely speaking, it is bound but valueless. It is an error to refer to a variable that is unbound.

Certain global variables are reserved as "named constants." They have a global value and may not be bound or assigned to. For example, the symbols t and nil are reserved. One may not assign a value to t or nil, and one may not bind t or nil. The global value of t is always t, and the global value of nil is always nil. Constant symbols defined by defconstant also become reserved and may not be further assigned to or bound (although they may be redefined, if necessary, by using defconstant again). Keyword symbols, which are notated with a leading colon, are reserved and may never be assigned to or bound; a keyword always evaluates to itself.

5.1.3. Special Forms

If a list is to be evaluated as a form, the first step is to examine the first element of the list. If the first element is one of the symbols appearing in Table 5-1, then the list is called a *special form*. (This use of the word "special" is unrelated to its use in the phrase "special variable.")

Special forms are generally environment and control constructs. Every special form has its own idiosyncratic syntax. An example is the if special form: (if p (+ x 4) 5) in COMMON LISP means what "**if** p **then** x + 4 **else** 5" would mean in ALGOL.

The evaluation of a special form normally produces a value or values, but the evaluation may instead call for a non-local exit; see return-from, go, and throw.

Table 5-1: Names of All COMMON LISP Special Forms

block	if	progv
catch	labels	quote
compiler-let	let	return-from
declare	let*	setq
eval-when	macrolet	tagbody
flet	multiple-value-call	the
function	multiple-value-prog1	throw
go	progn	unwind-protect

The set of special forms is fixed in COMMON LISP; no way is provided for the user to define more. The user can create new syntactic constructs, however, by defining macros.

The set of special forms in COMMON LISP is purposely kept very small because any program-analyzing program must have special knowledge about every type of special form. Such a program needs no special knowledge about macros because it is simple to expand the macro and operate on the resulting expansion. (This is not to say that many such programs, particularly compilers, will not have such special knowledge. A compiler may be able to produce much better code if it recognizes such constructs as `typecase` and `multiple-value-bind` and gives them customized treatment.)

An implementation is free to implement as a macro any construct described herein as a special form. Conversely, an implementation is free to implement as a special form any construct described herein as a macro if an equivalent macro definition is also provided. The practical consequence is that the predicates `macro-function` and `special-form-p` may both be true of the same symbol. It is recommended that a program-analyzing program process a form that is a list whose *car* is a symbol as follows:

1. If the program has particular knowledge about the symbol, process the form using special-purpose code. All of the symbols listed in Table 5-1 should fall into this category.

2. Otherwise, if `macro-function` is true of the symbol, apply either `macroexpand` or `macroexpand-1`, as appropriate, to the entire form and then start over.

3. Otherwise, assume it is a function call.

5.1.4. Macros

If a form is a list and the first element is not the name of a special form, it may be the name of a *macro*; if so, the form is said to be a *macro call*. A macro is essentially a function from forms to forms that will, given a call to that macro, compute a new form to be evaluated in place of the macro call. (This computation is sometimes referred to as *macro expansion*.) For example, the macro named `return` will take a form such as (`return` x) and from that form compute a new form (`return-from` nil x). We say that the old form *expands* into the new form. The new form is then evaluated in place of the original form; the value of the new form is returned as the value of the original form.

There are a number of standard macros in COMMON LISP, and the user can define more by using `defmacro`.

Macros provided by a COMMON LISP implementation as described herein may expand into code that is not portable among differing implementations. That is, a macro call may be implementation-independent because the macro is defined in this manual, but the expansion need not be.

Implementation note: Implementors are encouraged to implement the macros defined in this manual, as far as is possible, in such as way that the expansion will not contain any implementation-dependent special forms, nor contain as forms data objects that are not considered to be forms in COMMON LISP. The purpose of this restriction is to ensure that the expansion can be processed by a program-analyzing program in an implementation-independent manner. There is no problem with a macro expansion containing calls to implementation-dependent functions. This restriction is not a requirement of COMMON LISP; it is recognized that certain complex macros may be able to expand into significantly more efficient code in certain implementations by using implementation-dependent special forms in the macro expansion.

5.1.5. Function Calls

If a list is to be evaluated as a form and the first element is not a symbol that names a special form or macro, then the list is assumed to be a *function call*. The first element of the list is taken to name a function. Any and all remaining elements of the list are forms to be evaluated; one value is obtained from each form, and these values become the *arguments* to the function. The function is then *applied* to the arguments. The functional computation normally produces a value, but it may instead call for a non-local exit; see `throw`. A function that does return may produce no value or several values; see `values`. If and when the function returns, whatever values it returns become the values of the function-call form.

For example, consider the evaluation of the form (+ 3 (* 4 5)). The symbol + names the addition function, not a special form or macro. Therefore the two forms 3 and (* 4 5) are evaluated to produce arguments. The form 3 evaluates to 3, and the form (* 4 5) is a function call (to the multiplication function).

Therefore the forms 4 and 5 are evaluated, producing arguments 4 and 5 for the multiplication. The multiplication function calculates the number 20 and returns it. The values 3 and 20 are then given as arguments to the addition function, which calculates and returns the number 23. Therefore we say (+ 3 (* 4 5)) ⇒ 23.

5.2. Functions

There are two ways to indicate a function to be used in a function call form. One is to use a symbol that names the function. This use of symbols to name functions is completely independent of their use in naming special and lexical variables. The other way is to use a *lambda-expression*, which is a list whose first element is the symbol lambda. A lambda-expression is *not* a form; it cannot be meaningfully evaluated. Lambda-expressions and symbols, when used in programs as names of functions, can appear only as the first element of a function-call form, or as the second element of the function special form. Note that symbols and lambda-expressions are treated as *names* of functions in these two contexts. This should be distinguished from the treatment of symbols and lambda-expressions as *function objects*, that is, objects that satisfy the predicate functionp, as when giving such an object to apply or funcall to be invoked.

5.2.1. Named Functions

A name can be given to a function in one of two ways. A *global name* can be given to a function by using the defun construct. A *local name* can be given to a function by using the flet or labels special form. When a function is named, a lambda-expression is effectively associated with that name along with information about the entities that are lexically apparent at that point. If a symbol appears as the first element of a function-call form, then it refers to the definition established by the innermost flet or labels construct that textually contains the reference, or to the global definition (if any) if there is no such containing construct.

5.2.2. Lambda-Expressions

A *lambda-expression* is a list with the following syntax:

(lambda *lambda-list* . *body*)

The first element must be the symbol lambda. The second element must be a list. It is called the *lambda-list*, and specifies names for the *parameters* of the function.

When the function denoted by the lambda-expression is applied to arguments, the arguments are matched with the parameters specified by the lambda-list. The *body* may then refer to the arguments by using the parameter names. The *body* consists of any number of forms (possibly zero). These forms are evaluated in sequence, and the results of the *last* form only are returned as the results of the application (the value `nil` is returned if there are zero forms in the body). The complete syntax of a lambda-expression is:

```
(lambda ({var}*
         [&optional {var | (var [initform [svar]])}*]
         [&rest var]
         [&key {var | ({var | (keyword var)} [initform [svar]])}*
               [&allow-other-keys]]
         [&aux {var | (var [initform])}*])
   {declaration | documentation-string}*
   {form}*)
```

Each element of a lambda-list is either a *parameter specifier* or a *lambda-list keyword*; lambda-list keywords begin with &. (Note that lambda-list keywords are not keywords in the usual sense; they do not belong to the keyword package. They are ordinary symbols each of whose names begins with an ampersand. This terminology is unfortunately confusing but is retained for historical reasons.)

In all cases a *var* or *svar* must be a symbol, the name of a variable; each *keyword* must be a keyword symbol, such as `:start`. An *initform* may be any form.

A lambda-list has five parts, any or all of which may be empty:

- Specifiers for the *required* parameters. These are all the parameter specifiers up to the first lambda-list keyword; if there is no such lambda-list keyword, then all the specifiers are for required parameters.

- Specifiers for *optional* parameters. If the lambda-list keyword &optional is present, the *optional* parameter specifiers are those following the lambda-list keyword &optional up to the next lambda-list keyword or the end of the list.

- A specifier for a *rest* parameter. The lambda-list keyword &rest, if present, must be followed by a single *rest* parameter specifier, which in turn must be followed by another lambda-list keyword or the end of the lambda-list.

- Specifiers for *keyword* parameters. If the lambda-list keyword &key is present, all specifiers up to the next lambda-list keyword or the end of the list are *keyword* parameter specifiers. The keyword parameter specifiers may optionally be followed by the lambda-list keyword &allow-other-keys.

- Specifiers for *aux* variables. These are not really parameters. If the lambda-list keyword &aux is present, all specifiers after it are *auxiliary variable* specifiers.

When the function represented by the lambda-expression is applied to arguments, the arguments and parameters are processed in order from left to right. In the simplest case, only required parameters are present in the lambda-list; each is specified simply by a name *var* for the parameter variable. When the function is applied, there must be exactly as many arguments as there are parameters, and each parameter is bound to one argument. Here, and in general, the parameter is bound as a lexical variable unless a declaration has been made that it should be a special binding; see defvar, proclaim, and declare.

In the more general case, if there are *n* required parameters (*n* may be zero), there must be at least *n* arguments, and the required parameters are bound to the first *n* arguments. The other parameters are then processed using any remaining arguments.

If *optional* parameters are specified, then each one is processed as follows. If any unprocessed arguments remain, then the parameter variable *var* is bound to the next remaining argument, just as for a required parameter. If no arguments remain, however, then the *initform* part of the parameter specifier is evaluated, and the parameter variable is bound to the resulting value (or to nil if no *initform* appears in the parameter specifier). If another variable name *svar* appears in the specifier, it is bound to *true* if an argument was available, and to *false* if no argument remained (and therefore *initform* had to be evaluated). The variable *svar* is called a *supplied-p* parameter; it is bound not to an argument but to a value indicating whether or not an argument had been supplied for another parameter.

After all *optional* parameter specifiers have been processed, then there may or may not be a *rest* parameter. If there is a *rest* parameter, it is bound to a list of all as-yet-unprocessed arguments. (If no unprocessed arguments remain, the *rest* parameter is bound to the empty list.) If there is no *rest* parameter and there are no *keyword* parameters, then there should be no unprocessed arguments (it is an error if there are).

Next, any *keyword* parameters are processed. For this purpose the same arguments are processed that would be made into a list for a *rest* parameter. (Indeed, it is permitted to specify both &rest and &key. In this case the remaining arguments are used for both purposes; that is, all remaining arguments are made into a list for the &rest parameter, and are also processed for the &key parameters. This is the only situation in which an argument is used in the processing of more than one parameter specifier.) If &key is specified, there must remain an even number of arguments; these are considered as pairs, the first argument in each pair being interpreted as a keyword name and the second as the corresponding value. It is an error for the first object of each pair to be anything but a keyword.

Rationale: This last restriction is imposed so that a compiler may issue warnings about certain malformed calls to functions that take keyword arguments. It must be remembered that the arguments in a function call that evaluate to keywords are just like any other arguments, and may be any evaluable forms. A compiler could not, without additional context, issue a warning about the call

```
(fill seq item x y)
```

because in principle the variable x might have as its value a keyword such as :start. However, a compiler would be justified in issuing a warning about the call

```
(fill seq item 0 10)
```

because the constant 0 is definitely not a keyword. Similarly, if in the first case the variable x had been declared to be of type integer then type analysis could enable the compiler to justify a warning.

In each keyword parameter specifier must be a name *var* for the parameter variable. If an explicit *keyword* is specified, then that is the keyword name for the parameter. Otherwise the name *var* serves to indicate the keyword name, in that a keyword with the same name (in the keyword package) is used as the keyword. Thus

```
(defun foo (&key radix (type 'integer)) ...)
```

means exactly the same as

```
(defun foo (&key ((:radix radix)) ((:type type) 'integer)) ...)
```

The keyword parameter specifiers are, like all parameter specifiers, effectively processed from left to right. For each keyword parameter specifier, if there is an argument pair whose keyword name matches that specifier's keyword name (that is, the names are eq), then the parameter variable for that specifier is bound to the second item (the value) of that argument pair. If more than one such argument pair matches, it is not an error; the leftmost argument pair is used. If no such pair exists, then the *initform* for that specifier is evaluated and the parameter variable is bound to that value (or to nil if no *initform* was specified). The variable *svar* is treated as for ordinary *optional* parameters: it is bound to *true* if there was a matching argument pair, and to *false* otherwise.

It is an error if an argument pair has a keyword name not matched by any parameter specifier, unless at least one of the following two conditions is met:

- &allow-other-keys was specified in the lambda-list.

- Among the keyword argument pairs is a pair whose keyword is :allow-other-keys and whose value is not nil.

If either condition obtains, then it is not an error for an argument pair to match no parameter specified, and the argument pair is simply ignored (but such an argument pair is accessible through the &rest parameter if one was specified). The purpose of these mechanisms is to allow sharing of argument lists among several functions and to allow either the caller or the called function to specify that such sharing may be taking place.

After all parameter specifiers have been processed, the auxiliary variable specifiers (those following the lambda-list keyword &aux) are processed from left to right. For each one, the *initform* is evaluated and the variable *var* bound to that value (or to nil if no *initform* was specified). Nothing can be done with &aux variables that cannot be done with the special form let*:

```
(lambda (x y &aux (a (car x)) (b 2) c) ...)
   ≡ (lambda (x y) (let* ((a (car x)) (b 2) c) ...))
```

Which to use is purely a matter of style.

Whenever any *initform* is evaluated for any parameter specifier, that form may refer to any parameter variable to the left of the specifier in which the *initform* appears, including any supplied-p variables, and may rely on the fact that no other parameter variable has yet been bound (including its own parameter variable).

Once the lambda-list has been processed, the forms in the body of the lambda-expression are executed. These forms may refer to the arguments to the function by using the names of the parameters. On exit from the function, either by a normal return of the function's value(s) or by a non-local exit, the parameter bindings, whether lexical or special, are no longer in effect. (The bindings are not necessarily permanently discarded, for a lexical binding can later be reinstated if a "closure" over that binding was created, perhaps by using function, and saved before the exit occurred).

Examples of &optional and &rest parameters:

```
((lambda (a b) (+ a (* b 3))) 4 5) ⇒ 19
((lambda (a &optional (b 2)) (+ a (* b 3))) 4 5) ⇒ 19
((lambda (a &optional (b 2)) (+ a (* b 3))) 4) ⇒ 10
((lambda (&optional (a 2 b) (c 3 d) &rest x) (list a b c d x)))
   ⇒ (2 nil 3 nil nil)
```

```
((lambda (&optional (a 2 b) (c 3 d) &rest x) (list a b c d x))
 6)
   ⇒ (6 t 3 nil nil)
((lambda (&optional (a 2 b) (c 3 d) &rest x) (list a b c d x))
 6 3)
   ⇒ (6 t 3 t nil)
((lambda (&optional (a 2 b) (c 3 d) &rest x) (list a b c d x))
 6 3 8)
   ⇒ (6 t 3 t (8))
((lambda (&optional (a 2 b) (c 3 d) &rest x) (list a b c d x))
 6 3 8 9 10 11)
   ⇒ (6 t 3 t (8 9 10 11))
```

Examples of &key parameters:

```
((lambda (a b &key c d) (list a b c d)) 1 2)
   ⇒ (1 2 nil nil)
((lambda (a b &key c d) (list a b c d)) 1 2 :c 6)
   ⇒ (1 2 6 nil)
((lambda (a b &key c d) (list a b c d)) 1 2 :d 8)
   ⇒ (1 2 nil 8)
((lambda (a b &key c d) (list a b c d)) 1 2 :c 6 :d 8)
   ⇒ (1 2 6 8)
((lambda (a b, &key c d) (list a b c d)) 1 2 :d 8 :c 6)
   ⇒ (1 2 6 8)
((lambda (a b &key c d) (list a b c d)) :a 1 :d 8 :c 6)
   ⇒ (:a 1 6 8)
((lambda (a b &key c d) (list a b c d)) :a :b :c :d)
   ⇒ (:a :b :d nil)
```

Examples of mixtures:

```
((lambda (a &optional (b 3) &rest x &key c (d a))
   (list a b c d x))
 1)   ⇒ (1 3 nil 1 ())

((lambda (a &optional (b 3) &rest x &key c (d a))
   (list a b c d x))
 1 2)   ⇒ (1 2 nil 1 ())

((lambda (a &optional (b 3) &rest x &key c (d a))
   (list a b c d x))
 :c 7)   ⇒ (:c 7 nil :c ())
```

```
((lambda (a &optional (b 3) &rest x &key c (d a))
   (list a b c d x))
 1 6 :c 7)   ⇒ (1 6 7 1 (:c 7))

((lambda (a &optional (b 3) &rest x &key c (d a))
   (list a b c d x))
 1 6 :d 8)   ⇒ (1 6 nil 8 (:d 8))

((lambda (a &optional (b 3) &rest x &key c (d a))
   (list a b c d x))
 1 6 :d 8 :c 9 :d 10)   ⇒ (1 6 9 8 (:d 8 :c 9 :d 10))
```

All lambda-list keywords are permitted, but not terribly useful, in lambda-expressions appearing explicitly as the first element of a function-call form. They are extremely useful, however, in functions given global names by defun.

All symbols whose names begin with & are conventionally reserved for use as lambda-list keywords and should not be used as variable names. Implementations of COMMON LISP are free to provide additional lambda-list keywords.

lambda-list-keywords   [*Constant*]

The value of lambda-list-keywords is a list of all the lambda-list keywords used in the implementation, including the additional ones used only by defmacro. This list must contain at least the symbols &optional, &rest, &key, &allow-other-keys, &aux, &body, &whole, and &environment.

As an example of the use of &allow-other-keys and :allow-other-keys, consider a function that takes two keyword arguments of its own and also accepts additional keyword arguments to be passed to make-array:

```
(defun array-of-strings (str dims &rest keyword-pairs
                         &key (start 0) end &allow-other-keys)
   (apply #'make-array dims
          :initial-element (subseq str start end)
          :allow-other-keys t
          keyword-pairs))
```

This function takes a string and dimensioning information and returns an array of the specified dimensions, each of whose elements is the specified string. However, :start and :end keyword arguments may be used in the usual manner (see chapter 14) to specify that a substring of the given string should be used. In addition, the presence of &allow-other-keys in the lambda-list indicates that the caller may specify additional keyword arguments; the &rest argument provides access to them. These additional keyword arguments are fed to make-array. Now make-array normally does not allow the keywords :start and :end to be used, and it would be an error to specify such keyword arguments to make-array. However, the presence in the call to make-array of the keyword argument :allow-other-keys with a non-nil value causes any extraneous keyword arguments, including :start and :end, to be acceptable and ignored.

lambda-parameters-limit   *[Constant]*

The value of lambda-parameters-limit is a positive integer that is the upper exclusive bound on the number of distinct parameter names that may appear in a single lambda-list. This bound depends on the implementation but will not be smaller than 50. Implementors are encouraged to make this limit as large as practicable without sacrificing performance. See call-arguments-limit.

5.3. Top-Level Forms

The standard way for the user to interact with a COMMON LISP implementation is via a *read-eval-print loop*: the system repeatedly reads a form from some input source (such as a keyboard or a disk file), evaluates it, and then prints the value(s) to some output sink (such as a display screen or another disk file). Any form (evaluable data object) is acceptable; however, certain special forms are specifically designed to be convenient for use as *top-level* forms, rather than as forms embedded within other forms in the way that (+ 3 4) is embedded within (if p (+ 3 4) 6). These top-level special forms may be used to define globally named functions, to define macros, to make declarations, and to define global values for special variables.

It is not illegal to use these forms at other than top level, but whether it is meaningful to do so depends on context. Compilers, for example, may not recognize these forms properly in other than top-level contexts. (As a special case, however, if a progn form appears at top level, then all forms within that progn are considered by the compiler to be top-level forms.)

Compatibility note: In MacLisp, a top-level progn is considered to contain top-level forms only if the first form is (quote compile). This odd marker is unnecessary in COMMON LISP.

Macros are usually defined by using the special form defmacro. This facility is fairly complicated, and is described in chapter 8.

5.3.1. Defining Named Functions

The `defun` special form is the usual means of defining named functions.

`defun` *name lambda-list {declaration | doc-string}* {form}**   [*Macro*]

Evaluating a `defun` form causes the symbol *name* to be a global name for the function specified by the lambda-expression

(`lambda` *lambda-list {declaration | doc-string}* {form}**)

defined in the lexical environment in which the `defun` form was executed. Because `defun` forms normally appear at top level, this is normally the null lexical environment.

If the optional documentation string *doc-string* is present, then it is attached to the *name* as a documentation string of type `function`; see `documentation`. If *doc-string* is not followed by a declaration, it may be present only if at least one *form* is also specified, as it is otherwise taken to be a *form*. It is an error if more than one *doc-string* is present.

The *forms* constitute the body of the defined function; they are executed as an implicit `progn`.

The body of the defined function is implicitly enclosed in a `block` construct whose name is the same as the *name* of the function. Therefore `return-from` may be used to exit from the function.

Other implementation-dependent bookkeeping actions may be taken as well by `defun`. The *name* is returned as the value of the `defun` form. For example:

```
(defun discriminant (a b c)
  (declare (number a b c))
  "Compute the discriminant for a quadratic equation.
  Given a, b, and c, the value b^2-4*a*c is calculated.
  The quadratic equation a*x^2+b*x+c=0 has real, multiple,
  or complex roots depending on whether this calculated
  value is positive, zero, or negative, respectively."
  (- (* b b) (* 4 a c)))
  ⇒ discriminant
  and now (discriminant 1 2/3 -2) ⇒ 76/9
```

It is permissible to use `defun` to redefine a function, to install a corrected version of an incorrect definition, for example! It is permissible to redefine a macro as a function. It is an error to attempt to redefine the name of a special form (see Table 5-1) as a function.

5.3.2. Declaring Global Variables and Named Constants

The defvar and defparameter special forms are the usual means of specifying globally defined variables. The defconstant special form is used for defining named constants.

defvar *name* [*initial-value* [*documentation*]]	[*Macro*]
defparameter *name* *initial-value* [*documentation*]	[*Macro*]
defconstant *name* *initial-value* [*documentation*]	[*Macro*]

defvar is the recommended way to declare the use of a special variable in a program.

(defvar *variable*)

proclaims *variable* to be special (see proclaim), and may perform other system-dependent bookkeeping actions. If a second "argument" is supplied,

(defvar *variable initial-value*)

then *variable* is initialized to the result of evaluating the form *initial-value* unless it already has a value. The *initial-value* form is not evaluated unless it is used; this fact is useful if evaluation of the *initial-value* form does something expensive like creating a large data structure. The initialization is performed by assignment, and so assigns a global value to the variable unless there are currently special bindings of that variable. Normally there should not be any such special bindings.

defvar also provides a good place to put a comment describing the meaning of the variable, whereas an ordinary special proclamation offers the temptation to declare several variables at once and not have room to describe them all.

```
(defvar *visible-windows* 0
"Number of windows at least partially visible on the screen")
```

defparameter is similar to defvar, but defparameter requires an *initial-value* form, always evaluates the form, and assigns the result to the variable. The semantic distinction is that defvar is intended to declare a variable changed by the program, whereas defparameter is intended to declare a variable that is normally constant but can be changed (possibly at run time), where such a change is considered a change *to* the program. defparameter therefore does not indicate that the quantity *never* changes; in particular, it does not license the compiler to build assumptions about the value into programs being compiled.

defconstant is like defparameter but *does* assert that the value of the variable *name* is fixed and does license the compiler to build assumptions about the value into programs being compiled. (However, if the compiler chooses to replaces references to the name of the constant by the value of the constant in code to be compiled, perhaps in order to allow further optimization, the compiler must take care that such "copies" appear to be eql to the object that is the actual value of the constant. For example, the compiler may freely make copies of numbers but must exercise care when the value is a list.)

It is an error if there are any special bindings of the variable at the time the defconstant form is executed (but implementations may or may not check for this).

Once a name has been declared by defconstant to be constant, any further assignment to or binding of that special variable is an error. This is the case for such system-supplied constants as t and most-positive-fixnum. A compiler may also choose to issue warnings about bindings of the lexical variable of the same name.

For any of these constructs, the documentation should be a string. The string is attached to the name of the variable, parameter, or constant under the variable documentation type; see the documentation function.

These constructs are normally used only as top-level forms. The value returned by each of these constructs is the *name* declared.

5.3.3. Control of Time of Evaluation

The eval-when special form allows pieces of code to be executed only at compile time, only at load time, or when interpreted but not compiled. Its uses are relatively esoteric.

---

eval-when ({*situation*}*) {*form*}*   [*Special Form*]

The body of an eval-when form is processed as an implicit progn, but only in the situations listed. Each *situation* must be a symbol, either compile, load, or eval.

eval specifies that the interpreter should process the body. compile specifies that the compiler should evaluate the body at compile time in the compilation context. load specifies that the compiler should arrange to evaluate the forms in the body when the compiled file containing the eval-when form is loaded.

The eval-when construct may be more precisely understood in terms of a model of how the compiler processes forms in a file to be compiled. Successive forms are read from the file using the function read. These top-level forms are normally processed in what we shall call *not-compile-time* mode. There is another mode called *compile-time-too* mode. The eval-when special form controls which of these two modes to use.

Every form is processed as follows:

- If the form is an `eval-when` form:
  - If the situation `load` is specified:
    - If the situation `compile` is also specified, *or* if the current processing mode is *compile-time-too* and the situation `eval` is also specified, then process each of the forms in the body in *compile-time-too* mode.
    - Otherwise, process each of the forms in the body in *not-compile-time* mode.
  - If the situation `load` is not specified:
    - If the situation `compile` is specified, *or* if the current processing mode is *compile-time-too* and the situation `eval` is specified, then evaluate each of the forms in the body in the compiler's executing environment.
    - Otherwise, ignore the `eval-when` form entirely.
- If the form is not an `eval-when` form, then do two things. First, if the current processing mode is *compile-time-too* mode, then evaluate the form in the compiler's executing environment. Second, perform normal compiler processing of the form (compiling functions defined by `defun` forms, and so on).

One example of the use of `eval-when` is that if the compiler is to be able to properly read a file that uses user-defined reader macro characters, it is necessary to write

```
(eval-when (compile load eval)
  (set-macro-character #\$ #'(lambda (stream char)
                               (declare (ignore char))
                               (list 'dollar (read stream)))))
```

This causes the call to `set-macro-character` to be executed in the compiler's execution environment, thereby modifying its reader syntax table.

6

Predicates

A *predicate* is a function that tests for some condition involving its arguments and returns nil if the condition is false, or some non-nil value if the condition is true. One may think of a predicate as producing a Boolean value, where nil stands for *false* and anything else stands for *true*. Conditional control structures such as cond, if, when, and unless test such Boolean values. We say that a predicate *is true* when it returns a non-nil value, and *is false* when it returns nil; that is, it is true or false according to whether the condition being tested is true or false.

By convention, the names of predicates usually end in the letter p (which stands for "predicate"). COMMON LISP uses a uniform convention in hyphenating names of predicates. If the name of the predicate is formed by adding a p to an existing name, such as the name of a data type, a hyphen is placed before the final p if and only if there is a hyphen in the existing name. For example, number begets numberp but standard-char begets standard-char-p. On the other hand, if the name of a predicate is formed by adding a prefixing qualifier to the front of an existing predicate name, the two names are joined with a hyphen and the presence or absence of a hyphen before the final p is not changed. For example, the predicate string-lessp has no hyphen before the p because it is the string version of lessp (a MACLISP function that has been renamed < in COMMON LISP). The name string-less-p would incorrectly imply that it is a predicate that tests for a kind of object called a string-less, and the name stringlessp would connote a predicate that tests whether something has no strings (is "stringless")!

The control structures that test Boolean values only test for whether or not the value is nil, which is considered to be false. Any other value is considered to be true. Often a predicate will return nil if it "fails" and some *useful* value if it "succeeds"; such a function can be used not only as a test but also for the useful value provided in case of success. An example is member.

If no better non-nil value is available for the purpose of indicating success, by convention the symbol t is used as the "standard" true value.

6.1. Logical Values

The names `nil` and `t` are constants in COMMON LISP. Although they are symbols like any other symbols, and appear to be treated as variables when evaluated, it is not permitted to modify their values. See `defconstant`.

`nil` [*Constant*]

The value of `nil` is always `nil`. This object represents the logical *false* value and also the empty list. It can also be written `()`.

`t` [*Constant*]

The value of `t` is always `t`.

6.2. Data Type Predicates

Perhaps the most important predicates in LISP are those that deal with data types; that is, given a data object one can determine whether or not it belongs to a given type, or one can compare two type specifiers.

6.2.1. General Type Predicates

If a data type is viewed as the set of all objects belonging to the type, then the `typep` function is a set membership test, while `subtypep` is a subset test.

`typep` *object type* [*Function*]

`typep` is a predicate that is true if *object* is of type *type*, and is false otherwise. Note that an object can be "of" more than one type, since one type can include another. The *type* may be any of the type specifiers mentioned in chapter 4 *except* that it may not be or contain a type specifier list whose first element is `function` or `values`. A specifier of the form (`satisfies` *fn*) is handled simply by applying the function *fn* to *object* (see `funcall`); the *object* is considered to be of the specified type if the result is not `nil`.

`subtypep` *type1 type2* [*Function*]

The arguments must be type specifiers that are acceptable to `typep`. The two type specifiers are compared; this predicate is true if *type1* is definitely a (not necessarily proper) subtype of *type2*. If the result is `nil`, however, then *type1* may or may not

be a subtype of *type2* (sometimes it is impossible to tell, especially when satisfies type specifiers are involved). A second returned value indicates the certainty
of the result; if it is true, then the first value is an accurate indication of the subtype
relationship. Thus there are three possible result combinations:

t	t	*type1* is definitely a subtype of *type2*
nil	t	*type1* is definitely not a subtype of *type2*
nil	nil	subtypep could not determine the relationship

6.2.2. Specific Data Type Predicates

The following predicates test for individual data types.

null *object*   [*Function*]

null is true if its argument is (), and otherwise is false. This is the same operation
performed by the function not; however, not is normally used to invert a Boolean
value, whereas null is normally used to test for an empty list. The programmer
can therefore express *intent* by the choice of function name.

(null x) ≡ (typep x 'null) ≡ (eq x '())

symbolp *object*   [*Function*]

symbolp is true if its argument is a symbol, and otherwise is false.

(symbolp x) ≡ (typep x 'symbol)

Compatibility note: The INTERLISP equivalent of symbolp is called litatom.

---

atom *object*   [*Function*]

The predicate atom is true if its argument is not a cons, and otherwise is false.
Note that (atom '()) is true, because () ≡ nil.

(atom x) ≡ (typep x 'atom) ≡ (not (typep x 'cons))

Compatibility note: In some LISP dialects, notably INTERLISP, only symbols and numbers
are considered to be atoms; arrays and strings are considered to be neither atoms nor lists
(conses).

`consp` *object* [*Function*]

The predicate `consp` is true if its argument is a cons, and otherwise is false. Note that the empty list is not a cons, so `(consp '())` ≡ `(consp 'nil)` ⇒ `nil`.

`(consp x)` ≡ `(typep x 'cons)` ≡ `(not (typep x 'atom))`

Compatibility note: Some LISP implementations call this function `pairp` or `listp`. The name `pairp` was rejected for COMMON LISP because it emphasizes too strongly the dotted-pair notion rather than the usual usage of conses in lists. On the other hand, `listp` too strongly implies that the cons is in fact part of a list, which after all it might not be; moreover, `()` is a list, though not a cons. The name `consp` seems to be the appropriate compromise.

`listp` *object* [*Function*]

`listp` is true if its argument is a cons or the empty list `()`, and otherwise is false. It does not check for whether the list is a "true list" (one terminated by `nil`) or a "dotted list" (one terminated by a non-null atom).

`(listp x)` ≡ `(typep x 'list)` ≡ `(typep x '(or cons null))`

`numberp` *object* [*Function*]

`numberp` is true if its argument is any kind of number, and otherwise is false.

`(numberp x)` ≡ `(typep x 'number)`

`integerp` *object* [*Function*]

`integerp` is true if its argument is an integer, and otherwise is false.

`(integerp x)` ≡ `(typep x 'integer)`

Compatibility note: In MACLISP this is called `fixp`. Users have been confused as to whether this meant `integerp` or `fixnump`, and so the name `integerp` has been adopted here.

`rationalp` *object* [*Function*]

`rationalp` is true if its argument is a rational number (a ratio or an integer), and otherwise is false.

`(rationalp x)` ≡ `(typep x 'rational)`

floatp *object*   [*Function*]

floatp is true if its argument is a floating-point number, and otherwise is false.

(floatp x) ≡ (typep x 'float)

complexp *object*   [*Function*]

complexp is true if its argument is a complex number, and otherwise is false.

(complexp x) ≡ (typep x 'complex)

characterp *object*   [*Function*]

characterp is true if its argument is a character, and otherwise is false.

(characterp x) ≡ (typep x 'character)

stringp *object*   [*Function*]

stringp is true if its argument is a string, and otherwise is false.

(stringp x) ≡ (typep x 'string)

bit-vector-p *object*   [*Function*]

bit-vector-p is true if its argument is a bit-vector, and otherwise is false.

(bit-vector-p x) ≡ (typep x 'bit-vector)

vectorp *object*   [*Function*]

vectorp is true if its argument is a vector, and otherwise is false.

(vectorp x) ≡ (typep x 'vector)

simple-vector-p *object*   [*Function*]

vectorp is true if its argument is a simple general vector, and otherwise is false.

(simple-vector-p x) ≡ (typep x 'simple-vector)

simple-string-p *object*   [*Function*]

simple-string-p is true if its argument is a simple string, and otherwise is false.

(simple-string-p x) ≡ (typep x 'simple-string)

simple-bit-vector-p *object*   [*Function*]

simple-bit-vector-p is true if its argument is a simple bit-vector, and otherwise is false.

    (simple-bit-vector-p x) ≡ (typep x 'simple-bit-vector)

arrayp *object*   [*Function*]

arrayp is true if its argument is an array, and otherwise is false.

    (arrayp x) ≡ (typep x 'array)

packagep *object*   [*Function*]

packagep is true if its argument is an package, and otherwise is false.

    (packagep x) ≡ (typep x 'package)

functionp *object*   [*Function*]

functionp is true if its argument is suitable for applying to arguments, using for example the funcall or apply function. Otherwise functionp is false.

functionp is always true of symbols, lists whose *car* is the symbol lambda, any value returned by the function special form, and any values returned by the function compile when the first argument is nil.

compiled-function-p *object*   [*Function*]

compiled-function-p is true if its argument is any compiled code object, and otherwise is false.

    (compiled-function-p x) ≡ (typep x 'compiled-function)

commonp *object*   [*Function*]

commonp is true if its argument is any standard COMMON LISP data type, and otherwise is false.

    (commonp x) ≡ (typep x 'common)

See also standard-char-p, string-char-p, streamp, random-state-p, readtablep, hash-table-p, and pathnamep.

6.3. Equality Predicates

COMMON LISP provides a spectrum of predicates for testing for equality of two objects: eq (the most specific), eql, equal, and equalp (the most general). eq and equal have the meanings traditional in LISP. eql was added because it is frequently needed, and equalp was added primarily in order to have a version of equal that would ignore type differences when comparing numbers and case differences when comparing characters. If two objects satisfy any one of these equality predicates, then they also satisfy all those that are more general.

eq *x y*   [*Function*]

(eq *x y*) is true if and only if *x* and *y* are the same identical object. (Implementationally, *x* and *y* are usually eq if and only if they address the same identical memory location.)

It should be noted that things that print the same are not necessarily eq to each other. Symbols with the same print name usually are eq to each other because of the use of the intern function. However, numbers with the same value need not be eq, and two similar lists are usually not eq. For example:

```
(eq 'a 'b) is false.
(eq 'a 'a) is true.
(eq 3 3) might be true or false, depending on the implementation.
(eq 3 3.0) is false.
(eq 3.0 3.0) might be true or false, depending on the implementation.
(eq #c(3 -4) #c(3 -4))
  might be true or false, depending on the implementation.
(eq #c(3 -4.0) #c(3 -4)) is false.
(eq (cons 'a 'b) (cons 'a 'c)) is false.
(eq (cons 'a 'b) (cons 'a 'b)) is false.
(eq '(a . b) '(a . b)) might be true or false.
(progn (setq x (cons 'a 'b)) (eq x x)) is true.
(progn (setq x '(a . b)) (eq x x)) is true.
(eq #\A #\A) might be true or false, depending on the implementation.
(eq "Foo" "Foo") might be true or false.
(eq "Foo" (copy-seq "Foo")) is false.
(eq "FOO" "foo") is false.
```

In COMMON LISP, unlike some other LISP dialects, the implementation is permitted to make "copies" of characters and numbers at any time. (This permission is granted because it allows tremendous performance improvements in many common situations.) The net effect is that COMMON LISP makes no guarantee that eq will be true even when both its arguments are "the same thing" if that thing is a character or number. For example:

(let ((x 5)) (eq x x)) might be true or false.

The predicate eql is the same as eq, except that if the arguments are characters or numbers of the same type then their values are compared. Thus eql tells whether two objects are *conceptually* the same, whereas eq tells whether two objects are *implementationally* identical. It is for this reason that eql, not eq, is the default comparison predicate for the sequence functions defined in chapter 14.

Implementation note: eq simply compares the two given pointers, so any kind of object that is represented in an "immediate" fashion will indeed have like-valued instances satisfy eq. In some implementations, for example, fixnums and characters happen to "work." However, no program should depend on this, as other implementations of COMMON LISP might not use an immediate representation for these data types.

An additional problem with eq is that the implementation is permitted to "collapse" constants (or portions thereof) appearing in code to be compiled if they are equal. An object is considered to be a constant in code to be compiled if it is a self-evaluating form or is contained in a quote form. This is why (eq "Foo" "Foo") might be true or false; in interpreted code it would normally be false, because reading in the form (eq "Foo" "Foo") would construct distinct strings for the two arguments to eq, but the compiler might choose to use the same identical string or two distinct copies as the two arguments in the call to eq. Similarly, (eq '(a . b) '(a . b)) might be true or false, depending on whether the constant conses appearing in the quote forms were collapsed by the compiler. However, (eq (cons 'a 'b) (cons 'a 'b)) is always false, because every distinct call to the cons function necessarily produces a new and distinct cons.

eql *x y*   [*Function*]

The eql predicate is true if its arguments are eq, or if they are numbers of the same type with the same value, or if they are character objects that represent the same character. An example follows.

```
(eql 'a 'b) is false.
(eql 'a 'a) is true.
(eql 3 3) is true.
(eql 3 3.0) is false.
(eql 3.0 3.0) is true.
(eql #c(3 -4) #c(3 -4)) is true.
(eql #c(3 -4.0) #c(3 -4)) is false.
(eql (cons 'a 'b) (cons 'a 'c)) is false.
(eql (cons 'a 'b) (cons 'a 'b)) is false.
(eql '(a . b) '(a . b)) might be true or false.
(progn (setq x (cons 'a 'b)) (eql x x)) is true.
(progn (setq x '(a . b)) (eql x x)) is true.
(eql #\A #\A) is true.
(eql "Foo" "Foo") might be true or false.
(eql "Foo" (copy-seq "Foo")) is false.
(eql "FOO" "foo") is false.
```

Normally (eql 1.0s0 1.0d0) would be false, under the assumption that 1.0s0 and 1.0d0 are of distinct data types. However, implementations that do not provide four distinct floating-point formats are permitted to "collapse" the four formats into some smaller number of them; in such an implementation (eql 1.0s0 1.0d0) might be true. The predicate = will compare the values of two numbers even if the numbers are of different types.

If an implementation supports positive and negative zeros as distinct values (as in the IEEE proposed standard floating-point format), then (eql 0.0 -0.0) will be false. Otherwise, when the syntax -0.0 is read it will be interpreted as the value 0.0, and so (eql 0.0 -0.0) will be true. The predicate = differs from eql in that (= 0.0 -0.0) will always be true, because = compares the mathematical values of its operands, whereas eql compares the representational values, so to speak.

Two complex numbers are considered to be eql if their real parts are eql and their imaginary parts are eql. For example, (eql #c(4 5) #c(4 5)) is true and (eql #c(4 5) #c(4.0 5.0)) is false. Note that while (eql #c(5.0 0.0) 5.0) is false, (eql #c(5 0) 5) is true. In the case of (eql #c(5.0 0.0) 5.0) the two arguments are of different types, and so cannot satisfy eql; that's all there is to it. In the case of (eql #c(5 0) 5), however, #c(5 0) is not a complex number, but is always automatically reduced by the rule of complex canonicalization to the integer 5, just as the apparent ratio 20/4 is always simplified to 5.

The case of (eql "Foo" "Foo") is discussed above in the description of eq. While eql compares the values of numbers and characters, it does not compare

the contents of strings. To compare the characters of two strings, one should use
equal, equalp, string=, or string-equal.

Compatibility note: The COMMON LISP function eql is similar to the INTERLISP function eqp. However, eql considers 3 and 3.0 to be different, whereas eqp considers them to be the same; eqp behaves like the COMMON LISP = function, not like eql, when both arguments are numbers.

---

equal *x y*   [*Function*]

The equal predicate is true if its arguments are structurally similar (isomorphic) objects. A rough rule of thumb is that two objects are equal if and only if their printed representations are the same.

Numbers and characters are compared as for eql. Symbols are compared as for eq. This method of comparing symbols can violate the rule of thumb for equal and printed representations, but only in the infrequently occurring case of two distinct symbols with the same print name.

Certain objects that have components are equal if they are of the same type and corresponding components are equal. This test is implemented in a recursive manner and may fail to terminate for circular structures.

For conses, equal is defined recursively as the two *car*'s being equal and the two *cdr*'s being equal.

Two arrays are equal only if they are eq, with one exception: strings and bit-vectors are compared element-by-element. If either argument has a fill pointer, the fill pointer limits the number of elements examined by equal. Uppercase and lowercase letters in strings are considered by equal to be distinct. (In contrast, equalp ignores case distinctions in strings.)

Compatibility note: In ZETALISP, equal ignores the difference between uppercase and lowercase letters in strings. This violates the rule of thumb about printed representations, however, which is very useful, especially to novices. It is also inconsistent with the treatment of single characters, which in ZETALISP are represented as fixnums.

Two pathname objects are equal if and only if all the corresponding components (host, device, and so on) are equivalent. (Whether or not uppercase and lowercase letters are considered equivalent in strings appearing in components depends on the file name conventions of the file system.) Pathnames that are equal should be functionally equivalent.

```
(equal 'a 'b) is false.
(equal 'a 'a) is true.
(equal 3 3) is true.
(equal 3 3.0) is false.
(equal 3.0 3.0) is true.
(equal #c(3 -4) #c(3 -4)) is true.
(equal #c(3 -4.0) #c(3 -4)) is false.
(equal (cons 'a 'b) (cons 'a 'c)) is false.
(equal (cons 'a 'b) (cons 'a 'b)) is true.
(equal '(a . b) '(a . b)) is true.
(progn (setq x (cons 'a 'b)) (equal x x)) is true.
(progn (setq x '(a . b)) (equal x x)) is true.
(equal #\A #\A) is true.
(equal "Foo" "Foo") is true.
(equal "Foo" (copy-seq "Foo")) is true.
(equal "FOO" "foo") is false.
```

To compare a tree of conses, using eql (or any other desired predicate) on the leaves, use tree-equal.

equalp *x y*   [*Function*]

Two objects are equalp if they are equal; if they are characters and satisfy char-equal, which ignores alphabetic case and certain other attributes of characters; if they are numbers and have the same numerical value, even if they are of different types; or if they have components that are all equalp.

Objects that have components are equalp if they are of the same type and corresponding components are equalp. This test is implemented in a recursive manner and may fail to terminate for circular structures. For conses, equalp is defined recursively as the two *car*'s being equalp and the *two cdr*'s being equalp.

Two arrays are equalp if and only if they have the same number of dimensions, the dimensions match, and the corresponding components are equalp. The specializations need not match; for example, a string and a general array that happens to contain the same characters will be equalp (though definitely not equal). If either argument has a fill pointer, the fill pointer limits the number of elements examined by equalp. Because equalp performs element-by-element comparisons of strings and ignores the alphabetic case of characters, case distinctions are therefore also ignored when equalp compares strings.

Two symbols can be equalp only if they are eq, that is, the same identical object.

```
(equalp 'a 'b) is false.
(equalp 'a 'a) is true.
(equalp 3 3) is true.
(equalp 3 3.0) is true.
(equalp 3.0 3.0) is true.
(equalp #c(3 -4) #c(3 -4)) is true.
(equalp #c(3 -4.0) #c(3 -4)) is true.
(equalp (cons 'a 'b) (cons 'a 'c)) is false.
(equalp (cons 'a 'b) (cons 'a 'b)) is true.
(equalp '(a . b) '(a . b)) is true.
(progn (setq x (cons 'a 'b)) (equalp x x)) is true.
(progn (setq x '(a . b)) (equalp x x)) is true.
(equalp #\A #\A) is true.
(equalp "Foo" "Foo") is true.
(equalp "Foo" (copy-seq "Foo")) is true.
(equalp "FOO" "foo") is true.
```

6.4. Logical Operators

COMMON LISP provides three operators on Boolean values: and, or, and not. Of these, and and or are also control structures because their arguments are evaluated conditionally. The function not necessarily examines its single argument, and so is a simple function.

not *x*   [*Function*]

not returns t if *x* is nil, and otherwise returns nil. It therefore inverts its argument considered as a Boolean value.

null is the same as not; both functions are included for the sake of clarity. As a matter of style, it is customary to use null to check whether something is the empty list and to use not to invert the sense of a logical value.

and {*form*}*   [*Macro*]

(and *form1 form2* ...) evaluates each *form*, one at a time, from left to right. If any *form* evaluates to nil, the value nil is immediately returned without evaluating the remaining *forms*. If every *form* but the last evaluates to a non-nil value, and returns whatever the last *form* returns. Therefore in general and can be used both for logical operations, where nil stands for *false* and non-nil values stand for *true*, and as a conditional expression. An example follows.

```
(if (and (>= n 0)
         (< n (length a-simple-vector))
         (eq (elt a-simple-vector n) 'foo))
    (princ "Foo!"))
```

The above expression prints `Foo!` if element n of `a-simple-vector` is the symbol `foo`, provided also that n is indeed a valid index for `a-simple-vector`. Because `and` guarantees left-to-right testing of its parts, `elt` is not called if n is out of range.

To put it another way, the `and` special form does *short-circuit* Boolean evaluation, like the **and then** operator in ADA and what in some PASCAL-like languages is called **cand** (for "conditional and"); the LISP `and` special form is unlike the PASCAL or ADA **and** operator, which always evaluates both arguments.

In the previous example writing

```
(and (>= n 0)
     (< n (length a-simple-vector))
     (eq (elt a-simple-vector n) 'foo)
     (princ "Foo!"))
```

would accomplish the same thing. The difference is purely stylistic. Some programmers never use expressions containing side effects within `and`, preferring to use `if` or `when` for that purpose.

From the general definition, one can deduce that `(and x)` $\equiv$ `x`. Also, `(and)` evaluates to `t`, which is an identity for this operation.

One can define `and` in terms of `cond` in this way:

```
(and x y z ... w) ≡ (cond ((not x) nil)
                          ((not y) nil)
                          ((not z) nil)
                          ...
                          (t w))
```

See `if` and `when`, which are sometimes stylistically more appropriate than `and` for conditional purposes. If it is necessary to test whether a predicate is true of all elements of a list or vector (element 0 *and* element 1 *and* element 2 *and*...), then the function `every` may be useful.

---

or {*form*}*   [*Macro*]

(`or` *form1 form2* ...) evaluates each *form*, one at a time, from left to right. If any *form* other than the last evaluates to something other than `nil`, `or` immediately returns that non-`nil` value without evaluating the remaining *forms*. If every *form* but the last evaluates to `nil`, or returns whatever evaluation of the last of the *forms* returns. Therefore in general `or` can be used both for logical operations, where `nil` stands for *false* and non-`nil` values stand for *true*, and as a conditional expression.

To put it another way, the `or` special form does *short-circuit* Boolean evaluation, like the **or else** operator in ADA and what in some PASCAL-like languages is called **cor** (for "conditional or"); the LISP `or` special form is unlike the PASCAL or ADA **or** operator, which always evaluates both arguments.

From the general definition, one can deduce that $(\text{or } x) \equiv x$. Also, (or) evaluates to `nil`, which is the identity for this operation.

One can define `or` in terms of `cond` in this way:

$$(\text{or } x \ y \ z \ \ldots \ w) \equiv (\text{cond } (x) \ (y) \ (z) \ \ldots \ (\text{t } w))$$

See `if` and `unless`, which are sometimes stylistically more appropriate than `or` for conditional purposes. If it is necessary to test whether a predicate is true of one or more elements of a list or vector (element 0 *or* element 1 *or* element 2 *or*...), then the function `some` may be useful.

7

Control Structure

COMMON LISP provides a variety of special structures for organizing programs. Some have to do with flow of control (control structures), while others control access to variables (environment structures). Some of these features are implemented as special forms; other are implemented as macros, which typically expand into complex program fragments expressed in terms of special or other macros.

Function application is the primary method for construction of LISP programs. Operations are written as the application of a function to its arguments. Usually, LISP programs are written as a large collection of small functions, each of which implements a simple operation. These functions operate by calling one another, and so larger operations are defined in terms of smaller ones. LISP functions may call upon themselves recursively, either directly or indirectly.

While the LISP language is more applicative in style than statement-oriented, it nevertheless provides many operations that produce side effects, and consequently requires constructs for controlling the sequencing of side effects. The construct `progn`, which is roughly equivalent to an ALGOL **begin-end** block with all its semicolons, executes a number of forms sequentially, discarding the values of all but the last. Many LISP control constructs include sequencing implicitly, in which case they are said to provide an "implicit `progn`." Other sequencing constructs include `prog1` and `prog2`.

For looping, COMMON LISP provides the general iteration facility `do` as well as a variety of special-purpose iteration facilities for iterating or mapping over various data structures.

COMMON LISP provides the simple one-way conditionals `when` and `unless`, the simple two-way conditional `if`, and the more general multi-way conditionals such as `cond` and `case`. The choice of which form to use in any particular situation is a matter of taste and style.

Constructs for performing non-local exits with various scoping disciplines are provided: `block`, `return`, `return-from`, `catch`, and `throw`.

The multiple-value constructs provide an efficient way for a function to return more than one value; see `values`.

7.1. Constants and Variables

Because some LISP data objects are used to represent programs, one cannot always notate a constant data object in a program simply by writing the notation for the object unadorned; it would ambiguous whether a constant object or a program fragment was intended. The `quote` special form resolves this ambiguity.

There are two spaces of variables in COMMON LISP, in effect: ordinary variables and function names. There are some similarities between the two kinds, and in a few cases there are similar functions for dealing with them, for example `boundp` and `fboundp`. However, for the most part the two kinds of variables are used for very different purposes: one to name defined functions, macros, and special forms, and the other to name data objects.

7.1.1. Reference

The value of an ordinary variable may be obtained simply by writing the name of the variable as a form to be executed. Whether this is treated as the name of a special variable or a lexical variable is determined by the presence or absence of an applicable `special` declaration; see chapter 9.

The following functions and special forms allow reference to the values of constants and variables in other ways.

quote *object*   *[Special form]*

(`quote` *x*) simply returns *x*. The *object* is not evaluated and may be any LISP object whatsoever. This construct allows any LISP object to be written as a constant value in a program. For example:

```
(setq a 43)
(list a (cons a 3)) ⇒ (43 (43 . 3))
(list (quote a) (quote (cons a 3))) ⇒ (a (cons a 3))
```

Since `quote` forms are so frequently useful but somewhat cumbersome to type, a standard abbreviation is defined for them: any form *f* preceded by a single quote (`'`) character is assumed to have (`quote`) wrapped around it to make (`quote` *f*). For example:

```
(setq x '(the magic quote hack))
```

is normally interpreted by `read` to mean

```
(setq x (quote (the magic quote hack)))
```

See section 22.1.3.

---

function *fn*   [*Special form*]

The value of `function` is always the functional interpretation of *fn*; *fn* is interpreted as if it had appeared in the functional position of a function invocation. In particular, if *fn* is a symbol, the functional definition associated with that symbol is returned; see `symbol-function`. If *fn* is a lambda-expression, then a "lexical closure" is returned, that is, a function that when invoked will execute the body of the lambda-expression in such a way as to observe the rules of lexical scoping properly. For example:

```
(defun adder (x) (function (lambda (y) (+ x y))))
```

The result of (`adder` ∃) is a function that will add ∃ to its argument:

```
(setq add∃ (adder ∃))
(funcall add∃ 5) ⇒ 8
```

This works because `function` creates a closure of the inner lambda-expression that is able to refer to the value ∃ of the variable *x* even after control has returned from the function `adder`.

More generally, a lexical closure in effect retains the ability to refer to lexically visible *bindings*, not just values. Consider this code:

```
(defun two-funs (x)
  (list (function (lambda () x))
        (function (lambda (y) (setq x y)))))
(setq funs (two-funs 6))
(funcall (car funs)) ⇒ 6
(funcall (cadr funs) 43) ⇒ 43
(funcall (car funs)) ⇒ 43
```

The function `two-funs` returns a list of two functions, each of which refers to *the binding* of the variable *x* created on entry to the function `two-funs` when it was called with argument 6. This binding has the value 6 initially, but `setq` can alter a binding. The lexical closure created for the first lambda-expression does not "snapshot" the value ᒙ for x when the closure is created. The second function can be used to alter the binding (to 43, in the example), and this altered value then becomes accessible to the first function.

In situations where a closure of a lambda-expression over the same set of bindings may be produced more than once, the various resulting closures may or may not be eq, at the discretion of the implementation. For example:

```
(let ((x 5) (funs '()))
  (dotimes (j 10)
    (push #'(lambda (z)
              (if (null z) (setq x 0) (+ x z)))
          funs))
  funs)
```

The result of the above expression is a list of ten closures. Each logically requires only the binding of x. It is the same binding in each case, so the ten closures may or may not be the same identical (eq) object. On the other hand, the result of the expression

```
(let ((funs '()))
  (dotimes (j 10)
    (let ((x 5))
      (push (function (lambda (z)
                        (if (null z) (setq x 0) (+ x z))))
            funs)))
  funs)
```

is also a list of ten closures. However, in this case no two of the closures may be eq, because each closure is over a distinct binding of x, and these bindings can be behaviorally distinguished because of the use of setq.

The question of distinguishable behavior is important; the result of the simpler expression

```
(let ((funs '()))
  (dotimes (j 10)
    (let ((x 5))
      (push (function (lambda (z) (+ x z)))
            funs)))
  funs)
```

is a list of ten closures that *may* be pairwise eq. Although one might think that a different binding of x is involved for each closure (which is indeed the case), the bindings cannot be distinguished because their values are identical and immutable, there being no occurrence of setq on x. A compiler would therefore be justified in transforming the expression to

```
(let ((funs '()))
  (dotimes (j 10)
    (push (function (lambda (z) (+ 5 z)))
          funs))
  funs)
```

where clearly the closures may be the same after all. The general rule, then, is that the implementation is free to have two distinct evaluations of the same function form produce identical (eq) closures if it can prove that the two conceptually distinct resulting closures must in fact be behaviorally identical with respect to invocation. This is merely a permitted optimization; a perfectly valid implementation might simply cause every distinct evaluation of a function form to produce a new closure object not eq to any other.

Frequently a compiler can deduce that a closure in fact does not need to close over any variable bindings. For example, in the code fragment

```
(mapcar (function (lambda (x) (+ x 2))) y)
```

the function (lambda (x) (+ x 2)) contains no references to any outside entity. In this important special case, the same "closure" may be used as the value for all evaluations of the function special form. Indeed, this value need not be a closure object at all; it may be a simple compiled function containing no environment information. This example is simply a special case of the foregoing discussion and is included as a hint to implementors familiar with previous methods of implementing LISP. The distinction between closures and other kinds of functions is somewhat pointless, actually, as COMMON LISP defines no particular representation for closures and no way to distinguish between closures and non-closure functions. All that matters is that the rules of lexical scoping be obeyed.

Since function forms are so frequently useful but somewhat cumbersome to type, a standard abbreviation is defined for them: any form f preceded by #' (# followed by an apostrophe) is assumed to have (function) wrapped around it to make (function f). For example,

```
(remove-if #'numberp '(1 a b 3))
```

is normally interpreted by read to mean

```
(remove-if (function numberp) '(1 a b 3))
```

See section 22.1.4.

`symbol-value` *symbol*   *[Function]*

`symbol-value` returns the current value of the dynamic (special) variable named by *symbol*. An error occurs if the symbol has no value; see `boundp` and `makunbound`. Note that constant symbols are really variables that cannot be changed, and so `symbol-value` may be used to get the value of a named constant. In particular, `symbol-value` of a keyword will return that keyword.

   `symbol-value` cannot access the value of a lexical variable.

   This function is particularly useful for implementing interpreters for languages embedded in LISP. The corresponding assignment primitive is `set`; alternatively, `symbol-value` may be used with `setf`.

`symbol-function` *symbol*   *[Function]*

`symbol-function` returns the current global function definition named by *symbol*. An error is signalled if the symbol has no function definition; see `fboundp`. Note that the definition may be a function or may be an object representing a special form or macro. In the latter case, however, it is an error to attempt to invoke the object as a function. If it is desired to process macros, special forms, and functions equally well, as when writing an interpreter, it is best first to test the symbol with `macro-function` and `special-form-p` and then to invoke the functional value only if these two tests both yield false.

   This function is particularly useful for implementing interpreters for languages embedded in LISP.

   `symbol-function` cannot access the value of a lexical function name produced by `flet` or `labels`; it can access only the global function value.

   The global function definition of a symbol may be altered by using `setf` with `symbol-function`. Performing this operation causes the symbol to have *only* the specified definition as its global function definition; any previous definition, whether as a macro or as a function, is lost. It is an error to attempt to redefine the name of a special form (see Table 5-1).

`boundp` *symbol*   *[Function]*

`boundp` is true if the dynamic (special) variable named by *symbol* has a value; otherwise, it returns `nil`.

   See also `set` and `makunbound`.

`fboundp` *symbol*   *[Function]*

`fboundp` is true if the symbol has a global function definition. Note that `fboundp` is true when the symbol names a special form or macro. `macro-function` and `special-form-p` may be used to test for these cases.

See also `symbol-function` and `fmakunbound`.

`special-form-p` *symbol* [*Function*]

The function `special-form-p` takes a symbol. If the symbol globally names a special form, then a non-`nil` value is returned; otherwise `nil` is returned. A returned non-`nil` value is typically a function of implementation-dependent nature that can be used to interpret (evaluate) the special form.

It is possible for *both* `special-form-p` and `macro-function` to be true of a symbol. This is possible because an implementation is permitted to implement any macro also as a special form for speed. On the other hand, the macro definition must be available for use by programs that understand only the standard special forms listed in Table 5-1.

7.1.2. Assignment

The following facilities allow the value of a variable (more specifically, the value associated with the current binding of the variable) to be altered. Such alteration is different from establishing a new binding. Constructs for establishing new bindings of variables are described in section 7.5.

`setq` {*var form*}* [*Special form*]

The special form (`setq` *var1 form1 var2 form2* ...) is the "simple variable assignment statement" of LISP. First *form1* is evaluated and the result is stored in the variable *var1*, then *form2* is evaluated and the result stored in *var2*, and so forth. The variables are represented as symbols, of course, and are interpreted as referring to static or dynamic instances according to the usual rules. Therefore `setq` may be used for assignment of both lexical and special variables.

`setq` returns the last value assigned, that is, the result of the evaluation of its last argument. As a boundary case, the form (`setq`) is legal and returns `nil`. There must be an even number of argument forms. For example, in

```
(setq x (+ 3 2 1) y (cons x nil))
```

x is set to 6, y is set to (6), and the `setq` returns (6). Note that the first assignment is performed before the second form is evaluated, allowing that form to use the new value of x.

See also the description of `setf`, the COMMON LISP "general assignment statement" that is capable of assigning to variables, array elements, and other locations.

psetq *{var form}**   *[Macro]*

A psetq form is just like a setq form, except that the assignments happen in parallel. First all of the forms are evaluated, and then the variables are set to the resulting values. The value of the psetq form is nil. For example:

```
(setq a 1)
(setq b 2)
(psetq a b b a)
a ⇒ 2
b ⇒ 1
```

In this example, the values of a and b are exchanged by using parallel assignment. (If several variables are to be assigned in parallel in the context of a loop, the do construct may be appropriate.)

See also the description of setf, the COMMON LISP "general parallel assignment statement" that is capable of assigning to variables, array elements, and other locations.

set *symbol value*   *[Function]*

set allows alteration of the value of a dynamic (special) variable. set causes the dynamic variable named by *symbol* to take on *value* as its value. Only the value of the current dynamic binding is altered; if there are no bindings in effect, the most global value is altered. For example,

```
(set (if (eq a b) 'c 'd) 'foo)
```

will either set c to foo or set d to foo, depending on the outcome of the test (eq a b).

set returns *value* as its result.

set cannot alter the value of a local (lexically bound) variable. The special form setq is usually used for altering the values of variables (lexical or dynamic) in programs. set is particularly useful for implementing interpreters for languages embedded in LISP. See also progv, a construct that performs binding rather than assignment of dynamic variables.

makunbound *symbol*   *[Function]*
fmakunbound *symbol*   *[Function]*

makunbound causes the dynamic (special) variable named by *symbol* to become unbound (have no value). `fmakunbound` does the analogous thing for the global function definition named by *symbol*. For example:

```
(setq a 1)
a ⇒ 1
(makunbound 'a)
a ⇒ causes an error

(defun foo (x) (+ x 1))
(foo 4) ⇒ 5
(fmakunbound 'foo)
(foo 4) ⇒ causes an error
```

Both functions return *symbol* as the result value.

7.2. Generalized Variables

In LISP, a variable can remember one piece of data, that is, one LISP object. The main operations on a variable are to recover that object, and to alter the variable to remember a new object; these operations are often called *access* and *update* operations. The concept of variables named by symbols can be generalized to any storage location that can remember one piece of data, no matter how that location is named. Examples of such storage locations are the *car* and *cdr* of a cons, elements of an array, and components of a structure.

For each kind of generalized variable, typically there are two functions that implement the conceptual *access* and *update* operations. For a variable, merely mentioning the name of the variable accesses it, while the `setq` special form can be used to update it. The function `car` accesses the *car* of a cons, and the function `rplaca` updates it. The function `symbol-value` accesses the dynamic value of a variable named by a given symbol, and the function `set` updates it.

Rather than thinking about two distinct functions that respectively access and update a storage location somehow deduced from their arguments, we can instead simply think of a call to the access function with given arguments as a *name* for the storage location. Thus, just as x may be considered a name for a storage location (a variable), so (car x) is a name for the *car* of some cons (which is in turn named by x). Now, rather than having to remember two functions for each kind of generalized variable (having to remember, for example, that `rplaca` corresponds to `car`), we adopt a uniform syntax for updating storage locations named in this way, using the `setf` macro. This is analogous to the way we use the `setq` special form to convert the name of a variable (which is also a form that accesses it) into a form that updates it. The uniformity of this approach is illustrated in the following table.

Access function	Update function	Update using setf
x	(setq x datum)	(setf x datum)
(car x)	(rplaca x datum)	(setf (car x) datum)
(symbol-value x)	(set x datum)	(setf (symbol-value x) datum)

setf is actually a macro that examines an access form and produces a call to the corresponding update function.

Given the existence of setf in COMMON LISP, it is not necessary to have setq, rplaca, and set; they are redundant. They are retained in COMMON LISP because of their historical importance in LISP. However, most other update functions (such as putprop, the update function for get) have been eliminated from COMMON LISP in the expectation that setf will be uniformly used in their place.

---

setf   {*place newvalue*}*   [*Macro*]

(setf *place newvalue*) takes a form *place* that when evaluated *accesses* a data object in some location and "inverts" it to produce a corresponding form to *update* the location. A call to the setf macro therefore expands into an update form that stores the result of evaluating the form *newvalue* into the place referred to by the access-form.

If more than one *place-newvalue* pair is specified, the pairs are processed sequentially; that is,

```
(setf place1 newvalue1
      place2 newvalue2)
      ...
      placen newvaluen)
```

is precisely equivalent to

```
(progn (setf place1 newvalue1)
       (setf place2 newvalue2)
       ...
       (setf placen newvaluen))
```

For consistency, it is legal to write (setf), which simply returns nil.
The form *place* may be any one of the following:

• The name of a variable (either lexical or dynamic).

- A function call form whose first element is the name of any one of the following functions:

aref	car	svref	
nth	cdr	get	
elt	caar	getf	symbol-value
rest	cadr	gethash	symbol-function
first	cdar	documentation	symbol-plist
second	cddr	fill-pointer	macro-function
third	caaar	caaaar	cdaaar
fourth	caadr	caaadr	cdaadr
fifth	cadar	caadar	cdadar
sixth	caddr	caaddr	cdaddr
seventh	cdaar	cadaar	cddaar
eighth	cdadr	cadadr	cddadr
ninth	cddar	caddar	cdddar
tenth	cdddr	cadddr	cddddr

- A function call form whose first element is the name of a selector function constructed by defstruct.

- A function call form whose first element is the name of any one of the following functions, provided that the new value is of the specified type so that it can be used to replace the specified "location" (which is in each of these cases not truly a generalized variable):

Function name	Required type
char	string-char
schar	string-char
bit	bit
sbit	bit
subseq	sequence

In the case of subseq, the replacement value must be a sequence whose elements may be contained by the sequence argument to subseq. (Note that this is not so stringent as to require that the replacement value be a sequence of the same type as the sequence of which the subsequence is specified.) If the length of the replacement value does not equal the length of the subsequence to be replaced, then the shorter length determines the number of elements to be stored, as for the function replace.

- A function call form whose first element is the name of any one of the following functions, provided that the specified argument to that function is in turn a *place* form; in this case the new *place* has stored back into it the result of applying the specified "update" function (which is in each of these cases not a true update function):

Function name	Argument that is a *place*	Update function used
`char-bit`	first	`set-char-bit`
`ldb`	second	`dpb`
`mask-field`	second	`deposit-field`

- A `the` type declaration form, in which case the declaration is transferred to the *newvalue* form, and the resulting `setf` form is analyzed. For example,

```
(setf (the integer (cadr x)) (+ y 3))
```

is processed as if it were

```
(setf (cadr x) (the integer (+ y 3)))
```

- A call to `apply` where the first argument form is of the form *#'name*, that is, (`function` *name*), where *name* is the name of a function, calls to which are recognized as places by `setf`. Suppose that the use of `setf` with `apply` looks like this:

```
(setf (apply #'name x1 x2 ... xn rest) x0)
```

The `setf` method for the function *name* must be such that

```
(setf (name z1 z2 ... zm) z0)
```

expands into a store form

$$(storefn \; zi_1 \; zi_2 \; ... \; zi_k \; zm)$$

That is, it must expand into a function call such that all arguments but the last may be any permutation or subset of the new value *z0* and the arguments of the access form, but the *last* argument of the storing call must be the same as the last argument of the access call. See `define-setf-method` for more details on accessing and storing forms.

Given this, the `setf-of-apply` form shown above expands into

$$(apply \; #'storefn \; xi_1 \; xi_2 \; ... \; xi_k \; rest)$$

As an example, suppose that the variable `indexes` contains a list of subscripts for a multidimensional array *foo* whose rank is not known until run time. One may access the indicated element of the array by writing

```
(apply #'aref foo indexes)
```

and one may alter the value of the indicated element to that of `newvalue` by writing

```
(setf (apply #'aref foo indexes) newvalue)
```

- A macro call, in which case `setf` expands the macro call and then analyzes the resulting form.
- Any form for which a `defsetf` or `define-setf-method` declaration has been made.

`setf` carefully arranges to preserve the usual left-to-right order in which the various subforms are evaluated. On the other hand, the exact expansion for any particular form is not guaranteed and may even be implementation-dependent; all that is guaranteed is that the expansion of a `setf` form will be an update form that works for that particular implementation, and that the left-to-right evaluation of subforms is preserved.

The ultimate result of evaluating a `setf` form is the value of *newvalue*. Therefore `(setf (car x) y)` does not expand into precisely `(rplaca x y)`, but into something more like

```
(let ((G1 x) (G2 y)) (rplaca G1 G2) G2)
```

the precise expansion being implementation-dependent.

The user can define new `setf` expansions by using `defsetf`.

`psetf` *{place newvalue}**   [*Macro*]

`psetf` is like `setf` except that if more than one *place-newvalue* pair is specified then the assignments of new values to places are done in parallel. More precisely, all subforms that are to be evaluated are evaluated from left to right; after all evaluations have been performed, all of the assignments are performed in an unpredictable order. (The unpredictability matters only if more than one *place* form refers to the same place.) `psetf` always returns `nil`.

`shiftf` *{place}*+ *newvalue*   [*Macro*]

Each *place* form may be any form acceptable as a generalized variable to `setf`. In the form `(shiftf place1 place2 ... placen newvalue)`, the values in *place1* through *placen* are accessed and saved, and *newvalue* is evaluated, for a total of $n+1$ values in all. Values 2 through $n+1$ are then stored into *place1* through *placen*, and value 1 (the original value of *place1*) is returned. It is as if all the places form a shift register; the *newvalue* is shifted in from the right, all values shift over to the left one place, and the value shifted out of *place1* is returned.

For example:

```
(setq x (list 'a 'b 'c)) ⇒ (a b c)

(shiftf (cadr x) 'z) ⇒ b
   and now x ⇒ (a z c)

(shiftf (cadr x) (cddr x) 'q) ⇒ z
   and now x ⇒ (a (c) . q)
```

The effect of (shiftf *place1 place2 ... placen newvalue*) is equivalent to

```
(let ((var1 place1)
      (var2 place2)
       ...
      (varn placen))
  (setf place1 var2)
  (setf place2 var3)
   ...
  (setf placen newvalue)
  var1)
```

except that the latter would evaluate any subforms of each *place* twice, whereas
shiftf takes care to evaluate them only once. For example:

```
(setq n 0)
(setq x '(a b c d))
(shiftf (nth (setq n (+ n 1)) x) 'z) ⇒ b
   and now x ⇒ (a z c d)
```

but

```
(setq n 0)
(setq x '(a b c d))
(prog1 (nth (setq n (+ n 1)) x)
       (setf (nth (setq n (+ n 1)) x) 'z)) ⇒ b
   and now x ⇒ (a b z d)
```

Moreover, for certain *place* forms shiftf may be significantly more efficient than
the prog1 version.

Rationale: shiftf and rotatef have been included in COMMON LISP as generalizations
of two-argument versions formerly called swapf and exchf. The two-argument versions
have been found to be very useful, but the names were easily confused. The generalization
to many argument forms and the change of names were both inspired by the work of Suzuki
[19], which indicates that use of these primitives can make certain complex pointer-manipulation
programs clearer and easier to prove correct.

`rotatef` *{place}**   [*Macro*]

Each *place* form may be any form acceptable as a generalized variable to `setf`. In the form (`rotatef` *place1 place2* ... *placen*), the values in *place1* through *placen* are accessed and saved. Values 2 through *n* and value 1 are then stored into *place1* through *placen*. It is as if all the places form an end-around shift register that is rotated one place to the left, with the value of *place1* being shifted around the end to *placen*. Note that (`rotatef` *place1 place2*) exchanges the contents of *place* and *place2*.

The effect of (`rotatef` *place1 place2* ... *placen newvalue*) is roughly equivalent to

```
(psetf place1  place2
        place2  place3
        ...
        placen  place1)
```

except that the latter would evaluate any subforms of each *place* twice, whereas `rotatef` takes care to evaluate them only once. Moreover, for certain *place* forms `rotatef` may be significantly more efficient.

`rotatef` always returns `nil`.

Other macros that manipulate generalized variables include `getf`, `remf`, `incf`, `decf`, `push`, `pop`, `assert`, `ctypecase`, and `ccase`.

Macros that manipulate generalized variables must guarantee the "obvious" semantics: subforms of generalized-variable references are evaluated exactly as many times as they appear in the source program, and they are evaluated in exactly the same order as they appear in the source program.

In generalized-variable references such as `shiftf`, `incf`, `push`, and `setf` of `ldb`, the generalized variables are both read and written in the same reference. Preserving the source program order of evaluation and the number of evaluations is particularly important.

As an example of these semantic rules, in the generalized-variable reference (`setf` *reference value*) the *value* form must be evaluated *after* all the subforms of the reference because the *value* form appears to the right of them.

The expansion of these macros must consist of code that follows these rules or has the same effect as such code. This is accomplished by introducing temporary variables bound to the subforms of the reference. As an optimization in the implementation, temporary variables may be eliminated whenever it can be proven that removing them has no effect on the semantics of the program. For example, a constant need never be saved in a temporary variable. A variable, or any form that does not have side effects, need not be saved in a temporary variable if it can be proven that its value will not change within the scope of the generalized-variable reference.

COMMON LISP provides built-in facilities to take care of these semantic complications and optimizations. Since the required semantics can be guaranteed by these facilities, the user does not have to worry about writing correct code for them, especially in complex cases. Even experts can become confused and make mistakes while writing this sort of code.

Another reason for building in these functions is that the appropriate optimizations will differ from implementation to implementation. In some implementations most of the optimization is performed by the compiler, while in others a simpler compiler is used and most of the optimization is performed in the macros. The cost of binding a temporary variable relative to the cost of other LISP operations may differ greatly between one implementation and another, and some implementations may find it best never to remove temporary variables except in the simplest cases.

A good example of the issues involved can be seen in the following generalized-variable reference:

```
(incf (ldb byte-field variable))
```

This ought to expand into something like

```
(setq variable
      (dpb (1+ (ldb byte-field variable))
           byte-field
           variable))
```

In this expansion example we have ignored the further complexity of returning the correct value, which is the incremented byte, not the new value of variable. Note that the variable byte-field is evaluated twice, and the variable variable is referred to three times: once as the location in which to store a value, and twice during the computation of that value.

Now consider this expression:

```
(incf (ldb (aref byte-fields (incf i))
           (aref (determine-words-array) i)))
```

It ought to expand into something like this:

```
(let ((temp1 (aref byte-fields (incf i)))
      (temp2 (determine-words-array)))
  (setf (aref temp2 i)
        (dpb (1+ (ldb temp1 (aref temp2 i)))
             temp1
             (aref temp2 i))))
```

Again we have ignored the complexity of returning the correct value. What is important here is that the expressions (`incf i`) and (`determine-words-array`) must not be duplicated because each may have a side effect or be affected by side effects.

The COMMON LISP facilities provided to deal with these semantic issues include:

- Built-in macros such as `setf` and `push` that follow the semantic rules.

- The `define-modify-macro` macro, which allows new generalized-variable manipulating macros (of a certain restricted kind) to be defined easily. It takes care of the semantic rules automatically.

- The `defsetf` macro, which allows new types of generalized-variable references to be defined easily. It takes care of the semantic rules automatically.

- The `define-setf-method` macro and the `get-setf-method` function, which provide access to the internal mechanisms when it is necessary to define a complicated new type of generalized-variable reference or generalized-variable-manipulating macro.

`define-modify-macro` *name lambda-list function* [*doc-string*]   [*Macro*]

This macro defines a read-modify-write macro named *name*. An example of such a macro is `incf`. The first subform of the macro will be a generalized-variable reference. The *function* is literally the function to apply to the old contents of the generalized-variable to get the new contents; it is not evaluated. *lambda-list* describes the remaining arguments for the *function*; these arguments come from the remaining subforms of the macro after the generalized-variable reference. *lambda-list* may contain `&optional` and `&rest` markers. (The `&key` marker is not permitted here; `&rest` suffices for the purposes of `define-modify-macro`.) *doc-string* is documentation for the macro *name* being defined.

The expansion of a `define-modify-macro` is equivalent to the following, except that it generates code that follows the semantic rules outlined above.

```
(defmacro name (reference . lambda-list)
  doc-string
  `(setf ,reference
         (function ,reference ,arg1 ,arg2 ...)))
```

where *arg1*, *arg2*, ..., are the parameters appearing in *lambda-list*; appropriate provision is made for a `&rest` parameter.

As an example, `incf` could have been defined by:

```
(define-modify-macro incf (&optional (delta 1)) +)
```

An example of a possibly useful macro not predefined in COMMON LISP is:

```
(define-modify-macro unionf (other-set &rest keywords) union)
```

defsetf *access-fn* {*update-fn* [*doc-string*] | [*Macro*]
              lambda-list (*store-variable*)
              {*declaration* | *doc-string*}* {*form*}*}

This defines how to `setf` a generalized-variable reference of the form (*access-fn* ...). The value of a generalized-variable reference can always be obtained simply by evaluating it, so *access-fn* should be the name of a function or a macro.

The user of `defsetf` provides a description of how to store into the generalized-variable reference and return the value that was stored (because `setf` is defined to return this value). The implementation of `defsetf` takes care of ensuring that subforms of the reference are evaluated exactly once and in the proper left-to-right order. In order to do this, `defsetf` requires that *access-fn* be a function or a macro that evaluates its arguments, behaving like a function. Furthermore, a `setf` of a call on *access-fn* will also evaluate all of *access-fn*'s arguments; it cannot treat any of them specially. This means that `defsetf` cannot be used to describe how to store into a generalized variable that is a byte, such as (`ldb field reference`). To handle situations that do not fit the restrictions imposed by `defsetf`, use `define-setf-method`, which gives the user additional control at the cost of increased complexity.

A `defsetf` declaration may take one of two forms. The simple form of `defsetf` is

```
(defsetf access-fn update-fn [doc-string])
```

The *update-fn* must name a function (or macro) that takes one more argument than *access-fn* takes. When `setf` is given a *place* that is a call on *access-fn*, it expands into a call on *update-fn* that is given all the arguments to *access-fn* and also, as its last argument, the new value (which must be returned by *update-fn* as its value). For example, the effect of

```
(defsetf symbol-value set)
```

is built into the COMMON LISP system. This causes the form (`setf (symbol-value foo) fu`) to expand into (`set foo fu`). Note that

```
(defsetf car rplaca)
```

would be incorrect because `rplaca` does not return its last argument.

The complex form of `defsetf` looks like

(`defsetf` *access-fn lambda-list* (*store-variable*) . *body*)

and resembles `defmacro`. The *body* must compute the expansion of a `setf` of a call on *access-fn*.

The *lambda-list* describes the arguments of *access-fn*. `&optional`, `&rest`, and `&key` markers are permitted in *lambda-list*. Optional arguments may have defaults and "supplied-p" flags. The *store-variable* describes the value to be stored into the generalized-variable reference.

Rationale: The *store-variable* is enclosed in parentheses to provide for an extension to multiple store variables that would receive multiple values from the second subform of `setf`. The rules given below for coding `setf` methods discuss the proper handling of multiple store variables to allow for the possibility that this extension may be incorporated into COMMON LISP in the future.

The *body* forms can be written as if the variables in the *lambda-list* were bound to subforms of the call on *access-fn* and the *store-variable* were bound to the second subform of `setf`. However, this is not actually the case. During the evaluation of the *body* forms, these variables are bound to names of temporary variables, generated as if by `gensym` or `gentemp`, that will be bound by the expansion of `setf` to the values of those subforms. This binding permits the *body* forms to be written without regard for order-of-evaluation issues. `defsetf` arranges for the temporary variables to be optimized out of the final result in cases where that is possible. In other words, an attempt is made by `defsetf` to generate the best code possible in a particular implementation.

Note that the code generated by the *body* forms must include provision for returning the correct value (the value of *store-variable*). This is handled by the *body* forms rather than by `defsetf` because in many cases this value can be returned at no extra cost, by calling a function that simultaneously stores into the generalized variable and returns the correct value.

An example of the use of the complex form of `defsetf`:

```
(defsetf subseq (sequence start &optional end) (new-sequence)
  `(progn (replace ,sequence ,new-sequence
                   :start1 ,start :end1 ,end)
          ,new-sequence))
```

The underlying theory by which `setf` and related macros arrange to conform to the semantic rules given above is that from any generalized-variable reference one may derive its "`setf` method," which describes how to store into that reference and which subforms of it are evaluated.

Compatibility note: To avoid confusion, it should be noted that the use of the word "method" here in connection with `setf` has nothing to do with its use in ZETALISP in connection with message-passing and the ZETALISP "flavor system."

Given knowledge of the subforms of the reference, it is possible to avoid evaluating them multiple times or in the wrong order. A `setf` method for a given access form can be expressed as five values:

- A list of *temporary variables*.
- A list of *value forms* (subforms of the given form) to whose values the temporary variables are to be bound.
- A second list of temporary variables, called *store variables*.
- A *storing form*.
- An *accessing form*.

The temporary variables will be bound to the values of the value forms as if by `let*`; that is, the value forms will be evaluated in the order given and may refer to the values of earlier value forms by using the corresponding variables.

The store variables are to be bound to the values of the *newvalue* form, that is, the values to be stored into the generalized variable. In almost all cases only a single value is to be stored, and there is only one store variable.

The storing form and the accessing form may contain references to the temporary variables (and also, in the case of the storing form, to the store variables). The accessing form returns the value of the generalized variable. The storing form modifies the value of the generalized variable and guarantees to return the values of the store variables as its values; these are the correct values for `setf` to return. (Again, in most cases there is a single store variable and thus a single value to be returned.) The value returned by the accessing form is, of course, affected by execution of the storing form, but either of these forms may be evaluated any number of times, and therefore should be free of side effects (other than the storing action of the storing form).

The temporary variables and the store variables are generated names, as if by `gensym` or `gentemp`, so that there is never any problem of name clashes among them, or between them and other variables in the program. This is necessary to make the special forms that do more than one `setf` in parallel work properly; these are `psetf`, `shiftf`, and `rotatef`. Computation of the `setf` method must always create new variable names; it may not return the same ones every time.

Some examples of `setf` methods for particular forms:

- For a variable `x`:

```
()
()
(g0001)
(setq x g0001)
x
```

- For (`car` *exp*):

```
(g0002)
(exp)
(g0003)
(progn (rplaca g0002 g0003) g0003)
(car g0002)
```

- For (`subseq` *seq s e*):

```
(g0004 g0005 g0006)
(seq s e)
(g0007)
(progn (replace g0004 g0007 :start1 g0005 :end1 g0006)
       g0007)
(subseq g0004 g0005 g0006)
```

`define-setf-method` *access-fn lambda-list*   [*Macro*]
          {declaration | doc-string}* {form}*

This defines how to `setf` a generalized-variable reference that is of the form (*access-fn*...). The value of a generalized-variable reference can always be obtained simply by evaluating it, so *access-fn* should be the name of a function or a macro.

The *lambda-list* describes the subforms of the generalized-variable reference, as with `defmacro`. The result of evaluating the *forms* in the body must be five values representing the `setf` method, as described above. Note that `define-setf-method` differs from the complex form of defsetf in that while the body is being executed the variables in *lambda-list* are bound to parts of the generalized-variable reference, not to temporary variables that will be bound to the values of such parts. In addition, define-setf-method does not have defsetf's restriction that *access-fn* must be a function or a function-like macro; an arbitrary defmacro destructuring pattern is permitted in *lambda-list*.

By definition there are no good small examples of define-setf-method because the easy cases can all be handled by defsetf. A typical use is to define the setf method for ldb:

```
;;; SETF method for the form (LDB bytespec int).
;;; Recall that the int form must itself be suitable for SETF.

(define-setf-method ldb (bytespec int)
  (multiple-value-bind (temps vals stores
                        store-form access-form)
    (get-setf-method int)        ;Get SETF method for int.
    (let ((btemp (gensym))       ;Temp var for byte specifier.
          (store (gensym))       ;Temp var for byte to store.
          (stemp (first stores))) ;Temp var for int to store.
      ;; Return the SETF method for LDB as five values.
      (values (cons btemp temps)      ;Temporary variables.
              (cons bytespec vals)    ;Value forms.
              (list store)            ;Store variables.
              `(let ((,stemp (dpb ,store ,btemp ,access-form)))
                 ,store-form
                 ,store)              ;Storing form.
              `(ldb ,btemp ,access-form)  ;Accessing form.
              ))))
```

get-setf-method *form*   [*Function*]

get-setf-method returns five values constituting the setf method for *form*. The *form* must be a generalized-variable reference. get-setf-method takes care of error-checking and macro expansion and guarantees to return exactly one store-variable.

As an example, an extremely simplified version of setf, allowing no more and no fewer than two subforms, containing no optimization to remove unnecessary variables, and not allowing storing of multiple values, could be defined by:

```
(defmacro setf (reference value)
  (multiple-value-bind (vars vals stores store-form access-form)
      (get-setf-method reference)
    (declare (ignore access-form))
    `(let* ,(mapcar #'list
                    (append vars stores)
                    (append vals (list value)))
       ,store-form)))
```

get-setf-method-multiple-value *form*   [*Function*]

get-setf-method-multiple-value returns five values constituting the setf method for *form*. The *form* must be a generalized-variable reference. This is the same as get-setf-method except that it does not check the number of store-variables; use this in cases that allow storing multiple values into a generalized variable. There are no such cases in standard COMMON LISP, but this function is provided to allow for possible extensions.

7.3. Function Invocation

The most primitive form for function invocation in LISP of course has no name; any list that has no other interpretation as a macro call or special form is taken to be a function call. Other constructs are provided for less common but nevertheless frequently useful situations.

apply *function arg* &rest *more-args*   [*Function*]

This applies *function* to a list of arguments. *function* may be a compiled-code object, or a lambda-expression, or a symbol; in the latter case the global functional value of that symbol is used (but it is illegal for the symbol to be the name of a macro or special form). The arguments for the *function* consist of the last argument to apply appended to the end of a list of all the other arguments to apply but the *function* itself; it is as if all the arguments to apply except the *function* were given to list* to create the argument list. For example:

```
(setq f '+) (apply f '(1 2)) => 3
(setq f #'-) (apply f '(1 2)) => -1
(apply #'max 3 5 '(2 7 3)) => 7
(apply 'cons '((+ 2 3) 4)) =>
       ((+ 2 3) . 4)    not (5 . 4)
(apply #'+ '()) => 0
```

Note that if the function takes keyword arguments, the keywords as well as the corresponding values must appear in the argument list:

```
(apply #'(lambda (&key a b) (list a b)) '(:b 3)) ⇒ (nil 3)
```

This can be very useful in conjunction with the &allow-other-keys feature:

```
(defun foo (size &rest keys &key double &allow-other-keys)
  (let ((v (apply #'make-array size :allow-other-keys t keys)))
    (if double (concatenate (type-of v) v v) v)))

(foo 4 :initial-contents '(a b c d) :double t)
  ⇒ #(a b c d a b c d)
```

funcall *fn* &rest *arguments*   [*Function*]

(funcall *fn a1 a2 ... an*) applies the function *fn* to the arguments *a1*, *a2*, ..., *an*. *fn* may not be a special form nor a macro; this would not be meaningful. For example:

```
(cons 1 2) ⇒ (1 . 2)
(setq cons (symbol-function '+))
(funcall cons 1 2) ⇒ 3
```

The difference between funcall and an ordinary function call is that the function is obtained by ordinary LISP evaluation rather than by the special interpretation of the function position that normally occurs.

Compatibility note: The COMMON LISP function funcall corresponds roughly to the INTERLISP primitive apply*.

---

call-arguments-limit   [*Constant*]

The value of call-arguments-limit is a positive integer that is the upper exclusive bound on the number of arguments that may be passed to a function. This bound depends on the implementation, but will not be smaller than 50. (Implementors are encouraged to make this limit as large as practicable without sacrificing performance.) The value of call-arguments-limit must be as least as great as that of lambda-parameters-limit. See also multiple-values-limit.

7.4. Simple Sequencing

Each of the constructs in this section simply evaluates all the argument forms in order. They differ only in what results are returned.

`progn` *{form}**   [*Special form*]

The `progn` construct takes a number of forms and evaluates them sequentially, in order, from left to right. The values of all the forms but the last are discarded; whatever the last form returns is returned by the `progn` form. One says that all the forms but the last are evaluated for *effect*, because their execution is useful only for the side effects caused, but the last form is executed for *value*.

`progn` is the primitive control structure construct for "compound statements," such as **begin-end** blocks in ALGOL-like languages. Many LISP constructs are "implicit `progn`" forms, in that as part of their syntax each allows many forms to be written that are to be evaluated sequentially, discarding the results of all forms but the last and returning the results of the last form.

If the last form of the `progn` returns multiple values, then those multiple values are returned by the `progn` form. If there are no forms for the `progn`, then the result is `nil`. These rules generally hold for implicit `progn` forms as well.

`prog1` *first {form}**   [*Macro*]

`prog1` is similar to `progn`, but it returns the value of its *first* form. All the argument forms are executed sequentially; the value the first form produces is saved while all the others are executed and is then returned.

`prog1` is most commonly used to evaluate an expression with side effects and return a value that must be computed *before* the side effects happen. For example:

```
(prog1 (car x) (rplaca x 'foo))
```

alters the *car* of x to be `foo` and returns the old *car* of x.

`prog1` always returns a single value, even if the first form tries to return multiple values. As a consequence of this, `(prog1 x)` and `(progn x)` may behave differently if x can produce multiple values. See `multiple-value-prog1`. A point of style: although `prog1` can be used to force exactly a single value to be returned, it is conventional to use the function `values` for this purpose.

`prog2` *first second {form}**   [*Macro*]

`prog2` is similar to `prog1`, but it returns the value of its *second* form. All the argument forms are executed sequentially; the value of the second form is saved while all the other forms are executed and is then returned. `prog2` is provided mostly for historical compatibility.

```
(prog2 a b c ... z) ≡ (progn a (prog1 b c ... z))
```

Occasionally it is desirable to perform one side effect, then a value-producing operation, then another side effect. In such a peculiar case, prog2 is fairly perspicuous. For example:

```
(prog2 (open-a-file) (process-the-file) (close-the-file))
  ;value is that of process-the-file
```

prog2, like prog1, always returns a single value, even if the second form tries to return multiple values. As a consequence of this, (prog2 *x y*) and (progn *x y*) may behave differently if *y* can produce multiple values.

7.5. Establishing New Variable Bindings

During the invocation of a function represented by a lambda-expression (or a closure of a lambda-expression, as produced by function), new bindings are established for the variables that are the paremeters of the lambda-expression. These bindings initially have values determined by the parameter-binding protocol discussed in section 5.2.2.

The following constructs may also be used to establish bindings of variables, both ordinary and functional.

let ({*var* | (*var value*)}*) {*declaration*}* {*form*}*   [*Special form*]

A let form can be used to execute a series of forms with specified variables bound to specified values.

More precisely, the form

```
(let ((var1  value1)
      (var2  value2)
       . . .
      (varm  valuem))
  declaration1
  declaration2
   . . .
  declarationp
  body1
  body2
   . . .
  bodyn)
```

first evaluates the expressions *value1*, *value2*, and so on, in that order, saving the resulting values. Then all of the variables *varj* are bound to the corresponding values in parallel; each binding will be a lexical binding unless there is a `special` declaration to the contrary. The expressions *bodyk* are then evaluated in order; the values of all but the last are discarded (that is, the body of a `let` form is an implicit `progn`). The `let` form returns what evaluating *bodyn* produces (if the body is empty, which is fairly useless, `let` returns `nil` as its value). The bindings of the variables have lexical scope and indefinite extent.

Instead of a list (*varj valuej*), one may write simply *varj*. In this case *varj* is initialized to `nil`. As a matter of style, it is recommended that *varj* be written only when that variable will be stored into (such as by `setq`) before its first use. If it is important that the initial value is `nil` rather than some undefined value, then it is clearer to write out (*varj* `nil`) if the initial value is intended to mean "false" or (*varj* `'()`) if the initial value is intended to be an empty list. Note that the code

```
(let (x)
  (declare (integer x))
  (setq x (gcd y z))
  ...)
```

is incorrect; although x is indeed set before it is used, and is set to a value of the declared type `integer`, nevertheless x momentarily takes on the value `nil` in violation of the type declaration.

Declarations may appear at the beginning of the body of a `let`. See `declare`.

`let*` ({*var* | (*var value*)}*) {*declaration*}* {*form*}*   [*Special form*]

`let*` is similar to `let`, but the bindings of variables are performed sequentially rather than in parallel. This allows the expression for the value of a variable to refer to variables previously bound in the `let*` form.

More precisely, the form

```
(let* ((var1  value1)
       (var2  value2)
       ...
       (varm  valuem))
  declaration1
  declaration2
  ...
  declarationp
  body1
  body2
  ...
  bodyn)
```

first evaluates the expression *value1*, then binds the variable *var1* to that value; then it evaluates *value2* and binds *var2*; and so on. The expressions *bodyj* are then evaluated in order; the values of all but the last are discarded (that is, the body of a let* form is an implicit progn). The let* form returns the results of evaluating *bodyn* (if the body is empty, which is fairly useless, let* returns nil as its value). The bindings of the variables have lexical scope and indefinite extent.

Instead of a list ⟨*varj valuej*⟩, one may write simply *varj*. In this case *varj* is initialized to nil. As a matter of style, it is recommended that *varj* be written only when that variable will be stored into (such as by setq) before its first use. If it is important that the initial value is nil rather than some undefined value, then it is clearer to write out ⟨*varj* nil⟩ if the initial value is intended to mean "false" or ⟨*varj* '()⟩ if the initial value is intended to be an empty list.

Declarations may appear at the beginning of the body of a let*. See declare.

---

compiler-let ⟨ {*var* | (*var value*)}*⟩ {*form*}*   [*Special form*]

When executed by the LISP interpreter, compiler-let behaves exactly like let with all the variable bindings implicitly declared special. When the compiler processes this form, however, no code is compiled for the bindings; instead, the processing of the body by the compiler (including, in particular, the expansion of any macro calls within the body) is done with the special variables bound to the indicated values *in the execution context of the compiler*. This is primarily useful for communication among complicated macros.

Declarations may *not* appear at the beginning of the body of a compiler-let.

Rationale: Because of the unorthodox handling by compiler-let of its variable bindings, it would be complicated and confusing to permit declarations that apparently referred to the variables bound by compiler-let. Disallowing declarations eliminates the problem.

---

progv *symbols values* {*form*}*   [*Special form*]

progv is a special form that allows binding one or more dynamic variables whose names may be determined at run time. The sequence of forms (an implicit progn) is evaluated with the dynamic variables whose names are in the list *symbols* bound to corresponding values from the list *values*. (If too few values are supplied, the remaining symbols are bound and then made to have no value; see makunbound. If too many values are supplied, the excess values are ignored.) The results of the progv form are those of the last *form*. The bindings of the dynamic variables are undone on exit from the progv form. The lists of symbols and values are computed quantities; this is what makes progv different from, for example, let, where the variable names are stated explicitly in the program text.

progv is particularly useful for writing interpreters for languages embedded in LISP; it provides a handle on the mechanism for binding dynamic variables.

flet ({(*name lambda-list {declaration | doc-string}*   [*Special form*]
            {form}*)}*) {form}*
labels ({(*name lambda-list {declaration | doc-string}*   [*Special form*]
            {form}*)}*) {form}*
macrolet ({(*name varlist {declaration | doc-string}*   [*Special form*]
            {form}*)}*) {form}*

flet may be used to define locally named functions. Within the body of the flet form, function names matching those defined by the flet refer to the locally defined functions rather than to the global function definitions of the same name.

Any number of functions may be simultaneously defined. Each definition is similar in format to a defun form: first a name, then a parameter list (which may contain &optional, &rest, or &key parameters), then optional declarations and documentation string, and finally a body.

```
(flet ((safesqrt (x) (sqrt (abs x))))
  ;; The safesqrt function is used in two places.
  (safesqrt (apply #'+ (map 'list #'safesqrt longlist))))
```

The labels construct is identical in form to the flet construct. These constructs differ in that the scope of the defined function names for flet encompasses only the body, whereas for labels it encompasses the function definitions themselves. That is, labels can be used to define mutually recursive functions, but flet cannot. This distinction is useful. Using flet one can locally redefine a global function name, and the new definition can refer to the global definition; the same construction using labels would not have that effect.

```
(defun integer-power (n k)      ;A highly "bummed" integer
  (declare (integer n))         ; exponentiation routine.
  (declare (type (integer 0 *) k))
  (labels ((expt0 (x k a)
             (declare (integer x a) (type (integer 0 *) k))
             (cond ((zerop k) a)
                   ((evenp k) (expt1 (* x x) (floor k 2) a))
                   (t (expt0 (* x x) (floor k 2) (* x a)))))
           (expt1 (x k a)
             (declare (integer x a) (type (integer 1 *) k))
             (cond ((evenp k) (expt1 (* x x) (floor k 2) a))
                   (t (expt0 (* x x) (floor k 2) (* x a))))))
    (expt0 n k 1)))
```

`macrolet` is similar in form to `flet` but defines local macros, using the same format used by `defmacro`. The names established by `macrolet` as names for macros are lexically scoped.

Macros often must be expanded at "compile time" (more generally, at a time before the program itself is executed), and so the run-time values of variables are not available to macros defined by `macrolet`. The precise rule is that the macro-expansion functions defined by `macrolet` are defined in the *global* environment; lexically scoped entities that would ordinarily be lexically apparent are not visible within the expansion functions. However, lexically scoped entities *are* visible within the body of the `macrolet` form and *are* visible to the code that is the expansion of a macro call. The following example should make this clear:

```
(defun foo (x flag)
   (macrolet ((fudge (z)
                      ;The parameters x and flag are not accessible
                      ; at this point; a reference to flag would be to
                      ; the global variable of that name.
                     '(if flag (* ,z ,z) ,z)))
      ;The parameters x and flag are accessible here.
      (+ x
         (fudge x)
         (fudge (+ x 1))))))
```

The body of the `macrolet` becomes

```
(+ x
   (if flag (* x x) x))
   (if flag (* (+ x 1) (+ x 1)) (+ x 1)))
```

after macro expansion. The occurrences of x and flag legitimately refer to the parameters of the function `foo` because those parameters are visible at the site of the macro call which produced the expansion.

7.6. Conditionals

The traditional conditional construct in LISP is `cond`. However, `if` is much simpler and is directly comparable to conditional constructs in other programming languages, so it is considered to be primitive in COMMON LISP and is described first. COMMON

LISP also provides the dispatching constructs `case` and `typecase`, which are often more convenient than `cond`.

---

if *test then* [*else*]   [*Special form*]

The `if` special form corresponds to the **if-then-else** construct found in most algebraic programming languages. First the form *test* is evaluated. If the result is not `nil`, then the form *then* is selected; otherwise the form *else* is selected. Whichever form is selected is then evaluated, and `if` returns whatever evaluation of the selected form returns.

(`if` *test then else*) ≡ (`cond` (*test then*) (`t` *else*))

but `if` is considered more readable in some situations.

The *else* form may be omitted, in which case if the value of *test* is `nil` then nothing is done and the value of the `if` form is `nil`. If the value of the `if` form is important in this situation, then the `and` construct may be stylistically preferable, depending on the context. If the value is not important, but only the effect, then the `when` construct may be stylistically preferable.

---

when *test* {*form*}*   [*Macro*]

(`when` *test form1 form2* ...) first evaluates *test*. If the result is `nil`, then no *form* is evaluated, and `nil` is returned. Otherwise the *form*s constitute an implicit `progn` and are evaluated sequentially from left to right, and the value of the last one is returned.

(`when` *p a b c*) ≡ (`and` *p* (`progn` *a b c*))
(`when` *p a b c*) ≡ (`cond` (*p a b c*))
(`when` *p a b c*) ≡ (`if` *p* (`progn` *a b c*) `nil`)
(`when` *p a b c*) ≡ (`unless` (`not` *p*) *a b c*)

As a matter of style, `when` is normally used to conditionally produce some side effects, and the value of the `when`-form is normally not used. If the value is relevant, then it may be stylistically more appropriate to use `and` or `if`.

---

unless *test* {*form*}*   [*Macro*]

(`unless` *test form1 form2* ...) first evaluates *test*. If the result is *not* `nil`, then the *form*s are not evaluated, and `nil` is returned. Otherwise the *form*s constitute an implicit `progn` and are evaluated sequentially from left to right, and the value of the last one is returned.

```
(unless p a b c) ≡ (cond ((not p) a b c))
(unless p a b c) ≡ (if p nil (progn a b c))
(unless p a b c) ≡ (when (not p) a b c)
```

As a matter of style, `unless` is normally used to conditionally produce some side effects, and the value of the `unless`-form is normally not used. If the value is relevant, then it may be stylistically more appropriate to use `if`.

`cond {(`*test* `{`*form*`}*)}*`   [*Macro*]

A `cond` form has a number (possibly zero) of *clauses*, which are lists of forms. Each clause consists of a *test* followed by zero or more *consequents*. For example:

```
(cond (test-1 consequent-1-1 consequent-1-2 ...)
      (test-2)
      (test-3 consequent-3-1 ...)
      ... )
```

The first clause whose *test* evaluates to non-`nil` is selected; all other clauses are ignored, and the consequents of the selected clause are evaluated in order (as an implicit `progn`).

More specifically, `cond` processes its clauses in order from left to right. For each clause, the *test* is evaluated. If the result is `nil`, `cond` advances to the next clause. Otherwise, the *cdr* of the clause is treated as a list of forms, or consequents; these forms are evaluated in order from left to right, as an implicit `progn`. After evaluating the consequents, `cond` returns without inspecting any remaining clauses. The `cond` special form returns the results of evaluating the last of the selected consequents; if there were no consequents in the selected clause, then the single (and necessarily non-null) value of the *test* is returned. If `cond` runs out of clauses (every test produced `nil`, and therefore no clause was selected), the value of the `cond` form is `nil`.

If it is desired to select the last clause unconditionally if all others fail, the standard convention is to use `t` for the *test*. As a matter of style, it is desirable to write a last clause `(t nil)` if the value of the `cond` form is to be used for something. Similarly, it is in questionable taste to let the last clause of a `cond` be a "singleton clause"; an explicit `t` should be provided. (Note moreover that `(cond ... (x))` may behave differently from `(cond ... (t x))` if *x* might produce multiple values; the former always returns a single value, whereas the latter returns whatever values *x* returns. However, as a matter of style it is preferable to obtain this behavior by writing `(cond ... (t (values` *x*`)))`, using the `values` function explicitly to indicate the discarding of any excess values.) For example:

```
(setq z (cond (a 'foo) (b 'bar)))        ;Possibly confusing
(setq z (cond (a 'foo) (b 'bar) (t nil)))  ;Better
(cond (a b) (c d) (e))                   ;Possibly confusing
(cond (a b) (c d) (t e))                 ;Better
(cond (a b) (c d) (t (values e)))        ;Better (if one value
                                         ;   needed)
(cond (a b) (c))                         ;Possibly confusing
(cond (a b) (t c))                       ;Better
(if a b c)                               ;Also better
```

A LISP `cond` form may be compared to a continued **if-then-else** as found in many algebraic programming languages:

```
(cond (p ...)                          if p then ...
      (q ...)        roughly           else if q then ...
      (r ...)        corresponds       else if r then ...
      ...            to                ...
      (t ...))                         else ...
```

case *keyform* `{({({key}*) |` *key*`} {`*form*`}*)}*`   [*Macro*]

`case` is a conditional that chooses one of its clauses to execute by comparing a value to various constants, which are typically keyword symbols, integers, or characters (but may be any objects). Its form is as follows:

```
(case keyform
   (keylist-1 consequent-1-1 consequent-1-2 ...)
   (keylist-2 consequent-2-1 ...)
   (keylist-3 consequent-3-1 ...)
   ...)
```

Structurally `case` is much like `cond`, and it behaves like `cond` in selecting one clause and then executing all consequents of that clause. However, `case` differs in the mechanism of clause selection.

The first thing `case` does is to evaluate the form *keyform* to produce an object called the *key object*. Then `case` considers each of the clauses in turn. If *key* is in the *keylist* (that is, is `eql` to any item in the *keylist*) of a clause, the consequents of that clause are evaluated as an implicit `progn`; `case` returns what was returned by the last consequent (or `nil` if there are no consequents in that clause). If no clause is satisfied, `case` returns `nil`.

The keys in the keylists are *not* evaluated; literal key values must appear in the keylists. It is an error for the same key to appear in more than one clause; a consequence is that the order of the clauses does not affect the behavior of the case construct.

Instead of a *keylist*, one may write one of the symbols t and otherwise. A clause with such a symbol always succeeds and must be the last clause (this is an exception to the order-independence of clauses). See also ecase and ccase, each of which provides an implicit otherwise clause to signal an error if no clause is satisfied.

If there is only one key for a clause, then that key may be written in place of a list of that key, provided that no ambiguity results. Such a "singleton key" may not be nil (which is confusable with (), a list of no keys), t, otherwise, or a cons.

Compatibility note: The ZETALISP caseq construct uses eq for the comparison. In ZETALISP caseq therefore works for fixnums but not bignums. The MACLISP caseq construct simply prohibits the use of bignums; indeed, it permits only fixnums and symbols as clause keys. In the interest of hiding the fixnum-bignum distinction, and for general language consistency, case uses eql in COMMON LISP.

The INTERLISP selectq construct is similar to case.

---

typecase *keyform* {(*type* {*form*}*)}*   [*Macro*]

typecase is a conditional that chooses one of its clauses by examining the type of an object. Its form is as follows:

```
(typecase keyform
  (type-1 consequent-1-1 consequent-1-2 ...)
  (type-2 consequent-2-1 ...)
  (type-3 consequent-3-1 ...)
  ...)
```

Structurally typecase is much like cond or case, and it behaves like them in selecting one clause and then executing all consequents of that clause. It differs in the mechanism of clause selection.

The first thing typecase does is to evaluate the form *keyform* to produce an object called the key object. Then typecase considers each of the clauses in turn. The *type* that appears in each clause is a type specifier; it is not evaluated, but is a literal type specifier. The first clause for which the key is of that clause's specified *type* is selected, the consequents of this clause are evaluated as an implicit progn, and `typecase` returns what was returned by the last consequent (or `nil` if there are no consequents in that clause). If no clause is satisfied, `typecase` returns `nil`.

As for `case`, the symbol `t` or `otherwise` may be written for *type* to indicate that the clause should always be selected. See also `etypecase` and `ctypecase`, each of which provides an implicit `otherwise` clause to signal an error if no clause is satisfied.

It is permissible for more than one clause to specify a given type, particularly if one is a subtype of another; the earliest applicable clause is chosen. Thus for `typecase`, unlike `case`, the order of the clauses may affect the behavior of the construct. For example:

```
(typecase an-object
    (string ...)              ;This clause handles strings.
    ((array t) ...)           ;This clause handles general arrays.
    ((array bit) ...)         ;This clause handles bit arrays.
    (array ...)               ;This handles all other arrays.
    ((or list number) ...)    ;This handles lists and numbers.
    (t ...))                  ;This handles all other objects.
```

A COMMON LISP compiler may choose to issue a warning if a clause cannot be selected because it is completely shadowed by earlier clauses.

7.7. Blocks and Exits

The `block` and `return-from` constructs provide a structured lexical non-local exit facility. At any point lexically within a `block` construct, a `return-from` with the same name may be used to perform an immediate transfer of control that exits from the `block`. In the most common cases this mechanism is more efficient than the dynamic non-local exit facility provided by `catch` and `throw`, described in section 7.10.

block *name* {*form*}*   [*Special form*]

The `block` construct executes each *form* from left to right, returning whatever is returned by the last *form*. If, however, a `return` or `return-from` form that specifies the same *name* is executed during the execution of some *form*, then the results specified by the `return` or `return-from` are immediately returned as the value of the `block` construct, and execution proceeds as if the `block` had terminated normally. In this, `block` differs from `progn`; the `progn` construct has nothing to do with `return`.

The *name* is not evaluated; it must be a symbol. The scope of the *name* is lexical; only a `return` or `return-from` textually contained in some *form* can exit from the block. The extent of the name is dynamic. Therefore it is only possible to exit from a given run-time incarnation of a block once, either normally or by explicit return.

The `defun` form implicitly puts a `block` around the body of the function defined; the `block` has the same name as the function. Therefore one may use `return-from` to return prematurely from a function defined by `defun`.

The lexical scoping of the block name is fully general and has consequences that may be surprising to users and implementors of other LISP systems. For example, the `return-from` in the following example actually does "work" in COMMON LISP as one might expect:

```
(block loser
   (catch 'stuff
      (mapcar #'(lambda (x) (if (numberp x)
                                (hairyfun x)
                                (return-from loser nil)))
              items)))
```

Depending on the situation, a `return` in COMMON LISP may not be simple. A `return` can break up catchers if necessary to get to the block in question. It is possible for a "closure" created by `function` for a lambda-expression to refer to a block name as long as the name is lexically apparent.

`return-from` *name* [*result*]   [*Special form*]

`return` [*result*]   [*Macro*]

`return-from` is used to return from a `block` or from such constructs as `do` and `prog` that implicitly establish a `block`. The *name* is not evaluated and must be a symbol. A `block` construct with the same name must lexically enclose the occurrence of `return-from`; whatever the evaluation of *result* produces is immediately returned from the block. (If the *result* form is omitted, it defaults to `nil`. As a matter of style, this form ought to be used to indicate that the particular value returned doesn't matter.)

The `return-from` form itself never returns and cannot have a value; it causes results to be returned from a `block` construct. If the evaluation of *result* produces multiple values, those multiple values are returned by the construct exited.

(`return` *form*) is identical in meaning to (`return-from` `nil` *form*); it returns from a block named `nil`. Blocks established implicitly by iteration constructs such as `do` are named `nil`, so that `return` will exit properly from such a construct.

7.8. Iteration

COMMON LISP provides a number of iteration constructs. The `loop` construct provides a trivial iteration facility; it is little more than a `progn` with a branch from the bottom back to the top. The `do` and `do*` constructs provide a general iteration facility for controlling the variation of several variables on each cycle. For specialized iterations over the elements of a list or *n* consecutive integers, `dolist` and `dotimes` are provided. The `tagbody` construct is the most general, permitting arbitrary `go` statements within it. (The traditional `prog` construct is a synthesis of `tagbody`, `block`, and `let`.) Most of the iteration constructs permit statically defined non-local exits in the form of the `return-from` and `return` statements.

7.8.1. Indefinite Iteration

The `loop` construct is the simplest iteration facility. It controls no variables, and simply executes its body repeatedly.

loop   *{form}**   [*Macro*]

Each *form* is evaluated in turn from left to right. When the last *form* has been evaluated, then the first *form* is evaluated again, and so on, in a never-ending cycle. The `loop` construct never returns a value. Its execution must be terminated explicitly, using `return` or `throw`, for example.

`loop`, like most iteration constructs, establishes an implicit block named `nil`. Thus `return` may be used to exit from a `loop` with specified results.

A `loop` construct has this meaning only if every *form* is non-atomic (a list). The case where some *form* (possibly more than one) is atomic is reserved for future extensions.

Implementation note: There have been several proposals for a powerful iteration mechanism to be called `loop`. One version is provided in ZETALISP. Implementors are encouraged to experiment with extensions to the `loop` syntax, but users should be advised that in all likelihood some specific set of extensions to `loop` will be adopted in a future revision of COMMON LISP.

7.8.2. General Iteration

In contrast to `loop`, `do` and `do*` provide a powerful and general mechanism for repetitively recalculating many variables.

do ({(*var* [*init* [*step*]])}*) (*end-test* {*result*}*)   [*Macro*]
    {*declaration*}* {*tag* | *statement*}*
do* ({(*var* [*init* [*step*]])}*) (*end-test* {*form*}*)   [*Macro*]
    {*declaration*}* {*tag* | *statement*}*

The do special form provides a generalized iteration facility, with an arbitrary number of "index variables." These variables are bound within the iteration and stepped in parallel in specified ways. They may be used both to generate successive values of interest (such as successive integers) or to accumulate results. When an end condition is met, the iteration terminates with a specified value.

In general, a do loop looks like this:

```
(do ((var1 init1 step1)
     (var2 init2 step2)
      ...
     (varn initn stepn))
    (end-test . result)
  {declaration}*
  . tagbody)
```

A do* loop looks exactly the same except that the name do is replaced by do*.

The first item in the form is a list of zero or more index-variable specifiers. Each index-variable specifier is a list of the name of a variable *var*, an initial value *init*, and a stepping form *step*. If *init* is omitted, it defaults to nil. If *step* is omitted, the *var* is not changed by the do construct between repetitions (though code within the do is free to alter the value of the variable by using setq).

An index-variable specifier can also be just the name of a variable. In this case, the variable has an initial value of nil and is not changed between repetitions. As a matter of style, it is recommended that an unadorned variable name be written only when that variable will be stored into (such as by setq) before its first use. If it is important that the initial value is nil rather than some undefined value, then it is clearer to write out (*varj* nil) if the initial value is intended to mean "false" or (*varj* '()) if the initial value is intended to be an empty list.

Before the first iteration, all the *init* forms are evaluated, and each *var* is bound to the value of its respective *init*. This is a binding, not an assignment; when the loop terminates, the old values of those variables will be restored. For do, *all* of the *init* forms are evaluated *before* any *var* is bound; hence all the *init* forms may refer to the old bindings of all the variables (that is, to the values visible before beginning execution of the do construct). For do*, the first init form is evaluated, then the first var is bound to that value, then the second *init* form is evaluated, then the second *var* is bound, and so on; in general, the *initj* form can refer to the *new* binding *vark* if $k < j$, and otherwise to the *old* binding of *vark*.

The second element of the loop is a list of an end-testing predicate form *end-test* and zero or more *result* forms. This resembles a `cond` clause. At the beginning of each iteration, after processing the variables, the *end-test* is evaluated. If the result is `nil`, execution proceeds with the body of the `do` (or `do*`) form. If the result is not `nil`, the *result* forms are evaluated in order as an implicit `progn`, and then `do` returns. `do` returns the results of evaluating the last *result* form. If there are no *result* forms, the value of `do` is `nil`. Note that this is not quite analogous to the treatment of clauses in a `cond` form, because a `cond` clause with no result forms returns the (non-`nil`) result of the test.

At the beginning of each iteration other than the first, the index variables are updated as follows. All the *step* forms are evaluated, from left to right, and the resulting values are assigned to the respective index variables. Any variable that has no associated *step* form is not assigned to. For `do`, all the *step* forms are evaluated before any variable is updated; the assignment of values to variables is done in parallel, as if by `psetq`. Because *all* of the *step* forms are evaluated before *any* of the variables are altered, a step form when evaluated always has access to the *old* values of *all* the index variables, even if other step forms precede it. For `do*`, the first `step` form is evaluated, then the value is assigned to the first `var`, then the second *step* form is evaluated, then the value is assigned to the second `var`, and so on; the assignment of values to variables is done sequentially, as if by `setq`. For either `do` or `do*`, after the variables have been updated, the end-test is evaluated as described above, and the iteration continues.

If the end-test of a `do` form is `nil`, the test will never succeed. Therefore this provides an idiom for "do forever": the *body* of the `do` is executed repeatedly, stepping variables as usual. (The `loop` construct performs a "do forever" that steps no variables.) The infinite loop can be terminated by the use of `return`, `return-from`, `go` to an outer level, or `throw`. For example:

```
(do ((j 0 (+ j 1)))
    (nil)                          ;Do forever.
  (format t "~%Input ~D:" j)
  (let ((item (read)))
    (if (null item) (return)       ;Process items until nil seen.
        (format t "~&Output ~D: ~S" j (process item)))))
```

The remainder of the `do` form constitutes an implicit `tagbody`. Tags may appear within the body of a `do` loop for use by `go` statements appearing in the body (but such `go` statements may not appear in the variable specifiers, the *end-test*, or the *result* forms). When the end of a do body is reached, the next iteration cycle (beginning with the evaluation of *step* forms) occurs.

An implicit block named nil surrounds the entire do form. A return statement may be used at any point to exit the loop immediately.

declare forms may appear at the beginning of a do body. They apply to code in the do body, to the bindings of the do variables, to the *init* forms, to the *step* forms, to the *end-test*, and to the *result* forms.

Compatibility note: "Old-style" MacLisp do loops, that is, those of the form (do *var init step end-test . body*), are not supported in Common Lisp. Such old-style loops are considered obsolete, and in any case are easily converted to a new-style do with the insertion of three pairs of parentheses. In practice the compiler can catch nearly all instances of old-style do loops because they will not have a legal format anyway.

Here are some examples of the use of do:

```
(do ((i 0 (+ i 1))        ;Sets every null element of a-vector to zero.
     (n (length a-vector)))
    ((= i n))
  (when (null (aref a-vector i))
    (setf (aref a-vector i) 0)))
```

The construction

```
(do ((x e (cdr x))
     (oldx x x))
    ((null x))
  body)
```

exploits parallel assignment to index variables. On the first iteration, the value of oldx is whatever value x had before the do was entered. On succeeding iterations, oldx contains the value that x had on the previous iteration.

Very often an iterative algorithm can be most clearly expressed entirely in the *step* forms of a do, and the *body* is empty. For example,

```
(do ((x foo (cdr x))
     (y bar (cdr y))
     (z '() (cons (f (car x) (car y)) z)))
    ((or (null x) (null y))
     (nreverse z)))
```

does the same thing as (mapcar #'f foo bar). Note that the *step* computation for z exploits the fact that variables are stepped in parallel. Also, the body of the loop is empty. Finally, the use of `nreverse` to put an accumulated `do` loop result into the correct order is a standard idiom. Another example:

```
(defun list-reverse (list)
      (do ((x list (cdr x))
           (y '() (cons (car x) y)))
          ((endp x) y)))
```

Note the use of `endp` rather than `null` or `atom` to test for the end of a list; this may result in more robust code.

As an example of nested loops, suppose that `env` holds a list of conses. The *car* of each cons is a list of symbols, and the *cdr* of each cons is a list of equal length containing corresponding values. Such a data structure is similar to an association list, but is divided into "frames"; the overall structure resembles a rib-cage. A lookup function on such a data structure might be:

```
(defun ribcage-lookup (sym ribcage)
      (do ((r ribcage (cdr r)))
          ((null r) nil)
        (do ((s (caar r) (cdr s))
             (v (cdar r) (cdr v)))
            ((null s))
          (when (eq (car s) sym)
            (return-from ribcage-lookup (car v))))))
```

(Notice the use of indentation in the above example to set off the bodies of the `do` loops.)

A `do` loop may be explained in terms of the more primitive constructs `block`, `return`, `let`, `loop`, `tagbody`, and `psetq` as follows:

```
(block nil
  (let ((var1 init1)
        (var2 init2)
        ...
        (varn initn))
    {declaration}*
    (loop (when end-test (return (progn . result)))
          (tagbody . tagbody)
          (psetq var1 step1
                 var2 step2
                 ...
                 varn stepn))))
```

do* is exactly like do except that the bindings and steppings of the variables are performed sequentially rather than in parallel. It is as if, in the above explanation, let were replaced by let* and psetq were replaced by setq.

7.8.3. Simple Iteration Constructs

The constructs dolist and dotimes execute a body of code once for each value taken by a single variable. They are expressible in terms of do, but capture very common patterns of use.

Both dolist and dotimes perform a body of statements repeatedly. On each iteration a specified variable is bound to an element of interest that the body may examine. dolist examines successive elements of a list, and dotimes examines integers from 0 to $n-1$ for some specified positive integer n.

The value of any of these constructs may be specified by an optional result form, which if omitted defaults to the value nil.

The return statement may be used to return immediately from a dolist or dotimes form, discarding any following iterations that might have been performed; in effect, a block named nil surrounds the construct. The body of the loop is implicitly a tagbody construct; it may contain tags to serve as the targets of go statements. Declarations may appear before the body of the loop.

dolist (*var listform* [*resultform*]) {*declaration*}* {*tag* | *statement*}*   [*Macro*]

dolist provides straightforward iteration over the elements of a list. First dolist evaluates the form *listform*, which should produce a list. It then executes the body once for each element in the list, in order, with the variable *var* bound to the element. Then *resultform* (a single form, *not* an implicit progn) is evaluated, and the result is the value of the dolist form. (When the *resultform* is evaluated, the control variable *var* is still bound, and has the value nil.) If *resultform* is omitted, the result is nil.

```
(dolist (x '(a b c d)) (prin1 x) (princ " ")) ⇒ nil
    after printing "a b c d "
```

An explicit return statement may be used to terminate the loop and return a specified value.

dotimes (*var countform* [*resultform*]) {*declaration*}* {*tag* | *statement*}* [*Macro*]

dotimes provides straightforward iteration over a sequence of integers. The expression (dotimes (*var countform resultform*) . *progbody*) evaluates the form *countform*, which should produce an integer. It then performs *progbody* once for each integer from zero (inclusive) to *count* (exclusive), in order, with the variable *var* bound to the integer; if the value of *countform* is zero or negative, then the *progbody* is performed zero times. Finally, *resultform* (a single form, *not* an implicit `progn`) is evaluated, and the result is the value of the `dotimes` form. (When the *resultform* is evaluated, the control variable *var* is still bound, and has as its value the number of times the body was executed.) If *resultform* is omitted, the result is `nil`.

An explicit `return` statement may be used to terminate the loop and return a specified value.

Here is an example of the use of `dotimes` in processing strings:

```
;;; True if the specified subsequence of the string is a
;;; palindrome (reads the same forwards and backwards).
(defun palindromep (string &optional
                           (start 0)
                           (end (length string)))
  (dotimes (k (floor (- end start) 2) t)
    (unless (char-equal (char string (+ start k))
                        (char string (- end k 1)))
      (return nil))))

(palindromep "Able was I ere I saw Elba") ⇒ t

(palindromep "A man, a plan, a canal--Panama!") ⇒ nil

(remove-if-not #'alpha-char-p             ;Remove punctuation.
               "A man, a plan, a canal--Panama!")
  ⇒ "AmanaplanacanalPanama"

(palindromep
 (remove-if-not #'alpha-char-p
                "A man, a plan, a canal--Panama!")) ⇒ t

(palindromep
 (remove-if-not
  #'alpha-char-p
  "Unremarkable was I ere I saw Elba Kramer, nu?")) ⇒ t

(palindromep
 (remove-if-not
  #'alpha-char-p
  "A man, a plan, a cat, a ham, a yak,
                a yam, a hat, a canal--Panama!")) ⇒ t
```

Altering the value of *var* in the body of the loop (by using `setq`, for example) will have unpredictable, possibly implementation-dependent results. A COMMON LISP compiler may choose to issue a warning if such a variable appears in a `setq`.

Compatibility note: The `dotimes` construct is the closest thing in COMMON LISP to the INTERLISP `rptq` construct.

See also `do-symbols`, `do-external-symbols`, and `do-all-symbols`.

7.8.4. Mapping

Mapping is a type of iteration in which a function is successively applied to pieces of one or more sequences. The result of the iteration is a sequence containing the respective results of the function applications. There are several options for the way in which the pieces of the list are chosen and for what is done with the results returned by the applications of the function.

The function `map` may be used to map over any kind of sequence. The following functions operate only on lists.

`mapcar` *function list* &rest *more-lists*	[*Function*]
`maplist` *function list* &rest *more-lists*	[*Function*]
`mapc` *function list* &rest *more-lists*	[*Function*]
`mapl` *function list* &rest *more-lists*	[*Function*]
`mapcan` *function list* &rest *more-lists*	[*Function*]
`mapcon` *function list* &rest *more-lists*	[*Function*]

For each these mapping functions, the first argument is a function and the rest must be lists. The function must take as many arguments as there are lists.

`mapcar` operates on successive elements of the lists. First the function is applied to the *car* of each list, then to the *cadr* of each list, and so on. (Ideally all the lists are the same length; if not, the iteration terminates when the shortest list runs out, and excess elements in other lists are ignored.) The value returned by `mapcar` is a list of the results of the successive calls to the function. For example:

```
(mapcar #'abs '(3 -4 2 -5 -6)) => (3 4 2 5 6)
(mapcar #'cons '(a b c) '(1 2 3)) => ((a . 1) (b . 2) (c . 3))
```

`maplist` is like `mapcar` except that the function is applied to the list and successive *cdr*'s of that list rather than to successive elements of the list. For example:

```
(maplist #'(lambda (x) (cons 'foo x))
           '(a b c d))
  ⇒ ((foo a b c d) (foo b c d) (foo c d) (foo d))
(maplist #'(lambda (x) (if (member (car x) (cdr x)) 0 1)))
           '(a b a c d b c))
  ⇒ (0 0 1 0 1 1 1)
  ;An entry is 1 if the corresponding element of the input
  ;  list was the last instance of that element in the input list.
```

mapl and mapc are like maplist and mapcar respectively, except that they do not
accumulate the results of calling the function.

Compatibility note: In all LISP systems since LISP 1.5, mapl has been called map. In the
chapter on sequences it is explained why this was a bad choice. Here the name map is used
for the far more useful generic sequence mapper, in closer accordance to the computer
science literature, especially the growing body of papers on functional programming.

These functions are used when the function is being called merely for its side
effects, rather than its returned values. The value returned by mapl or mapc is the
second argument, that is, the first sequence argument.

   mapcan and mapcon are like mapcar and maplist respectively, except that they
combine the results of the function using nconc instead of list. That is,

```
(mapcon f x1 ... xn)
  ≡ (apply #'nconc (maplist f x1 ... xn))
```

and similarly for the relationship between mapcan and mapcar. Conceptually, these
functions allow the mapped function to return a variable number of items to be put
into the output list. This is particularly useful for effectively returning zero or one
item:

```
(mapcan #'(lambda (x) (and (numberp x) (list x)))
         '(a 1 b c 3 4 d 5))
  ⇒ (1 3 4 5)
```

In this case the function serves as a filter; this is a standard LISP idiom using
mapcan. (The function remove-if-not might have been useful in this particular
context, however.) Remember that nconc is a destructive operation, and therefore
so are mapcan and mapcon; the lists returned by the *function* are altered in order
to concatenate them.

Sometimes a `do` or a straightforward recursion is preferable to a mapping operation; however, the mapping functions should be used wherever they naturally apply because this increases the clarity of the code.

The functional argument to a mapping function must be acceptable to `apply`; it cannot be a macro or the name of a special form. Of course, there is nothing wrong with using a function that has `&optional` and `&rest` parameters as the functional argument.

7.8.5. The "Program Feature"

LISP implementations since LISP 1.5 have had what was originally called "the program feature," as if it were impossible to write programs without it! The `prog` construct allows one to write in an ALGOL-like or FORTRAN-like statement-oriented style, using `go` statements that can refer to tags in the body of the `prog`. Modern LISP programming style tends to use `prog` rather infrequently. The various iteration constructs, such as `do`, have bodies with the characteristics of a `prog`. (However, the ability to use `go` statements within iteration constructs is very seldom used in practice.)

Three distinct operations are performed by `prog`: it binds local variables, it permits use of the `return` statement, and it permits use of the `go` statement. In COMMON LISP, these three operations have been separated into three distinct constructs: `let`, `block`, and `tagbody`. These three constructs may be used independently as building blocks for other types of constructs.

`tagbody {tag | statement}*`   [*Special form*]

The part of a `tagbody` after the variable list is called the *body*. An item in the body may be a symbol or an integer, in which case it is called a *tag*, or an item in the body may be a list, in which case it is called a *statement*.

Each element of the body is processed from left to right. A *tag* is ignored; a *statement* is evaluated, and its results are discarded. If the end of the body is reached, the `tagbody` returns `nil`.

If (`go tag`) is evaluated, control jumps to the part of the body labelled with the *tag*.

Compatibility note: The "computed `go`" feature of MACLISP is not supported. The syntax of a computed `go` is idiosyncratic, and the feature is not supported by ZETALISP, NIL, or INTERLISP. The computed `go` has been infrequently used in MACLISP anyway, and is easily simulated with no loss of efficiency by using a `case` statement each of whose clauses performs a (non-computed) `go`.

The scope of the tags established by a tagbody is lexical, and the extent is dynamic. Once a tagbody construct has been exited, it is no longer legal to go to a *tag* in its body. It is permissible for a go to jump to a tagbody that is not the innermost tagbody construct containing that go; the tags established by a tagbody will only shadow other tags of like name.

The lexical scoping of the go targets named by tags is fully general and has consequences that may be surprising to users and implementors of other LISP systems. For example, the go in the following example actually does "work" in COMMON LISP as one might expect:

```
(tagbody
   (catch 'stuff
      (mapcar #'(lambda (x) (if (numberp x)
                                (hairyfun x)
                                (go lose)))
              items))
   (return)
lose
   (error "I lost big!"))
```

Depending on the situation, a go in COMMON LISP does not necessarily correspond to a simple machine "jump" instruction! A go can break up catchers if necessary to get to the target. It is possible for a "closure" created by function for a lambda-expression to refer to a go target as long as the tag is lexically apparent. See chapter 3 for an elaborate example of this.

prog ({*var* | (*var* [*init*])}*) {*declaration*}* {*tag* | *statement*}*   [*Macro*]
prog* ({*var* | (*var* [*init*])}*) {*declaration*}* {*tag* | *statement*}*   [*Macro*]

The prog construct is a synthesis of let, block, and tagbody, allowing bound variables and the use of return and go within a single construct. A typical prog construct looks like this:

```
(prog (var1 var2 (var3 init3) var4 (var5 init5))
      {declaration}*
      statement1
tag1
      statement2
      statement3
      statement4
tag2
      statement5
      ...
      )
```

The list after the keyword prog is a set of specifications for binding *var1*, *var2*, etc., which are temporary variables bound locally to the prog. This list is processed exactly as the list in a let statement: first all the *init* forms are evaluated from left to right (where nil is used for any omitted *init* form), and then the variables are all bound in parallel to the respective results. Any *declaration* appearing in the prog is used as if appearing at the top of the let body.

The body of the prog is executed as if it were a tagbody construct; the go statement may be used to transfer control to a *tag*.

A prog implicitly establishes a block named nil around the entire prog construct, so that return may be used at any time to exit from the prog construct.

Here is a fine example of what can be done with prog:

```
(defun king-of-confusion (w)
   "Take a cons of two lists and make a list of conses.
    Think of this function as being like a zipper."
   (prog (x y z)                ;Initialize x, y, z to nil
         (setq y (car w) z (cdr w))
     loop
         (cond ((null y) (return x))
               ((null z) (go err)))
     rejoin
         (setq x (cons (cons (car y) (car z)) x))
         (setq y (cdr y) z (cdr z))
         (go loop)
     err
         (cerror "Will self-pair extraneous items"
                 "Mismatch - gleep! S" y)
         (setq z y)
         (go rejoin)))
```

which is accomplished somewhat more perspicuously by:

```
(defun prince-of-clarity (w)
  "Take a cons of two lists and make a list of conses.
   Think of this function as being like a zipper."
  (do ((y (car w) (cdr y))
       (z (cdr w) (cdr z))
       (x '() (cons (cons (car y) (car z)) x)))
      ((null y) x)
    (when (null z)
      (cerror "Will self-pair extraneous items"
              "Mismatch - gleep! S" y)
      (setq z y))))
```

The `prog` construct may be explained in terms of the simpler constructs `block`, `let`, and `tagbody` as follows:

(prog *variable-list* {*declaration*}* . *body*)
    ≡ (block nil (let *variable-list* {*declaration*}* (tagbody . *body*)))

The `prog*` special form is almost the same as `prog`. The only difference is that the binding and initialization of the temporary variables is done *sequentially*, so that the *init* form for each one can use the values of previous ones. Therefore `prog*` is to `prog` as `let*` is to `let`. For example,

(prog* ((y z) (x (car y)))
    (return x))

returns the *car* of the value of z.

go *tag*   *[Special form]*

The (go *tag*) special form is used to do a "go to" within a `tagbody` construct. The *tag* must be a symbol or an integer; the *tag* is not evaluated. go transfers control to the point in the body labelled by a tag `eql` to the one given. If there is no such tag in the body, the bodies of lexically containing `tagbody` constructs (if any) are examined as well. It is an error if there is no matching tag lexically visible to the point of the go.

The go form does not ever return a value.

As a matter of style, it is recommended that the user think twice before using a go. Most purposes of go can be accomplished with one of the iteration primitives, nested conditional forms, or `return-from`. If the use of go seems to be unavoidable, perhaps the control structure implemented by go should be packaged as a macro definition.

7.9. Multiple Values

Ordinarily the result of calling a LISP function is a single LISP object. Sometimes, however, it is convenient for a function to compute several objects and return them. COMMON LISP provides a mechanism for handling multiple values directly. This mechanism is cleaner and more efficient than the usual tricks involving returning a list of results or stashing results in global variables.

7.9.1. Constructs for Handling Multiple Values

Normally multiple values are not used. Special forms are required both to *produce* multiple values and to *receive* them. If the caller of a function does not request multiple values, but the called function produces multiple values, then the first value is given to the caller and all others are discarded; if the called function produces zero values, then the caller gets `nil` as a value.

The primary primitive for producing multiple values is `values`, which takes any number of arguments and returns that many values. If the last form in the body of a function is a `values` with three arguments, then a call to that function will return three values. Other special forms also produce multiple values, but they can be described in terms of `values`. Some built-in COMMON LISP functions, such as `floor`, return multiple values; those that do are so documented.

The special forms and macros for receiving multiple values are as follows:

```
multiple-value-list
multiple-value-call
multiple-value-prog1
multiple-value-bind
multiple-value-setq
```

These specify a form to evaluate and an indication of where to put the values returned by that form.

---

values &rest *args*   [*Function*]

All of the arguments are returned, in order, as values. For example:

```
(defun polar (x y)
  (values (sqrt (+ (* x x) (* y y))) (atan y x)))

(multiple-value-bind (r theta) (polar 3.0 4.0)
  (vector r theta))
   ⇒ #(5.0 0.9272952)
```

The expression `(values)` returns zero values. This is the standard idiom for returning no values from a function.

Sometimes it is desirable to indicate explicitly that a function will return exactly one value. For example, the function

```
(defun foo (x y)
  (floor (+ x y) y))
```

will return two values because `floor` returns two values. It may be that the second value makes no sense, or that for efficiency reasons it is desired not to compute the second value. The `values` function is the standard idiom for indicating that only one value is to be returned, as shown in the following example.

```
(defun foo (x y)
  (values (floor (+ x y) y)))
```

This works because `values` returns exactly *one* value for each of its argument forms; as for any function call, if any argument form to `values` produces more than one value, all but the first are discarded.

There is absolutely no way in COMMON LISP for a caller to distinguish between returning a single value in the ordinary manner and returning exactly one "multiple value." For example, the values returned by the expressions `(+ 1 2)` and `(values (+ 1 2))` are identical in every respect: the single value `3`.

`multiple-values-limit`   [*Constant*]

The value of `multiple-values-limit` is a positive integer that is the upper exclusive bound on the number of values that may be returned from a function. This bound depends on the implementation, but will not be smaller than 20. (Implementors are encouraged to make this limit as large as practicable without sacrificing performance.) See `lambda-parameters-limit` and `call-arguments-limit`.

`values-list` *list*   [*Function*]

All of the elements of *list* are returned as multiple values. For example:

`(values-list (list a b c))` ≡ `(values a b c)`

In general,

`(values-list `*list*`)` ≡ `(apply #'values `*list*`)`

but `values-list` may be clearer or more efficient.

`multiple-value-list` *form*   [*Macro*]

`multiple-value-list` evaluates *form* and returns a list of the multiple values it returned. For example:

`(multiple-value-list (floor -3 4))` ⇒ `(-1 1)`

`multiple-value-list` and `values-list` are therefore inverses of each other.

`multiple-value-call` *function* {*form*}*   [*Special form*]

`multiple-value-call` first evaluates *function* to obtain a function and then evaluates all of the *forms*. All the values of the *forms* are gathered together (not just one value from each) and are all given as arguments to the function. The result of `multiple-value-call` is whatever is returned by the function. For example:

```
(+ (floor 5 3) (floor 19 4))
  ≡ (+ 1 4) ⇒ 5
(multiple-value-call #'+ (floor 5 3) (floor 19 4))
  ≡ (+ 1 2 4 3) ⇒ 10
(multiple-value-list form) ≡ (multiple-value-call #'list form)
```

`multiple-value-prog1` *form {form}**   [*Special form*]

`multiple-value-prog1` evaluates the first *form* and saves all the values produced by that form. It then evaluates the other *form*s from left to right, discarding their values. The values produced by the first *form* are returned by `multiple-value-prog1`. See `prog1`, which always returns a single value.

`multiple-value-bind` (*{var}**) *values-form {declaration}* {form}**   [*Macro*]

The *values-form* is evaluated, and each of the variables *var* is bound to the respective value returned by that form. If there are more variables than values returned, extra values of `nil` are given to the remaining variables. If there are more values than variables, the excess values are simply discarded. The variables are bound to the values over the execution of the forms, which make up an implicit `progn`. For example:

```
(multiple-value-bind (x) (floor 5 3) (list x)) ⇒ (1)
(multiple-value-bind (x y) (floor 5 3) (list x y)) ⇒ (1 2)
(multiple-value-bind (x y z) (floor 5 3) (list x y z))
  ⇒ (1 2 nil)
```

`multiple-value-setq` *variables form*   [*Macro*]

The *variables* must be a list of variables. The *form* is evaluated, and the variables are *set* (not bound) to the values returned by that form. If there are more variables than values returned, extra values of `nil` are assigned to the remaining variables. If there are more values than variables, the excess values are simply discarded.

Compatibility note: In ZETALISP this is called `multiple-value`. The added clarity of the name `multiple-value-setq` in COMMON LISP was deemed worth the incompatibility with ZETALISP.

`multiple-value-setq` always returns a single value, which is the first value returned by *form*, or `nil` if *form* produces zero values.

7.9.2. Rules Governing the Passing of Multiple Values

It is often the case that the value of a special form or macro call is defined to be the value of one of its subforms. For example, the value of a `cond` is the value of the last form in the selected clause. In most such cases, if the subform produces multiple values, then the original form will also produce all of those values. This *passing back* of multiple values of course has no effect unless eventually one of the special forms for receiving multiple values is reached.

To be explicit, multiple values can result from a special form under precisely these circumstances:

Evaluation and Application

- `eval` returns multiple values if the form given it to evaluate produces multiple values.

- `apply`, `funcall`, and `multiple-value-call` pass back multiple values from the function applied or called.

Implicit `progn` contexts

- The special form `progn` passes backs multiple values resulting from evaluation of the last subform. Other situations referred to as "implicit `progn`," where several forms are evaluated and the results of all but the last form are discarded, also pass back multiple values from the last form. These situations include the body of a lambda-expression, in particular those constructed by `defun`, `defmacro`, and `deftype`. Also included are bodies of the constructs `eval-when`, `progv`, `let`, `let*`, `when`, `unless`, `block`, `multiple-value-bind`, and `catch`, as well as clauses in such conditional constructs as `case`, `typecase`, `ecase`, `etypecase`, `ccase`, and `ctypecase`.

Conditional constructs

- `if` passes back multiple values from whichever subform is selected (the *then* form or the *else* form).

- `and` and `or` pass back multiple values from the last subform but not from subforms other than the last.

- `cond` passes back multiple values from the last subform of the implicit `progn` of the selected clause. If, however, the clause selected is a singleton clause, then only a single value (the non-`nil` predicate value) is returned. This is true even if the singleton clause is the last clause of the `cond`. It is *not* permitted to treat a final clause `(x)` as being the same as `(t x)` for this reason; the latter passes back multiple values from the form x.

Returning from a block

- The `block` construct passes back multiple values from its last subform when it exits normally. If `return-from` (or `return`) is used to terminate the `block` prematurely, then `return-from` passes back multiple values from its subform as the values of the terminated `block`. Other constructs that create implicit blocks, such as `do`, `dolist`, `dotimes`, `prog`, and `prog*`, also pass back multiple values specified by `return-from` (or `return`).

- `do` passes back multiple values from the last form of the exit clause, exactly as if the exit clause were a `cond` clause. Similarly, `dolist` and `dotimes` pass back multiple values from the *resultform* if that is executed. These situations are all examples of implicit uses of `return-from`.

Throwing out of a catch

- The `catch` construct returns multiple values if the result form in a `throw` exiting from such a catch produces multiple values.

Miscellaneous situations

- `multiple-value-prog1` passes back multiple values from its first subform. However, `prog1` always returns a single value.
- `unwind-protect` returns multiple values if the form it protects returns mutliple values.
- `the` returns multiple values if the form it contains returns multiple values.

Among special forms that *never* pass back multiple values are `setq`, `multiple-value-setq`, `prog1`, and `prog2`. The conventional way to force only one value to be returned from a form x is to write `(values x)`.

The most important rule about multiple values is: **No matter how many values a form produces, if the form is an argument form in a function call, then exactly *one* value (the first one) is used.**

For example, if you write (cons (floor x)), then cons will always receive *exactly* one argument (which is of course an error), even though floor returns two values. To pass both values from floor to cons, one must write something like (multiple-value-call #'cons (floor x)). In an ordinary function call, each argument form produces exactly *one* argument; if such a form returns zero values, nil is used for the argument, and if more than one value, all but the first are discarded. Similarly, conditional constructs such as if that test the value of a form will use exactly one value, the first one, from that form and discard the rest; such constructs will use nil as the test value if zero values are returned.

7.10. Dynamic Non-local Exits

COMMON LISP provides a facility for exiting from a complex process in a non-local, dynamically scoped manner. There are two classes of special forms for this purpose, called *catch* forms and *throw* forms, or simply *catches* and *throws*. A catch form evaluates some subforms in such a way that, if a throw form is executed during such evaluation, the evaluation is aborted at that point and the catch form immediately returns a value specified by the throw. Unlike block and return (section 7.7), which allow for exiting a block form from any point lexically within the body of the block, the catch/throw mechanism works even if the throw form is not textually within the body of the catch form. The throw need only occur within the extent (time span) of the evaluation of the body of the catch. This is analogous to the distinction between dynamically bound (special) variables and lexically bound (local) variables.

catch *tag* {*form*}*   [*Special form*]

The catch special form serves as a target for transfer of control by throw. The form *tag* is evaluated first to produce an object that names the catch; it may be any LISP object. A catcher is then established with the object as the tag. The *forms* are evaluated as an implicit progn, and the results of the last form are returned, except that if during the evaluation of the *forms* a throw should be executed such that the tag of the throw matches (is eq to) the tag of the catch and the catcher is the most recent outstanding catcher with that tag, then the evaluation of the *forms* is aborted and the results specified by the throw are immediately returned from the catch expression. The catcher established by the catch expression is disestablished just before the results are returned.

The tag is used to match throws with catches. (catch 'foo *form*) will catch a (throw 'foo *form*) but not a (throw 'bar *form*). It is an error if throw is done when there is no suitable catch ready to catch it.

Catch tags are compared using eq, not eql; therefore numbers and characters should not be used as catch tags.

Compatibility note: The name catch comes from MacLisp, but the syntax of catch in Common Lisp is different. The MacLisp syntax was (catch *form tag*), where the *tag* was not evaluated.

---

unwind-protect *protected-form* {*cleanup-form*}*   [*Special form*]

Sometimes it is necessary to evaluate a form and make sure that certain side effects take place after the form is evaluated; a typical example is:

```
(progn (start-motor)
       (drill-hole)
       (stop-motor))
```

The non-local exit facility of Common Lisp creates a situation in which the above code won't work, however: if drill-hole should do a throw to a catch that is outside of the progn form (perhaps because the drill bit broke), then (stop-motor) will never be evaluated (and the motor will presumably be left running). This is particularly likely if drill-hole causes a Lisp error and the user tells the error-handler to give up and abort the computation. (A possibly more practical example might be:

```
(prog2 (open-a-file)
       (process-file)
       (close-the-file))
```

where it is desired always to close the file when the computation is terminated for whatever reason. This case is so important that Common Lisp provides the special form with-open-file for this purpose.)

In order to allow the example hole-drilling program to work, it can be rewritten using unwind-protect as follows:

```
(unwind-protect
  (progn (start-motor)
         (drill-hole))
  (stop-motor))
```

If drill-hole does a throw that attempts to quit out of the unwind-protect, then (stop-motor) will be executed.

This example assumes that it is correct to call stop-motor even if the motor has not yet been started. Remember that an error or interrupt may cause an exit even before any initialization forms have been executed. Any state restoration code should operate correctly no matter where in the protected code an exit occurred. For example, the following code is not correct:

```
(unwind-protect
  (progn (incf *access-count*)
         (perform-access))
  (decf *access-count*))
```

If an exit occurs before completion of the incf operation the decf operation will be executed anyway, resulting in an incorrect value for *access-count*. The correct way to code this is as follows:

```
(let ((old-count *access-count*))
  (unwind-protect
    (progn (incf *access-count*)
           (perform-access))
    (setq *access-count* old-count)))
```

As a general rule, unwind-protect guarantees to execute the *cleanup-forms* before exiting, whether it terminates normally or is aborted by a throw of some kind. (If, however, an exit occurs during execution of the *cleanup-forms*, no special action is taken. The *cleanup-forms* of an unwind-protect are not protected by that unwind-protect, though they may be protected if that unwind-protect occurs within the protected form of another unwind-protect.) unwind-protect returns whatever results from evaluation of the *protected-form* and discards all the results from the *cleanup-forms*.

It should be emphasized that unwind-protect protects against *all* attempts to exit from the protected form, including not only such "dynamic exit" facilities such as throw but also such "lexical exit" facilities as go and return-from. Consider this situation:

```
(tagbody
  (let ((x 3))
    (unwind-protect
      (if (numberp x) (go out))
      (print x)))
  out
    ...)
```

When the `go` is executed, the call to `print` is executed first, and then the transfer of control to the tag `out` is completed.

`throw` *tag result*   [*Special form*]

The `throw` special form transfers control to a matching `catch` construct. The *tag* is evaluated first to produce an object called the throw tag; then the *result* form is evaluated, and its results are saved (if the *result* form produces multiple values, then *all* the values are saved). The most recent outstanding catch whose tag matches the throw tag is exited; the saved results are returned as the value(s) of the catch. A `catch` matches only if the catch tag is `eq` to the throw tag.

In the process, dynamic variable bindings are undone back to the point of the catch, and any intervening `unwind-protect` cleanup code is executed. The *result* form is evaluated before the unwinding process commences, and whatever results it produces are returned from the catch.

If there is no outstanding catcher whose tag matches the throw tag, no unwinding of the stack is performed, and an error is signalled. When the error is signalled, the outstanding catchers and the dynamic variable bindings are those in force at the point of the throw.

Implementation note: These requirements imply that throwing should typically make two passes over the control stack. In the first pass it simply searches for a matching catch. In this search every `catch` must be considered, but every `unwind-protect` should be ignored. On the second pass the stack is actually unwound, one frame at a time, undoing dynamic bindings and outstanding `unwind-protect` constructs in reverse order of creation until the matching catch is reached.

Compatibility note: The name `throw` comes from MacLisp, but the syntax of `throw` in Common Lisp is different. The MacLisp syntax was (`throw` *form tag*), where the *tag* was not evaluated.

8

Macros

The COMMON LISP macro facility allows the user to define arbitrary functions that convert certain LISP forms into different forms before evaluating or compiling them. This is done at the expression level, not at the character-string level as in most other languages. Macros are important in the writing of good code: they make it possible to write code that is clear and elegant at the user level, but that is converted to a more complex or more efficient internal form for execution.

When `eval` is given a list whose *car* is a symbol, it looks for local definitions of that symbol (by `flet`, `labels`, and `macrolet`); if that fails, it looks for a global definition. If the definition is a macro definition, then the original list is said to be a *macro call*. Associated with the definition will be a function of two arguments, called the *expansion function*. This function is called with the entire macro call as its first argument (the second argument is a lexical environment); it must return some new LISP form, called the *expansion* of the macro call. (Actually, a more general mechanism is involved; see `macroexpand`.) This expansion is then evaluated in place of the original form.

When a function is being compiled, any macros it contains are expanded at compilation time. This means that a macro definition must be seen by the compiler before the first use of the macro.

More generally, an implementation of COMMON LISP has great latitude in deciding exactly when to expand macro calls within a program. For example, it is acceptable for the `defun` special form to expand all macro calls within its body at the time the `defun` form is executed and record the fully expanded body as the body of the function being defined. (An implementation might even choose always to compile functions defined by `defun`, even when operating in an "interpretive" mode!)

Macros should be written in such a way as to depend as little as possible on the execution environment to produce a correct expansion. To ensure consistent behavior, it is best to ensure that all macro definitions are available, whether to the interpreter or compiler, before any code containing calls to those macros is introduced.

In COMMON LISP, macros are not functions. In particular, macros cannot be used as functional arguments to such functions as `apply`, `funcall`, or `map`; in such situations, the list representing the "original macro call" does not exist, and cannot exist, because in some sense the arguments have already been evaluated.

8.1. Macro Definition

The function `macro-function` determines whether a given symbol is the name of a macro. The `defmacro` construct provides a convenient way to define new macros.

`macro-function` *symbol*   [*Function*]

The argument must be a symbol. If the symbol has a global function definition that is a macro definition, then the expansion function (a function of two arguments, the macro-call form and an environment) is returned. If the symbol has no global function definition, or has a definition as an ordinary function or as a special form but not as a macro, then `nil` is returned. The function `macroexpand` is the best way to invoke the expansion function.

It is possible for *both* `macro-function` and `special-form-p` to be true of a symbol. This is possible because an implementation is permitted to implement any macro also as a special form for speed. On the other hand, the macro definition must be available for use by programs that understand only the standard special forms listed in Table 5-1.

`macro-function` cannot be used to determine whether a symbol names a locally defined macro established by `macrolet`; `macro-function` can examine only global definitions.

`setf` may be used with `macro-function` to install a macro as a symbol's global function definition:

```
(setf (macro-function symbol) fn)
```

The value installed must be a function that accepts two arguments, an entire macro call and an environment, and computes the expansion for that call. Performing this operation causes the symbol to have *only* that macro definition as its global function definition; any previous definition, whether as a macro or as a function, is lost. It is an error to attempt to redefine the name of a special form (see Table 5-1).

`defmacro` *name lambda-list {declaration | doc-string}* {form}** [*Macro*]

`defmacro` is a macro-defining macro that arranges to decompose the macro-call form in an elegant and useful way. `defmacro` has essentially the same syntax as `defun`: *name* is the symbol whose macro definition we are creating, *lambda-list* is similar in form to a lambda-list, and the *forms* constitute the body of the expander function. The `defmacro` construct arranges to install this expander function, as the global macro definition of *name*. The expander function is effectively defined in the *global* environment; lexically scoped entities established outside the `defmacro` form that would ordinarily be lexically apparent are not visible within the body of the expansion function. The *name* is returned as the value of the `defmacro` form.

If we view the macro call as a list containing a function name and some argument forms, in effect the expander function and the list of (unevaluated) argument forms is given to `apply`. The parameter specifiers are processed as for any lambda-expression, using the macro-call argument forms as the arguments. Then the body forms are evaluated as an implicit `progn`, and the value of the last form is returned as the expansion of the macro call.

If the optional documentation string *doc-string* is present (if not followed by a declaration, it may be present only if at least one *form* is also specified, as it is otherwise taken to be a *form*), then it is attached to the *name* as a documentation string of type `function`; see `documentation`.

Like the lambda-list in a `defun`, a `defmacro` *lambda-list* may contain the lambda-list keywords `&optional`, `&rest`, `&key`, `&allow-other-keys`, and `&aux`. For `&optional` and `&key` parameters, initialization forms and "supplied-p" parameters may be specified, just as for `defun`. Three additional markers are allowed in `defmacro` variable lists only:

`&body`   This is identical in function to `&rest`, but it informs certain output-formatting and editing functions that the remainder of the form is treated as a body, and should be indented accordingly. (Only one of `&body` or `&rest` may be used.)

`&whole`   This is followed by a single variable that is bound to the entire macro-call form; this is the value that the macro definition function receives as its single argument. `&whole` and the following variable should appear first in the lambda-list, before any other parameter or lambda-list keyword.

This is followed by a single variable that is bound to an environment representing the lexical environment in which the macro call is to be interpreted. This environment may not be the complete lexical environment; it should be used only with the function `macroexpand` for the sake of any local macro definitions that the `macrolet` construct may have established within that lexical environment. This is useful primarily in the rare cases where a macro definition must explicitly expand any macros in a subform of the macro call before computing its own expansion.

See `lambda-list-keywords`.

`defmacro`, unlike any other COMMON LISP construct that has a lambda-list as part of its syntax, provides an additional facility known as *destructuring*. Anywhere in the lambda-list where a parameter name may appear, and where ordinary lambda-list syntax (as described in section 5.2.2) does not otherwise allow a list, a lambda-list may appear in place of the parameter name. When this is done, then the argument form that would match the parameter is treated as a (possibly dotted) list, to be used as an argument forms list for satisfying the parameters in the embedded lambda-list. As an example, one could write the macro definition for `dolist` in this manner:

```
(defmacro dolist ((var listform &optional resultform)
                  &rest body)
  ...)
```

More examples of embedded lambda-lists in `defmacro` are shown below.

Another destructuring rule is that `defmacro` allows any lambda-list (whether top-level or embedded) to be dotted, ending in a parameter name. This situation is treated exactly as if the parameter name that ends the list had appeared preceded by `&rest`. For example, the definition skeleton for `dolist` shown above could instead have been written

```
(defmacro dolist ((var listform &optional resultform)
                  . body)
  ...)
```

If the compiler encounters a `defmacro`, the new macro is added to the compilation environment, and a compiled form of the expansion function is also added to the output file so that the new macro will be operative at runtime. If this is not the desired effect, the `defmacro` form can be wrapped in an `eval-when` construct.

It is permissible to use `defmacro` to redefine a macro (for example, to install a corrected version of an incorrect definition!), or to redefine a function as a macro. It is an error to attempt to redefine the name of a special form (see Table 5-1) as a macro.

See also `macrolet`, which establishes macro definitions over a restricted lexical scope.

Suppose, for the sake of example, that it were desirable to implement a conditional construct analogous to the FORTRAN arithmetic IF statement. (This of course requires a certain stretching of the imagination and suspension of disbelief.) The construct should accept four forms: a *test-value*, a *neg-form*, a *zero-form*, and a *pos-form*. One of the last three forms is chosen to be executed according to whether the value of the *test-form* is positive, negative, or zero. Using `defmacro`, a definition for such a construct might look like this:

```
(defmacro arithmetic-if (test neg-form zero-form pos-form)
  (let ((var (gensym)))
    `(let ((,var ,test))
       (cond ((< ,var 0) ,neg-form)
             ((= ,var 0) ,zero-form)
             (t ,pos-form)))))
```

Note the use of the backquote facility in this definition. See section 22.1.3. Also note the use of `gensym` to generate a new variable name. This is necessary to avoid conflict with any variables that might be referred to in *neg-form*, *zero-form*, or *pos-form*.

If the form is executed by the interpreter, it will cause the function definition of the symbol `arithmetic-if` to be a macro associated with which is a two-argument expansion function roughly equivalent to:

```
(lambda (calling-form environment)
  (declare (ignore environment))
  (let ((var (gensym)))
    (list 'let
          (list (list 'var (cadr calling-form)))
          (list 'cond
                (list (list '< var '0) (caddr calling-form))
                (list (list '= var '0) (cadddr calling-form))
                (list 't (fifth calling-form))))))
```

The lambda-expression is produced by the `defmacro` declaration. The calls to `list` are the (hypothetical) result of the backquote (`) macro character and its associated commas. The precise macro expansion function may depend on the implementation, for example providing some degree of explicit error checking on the number of argument forms in the macro call.

Now, if `eval` encounters

Now, if `eval` encounters

```
(arithmetic-if (- x 4.0)
               (- x)
               (error "Strange zero")
               x)
```

this will be expanded into something like

```
(let ((g407 (- x 4.0)))
  (cond ((< g407 0) (- x))
        ((= g407 0) (error "Strange zero"))
        (t x)))
```

and `eval` tries again on this new form. (It should be clear now that the backquote facility is very useful in writing macros, since the form to be returned is normally a complex list structure, typically consisting of a mostly constant template with a few evaluated forms here and there. The backquote template provides a "picture" of the resulting code, with places to be filled in indicated by preceding commas.)

To expand on this example, stretching credibility to its limit, we might allow the *pos-form* and *zero-form* to be omitted, allowing their values to default to nil, in much the same way that the *else* form of a COMMON LISP `if` construct may be omitted:

```
(defmacro arithmetic-if (test neg-form
                              &optional zero-form pos-form)
  (let ((var (gensym)))
    `(let ((,var ,test))
       (cond ((< ,var 0) ,neg-form)
             ((= ,var 0) ,zero-form)
             (t ,pos-form)))))
```

Then one could write

```
(arithmetic-if (- x 4.0) (print x))
```

which would be expanded into something like

```
(let ((g408 (- x 4.0)))
  (cond ((< g408 0) (print x))
        ((= g408 0) nil)
        (t nil)))
```

The resulting code is correct but rather silly-looking. One might rewrite the macro definition to produce better code when *pos-form* and possibly *zero-form* are omitted, or one might simply rely on the COMMON LISP implementation to provide a compiler smart enough to improve the code itself.

Destructuring is a very powerful facility that allows the `defmacro` lambda-list to express the structure of a complicated macro-call syntax. If no lambda-list keywords appear, then the `defmacro` lambda-list is simply a list, nested to some extent, containing parameter names at the leaves. The macro-call form must have the same list structure. For example, consider this macro definition:

```
(defmacro halibut ((mouth eye1 eye2)
                   ((fin1 length1) (fin2 length2))
                   tail)
   ...)
```

Now consider this macro call:

```
(halibut (m (car eyes) (cdr eyes))
         ((f1 (count-scales f1)) (f2 (count-scales f2)))
         my-favorite-tail)
```

This would cause the expansion function to receive the following values for its parameters:

Parameter	*Value*
mouth	m
eye1	(car eyes)
eye2	(cdr eyes)
fin1	f1
length1	(count-scales f1)
fin2	f2
length2	(count-scales f2)
tail	my-favorite-tail

The following macro call would be in error because there would be no argument form to match the parameter length1:

```
(halibut (m (car eyes) (cdr eyes))
         ((f1) (f2 (count-scales f2)))
         my-favorite-tail)
```

The following macro call would be in error because a symbol appears in the call where the structure of the lambda-list requires a list.

```
(halibut my-favorite-head
         ((f1 (count-scales f1)) (f2 (count-scales f2)))
         my-favorite-tail)
```

The fact that the value of the variable `my-favorite-head` might happen to be a list is irrelevant here. It is the macro call itself whose structure must match that of the `defmacro` lambda-list.

The use of lambda-list keywords adds even greater flexibility. For example, suppose it is convenient within the expansion function for `halibut` to be able to refer to the list whose components are called `mouth`, `eye1`, and `eye2` as `head`. One may write this:

```
(defmacro halibut ((&whole head mouth eye1 eye2)
                   ((fin1 length1) (fin2 length2))
                   tail)
```

Now consider the same valid macro call as before:

```
(halibut (m (car eyes) (cdr eyes))
         ((f1 (count-scales f1)) (f2 (count-scales f2)))
         my-favorite-tail)
```

This would cause the expansion function to receive the same values for its parameters and also a value for the parameter `head`:

Parameter	*Value*
head	(m (car eyes) (cdr eyes))

The stipulation, that an embedded lambda-list is permitted only where ordinary lambda-list syntax would permit a parameter name but not a list, is made to prevent ambiguity. For example, one may not write

```
(defmacro loser (x &optional (a b &rest c) &rest z)
  ...)
```

because ordinary lambda-list syntax does permit a list following `&optional`; the list `(a b &rest c)` would be interpreted as describing an optional parameter named a whose default value is that of the form b, with a supplied-p parameter named `&rest` (not legal), and an extraneous symbol c in the list (also not legal). An almost correct way to express this is

```
(defmacro loser (x &optional ((a b &rest c)) &rest z)
  ...)
```

The extra set of parentheses removes the ambiguity. However, the definition is now incorrect because a macro call such as (loser (car pool)) would not provide any argument form for the lambda-list (a b &rest c), and so the default value against which to match the lambda-list would be nil because no explicit default value was specified. This is in error because nil is an empty list; it does not have forms to satisfy the parameters a and b. The fully correct definition would be either

```
(defmacro loser (x &optional ((a b &rest c) '(nil nil)) &rest z)
  ...)
```

or

```
(defmacro loser (x &optional ((&optional a b &rest c)) &rest z)
  ...)
```

These differ slightly: the first requires that if the macro call specifies a explicitly then it must also specify b explicitly, whereas the second does not have this requirement. For example,

```
(loser (car pool) ((+ x 1)))
```

would be a valid call for the second definition but not for the first.

8.2. Macro Expansion

The macroexpand function is the conventional means for expanding a macro call. A hook is provided for a user function to gain control during the expansion process.

macroexpand *form* &optional *env*   [*Function*]
macroexpand-1 *form* &optional *env*   [*Function*]

If *form* is a macro call, then macroexpand-1 will expand the macro call *once* and return two values: the expansion and t. If *form* is not a macro call, then the two values *form* and nil are returned.

A *form* is considered to be a macro call only if it is a cons whose *car* is a symbol that names a macro. The environment *env* is similar to that used within the evaluator (see evalhook); it defaults to a null environment. Any local macro definitions established within *env* by macrolet will be considered. If only *form* is given as an argument, then the environment is effectively null, and only global macro definitions (as established by defmacro) will be considered.

Macro expansion is carried out as follows. Once macroexpand-1 has determined that a symbol names a macro, it obtains the expansion function for that macro. The value of the variable *macroexpand-hook* is then called as a function of three arguments: the expansion function, the *form*, and the environment *env*. The value returned from this call is taken to be the expansion of the macro call. The initial value of *macroexpand-hook* is funcall, and the net effect is to invoke the expansion function, giving it *form* and *env* as its two arguments. (The purpose of *macroexpand-hook* is to facilitate various techniques for improving interpretation speed by caching macro expansions.)

The evaluator expands macro calls as if through the use of macroexpand-1; the point is that eval also uses *macroexpand-hook*.

macroexpand is similar to macroexpand-1, but repeatedly expands *form* until it is no longer a macro call. (In effect, macroexpand simply calls macroexpand-1 repeatedly until the second value returned is nil.) A second value of t or nil is returned as for macroexpand-1, indicating whether the original *form* was a macro call.

macroexpand-hook   [*Variable*]

The value of *macroexpand-hook* is used as the expansion interface hook by macroexpand-1.

9

Declarations

Declarations allow you to specify extra information about your program to the LISP system. With one exception, declarations are completely optional and correct declarations do not affect the meaning of a correct program. The exception is that special declarations *do* affect the interpretation of variable bindings and references, and so *must* be specified where appropriate. All other declarations are of an advisory nature, and may be used by the LISP system to aid the programmer by performing extra error checking or producing more efficient compiled code. Declarations are also a good way to add documentation to a program.

Note that it is considered an error for a program to violate a declaration (such as a type declaration), but an implementation is not required to detect such errors (though such detection, where feasible, is to be encouraged).

9.1. Declaration Syntax

The declare construct is used for embedding declarations within executable code. Global declarations and declarations that are computed by a program are established by the proclaim construct.

declare {*decl-spec*}*   *[Special form]*

A declare form is known as a *declaration*. Declarations may occur only at the beginning of the bodies of certain special forms; that is, a declaration may occur only as a statement of such a special form, and all statements preceding it (if any) must also be declare forms (or possibly documentation strings, in some cases). Declarations may occur in lambda-expressions and in the forms listed here.

```
defmacro                dotimes
defsetf                 flet
deftype                 labels
defun                   let
do*                     let*
do-all-symbols          locally
do-external-symbols     macrolet
do-symbols              multiple-value-bind
do                      prog
dolist                  prog*
```

It is an error to attempt to evaluate a declaration. Those special forms that permit declarations to appear perform explicit checks for their presence.

Compatibility note: In MacLisp, `declare` is a special form that does nothing but return the symbol `declare` as its result. The MacLisp interpreter knows nothing about declarations but just blindly evaluates them, effectively ignoring them. The MacLisp compiler recognizes declarations but processes them simply by evaluating the subforms of the declaration in the compilation context. In Common Lisp it is important that both the interpreter and compiler recognize declarations (especially `special` declarations) and treat them consistently, and so the rules about the structure and use of declarations have been made considerably more stringent. The odd tricks played in MacLisp by writing arbitrary forms to be evaluated within a `declare` form are better done in both MacLisp and Common Lisp by using `eval-when`.

It is permissible for a macro call to expand into a declaration and be recognized as such, provided that the macro call appears where a declaration may legitimately appear. (However, a macro call may not appear in place of a *decl-spec*.)

Each *decl-spec* is a list whose *car* is a symbol specifying the kind of declaration to be made. Declarations may be divided into two classes: those that concern the bindings of variables, and those that do not. (The `special` declaration is the sole exception: it effectively falls into both classes, as explained below.) Those that concern variable bindings apply only to the bindings made by the form at the head of whose body they appear. For example, in

```
(defun foo (x)
  (declare (type float x)) ...
  (let ((x 'a)) ...)
  ...)
```

the `type` declaration applies only to the outer binding of x, and not to the binding made in the `let`.

Compatibility note: This represents a difference from MACLISP, in which type declarations are pervasive.

Declarations that do not concern themselves with variable bindings are pervasive, affecting all code in the body of the special form. As an example of a pervasive declaration,

```
(defun foo (x y) (declare (notinline floor)) ...)
```

advises that everywhere within the body of `foo` the function `floor` should not be open-coded but called as an out-of-line subroutine.

Some special forms contain pieces of code that, properly speaking, are not part of the body of the special form. Examples of this are initialization forms that provide values for bound variables, and the result forms of iteration constructs. In all cases such additional code is within the scope of any pervasive declarations appearing before the body of the special form. Non-pervasive declarations have no effect on such code, except (of course) in those situations where the code is defined to be within the scope of the variables affected by such non-pervasive declarations. For example:

```
(defun few (x &optional (y *print-circle*))
  (declare (special *print-circle*))
  ...)
```

The reference to *print-circle* in the first line of this example is special because of the declaration in the second line.

```
(defun nonsense (k x z)
  (foo z x)                          ;First call to foo
  (let ((j (foo k x))                ;Second call to foo
        (x (* k k)))
    (declare (inline foo) (special x z))
    (foo x j z)))                    ;Third call to foo
```

In this rather nonsensical example, the `inline` declaration applies to the second and third calls to `foo`, but not to the first one. The `special` declaration of x causes the `let` form to make a special binding for x, and causes the reference to x in the body of the `let` to be a special reference. The reference to x in the second call to foo is also a special reference. The reference to x in the first call to foo is a local reference, not a special one. The special declaration of z causes the reference to z in the call to foo to be a special reference; it will not refer to the parameter to nonsense named z, because that parameter binding has not been declared to be special. (The special declaration of z does not appear in the body of the defun, but in an inner construct, and therefore does not affect the binding of the parameter.)

locally *{declaration}* {form}**   [*Macro*]

This special form may be used to make local pervasive declarations where desired. It does not bind any variables and therefore cannot be used meaningfully for declarations of variable bindings. (Note that the special declaration may be used with locally to pervasively affect references to, rather than bindings of, variables.) For example:

```
(locally (declare (inline floor) (notinline car cdr))
         (declare (optimize space))
  (floor (car x) (cdr y)))
```

proclaim *decl-spec*   [*Function*]

The function proclaim takes a *decl-spec* as its argument and puts it into effect globally. (Such a global declaration is called a *proclamation*.) Because proclaim is a function, its argument is always evaluated. This allows a program to compute a declaration and then put it into effect by calling proclaim.

Any variable names mentioned are assumed to refer to the dynamic values of the variable. For example, the proclamation

```
(proclaim '(type float tolerance))
```

once executed, specifies that the dynamic value of tolerance should always be a floating-point number. Similarly, any function names mentioned are assumed to refer to the global function definition.

A proclamation constitutes a universal declaration, always in force unless locally shadowed. For example,

```
(proclaim '(inline floor))
```

advises that floor should normally be open-coded in-line by the compiler (but in the situation

```
(defun foo (x y) (declare (notinline floor)) ...)
```

it will be compiled out-of-line anyway in the body of `foo`, because of the shadowing local declaration to that effect).

As a special case (so to speak), `proclaim` treats a `special` *declaration-form* as applying to all bindings as well as to all references of the mentioned variables. For example, after

```
(proclaim '(special x))
```

then in a function definition such as

```
(defun example (x) ...)
```

the parameter `x` will be bound as a special (dynamic) variable rather than as a lexical (static) variable. This facility should be used with caution. The usual way to define a globally special variable is with `defvar` or `defparameter`.

9.2. Declaration Specifiers

Here is a list of valid declaration specifiers for use in `declare`. A construct is said to be "affected" by a declaration if it occurs within the scope of a declaration.

special

(`special` *var1 var2* ...) specifies that all of the variables named are to be considered *special*. This specifier affects variable bindings but also pervasively affects references. All variable bindings affected are made to be dynamic bindings, and affected variable references refer to the current dynamic binding rather than the current local binding. For example:

```
(defun hack (thing *mod*)          ;The binding of the parameter
  (declare (special *mod*))        ; *mod* is visible to hack1,
  (hack1 (car thing)))             ; but not that of thing.

(defun hack1 (arg)
  (declare (special *mod*))        ;Declare references to *mod*
                                   ; within hack1 to be special.
  (if (atom arg) *mod*
      (cons (hack1 (car arg)) (hack1 (cdr arg)))))
```

Note that it is conventional, though not required, to give special variables names that begin and end with an asterisk.

A `special` declaration does *not* affect bindings pervasively. Inner bindings of a variable implicitly shadow a `special` declaration and must be explicitly re-declared to be special. (However, a `special` proclamation *does* pervasively affect bindings; this exception is made for reasons of convenience and compatibility with MacLisp.) For example:

```
(proclaim '(special x))              ;x is always special.

(defun example (x y)
  (declare (special y))
  (let ((y 3) (x (* x 2)))
    (print (+ y (locally (declare (special y)) y)))
    (let ((y 4)) (declare (special y)) (foo x))))
```

In the contorted code above, the outermost and innermost bindings of y are special and therefore dynamically scoped, but the middle binding is lexically scoped. The two arguments to + are different, one being the value, which is 3, of the lexically bound variable y, and the other being the value of the special variable named y (a binding of which happens, coincidentally, to lexically surround it at an outer level). All the bindings of x and references to x are special, however, because of the proclamation that x is always `special`.

As a matter of style, use of `special` proclamations should be avoided. The `defvar` and `defparameter` macros are the conventional means for proclaiming special variables in a program.

type

(`type` *type var1 var2* ...) affects only variable bindings and specifies that the variables mentioned will take on values only of the specified type. In particular, values assigned to the variables by `setq`, as well as the initial values of the variables, must be of the specified type.

type

(*type var1 var2* ...) is an abbreviation for (`type` *type var1 var2* ...), provided that *type* is one of the symbols appearing in Table 4-1.

ftype

(`ftype` *type function-name-1 function-name-2* ...) specifies that the named functions will be of the functional type *type*, an example of which follows.

```
(declare (ftype (function (integer list) t) nth)
         (ftype (function (number) float) sin cos))
```

Note that rules of lexical scoping are observed; if one of the functions mentioned has a lexically apparent local definition (as made by `flet` or `labels`), then the declaration applies to that local definition and not to the global function definition.

`function`

(function *name arglist result-type1 result-type2* ...) is entirely equivalent to

(ftype (function *arglist result-type1 result-type2* ...) *name*)

but may be more convenient for some purposes. For example:

```
(declare (function nth (integer list) t)
         (function sin (number) float)
         (function cos (number) float))
```

The syntax mildly resembles that of `defun`: a function name, then an argument list, then a specification of results.

Note that rules of lexical scoping are observed; if one of the functions mentioned has a lexically apparent local definition (as made by `flet` or `labels`), then the declaration applies to that local definition and not to the global function definition.

`inline`

(inline *function1 function2* ...) specifies that it is desirable for the compiler to open-code calls to the specified functions; that is, the code for a specified function should be integrated into the calling routine, appearing "in line" in place of a procedure call. This may achieve extra speed at the expense of debuggability (calls to functions compiled in-line cannot be traced, for example). This declaration is pervasive. Remember that a compiler is free to ignore this declaration.

Note that rules of lexical scoping are observed; if one of the functions mentioned has a lexically apparent local definition (as made by `flet` or `labels`), then the declaration applies to that local definition and not to the global function definition.

`notinline`

(notinline *function1 function2* ...) specifies that it is *undesirable* to compile the specified functions in-line. This declaration is pervasive. A compiler is *not* free to ignore this declaration.

Note that rules of lexical scoping are observed; if one of the functions mentioned has a lexically apparent local definition (as made by `flet` or `labels`), then the declaration applies to that local definition and not to the global function definition.

ignore

(`ignore` *var1 var2 ... varn*) affects only variable bindings and specifies that the bindings of the specified variables are never used. It is desirable for a compiler to issue a warning if a variable so declared is ever referred to or is also declared special, or if a variable is lexical, never referred to, and not declared to be ignored.

optimize

(`optimize` (*quality1 value1*) (*quality2 value2*)...) advises the compiler that each *quality* should be given attention according to the specified corresponding *value*. A quality is a symbol; standard qualities include `speed` (of the object code), `space` (both code size and run-time space), `safety` (run-time error checking), and `compilation-speed` (speed of the compilation process). Other qualities may be recognized by particular implementations. A *value* should be a non-negative integer, normally in the range ◻ to ◰. The value ◻ means that the quality is totally unimportant, and ◰ that the quality is extremely important; ı and ᴤ are intermediate values, with ı the "normal" or "usual" value. One may abbreviate (*quality* ◰) to simply *quality*. This declaration is pervasive. For example:

```
(defun often-used-subroutine (x y)
  (declare (optimize (safety ᴤ)))
  (error-check x y)
  (hairy-setup x)
  (do ((i ◻ (+ i ı))
       (z x (cdr z)))
      ((null z) i)
    ;; This inner loop really needs to burn.
    (declare (optimize speed))
    (declare (fixnum i))
    )))
```

declaration

(`declaration` *name1 name2* ...) advises the compiler that each *namej* is a valid but non-standard declaration name. The purpose of this is to tell one compiler not to issue warnings for declarations meant for another compiler or other program processor. This kind of declaration may be used only as a proclamation. For example:

```
(proclaim '(declaration author
                         target-language
                         target-machine))

(proclaim '(target-language ada))

(proclaim '(target-machine IBM-b50))

(defun strangep (x)
  (declare (author "Harry Tweeker"))
  (member x '(strange weird odd peculiar)))
```

An implementation is free to support other (implementation-dependent) declaration specifiers as well. On the other hand, a COMMON LISP compiler is free to ignore entire classes of declaration specifiers (for example, implementation-dependent declaration specifiers not supported by that compiler's implementation!), except for the `declaration` declaration specifier. Compiler implementors are encouraged, however, to program the compiler to issue by default a warning if the compiler finds a declaration specifier of a kind it never uses. Such a warning is required in any case if a declaration specifier is not one of those defined above and has not been declared in a `declaration` declaration.

9.3. Type Declaration for Forms

Frequently it is useful to declare that the value produced by the evaluation of some form will be of a particular type. Using `declare` one can declare the type of the value held by a bound variable, but there is no easy way to declare the type of the value of an unnamed form. For this purpose the `the` special form is defined; `(the type form)` means that the value of *form* is declared to be of type *type*.

`the` *value-type form*   [*Special Form*]

The *form* is evaluated; whatever it produces is returned by the `the` form. In addition, it is an error if what is produced by the *form* does not conform to the data type specified by *value-type* (which is not evaluated). (A given implementation may or may not actually check for this error. Implementations are encouraged to make an explicit error check when running interpretively.) In effect, this declares that the user undertakes to guarantee that the values of the form will always be of the specified type. For example:

```
(the string (copy-seq x))          ;The result will be a string.
(the integer (+ x 3))              ;The result of + will be an integer.
(+ (the integer x) 3)              ;The value of x will be an integer.
(the (complex rational) (* z 3))
(the (unsigned-byte 8) (logand x mask))
```

The `values` type specifier may be used to indicate the types of multiple values:

```
(the (values integer integer) (floor x y))
(the (values string t)
     (gethash the-key the-string-table))
```

Compatibility note: This construct is borrowed from the INTERLISP DECL package; INTERLISP, however, allows an implicit `progn` after the type specifier rather than just a single form. The MACLISP `fixnum-identity` and `flonum-identity` constructs can be expressed as (the fixnum *x*) and (the single-float *x*).

10

Symbols

A LISP symbol is a data object that has three user-visible components:

- The *property list* is a list that effectively provides each symbol with many modifiable named components.

- The *print name* must be a string, which is the sequence of characters used to identify the symbol. Symbols are of great use because a symbol can be located once its name is given (typed, say, on a keyboard). It is ordinarily not permitted to alter a symbol's print name.

- The *package cell* must refer to a package object. A package is a data structure used to locate a symbol once given the symbol's name. A symbol is uniquely identified by its name only when considered relative to a package. A symbol may appear in many packages, but it can be *owned* by at most one package. The package cell points to the owner, if any. Package cells are discussed along with packages in chapter 11.

A symbol may actually have other components for use by the implementation. One of the more important uses of symbols is as names for program variables; it is frequently desirable for the implementor to use certain components of a symbol to implement the semantics of variables. See `symbol-value` and `symbol-function`. However, there are several possible implementation strategies, and so such possible components are not described here.

10.1. The Property List

Since its inception, LISP has associated with each symbol a kind of tabular data structure called a *property list* (*plist* for short). A property list contains zero or more entries; each entry associates with a key (called the *indicator*), which is typically a symbol, an arbitrary LISP object (called the *value* or, sometimes, the *property*). There are no duplications among the indicators; a property list may only have one property at a time with a given name. In this way, given a symbol and an indicator (another symbol), an associated value can be retrieved.

A property list is very similar in purpose to an association list. The difference is that a property list is an object with a unique identity; the operations for adding and removing property-list entries are destructive operations that alter the property list rather than making a new one. Association lists, on the other hand, are normally augmented non-destructively (without side effects) by adding new entries to the front (see `acons` and `pairlis`).

A property list is implemented as a memory cell containing a list with an even number (possibly zero) of elements. (Usually this memory cell is the property-list cell of a symbol, but any memory cell acceptable to `setf` can be used if `getf` and `remf` are used.) Each pair of elements in the list constitutes an entry; the first item is the indicator, and the second is the value. Because property-list functions are given the symbol and not the list itself, modifications to the property list can be recorded by storing back into the property-list cell of the symbol.

When a symbol is created, its property list is initially empty. Properties are created by using `get` within a `setf` form.

COMMON LISP does not use a symbol's property list as extensively as earlier LISP implementations did. Less-used data, such as compiler, debugging, and documentation information, is kept on property lists in COMMON LISP.

Compatibility note: In older LISP implementations, the print name, value, and function definition of a symbol were kept on its property list. The value cell was introduced into MACLISP and INTERLISP to speed up access to variables; similarly for the print-name cell and function cell (MACLISP does not use a function cell). Recent LISP implementations such as SPICE LISP, ZETALISP, and NIL have introduced all of these cells plus the package cell. None of the MACLISP system property names (`expr`, `fexpr`, `macro`, `array`, `subr`, `lsubr`, `fsubr`, and in former times `value` and `pname`) exist in COMMON LISP.

In COMMON LISP, the notion of "disembodied property list" introduced in MACLISP is eliminated. It tended to be used for rather kludgy things, and in ZETALISP is often associated with the use of locatives (to make it "off by one" for searching alternating keyword lists). In COMMON LISP special `setf`-like property-list functions are introduced: `getf` and `remf`.

`get` *symbol indicator* &optional *default*   [*Function*]

get searches the property list of *symbol* for an indicator eq to *indicator*. The first argument must be a symbol. If one is found, then the corresponding value is returned; otherwise *default* is returned. If *default* is not specified, then `nil` is used for *default*. Note that there is no way to distinguish an absent property from one whose value is *default*.

```
(get x y) ≡ (getf (symbol-plist x) y)
```

Suppose that the property list of foo is (bar t baz 3 hunoz "Huh?"). Then, for example:

```
(get 'foo 'baz) ⇒ 3
(get 'foo 'hunoz) ⇒ "Huh?"
(get 'foo 'zoo) ⇒ nil
```

Compatibility note: In MACLISP, the first argument to get could be a list, in which case the *cdr* of the list was treated as a so-called "disembodied property list." The first argument to get could also be any other object, in which case get would always return nil. In COMMON LISP, it is an error to give anything but a symbol as the first argument to get.

What COMMON LISP calls get, INTERLISP calls getprop.

What MACLISP and INTERLISP call putprop is accomplished in COMMON LISP by using get with setf.

setf may be used with get to create a new property-value pair, possibly replacing an old pair with the same property name. For example:

```
(get 'clyde 'species) ⇒ nil
(setf (get 'clyde 'species) 'elephant) ⇒ elephant
and now (get 'clyde 'species) ⇒ elephant
```

The *default* argument may be specified to get in this context; it is ignored by setf, but may be useful in such macros as push that are related to setf:

```
(push item (get sym 'token-stack '(initial-item)))
```

means the approximately the same as

```
(setf (get sym 'token-stack '(initial-item))
      (cons item (get sym 'token-stack '(initial-item))))
```

which in turn would be treated as simply

```
(setf (get sym 'token-stack)
      (cons item (get sym 'token-stack '(initial-item))))
```

remprop *symbol indicator*   [*Function*]

This removes from *symbol* the property with an indicator eq to *indicator*. The
property indicator and the corresponding value are removed by destructively splicing
the property list. It returns nil if no such property was found, or non-nil if a
property was found.

```
(remprop x y) ≡ (remf (symbol-plist x) y)
```

For example, if the property list of foo is initially

```
(color blue height 6.3 near-to bar)
```

then the call

```
(remprop 'foo 'height)
```

returns a non-nil value after altering foo's property list to be

```
(color blue near-to bar)
```

symbol-plist *symbol*   [*Function*]

This returns the list that contains the property pairs of *symbol*; the contents of the
property-list cell are extracted and returned.

   Note that using get on the result of symbol-plist does *not* work. One must
give the symbol itself to get or else use the function getf.

   setf may be used with symbol-plist to destructively replace the entire property
list of a symbol. This is a relatively dangerous operation, as it may destroy important information that the implementation may happen to store in property lists.
Also, care must be taken that the new property list is in fact a list of even length.

Compatibility note: In MACLISP, this function is called plist; in INTERLISP, it is called
getproplist.

---

getf *place indicator* &optional *default*   [*Function*]

getf searches the property list stored in *place* for an indicator eq to *indicator*. If
one is found, then the corresponding value is returned; otherwise *default* is returned.
If *default* is not specified, then nil is used for *default*. Note that there is no way
to distinguish an absent property from one whose value is *default*. Often *place* is
computed from a generalized variable acceptable to setf.

setf may be used with getf, in which case the *place* must indeed be acceptable as a *place* to setf. The effect is to add a new property-value pair, or update an existing pair, in the property list kept in the *place*. The *default* argument may be specified to getf in this context; it is ignored by setf but may be useful in such macros as push that are related to setf. See the description of get for an example of this.

Compatibility note: The INTERLISP function listget is similar to getf. The INTERLISP function listput is similar to using getf with setf.

---

remf *place indicator*   [*Macro*]

This removes from the property list stored in *place* the property with an indicator eq to *indicator*. The property indicator and the corresponding value are removed by destructively splicing the property list. remf returns nil if no such property was found, or some non-nil value if a property was found. The form *place* may be any generalized variable acceptable to setf. See remprop.

get-properties *place indicator-list*   [*Function*]

get-properties is like getf, except that the second argument is a list of indicators. get-properties searches the property list stored in *place* for any of the indicators in *indicator-list* until it finds the first property in the property list whose indicator is one of the elements of *indicator-list*. Normally *place* is computed from a generalized variable acceptable to setf.

get-properties returns three values. If any property was found, then the first two values are the indicator and value for the first property whose indicator was in *indicator-list*, and the third is that tail of the property list whose *car* was the indicator (and whose *cadr* is therefore the value). If no property was found, all three values are nil. Thus the third value serves as a flag indicating success or failure and also allows the search to be restarted after the property found if desired.

10.2. The Print Name

Every symbol has an associated string called the *print name*. This string is used as the external representation of the symbol: if the characters in the string are typed in to read (with suitable escape conventions for certain characters), it is interpreted as a reference to that symbol (if it is interned); and if the symbol is printed, print types out the print name. For more information, see the sections on the *reader* (section 22.1.1) and *printer* (section 22.1.6).

`symbol-name` *sym*   [*Function*]

This returns the print name of the symbol *sym*. For example:

`(symbol-name 'xyz)` ⇒ `"XYZ"`

It is an extremely bad idea to modify a string being used as the print name of a symbol. Such a modification may tremendously confuse the function `read` and the package system.

10.3. Creating Symbols

Symbols can be used in two rather different ways. An *interned* symbol is one that is indexed by its print name in a catalogue called a *package*. Every time anyone asks for a symbol with that print name, he gets the same (`eq`) symbol. Every time input is read with the function `read`, and that print name appears, it is read as the same symbol. This property of symbols makes them appropriate to use as names for things and as hooks on which to hang permanent data objects (using the property list, for example).

Interned symbols are normally created automatically; the first time something (such as the function `read`) asks the package system for a symbol with a given print name, that symbol is automatically created. The function used to ask for an interned symbol is `intern`, or one of the functions related to `intern`.

Although interned symbols are the most commonly used, they will not be discussed further here. For more information, see chapter 11.

An *uninterned* symbol is a symbol used simply as a data object, with no special cataloguing (it belongs to no particular package). An uninterned symbol is printed as *#:* followed by its print name. The following are some functions for creating uninterned symbols.

`make-symbol` *print-name*   [*Function*]

(`make-symbol` *print-name*) creates a new uninterned symbol, whose print name is the string *print-name*. The value and function bindings will be unbound and the property list will be empty.

The string actually installed in the symbol's print-name component may be the given string *print-name* or may be a copy of it, at the implementation's discretion.

The user should not assume that `(symbol-name (make-symbol x))` is eq to x, but also should not alter a string once it has been given as an argument to `make-symbol`.

Implementation note: An implementation might choose, for example, to copy the string to some read-only area, in the expectation that it will never be altered.

`copy-symbol` *sym* &optional *copy-props*   [*Function*]

This returns a new uninterned symbol with the same print name as *sym*. If *copy-props* is non-`nil`, then the initial value and function definition of the new symbol will be the same as those of *sym*, and the property list of the new symbol will be a copy of *sym*'s. If *copy-props* is `nil` (the default), then the new symbol will be unbound and undefined, and its property list will be empty.

`gensym` &optional *x*   [*Function*]

`gensym` invents a print name and creates a new symbol with that print name. It returns the new, uninterned symbol.

The invented print name consists of a prefix (which defaults to G), followed by the decimal representation of a number. The number is increased by one every time `gensym` is called.

If the argument *x* is present and is an integer, then *x* must be non-negative, and the internal counter is set to *x* for future use; otherwise the internal counter is incremented. If *x* is a string, then that string is made the default prefix for this and future calls to `gensym`. After handling the argument, `gensym` creates a symbol as it would with no argument. For example:

```
(gensym) ⇒ G7
(gensym "FOO-") ⇒ FOO-8
(gensym 32) ⇒ FOO-32
(gensym) ⇒ FOO-33
(gensym "GARBAGE-") ⇒ GARBAGE-34
```

`gensym` is usually used to create a symbol that should not normally be seen by the user and whose print name is unimportant except to allow easy distinction by eye between two such symbols. The optional argument is rarely supplied. The name comes from "generate symbol," and the symbols produced by it are often called "gensyms."

Compatibility note: In earlier versions of LISP, such as MACLISP and INTERLISP, the print name of a gensym was of fixed length, consisting of a single letter and a fixed-length decimal representation with leading zeros if necessary, for example, G0007. This convention was motivated by an implementation consideration, namely that the name should fit into a single machine word, allowing a quick and clever implementation. Such considerations are less relevant in COMMON LISP. The consistent use of a mnemonic prefixes can make it easier for the programmer, when debugging, to determine what code generated a particular symbol. The elimination of the fixed-length decimal representation prevents the same name from being used twice unless the counter is explicitly reset.

If it is desirable for the generated symbols to be interned, and yet guaranteed to be symbols distinct from all others, then the function `gentemp` may be more appropriate to use.

`gentemp` &optional *prefix package*   [*Function*]

`gentemp`, like `gensym`, creates and returns a new symbol. `gentemp` differs from `gensym` in that it interns the symbol (see `intern`) in the *package* (which defaults to the current package; see `*package*`). `gentemp` guarantees the symbol will be a new one not already existing in the package. It does this by using a counter as `gensym` does, but if the generated symbol is not really new, then the process is repeated until a new one is created. There is no provision for resetting the `gentemp` counter. Also, the prefix for `gentemp` is not remembered from one call to the next; if *prefix* is omitted, the default prefix T is used.

`symbol-package` *sym*   [*Function*]

Given a symbol *sym*, `symbol-package` returns the contents of the package cell of that symbol. This will be a package object or `nil`.

`keywordp` *object*   [*Function*]

The argument may be any LISP object. The predicate `keywordp` is true if the argument is a symbol and that symbol is a keyword (that is, belongs to the keyword package). Keywords are those symbols that are written with a leading colon. Every keyword is a constant, in the sense that it always evaluates to itself. See `constantp`.

11

Packages

One problem with earlier LISP systems is the use of a single name space for all symbols. In large LISP systems, with modules written by many different programmers, accidental name collisions become a serious problem. COMMON LISP addresses this problem through the *package system*, derived from an earlier package system developed for ZETALISP [21]. In addition to preventing name-space conflicts, the package system makes the modular structure of large LISP systems more explicit.

A *package* is a data structure that establishes a mapping from print names (strings) to symbols. The package thus replaces the "oblist" or "obarray" machinery of earlier LISP systems. At any given time one package is current, and this package is used by the LISP reader in translating strings into symbols. The current package is, by definition, the one that is the value of the global variable *package*. It is possible to refer to symbols in packages other than the current one through the use of *package qualifiers* in the printed representation of the symbol. For example, foo:bar, when seen by the reader, refers to the symbol whose name is bar in the package whose name is foo. (Actually, this is true only if bar is an external symbol of foo, that is, a symbol that is supposed to be visible outside of foo. A reference to an internal symbol requires the intentionally clumsier syntax foo::bar.)

The string-to-symbol mappings available in a given package are divided into two classes, *external* and *internal*. We refer to the symbols accessible via these mappings as being *external* and *internal* symbols of the package in question, though really it is the mappings that are different and not the symbols themselves. Within a given package, a name refers to one symbol or to none; if it does refer to a symbol, then it is either external or internal in that package, but not both.

External symbols are part of the package's public interface to other packages. External symbols are supposed to be chosen with some care and are advertised to users of the package. Internal symbols are for internal use only, and these symbols are normally hidden from other packages. Most symbols are created as internal symbols; they become external only if they appear explicitly in an export command for the package.

A symbol may appear in many packages. It will always have the same name wherever it appears, but it may be external in some packages and internal in others. On the other hand, the same name (string) may refer to different symbols in different packages.

Normally, a symbol that appears in one or more packages will be *owned* by one particular package, called the *home package* of the symbol; that package is said to *own* the symbol. Every symbol has a component called the *package cell* that contains a pointer to its home package. A symbol that is owned by some package is said to be *interned*. Some symbols are not owned by any package; such a symbol is said to be *uninterned*, and its package cell contains `nil`.

Packages may be built up in layers. From the point of view of a package's user, the package is a single collection of mappings from strings into internal and external symbols. However, some of these mappings may be established within the package itself, while other mappings are inherited from other packages via the `use-package` construct. (The mechanisms responsible for this inheritance are described below.) In what follows, we will refer to a symbol as being *accessible* in a package if it can be referred to without a package qualifier when that package is current, regardless of whether the mapping occurs within that package or via inheritance. We will refer to a symbol as being *present* in a package if the mapping is in the package itself and is not inherited from somewhere else.

A symbol is said to be *interned in a package* if it is accessible in that package and also is owned (by either that package or some other package). Normally all the symbols accessible in a package will in fact be owned by some package, but the terminology is useful when discussing the pathological case of an accessible but unowned (uninterned) symbol.

As a verb, to *intern* a symbol in a package means to cause the symbol to be interned in the package if it was not already; this process is performed by the function `intern`. If the symbol was previously unowned, then the package it is being interned in becomes its owner (home package); but if the symbol was previously owned by another package, that other package continues to own the symbol.

To *unintern* a symbol from the package means to cause it to be not present and, additionally, to make the symbol uninterned if the package was the symbol's home package (owner). This process is performed by the function `unintern`.

11.1. Consistency Rules

Package-related bugs can be very subtle and confusing: things are not what they appear to be. The COMMON LISP package system is designed with a number of safety features to prevent most of the common bugs that would otherwise occur in normal use. This may seem over-protective, but experience with earlier package systems has shown that such safety features are needed.

In dealing with the package system, it is useful to keep in mind the following consistency rules, which remain in force as long as the value of *package* is not changed by the user or his code:

- *Read-read consistency:* Reading the same print name always results in the same (eq) symbol.

- *Print-read consistency:* An interned symbol always prints as a sequence of characters that, when read back in, yields the same (eq) symbol.

- *Print-print consistency:* If two interned symbols are not eq, then their printed representations will be different sequences of characters.

These consistency rules remain true in spite of any amount of implicit interning caused by typing in LISP forms, loading files, etc. This has the important implication that, as long as the current package is not changed, results are reproducible regardless of the order of loading files or the exact history of what symbols were typed in when. The rules can only be violated by explicit action: changing the value of *package*, forcing some action by continuing from an error, or calling one of the "dangerous" functions unintern, unexport, shadow, shadowing-import, or unuse-package.

11.2. Package Names

Each package has a name (a string) and perhaps some nicknames. These are assigned when the package is created, though they can be changed later. A package's name should be something long and self-explanatory, like editor; there might be a nickname that is shorter and easier to type, such as ed.

There is a single name space for packages. The function find-package translates a package name or nickname into the associated package. The function package-name returns the name of a package. The function package-nicknames returns a list of all nicknames for a package. The function rename-package removes a package's current name and nicknames and replaces them with new ones specified by the user. Package renaming is occasionally useful when, for development purposes, it is desirable to load two versions of a package into the same LISP. One can load the first version, rename it, and then load the other version, without getting a lot of name conflicts.

When the LISP reader sees a qualified symbol, it handles the package-name part in the same way as the symbol part with respect to capitalization. Lowercase characters in the package name are converted to corresponding uppercase characters unless preceded by the escape character \ or surrounded by ! characters. The lookup done by the find-package function is case-sensitive, like that done for symbols. Note that ¡Foo¡::¡Bar¡ refers to a symbol whose name is Bar in a package whose name is Foo. By contrast, ¡Foo:Bar¡ refers to a seven-character symbol that has a colon in its name (as well as two uppercase letters and four lowercase letters) and is interned in the current package. Following the convention used in this manual for symbols, we will show ordinary package names using lowercase letters, even though the name string is internally represented with uppercase letters.

Most of the functions that require a package-name argument from the user accept either a symbol or a string. If the user supplies a symbol, its print name will be used; the print name will already have undergone case-conversion by the usual rules. If the user supplies a string, he must be careful to capitalize the string so as to match exactly the string that names the package.

11.3. Translating Strings to Symbols

The value of the special variable *package* must always be a package object (not a name). Whatever package object is currently the value of *package* is referred to as the *current package*.

When the LISP reader has, by parsing, obtained a string of characters thought to name a symbol, that name is looked up in the current package. This lookup may involve looking in other packages whose external symbols are inherited by the current package. If the name is found, the corresponding symbol is returned. If the name is not found (that is, there is no symbol of that name accessible in the current package), a new symbol is created for it and is placed in the current package as an internal symbol. Moreover, the current package becomes the owner (home package) of the symbol, and so the symbol becomes interned in the current package. If the name is later read again while this same package is current, the same symbol will then be found and returned.

Often it is desirable to refer to an external symbol in some package other than the current one. This is done through the use of a *qualified name*, consisting of a package name, then a colon, then the name of the symbol. This causes the symbol's name to be looked up in the specified package, rather than in the current one. For example, editor:buffer refers to the external symbol named buffer accessible in the package named editor, regardless of whether there is a symbol named buffer in the current package. If there is no package named editor, or if no symbol named buffer is accessible in editor, or if buffer is an internal symbol in editor, the LISP reader will signal a correctable error to ask the user what he really wants to do.

On rare occasions, a user may need to refer to an *internal* symbol of some package other than the current one. It is illegal to do this with the colon qualifier, since accessing an internal symbol of some other package is usually a mistake. However, this operation is legal if a doubled colon `::` is used as the separator in place of the usual single colon. If `editor::buffer` is seen, the effect is exactly the same as reading `buffer` with `*package*` temporarily rebound to the package whose name is `editor`. This special-purpose qualifier should be used with caution.

The package named `keyword` contains all keyword symbols used by the LISP system itself and by user-written code. Such symbols must be easily accessible from any package, and name conflicts are not an issue because these symbols are used only as labels and never to carry package-specific values or properties. Because keyword symbols are used so frequently, COMMON LISP provides a special reader syntax for them. Any symbol preceded by a colon but no package name (for example `:foo`) is added to (or looked up in) the `keyword` package as an *external* symbol. The `keyword` package is also treated specially in that whenever a symbol is added to the `keyword` package the symbol is always made external; the symbol is also automatically declared to be a constant (see `defconstant`) and made to have itself as its value. This is why every keyword evaluates to itself. As a matter of style, keywords should always be accessed using the leading-colon convention; the user should never import or inherit keywords into any other package. It is an error to try to apply `use-package` to the `keyword` package.

Each symbol contains a package cell that is used to record the home package of the symbol, or `nil` if the symbol is uninterned. This cell may be accessed by using the function `symbol-package`. When an interned symbol is printed, if it is a symbol in the keyword package, then it is printed with a preceding colon; otherwise, if it is accessible (directly or by inheritance) in the current package, it is printed without any qualification; otherwise, it is printed with the name of the home package as the qualifier, using `:` as the separator if the symbol is external and `::` if not.

A symbol whose package slot contains `nil` (that is, has no home package) is printed preceded by `#:`. It is possible, by the use of `import` and `unintern`, to create a symbol that has no recorded home package, but that in fact is accessible in some package. The system does not check for this pathological case, and such symbols will always be printed preceded by `#:`.

In summary, the following four uses of symbol qualifier syntax are defined.

```
foo:bar
```

When read, looks up BAR among the external symbols of the package named FOO. Printed when symbol `bar` is external in its home package `foo` and is not accessible in the current package.

`foo::bar`

When read, interns BAR as if FOO were the current package. Printed when symbol bar is internal in its home package foo and is not accessible in the current package.

`:bar`

When read, interns BAR as an external symbol in the keyword package, and makes it evaluate to itself. Printed when the home package of symbol bar is keyword.

`#:bar`

When read, creates a new uninterned symbol named BAR. Printed when the symbol bar is uninterned (has no home package), even in the pathological case that *bar* is uninterned but nevertheless somehow accessible in the current package.

All other uses of colons within names of symbols are not defined by COMMON LISP but are reserved for implementation-dependent use; this includes names that end in a colon, contain two or more colons, or consist of just a colon.

11.4. Exporting and Importing Symbols

Symbols from one package may be made accessible in another package in two ways.

First, any individual symbol may be added to a package by use of the function import. The form (import 'editor:buffer) takes the external symbol named buffer in the editor package (this symbol was located when the form was read by the LISP reader) and adds it to the current package as an internal symbol. The symbol is then present in the current package. The imported symbol is not automatically exported from the current package, but if it is already present and external, then the fact that it is external is not changed. After the call to import it is possible to refer to buffer in the importing package without any qualifier. The status of buffer in the package named editor is unchanged, and editor remains the home package for this symbol. Once imported, a symbol is *present* in the importing package and can be removed only by calling unintern.

If the symbol is already present in the importing package, import has no effect. If a distinct symbol with the name buffer is accessible in the importing package (directly or by inheritance), then a correctable error is signalled, as described in section 11.5, because import avoids letting one symbol shadow another.

A symbol is said to be *shadowed* by another symbol in some package if the first symbol would be accessible by inheritance if not for the presence of the second symbol. If the user really wants to import a symbol without the possibility of getting an error because of shadowing, he should use the function shadowing-import. This inserts the symbol into the specified package as an internal symbol, regardless of whether another symbol of the same name will be shadowed by this action. If a different symbol of the same name is already present in the package, that symbol will first be uninterned from the package (see unintern). The new symbol is added to the package's shadowing-symbols list. shadowing-import should be used with caution. It changes the state of the package system in such a way that the consistency rules do not hold across the change.

The second mechanism is provided by the function use-package. This causes a package to inherit all of the external symbols of some other package. These symbols become accessible as *internal* symbols of the using package. That is, they can be referred to without a qualifier while this package is current, but they are not passed along to any other package that uses this package. Note that use-package, unlike import, does not cause any new symbols to be *present* in the current package but only makes them *accessible* by inheritance. use-package checks carefully for name conflicts between the newly imported symbols and those already accessible in the importing package. This is described in detail in section 11.5.

Typically a user, working by default in the user package, will load a number of packages into his LISP to provide an augmented working environment; then he will call use-package on each of these packages so that he can easily access their external symbols. unuse-package undoes the effects of a previous use-package. The external symbols of the used package are no longer inherited. However, any symbols that have been imported into the using package continue to be present in that package.

There is no way to inherit the *internal* symbols of another package; to refer to an internal symbol, the user must either make that symbol's home package current, use a qualifier, or import that symbol into the current package.

When intern or some other function wants to look up a symbol in a given package, it first looks for the symbol among the external and internal symbols of the package itself; then it looks through the external symbols of the used packages in some unspecified order. The order does not matter; according to the rules for handling name conflicts (see below), if conflicting symbols appear in two or more packages inherited by package X, a symbol of this name must also appear in X itself as a shadowing symbol. Of course, implementations are free to choose other, more efficient ways of implementing this search, as long as the user-visible behavior is equivalent to what is described here.

The function export takes a symbol that is accessible in some specified package (directly or by inheritance) and makes it an external symbol of that package. If the symbol is already accessible as an external symbol in the package, `export` has no effect. If the symbol is directly present in the package as an internal symbol, it is simply changed to external status. If it is accessible as an internal symbol via `use-package`, the symbol is first imported into the package, then exported. (The symbol is then present in the specified package whether or not the package continues to use the package through which the symbol was originally inherited.) If the symbol is not accessible at all in the specified package, a correctable error is signalled that, upon continuing, asks the user whether the symbol should be imported.

The function `unexport` is provided mainly as a way to undo erroneous calls to `export`. It works only on symbols directly present in the current package, switching them back to internal status. If `unexport` is given a symbol already accessible as an internal symbol in the current package, it does nothing; if it is given a symbol not accessible in the package at all, it signals an error.

11.5. Name Conflicts

A fundamental invariant of the package system is that within one package any particular name can refer to at most one symbol. A *name conflict* is said to occur when there is more than one candidate symbol and it is not obvious which one to choose. If the system does not always choose the same way, the read-read consistency rule would be violated. For example, some programs or data might have been read in under a certain mapping of the name to a symbol. If the mapping changes to a different symbol, and subsequently additional programs or data are read, then the two programs will not access the same symbol even though they use the same name. Even if the system did always choose the same way, a name conflict is likely to result in a mapping from names to symbols different from what was expected by the user, causing programs to execute incorrectly. Therefore, any time a name conflict is about to occur, an error is signalled. The user may continue from the error and tell the package system how to resolve the conflict.

It may be that the same symbol is accessible to a package through more than one path. For example, the symbol might be an external symbol of more than one used package, or the symbol might be directly present in a package and also inherited from another package. In such cases there is no name conflict. The same identical symbol cannot conflict with itself. Name conflicts occur only between distinct symbols with the same name.

The creator of a package can tell the system in advance how to resolve a name conflict through the use of *shadowing*. Every package has a list of shadowing symbols. A shadowing symbol takes precedence over any other symbol of the same name that would otherwise be accessible to the package. A name conflict involving a shadowing symbol is always resolved in favor of the shadowing symbol, without signalling an error (except for one exception involving `import` described below). The functions `shadow` and `shadowing-import` may be used to declare shadowing symbols.

Name conflicts are detected when they become possible, that is, when the package structure is altered. There is no need to check for name conflicts during every name lookup.

The functions `use-package`, `import`, and `export` check for name conflicts. `use-package` makes the external symbols of the package being used accessible to the using package; each of these symbols is checked for name conflicts with the symbols already accessible. `import` adds a single symbol to the internals of a package, checking for a name conflict with an existing symbol either present in the package or accessible to it. `import` signals a name conflict error even if the conflict is with a shadowing symbol, the rationale being that the user has given two explicit and inconsistent directives. `export` makes a single symbol accessible to all the packages that use the package from which the symbol is exported. All of these packages are checked for name conflicts: (`export` *s p*) does (`find-symbol` (`symbol-name` *s*) *q*) for each package *q* in (`package-used-by-list` *p*). Note that in the usual case of an `export` during the initial definition of a package, the result of `package-used-by-list` will be `nil` and the name-conflict checking will take negligible time.

The function `intern`, which is the one used most frequently by the LISP reader for looking up names of symbols, does not need to do any name-conflict checking, because it never creates a new symbol if there is already an accessible symbol with the name given.

`shadow` and `shadowing-import` never signal a name-conflict error because the user, by calling these functions, has specified how any possible conflict is to be resolved. `shadow` does name-conflict checking to the extent that it checks whether a distinct existing symbol with the specified name is accessible and, if so, whether it is directly present in the package or inherited. In the latter case, a new symbol is created to shadow it. `shadowing-import` does name-conflict checking to the extent that it checks whether a distinct existing symbol with the same name is accessible; if so, it is shadowed by the new symbol, which implies that it must be uninterned if it was directly present in the package.

`unuse-package`, `unexport`, and `unintern` (when the symbol being uninterned is not a shadowing symbol) do not need to do any name-conflict checking because they only remove symbols from a package; they do not make any new symbols accessible.

Giving a shadowing symbol to `unintern` can uncover a name conflict that had previously been resolved by the shadowing. If package A uses packages B and C, A contains a shadowing symbol x, and B and C each contain external symbols named x, then removing the shadowing symbol x from A will reveal a name conflict between `b:x` and `c:x` if those two symbols are distinct. In this case `unintern` will signal an error.

Aborting from a name-conflict error leaves the original symbol accessible. Package functions always signal name-conflict errors before making any change to the package structure. When multiple changes are to be made, however, for example when `export` is given a list of symbols, it is permissible for the implementation to process each change separately, so that aborting from a name conflict caused by the second symbol in the list will not unexport the first symbol in the list. However, aborting from a name-conflict error caused by `export` of a single symbol will not leave that symbol accessible to some packages and inaccessible to others; with respect to each symbol processed, `export` behaves as if it were as an atomic operation.

Continuing from a name-conflict error should offer the user a chance to resolve the name conflict in favor of either of the candidates. The package structure should be altered to reflect the resolution of the name conflict, via `shadowing-import`, `unintern`, or `unexport`.

A name conflict in `use-package` between a symbol directly present in the using package and an external symbol of the used package may be resolved in favor of the first symbol by making it a shadowing symbol, or in favor of the second symbol by uninterning the first symbol from the using package. The latter resolution is dangerous if the symbol to be uninterned is an external symbol of the using package, since it will cease to be an external symbol.

A name conflict in `use-package` between two external symbols inherited by the using package from other packages may be resolved in favor of either symbol by importing it into the using package and making it a shadowing symbol.

A name conflict in `export` between the symbol being exported and a symbol already present in a package that would inherit the newly-exported symbol may be resolved in favor of the exported symbol by uninterning the other one, or in favor of the already-present symbol by making it a shadowing symbol.

A name conflict in `export` or `unintern` due to a package inheriting two distinct symbols with the same name from two other packages may be resolved in favor of either symbol by importing it into the using package and making it a shadowing symbol, just as with `use-package`.

A name conflict in `import` between the symbol being imported and a symbol inherited from some other package may be resolved in favor of the symbol being imported by making it a shadowing symbol, or in favor of the symbol already accessible by not doing the `import`. A name conflict in `import` with a symbol already present in the package may be resolved by uninterning that symbol, or by not doing the `import`.

Good user-interface style dictates that `use-package` and `export`, which can cause many name conflicts simultaneously, first check for all of the name conflicts before presenting any of them to the user. The user may then choose to resolve all of them wholesale or to resolve each of them individually, the latter requiring a lot of interaction but permitting different conflicts to be resolved different ways.

Implementations may offer other ways of resolving name conflicts. For instance, if the symbols that conflict are not being used as objects but only as names for functions, it may be possible to "merge" the two symbols by putting the function definition onto both symbols. References to either symbol for purposes of calling a function would be equivalent. A similar merging operation can be done for variable values and for things stored on the property list. In ZETALISP, for example, one can also *forward* the value, function, and property cells so that future changes to either symbol will propagate to the other one. Some other implementations are able to do this with value cells but not with property lists. Only the user can know whether this way of resolving a name conflict is adequate, because it will work only if the use of two non-eq symbols with the same name will not prevent the correct operation of his program. The value of offering symbol-merging as a way of resolving name conflicts is that it can avoid the need to throw away the whole LISP world, correct the package-definition forms that caused the error, and start over from scratch.

11.6. Built-in Packages

The following packages, at least, are built into every COMMON LISP system:

`lisp`

The package named `lisp` contains the primitives of the COMMON LISP system. Its external symbols include all of the user-visible functions and global variables that are present in the COMMON LISP system, such as `car`, `cdr`, `*package*`, etc. Almost all other packages will want to use `lisp` so that these symbols will be accessible without qualification.

`user`

The `user` package is, by default, the current package at the time a COMMON LISP system starts up. This package uses the `lisp` package.

`keyword`

This package contains all of the keywords used by built-in or user-defined LISP functions. Printed symbol representations that start with a colon are interpreted as referring to symbols in this package, which are always external symbols. All symbols in this package are treated as constants that evaluate to themselves, so that the user can type `:foo` instead of `':foo`.

`system`

This package name is reserved to the implementation. Normally this is used to contain names of implementation-dependent system-interface functions. This package uses `lisp` and has the nickname `sys`.

11.7. Package System Functions and Variables

Some of the functions and variables in this section are described in previous sections but are included here for completeness.

It is up to each implementation's compiler to ensure that when a compiled file is loaded, all of the symbols in the file end up in the same packages that they would occupy if the LISP source file were loaded. In most compilers, this will be accomplished by treating certain package operations as though they are surrounded by `(eval-when (compile load eval) ...)`; see eval-when. These operations are `make-package`, `in-package`, `shadow`, `shadowing-import`, `export`, `unexport`, `use-package`, `unuse-package`, and `import`. To guarantee proper compilation in all COMMON LISP implementations, these functions should appear only at top level within a file. As a matter of style, it is suggested that each file contain only one package, and that all of the package setup forms appear near the start of the file. This is discussed in more detail, with examples, in section 11.9.

Implementation note: In the past, some LISP compilers have read the entire file into LISP before processing any of the forms. Other compilers have arranged for the loader to do all of its intern operations before evaluating any of the top-level forms. Neither of these techniques will work in a straightforward way in COMMON LISP because of the presence of multiple packages.

For the functions described here, all optional arguments named *package* default to the current value of `*package*`. Where a function takes an argument that is either a symbol or a list of symbols, an argument of `nil` is treated as an empty list of symbols. Any argument described as a package name may be either a string or a symbol. If a symbol is supplied, its print name will be used as the package name; if a string is supplied, the user must be take care to specify the same capitalization used in the package name, normally all capitals.

package   [*Variable*]

The value of this variable must be a package; this package is said to be the current package. The initial value of *package* is the user package.

   The function load rebinds *package* to its current value. If some form in the file changes the value of *package* during loading, the old value will be restored when the loading is completed.

make-package *package-name* &key :nicknames :use   [*Function*]

This creates and returns a new package with the specified package name. As described above, this argument may be either a string or a symbol. The :nicknames argument must be a list of strings to be used as alternative names for the package. Once again, the user may supply symbols in place of the strings, in which case the print names of the symbols are used. These names and nicknames must not conflict with any existing package names; if they do, a correctable error is signalled.

   The :use argument is a list of packages or the names (strings or symbols) of packages whose external symbols are to be inherited by the new package. These packages must already exist. If not supplied, :use defaults to a list of one package, the lisp package.

in-package *package-name* &key :nicknames :use   [*Function*]

The in-package function is intended to be placed at the start of a file containing a subsystem that is to be loaded into some package other than user. If there is not already a package named *package-name*, this function is similar to make-package, except that after the new package is created, *package* is set to it. This binding will remain in force until changed by the user (perhaps with another in-package call) or until the *package* variable reverts to its old value at the completion of a load operation.

   If there is an existing package whose name is *package-name*, the assumption is that the user is re-loading a file after making some changes. The existing package is augmented to reflect any new nicknames or new packages in the :use list (with the usual error checking), and *package* is then set to this package.

find-package *name*   [*Function*]

The *name* must be a string that is the name or nickname for a package. This argument may also be a symbol, in which case the symbol's print name is used. The package with that name or nickname is returned; if no such package exists, find-package returns nil. The matching of names observes case (as in string=).

`package-name` *package*   [*Function*]

The argument must be a package. This function returns the string that names that package.

`package-nicknames` *package*   [*Function*]

The argument must be a package. This function returns the list of nickname strings for that package, not including the primary name.

`rename-package` *package new-name* &optional *new-nicknames*   [*Function*]

The old name and all of the old nicknames of *package* are eliminated and are replaced by *new-name* and *new-nicknames*. The *new-name* argument is a string or symbol; the *new-nicknames* argument, which defaults to `nil`, is a list of strings or symbols.

`package-use-list` *package*   [*Function*]

A list of other packages used by the argument package is returned.

`package-used-by-list` *package*   [*Function*]

A list of other packages that use the argument package is returned.

`package-shadowing-symbols` *package*   [*Function*]

A list is returned of symbols that have been declared as shadowing symbols in this package by `shadow` or `shadowing-import`. All symbols on this list are present in the specified package.

`list-all-packages`   [*Function*]

This function returns a list of all packages that currently exist in the LISP system.

`intern` *string* &optional *package*   [*Function*]

The *package*, which defaults to the current package, is searched for a symbol with the name specified by the *string* argument. This search will include inherited symbols, as described in section 11.4. If a symbol with the specified name is found, it is returned. If no such symbol is found, one is created and is installed in the specified package as an internal symbol (as an external symbol if the package is the `keyword` package); the specified package becomes the home package of the created symbol.

Two values are returned. The first is the symbol that was found or created. The second value is `nil` if no pre-existing symbol was found, and takes on one of three values if a symbol was found:

`:internal`   The symbol was directly present in the package as an internal symbol.

`:external`   The symbol was directly present as an external symbol.

`:inherited`   The symbol was inherited via `use-package` (which implies that the symbol is internal).

Compatibility note: Conceptually, `intern` translates a string to a symbol. In MacLisp and several other dialects of Lisp, `intern` can take either a string or a symbol as its argument; in the latter case, the symbol's print name is extracted and used as the string. However, this leads to some confusing issues about what to do if `intern` finds a symbol that is not `eq` to the argument symbol. To avoid such confusion, Common Lisp requires the argument to be a string.

`find-symbol` *string* &optional *package*   [*Function*]

This is identical to `intern`, but it never creates a new symbol. If a symbol with the specified name is found in the specified package, directly or by inheritance, the symbol found is returned as the first value and the second value is as specified for `intern`. If the symbol is not accessible in the specified package, both values are `nil`.

`unintern` *symbol* &optional *package*   [*Function*]

If the specified symbol is present in the specified *package*, it is removed from that package and also from the package's shadowing-symbols list if it is present there. Moreover, if the *package* is the home package for the symbol, the symbol is made to have no home package. Note that in some circumstances the symbol may continue to be accessible in the specified package by inheritance. `unintern` returns `t` if it actually removed a symbol, and `nil` otherwise.

`unintern` should be used with caution. It changes the state of the package system in such a way that the consistency rules do not hold across the change.

Compatibility note: The equivalent of this in MacLisp is `remob`.

`export` *symbols* &optional *package* [*Function*]

The *symbols* argument should be a list of symbols, or possibly a single symbol. These symbols become accessible as external symbols in *package*. See section 11.4 for details. `export` returns `t`.

By convention, a call to `export` listing all exported symbols is placed near the start of a file to advertise which of the symbols mentioned in the file are intended to be used by other programs.

`unexport` *symbols* &optional *package* [*Function*]

The argument should be a list of symbols, or possibly a single symbol. These symbols become internal symbols in *package*. It is an error to unexport a symbol from the `keyword` package. See section 11.4 for details. `unexport` returns `t`.

`import` *symbols* &optional *package* [*Function*]

The argument should be a list of symbols, or possibly a single symbol. These symbols become internal symbols in *package* and can therefore be referred to without having to use qualified-name (colon) syntax. `import` signals a correctable error if any of the imported symbols has the same name as some distinct symbol already accessible in the package. See section 11.4 for details. `import` returns `t`.

`shadowing-import` *symbols* &optional *package* [*Function*]

This is like import, but it does not signal an error even if the importation of a symbol would shadow some symbol already accessible in the package. In addition to being imported, the symbol is placed on the shadowing-symbols list of *package*. See section 11.5 for details. `shadowing-import` returns `t`.

`shadowing-import` should be used with caution. It changes the state of the package system in such a way that the consistency rules do not hold across the change.

`shadow` *symbols* &optional *package* [*Function*]

The argument should be a list of symbols, or possibly a single symbol. The print name of each symbol is extracted, and the specified package is searched for a symbol of that name. If such a symbol is present in this package (directly, not by inheritance), then nothing is done. Otherwise, a new symbol is created with this print name, and it is inserted in the specified package as an internal symbol. The symbol is also placed on the shadowing-symbols list of *package*. See section 11.5 for details. `shadow` returns `t`.

shadow should be used with caution. It changes the state of the package system in such a way that the consistency rules do not hold across the change.

---

use-package *packages-to-use* &optional *package*   [*Function*]

The *packages-to-use* argument should be a list of packages or package names, or possibly a single package or package name. These packages are added to the use-list of *package* if they are not there already. All external symbols in the packages to use become accessible in *package* as internal symbols. See section 11.4 for details. It is an error to try to use the *keyword* package. use-package returns t.

---

unuse-package *packages-to-unuse* &optional *package*   [*Function*]

The *packages-to-unuse* argument should be a list of packages or package names, or possibly a single package or package name. These packages are removed from the use-list of *package*. unuse-package returns t.

---

find-all-symbols *string-or-symbol*   [*Function*]

find-all-symbols searches every package in the LISP system to find every symbol whose print name is the specified string. A list of all such symbols found is returned. This search is case-sensitive. If the argument is a symbol, its print name supplies the string to be searched for.

---

do-symbols (*var* [*package* [*result-form*]]) {*declaration*}*   [*Macro*]
                                  {*tag* | *statement*}*

do-symbols provides straightforward iteration over the symbols of a package. The body is performed once for each symbol accessible in the *package*, in no particular order, with the variable *var* bound to the symbol. Then *result-form* (a single form, *not* an implicit progn) is evaluated, and the result is the value of the do-symbols form. (When the *result-form* is evaluated, the control variable *var* is still bound and has the value nil.) If the *result-form* is omitted, the result is nil. return may be used to terminate the iteration prematurely. If execution of the body affects which symbols are contained in the *package*, other than possibly to remove the symbol currently the value of *var* by using unintern, the effects are unpredictable.

---

do-external-symbols (*var* [*package* [*result*]]) {*declaration*}*   [*Macro*]
                                  {*tag* | *statement*}*

do-external-symbols is just like do-symbols, except that only the external symbols of the specified package are scanned.

`do-all-symbols` (*var* [*result-form*]) {*declaration*}* {*tag* | *statement*}*   [*Macro*]

This is similar to `do-symbols` but executes the body once for every symbol contained in every package. (This will not process every symbol whatsoever, because a symbol not accessible in any package will not be processed. Normally, uninterned symbols are not accessible in any package.) It is *not* in general the case that each symbol is processed only once, because a symbol may appear in many packages.

11.8. Modules

A *module* is a COMMON LISP subsystem that is loaded from one or more files. A module is normally loaded as a single unit, regardless of how many files are involved. A module may consist of one package or several packages. The file-loading process is necessarily implementation-dependent, but COMMON LISP provides some very simple portable machinery for naming modules, for keeping track of which modules have been loaded, and for loading modules as a unit.

`*modules*`   [*Variable*]

The variable `*modules*` is a list of names of the modules that have been loaded into the LISP system so far. This list is used by the functions `provide` and `require`.

`provide` *module-name*   [*Function*]
`require` *module-name* &optional *pathname*   [*Function*]

Each module has a unique name (a string). The `provide` and `require` functions accept either a string or a symbol as the *module-name* argument. If a symbol is provided, its print name is used as the module name. If the module consists of a single package, it is customary for the package and module names to be the same.

The `provide` function adds a new module name to the list of modules maintained in the variable `*modules*`, thereby indicating that the module in question has been loaded.

The `require` function tests whether a module is already present (using a case-sensitive comparison); if the module is not present, `require` proceeds to load the appropriate file or set of files. The pathname argument, if present, is a single pathname or a list of pathnames whose files are to be loaded in order, left to right. If the pathname argument is `nil` or is not provided, the system will attempt to determine, in some system-dependent manner, which files to load. This will typically involve some central registry of module names and the associated file lists.

Implementation note: One way to implement such a registry on many operating systems is simply to use a distinguished "library" directory within the file system, where the name of each file is the same as the module it contains.

Table 11-1: An Initialization File

```
;;;; Lisp init file for I. Newton.

;;; Set up the USER package the way I like it.

(require 'calculus)                  ;I use CALCULUS a lot. Load it.
(use-package 'calculus)              ;Get easy access to its
                                     ; exported symbols.

(require 'newtonian-mechanics) ;Ditto for NEWTONIAN-MECHANICS.
(use-package 'newtonian-mechanics)

;;; I just want a few thing from RELATIVITY,
;;; and other things conflict.
;;; Import only what I need into the USER package.

(require 'relativity)
(import '(relativity:speed-of-light
          relativity:ignore-small-errors))

;;; These are worth loading, but I will use qualified names,
;;; such as PHLOGISTON:MAKE-FIRE-BOTTLE, to get at any symbols
;;; I might need from these packages.

(require 'phlogiston)
(require 'alchemy)

;;; End of Lisp init file for I. Newton.
```

11.9. An Example

Most users will want to load and use packages but will never need to build one. Often a user will load a number of packages into the user package whenever he uses COMMON LISP. Typically an implementation might provide some sort of initialization file mechanism to make such setup automatic when the LISP starts up. Table 11-1 shows such an initialization file, one that simply causes other facilities to be loaded.

When each of two files uses some symbols from the other, one must be careful to arrange the contents of the file in the proper order. Typically each file contains a single package that is a complete module. The contents of such a file should include the following items, in order:

1. A call to provide that announces the module name.
2. A call to in-package that establishes the package.
3. A call to shadow that establishes any local symbols that will shadow symbols that would otherwise be inherited from packages that this package will use.

Table 11-2: File `alchemy`

```
;;;; Alchemy functions, written and maintained by Merlin, Inc.

(provide 'alchemy)                ;The module is named ALCHEMY.
(in-package 'alchemy)             ;So is the package.

;;; There is nothing to shadow.

;;; Here is the external interface.

(export '(lead-to-gold gold-to-lead
          antimony-to-zinc elixir-of-life))

;;; This package/module needs a function from
;;; the PHLOGISTON package/module.

(require 'phlogiston)

;;; We don't frequently need most of the external symbols from
;;; PHLOGISTON, so it's not worth doing a USE-PACKAGE on it.
;;; We'll just use qualified names as needed. But we use
;;; one function, MAKE-FIRE-BOTTLE, a lot, so import it.
;;; It's external in PHLOGISTON, and so can be referred to
;;; here using ":" qualified-name syntax.

(import '(phlogiston:make-fire-bottle))

;;; Now for the real contents of this file.

(defun lead-to-gold (x)
  "Takes a quantity of lead and returns gold."
  (when (> (phlogiston:heat-flow x) ;Using a qualified symbol.
           3)
    (make-fire-bottle x))          ;Using an imported symbol.
  (gild x))

;;; And so on ...
```

4. A call to `export` that establishes all of this package's external symbols.
5. Any number of calls to `require` to load other modules that the contents of this file might want to use or refer to. (Because the calls to `require` follow the calls to `in-package`, `shadow`, and `export`, it is possible for the packages that may be loaded to refer to external symbols in this package.)
6. Any number of calls to `use-package`, to make external symbols from other packages accessible in this package.
7. Any number of calls to `import`, to make symbols from other packages present in this package.
8. Finally, the definitions making up the contents of this package/module.

Table 11-3: File `phlogiston`

```
;;; Phlogiston functions, by Thermofluidics, Ltd.

(provide 'phlogiston)           ;The module is named PHLOGISTON.
(in-package 'phlogiston)        ;So is the package.

;;; There is nothing to shadow.

;;; Here is the external interface.

(export '(heat-flow cold-flow mix-fluids separate-fluids
          burn make-fire-bottle))

;;; This file uses functions from the ALCHEMY package/module.

(require 'alchemy)

;;; We use alchemy functions a lot, so use the package.
;;; This will allow symbols exported from the ALCHEMY package
;;; to be referred to here without the need for qualified names.

(use-package 'alchemy)

;;; No calls to IMPORT are needed here.

;;; The real contents of this package/module.

(defun heat-flow (amount x y)
  "Make some amount of heat flow from x to y."
  (when feeling-weak
    (quaff (elixir-of-life)))        ;No qualifier needed.
  (push-heat amount x y))

;;; And so on ...
```

The following mnemonic sentence may be helpful in remembering the proper order of these calls:

Put in seven extremely random user interface commands.

Each word of the sentence corresponds to one item in the above ordering:

Put	`Provide`
IN	`IN-package`
Seven	`Shadow`
EXtremely	`EXport`
Random	`Require`
USEr	`USE-package`
Interface	`Import`
COmmands	`COntents of package/module`

The sentence says what it helps you to do.

Now, suppose for the sake of example that the `phlogiston` and `alchemy` packages are single-file, single-package modules as described above. The `phlogiston` package needs to use the `alchemy` package, and the `alchemy` package needs to use several external symbols from the `phlogiston` package. The definitions in the `alchemy` and `phlogiston` files (see Tables 11-2 and 11-3) allow a user to specify `require` statements for either of these modules, or for both of them in either order, and all relevant information will be loaded automatically and in the correct order.

For very large modules whose contents are spread over several files (the `lisp` package is an example), it is recommended that the user create the package and declare all of the shadows and external symbols in a separate file, so that this can be loaded before anything that might use symbols from this package.

12

Numbers

Common Lisp provides several different representations for numbers. These representations may be divided into four categories: integers, ratios, floating-point numbers, and complex numbers. Many numeric functions will accept any kind of number; they are *generic*. Other functions accept only certain kinds of numbers.

In general, numbers in Common Lisp are not true objects; eq cannot be counted upon to operate on them reliably. In particular, it is possible that the expression

```
(let ((x z) (y z)) (eq x y))
```

may be false rather than true if the value of z is a number.

Rationale: This odd breakdown of eq in the case of numbers allows the implementor enough design freedom to produce exceptionally efficient numerical code on conventional architectures. MacLisp requires this freedom, for example, in order to produce compiled numerical code equal in speed to FORTRAN. Common Lisp makes this same restriction, if not for this freedom, then at least for the sake of compatibility.

If two objects are to be compared for "identity," but either might be a number, then the predicate eql is probably appropriate; if both objects are known to be numbers, then = may be preferable.

12.1. Precision, Contagion, and Coercion

In general, computations with floating-point numbers are only approximate. The *precision* of a floating-point number is not necessarily correlated at all with the *accuracy* of that number. For instance, 3.142857142857142857 is a more precise approximation to π than 3.14159, but the latter is more accurate. The precision refers to the number of bits retained in the representation. When an operation combines a short floating-point number with a long one, the result will be a long floating-point number. This rule is made to ensure that as much accuracy as possible is preserved; however, it is by no means a guarantee. COMMON LISP numerical routines do assume, however, that the accuracy of an argument does not exceed its precision. Therefore when two small floating-point numbers are combined, the result will always be a small floating-point number. This assumption can be overridden by first explicitly converting a small floating-point number to a larger representation. (COMMON LISP never converts automatically from a larger size to a smaller one.)

Rational computations cannot overflow in the usual sense (though of course there may not be enough storage to represent one), as integers and ratios may in principle be of any magnitude. Floating-point computations may get exponent overflow or underflow; this is an error.

When rational and floating-point numbers are compared or combined by a numerical function, the rule of *floating-point contagion* is followed: when a rational meets a floating-point number, the rational is first converted to a floating-point number of the same format. For functions such as + that take more than two arguments, it may be that part of the operation is carried out exactly using rationals and then the rest is done using floating-point arithmetic.

For functions that are mathematically associative (and possibly commutative), a COMMON LISP implementation may process the arguments in any manner consistent with associative (and possibly commutative) rearrangement. This does not affect the order in which the argument forms are evaluated, of course; that order is always left to right, as in all COMMON LISP function calls. What is left loose is the order in which the argument values are processed. The point of all this is that implementations may differ in which automatic coercions are applied because of differing orders of argument processing. As an example, consider this expression:

```
(+ 1/3 2/3 1.0D0 1.0 1.0E-15)
```

One implementation might process the arguments from left to right, first adding 1/3 and 2/3 to get 1, then converting that to a double-precision floating-point number for combination with 1.0D0, then successively converting and adding 1.0 and 1.0E-15. Another implementation might process the arguments from right to left, first performing a single-precision floating-point addition of 1.0 and 1.0E-15 (and probably losing some accuracy in the process!), then converting the sum to double precision and adding 1.0D0, then converting 2/3 to double-precision floating-point and adding it, and then converting 1/3 and adding that. A third implementation might first scan all the arguments, process all the rationals first to keep that part of the computation exact, then find an argument of the largest floating-point format among all the arguments and add that, and then add in all other arguments, converting each in turn (all in a perhaps misguided attempt to make the computation as accurate as possible). In any case, all three strategies are legitimate. The user can of course control the order of processing explicitly by writing several calls; for example:

```
(+ (+ 1/3 2/3) (+ 1.0D0 1.0E-15) 1.0)
```

The user can also control all coercions simply by writing calls to coercion functions explicitly.

In general, then, the type of the result of a numerical function is a floating-point number of the largest format among all the floating-point arguments to the function; but if the arguments are all rational, then the result is rational (except for functions that can produce mathematically irrational results, in which case a single-format floating-point number may result).

There is a separate rule of complex contagion. As a rule, complex numbers never result from a numerical function unless one or more of the arguments is complex. (Exceptions to this rule occur among the irrational and transcendental functions, specifically `expt`, `log`, `sqrt`, `asin`, `acos`, `acosh`, and `atanh`; see section 12.5.) When a non-complex number meets a complex number, the non-complex number is in effect first converted to a complex number by providing an imaginary part of 0.

If any computation produces a result that is a ratio of two integers such that the denominator evenly divides the numerator, then the result is immediately converted to the equivalent integer. This is called the rule of *rational canonicalization*.

If the result of any computation would be a complex rational with a zero imaginary part, the result is immediately converted to a non-complex rational number by taking the real part. This is called the rule of *complex canonicalization*. Note that this rule does *not* apply to complex numbers whose components are floating-point numbers. Whereas `#C(5 0)` and `5` are not distinct values in COMMON LISP (they are always eql), `#C(5.0 0.0)` and `5.0` are always distinct values in COMMON LISP (they are never eql, although they are equalp).

12.2. Predicates on Numbers

Each of the following functions tests a single number for a specific property. Each function requires that its argument be a number; to call one with a non-number is an error.

zerop *number*   [*Function*]

This predicate is true if *number* is zero (either the integer zero, a floating-point zero, or a complex zero), and is false otherwise. Regardless of whether an implementation provides distinct representations for positive and negative floating-point zeros, (zerop -0.0) is always true. It is an error if the argument *number* is not a number.

---

plusp *number*   [*Function*]

This predicate is true if *number* is strictly greater than zero, and is false otherwise. It is an error if the argument *number* is not a non-complex number.

---

minusp *number*   [*Function*]

This predicate is true if *number* is strictly less than zero, and is false otherwise. Regardless of whether an implementation provides distinct representations for positive and negative floating-point zeros, (minusp -0.0) is always false. (The function float-sign may be used to distinguish a negative zero.) It is an error if the argument *number* is not a non-complex number.

---

oddp *integer*   [*Function*]

This predicate is true if the argument *integer* is odd (not divisible by two), and otherwise is false. It is an error if the argument is not an integer.

---

evenp *integer*   [*Function*]

This predicate is true if the argument *integer* is even (divisible by two), and otherwise is false. It is an error if the argument is not an integer.

See also the data-type predicates integerp, rationalp, floatp, complexp, and numberp.

12.3. Comparisons on Numbers

Each of the functions in this section requires that its arguments all be numbers; to call one with a non-number is an error. Unless otherwise specified, each works on all types of numbers, automatically performing any required coercions when arguments are of different types.

= *number* &rest *more-numbers*	[*Function*]
/= *number* &rest *more-numbers*	[*Function*]
< *number* &rest *more-numbers*	[*Function*]
> *number* &rest *more-numbers*	[*Function*]
<= *number* &rest *more-numbers*	[*Function*]
>= *number* &rest *more-numbers*	[*Function*]

These functions each take one or more arguments. If the sequence of arguments satisfies a certain condition:

=	all the same
/=	all different
<	monotonically increasing
>	monotonically decreasing
<=	monotonically nondecreasing
>=	monotonically nonincreasing

then the predicate is true, and otherwise is false. Complex numbers may be compared using = and /=, but the others require non-complex arguments. Two complex numbers are considered equal by = if their real parts are equal and their imaginary parts are equal according to =. A complex number may be compared to a non-complex number with = or /=. For example:

(= 3 3) is true.   (/= 3 3) is false.
(= 3 5) is false.   (/= 3 5) is true.
(= 3 3 3 3) is true.   (/= 3 3 3 3) is false.
(= 3 3 5 3) is false.   (/= 3 3 5 3) is false.
(= 3 6 5 2) is false.   (/= 3 6 5 2) is true.
(= 3 2 3) is false.   (/= 3 2 3) is false.
(< 3 5) is true.   (<= 3 5) is true.
(< 3 -5) is false.   (<= 3 -5) is false.
(< 3 3) is false.   (<= 3 3) is true.
(< 0 3 4 6 7) is true.   (<= 0 3 4 6 7) is true.
(< 0 3 4 4 6) is false.   (<= 0 3 4 4 6) is true.
(> 4 3) is true.   (>= 4 3) is true.
(> 4 3 2 1 0) is true.   (>= 4 3 2 1 0) is true.
(> 4 3 3 2 0) is false.   (>= 4 3 3 2 0) is true.
(> 4 3 1 2 0) is false.   (>= 4 3 1 2 0) is false.
(= 3) is true.   (/= 3) is true.
(< 3) is true.   (<= 3) is true.
(= 3.0 #C(3.0 0.0)) is true.   (/= 3.0 #C(3.0 1.0)) is true.
(= 3 3.0) is true.   (= 3.0s0 3.0d0) is true.
(= 0.0 -0.0) is true.   (= 5/2 2.5) is true.
(> 0.0 -0.0) is false.   (= 0 -0.0) is true.

With two arguments, these functions perform the usual arithmetic comparison tests. With three or more arguments, they are useful for range checks as shown in the following example:

`(<= 0 x 9)`	;true if `x` is between 0 and 9, inclusive
`(< 0.0 x 1.0)`	;true if `x` is between 0.0 and 1.0, exclusive
`(< -1 j (length s))`	;true if `j` is a valid index for `s`
`(<= 0 j k (- (length s) 1))`	;true if `j` and `k` are each valid
	; indices for `s` and also `j≤k`

Rationale: The "unequality" relation is called `/=` rather than `<>` (the name used in PASCAL) for two reasons. First, `/=` of more than two arguments is not the same as the `or` of `<` and `>` of those same arguments. Second, unequality is meaningful for complex numbers even though `<` and `>` are not. For both reasons it would be misleading to associate unequality with the names of `<` and `>`.

Compatibility note: In COMMON LISP, the comparison operations perform "mixed-mode" comparisons: `(= 3 3.0)` is true. In MACLISP, there must be exactly two arguments, and they must be either both fixnums or both floating-point numbers. To compare two numbers for numerical equality and type equality, use `eql`.

`max` *number* &rest *more-numbers*	*[Function]*
`min` *number* &rest *more-numbers*	*[Function]*

The arguments may be any non-complex numbers. `max` returns the argument that is greatest (closest to positive infinity). `min` returns the argument that is least (closest to negative infinity).

For `max`, if the arguments are a mixture of rationals and floating-point numbers, and the largest argument is a rational, then the implementation is free to produce either that rational or its floating-point approximation; if the largest argument is a floating-point number of a smaller format than the largest format of any floating-point argument, then the implementation is free to return the argument in its given format or expanded to the larger format. More concisely, the implementation has the choice of returning the largest argument as is or applying the rules of floating-point contagion, taking all the arguments into consideration for contagion purposes. Also, if one or more of the arguments are equal, then any one of them may be chosen as the value to return. Similar remarks apply to `min` (replacing "largest argument" by "smallest argument").

`(max 6 12)` ⇒ `12`	`(min 6 12)` ⇒ `6`
`(max -6 -12)` ⇒ `-6`	`(min -6 -12)` ⇒ `-12`
`(max 1 3 2 -7)` ⇒ `3`	`(min 1 3 2 -7)` ⇒ `-7`
`(max -2 3 0 7)` ⇒ `7`	`(min -2 3 0 7)` ⇒ `-2`
`(max 3)` ⇒ `3`	`(min 3)` ⇒ `3`

```
(max 5.0 2) ⇒ 5.0                      (min 5.0 2) ⇒ 2 or 2.0
(max 3.0 7 1) ⇒ 7 or 7.0               (min 3.0 7 1) ⇒ 1 or 1.0
(max 1.0s0 7.0d0) ⇒ 7.0d0
(min 1.0s0 7.0d0) ⇒ 1.0s0 or 1.0d0
(max 3 1 1.0s0 1.0d0) ⇒ 3 or 3.0d0
(min 3 1 1.0s0 1.0d0) ⇒ 1 or 1.0s0 or 1.0d0
```

12.4. Arithmetic Operations

Each of the functions in this section requires that its arguments all be numbers; to call one with a non-number is an error. Unless otherwise specified, each works on all types of numbers, automatically performing any required coercions when arguments are of different types.

+ &rest *numbers*   [*Function*]

This returns the sum of the arguments. If there are no arguments, the result is 0, which is an identity for this operation.

Compatibility note: While + is compatible with its use in ZETALISP, it is incompatible with MACLISP, which uses + for fixnum-only addition.

- *number* &rest *more-numbers*   [*Function*]

The function -, when given one argument, returns the negative of that argument.

The function -, when given more than one argument, successively subtracts from the first argument all the others, and returns the result. For example, (- 3 4 5) ⇒ -6.

Compatibility note: While - is compatible with its use in ZETALISP, it is incompatible with MACLISP, which uses - for fixnum-only subtraction. Also, - differs from difference as used in most LISP systems in the case of one argument.

---

* &rest *numbers*   [*Function*]

This returns the product of the arguments. If there are no arguments, the result is 1, which is an identity for this operation.

Compatibility note: While * is compatible with its use in ZETALISP, it is incompatible with MACLISP, which uses * for fixnum-only multiplication.

/ *number* &rest *more-numbers*   [*Function*]

The function /, when given more than one argument, successively divides the first argument by all the others and returns the result.

With one argument, / reciprocates the argument.

/ will produce a ratio if the mathematical quotient of two integers is not an exact integer. For example:

```
(/ 12 4) ⇒ 3
(/ 13 4) ⇒ 13/4
(/ -8) ⇒ -1/8
(/ 3 4 5) ⇒ 3/20
```

To divide one integer by another producing an integer result, use one of the functions floor, ceiling, truncate, or round.

If any argument is a floating-point number, then the rules of floating-point contagion apply.

Compatibility note: What / does is totally unlike what the usual // or quotient operator does. In most LISP systems, quotient behaves like / except when dividing integers, in which case it behaves like truncate of two arguments; this behavior is mathematically intractable, leading to such anomalies as

(quotient 1.0 2.0) ⇒ 0.5 but (quotient 1 2) ⇒ 0

In contrast, the COMMON LISP function / produces these results:

(/ 1.0 2.0) ⇒ 0.5 and (/ 1 2) ⇒ 1/2

In practice quotient is used only when one is sure that both arguments are integers, *or* when one is sure that at least one argument is a floating-point number. / is tractable for its purpose and "works" for *any* numbers.

1+ *number*   [*Function*]

1- *number*   [*Function*]

(1+ x) is the same as (+ x 1).

(1- x) is the same as (- x 1). Note that the short name may be confusing: (1- x) does *not* mean $1 - x$; rather, it means $x - 1$.

Rationale: These are included primarily for compatibility with MACLISP and ZETALISP. Some programmers prefer always to write (+ x 1) and (- x 1) instead of (1+ x) and (1- x).

Implementation note: Compiler writers are very strongly encouraged to ensure that `(1+ x)` and `(+ x 1)` compile into identical code, and similarly for `(1- x)` and `(- x 1)`, to avoid pressure on a LISP programmer to write possibly less clear code for the sake of efficiency. This can easily be done as a source-language transformation.

---

incf *place* [*delta*]   [*Macro*]
decf *place* [*delta*]   [*Macro*]

The number produced by the form *delta* is added to (`incf`) or subtracted from (`decf`) the number in the generalized variable named by *place*, and the sum is stored back into *place* and returned. The form *place* may be any form acceptable as a generalized variable to `setf`. If *delta* is not supplied, then the number in *place* is changed by 1. For example:

```
(setq n 0)
(incf n) => 1          and now n => 1
(decf n 3) => -2       and now n => -2
(decf n -5) => 3       and now n => 3
(decf n) => 2          and now n => 2
```

The effect of (`incf` *place delta*) is roughly equivalent to

```
(setf place (+ place delta))
```

except that the latter would evaluate any subforms of *place* twice, whereas `incf` takes care to evaluate them only once. Moreover, for certain *place* forms `incf` may be significantly more efficient than the `setf` version.

conjugate *number*   [*Function*]

This returns the complex conjugate of *number*. The conjugate of a non-complex number is itself. For a complex number z,

```
(conjugate z) ≡ (complex (realpart z) (- (imagpart z)))
```

For example:

```
(conjugate #C(3/5 4/5)) => #C(3/5 -4/5)
(conjugate #C(0.0D0 -1.0D0)) => #C(0.0D0 1.0D0)
(conjugate 3.7) => 3.7
```

gcd &rest *integers*   [*Function*]

This returns the greatest common divisor of all the arguments, which must be integers. The result of gcd is always a non-negative integer. If one argument is given, its absolute value is returned. If no arguments are given, gcd returns 0, which is an identity for this operation. For three or more arguments,

(gcd *a b c* ... *z*) ≡ (gcd (gcd *a b*) *c* ... *z*)

Here are some examples of the use of gcd:

```
(gcd 91 -49) ⇒ 7
(gcd 63 -42 35) ⇒ 7
(gcd 5) ⇒ 5
(gcd -4) ⇒ 4
(gcd) ⇒ 0
```

lcm *integer* &rest *more-integers*   [*Function*]

This returns the least common multiple of its arguments, which must be integers. The result of lcm is always a non-negative integer. For two arguments that are not both zero,

(lcm *a b*) ≡ (/ (abs (* *a b*)) (gcd *a b*))

If one or both arguments are zero,

(lcm *a* 0) ≡ (lcm 0 *a*) ≡ 0

For one argument, lcm returns the absolute value of that argument. For three or more arguments,

(lcm *a b c* ... *z*) ≡ (lcm (lcm *a b*) *c* ... *z*)

Some examples:

```
(lcm 14 35) ⇒ 70
(lcm 0 5) ⇒ 0
(lcm 1 2 3 4 5 6) ⇒ 60
```

Mathematically, (lcm) should return infinity. Because COMMON LISP does not have a representation for infinity, lcm, unlike gcd, always requires at least one argument.

12.5. Irrational and Transcendental Functions

COMMON LISP provides no data type that can accurately represent irrational numerical values. The functions in this section are described as if the results were mathematically accurate, but actually they all produce floating-point approximations to the true mathematical result in the general case. In some places mathematical identities are set forth that are intended to elucidate the meanings of the functions; however, two mathematically identical expressions may be computationally different because of errors inherent in the floating-point approximation process.

When the arguments to a function in this section are all rational and the true mathematical result is also (mathematically) rational, then unless otherwise noted an implementation is free to return either an accurate result of type `rational` or a single-precision floating-point approximation. If the arguments are all rational but the result cannot be expressed as a rational number, then a single-precision floating-point approximation is always returned.

The rules of floating-point contagion and complex contagion are effectively obeyed by all the functions in this section except `expt`, which treats some cases of rational exponents specially. When, possibly after contagious conversion, all of the arguments are of the same floating-point or complex floating-point type, then the result will be of that same type unless otherwise noted.

Implementation note: There is a "floating-point cookbook" by Cody and Waite [4] that may be a useful aid in implementing the functions defined in this section.

12.5.1. Exponential and Logarithmic Functions

Along with the usual one-argument and two-argument exponential and logarithm functions, `sqrt` is considered to be an exponential function, because it raises a number to the power 1/2.

exp *number*   [*Function*]

Returns *e* raised to the power *number*, where *e* is the base of the natural logarithms.

expt *base-number power-number*   [*Function*]

Returns *base-number* raised to the power *power-number*. If the *base-number* is of type `rational` and the *power-number* is an `integer`, the calculation will be exact and the result will be of type `rational`; otherwise a floating-point approximation may result.

When *power-number* is ◻ (a zero of type integer), then the result is always the value one in the type of *base-number*, even if the *base-number* is zero (of any type). That is:

```
(expt x 0) ≡ (coerce 1 (type-of x))
```

If the *power-number* is a zero of any other data type, then the result is also the value one, in the type of the arguments after the application of the contagion rules, with one exception: it is an error if *base-number* is zero when the *power-number* is a zero not of type integer.

Implementations of expt are permitted to use different algorithms for the cases of a rational *power-number* and a floating-point *power-number*; the motivation is that in many cases greater accuracy can be achieved for the case of a rational *power-number*. For example, (expt pi 16) and (expt pi 16.0) may yield slightly different results if the first case is computed by repeated squaring and the second by the use of logarithms. Similarly, an implementation might choose to compute (expt x 3/2) as if it had been written (sqrt (expt x 3)), perhaps producing a more accurate result than would (expt x 1.5). It is left to the implementor to determine the best strategies.

The result of expt can be a complex number, even when neither argument is complex, if *base-number* is negative and *power-number* is not an integer. The result is always the principal complex value. Note that (expt -8 1/3) is not permitted to return -2; while -2 is indeed one of the cube roots of -8, it is not the principal cube root, which is a complex number approximately equal to #C(0.5 1.73205).

---

log *number* &optional *base*   [*Function*]

Returns the logarithm of *number* in the base *base*, which defaults to *e*, the base of the natural logarithms. For example:

```
(log 8.0 2) ⇒ 3.0
(log 100.0 10) ⇒ 2.0
```

The result of (log 8 2) may be either 3 or 3.0, depending on the implementation.

Note that log may return a complex result when given a non-complex argument if the argument is negative. For example:

```
(log -1.0) ≡ (complex 0.0 (float pi 0.0))
```

sqrt *number*   [*Function*]

Returns the principal square root of *number*. If the *number* is not complex but is negative, then the result will be a complex number. For example:

```
(sqrt 9.0) ⇒ 3.0
(sqrt -9.0) ⇒ #c(0.0 3.0)
```

The result of (sqrt 9) may be either 3 or 3.0, depending on the implementation. The result of (sqrt -9) may be either #c(0 3) or #c(0.0 3.0).

isqrt *integer*   [*Function*]

Integer square root: the argument must be a non-negative integer, and the result is the greatest integer less than or equal to the exact positive square root of the argument. For example:

```
(isqrt 9) ⇒ 3
(isqrt 12) ⇒ 3
(isqrt 300) ⇒ 17
(isqrt 325) ⇒ 18
```

12.5.2. Trigonometric and Related Functions

Some of the functions in this section, such as abs and signum, are apparently unrelated to trigonometric functions when considered as functions of real numbers only. The way in which they are extended to operate on complex numbers makes the trigonometric connection clear.

abs *number*   [*Function*]

Returns the absolute value of the argument. For a non-complex number,

```
(abs x) ≡ (if (minusp x) (- x) x)
```

and the result is always of the same type as the argument.

For a complex number z, the absolute value may be computed as

```
(sqrt (+ (expt (realpart z) 2) (expt (imagpart z) 2)))
```

Implementation note: The careful implementor will not use this formula directly for all complex numbers but will instead handle very large or very small components specially to avoid intermediate overflow or underflow.

For example:

```
(abs #c(3.0 -4.0)) ⇒ 5.0
```

The result of (abs #c(3 4)) may be either 5 or 5.0, depending on the implementation.

---

phase *number*   [*Function*]

The phase of a number is the angle part of its polar representation as a complex number. That is,

```
(phase x) ≡ (atan (imagpart x) (realpart x))
```

The result is in radians, in the range $-\pi$ (exclusive) to π (inclusive). The phase of a positive non-complex number is zero; that of a negative non-complex number is π. The phase of zero is arbitrarily defined to be zero.

If the argument is a complex floating-point number, the result is a floating-point number of the same type as the components of the argument. If the argument is a floating-point number, the result is a floating-point number of the same type. If the argument is a rational number or complex rational number, the result is a single-format floating-point number.

---

signum *number*   [*Function*]

By definition,

```
(signum x) ≡ (if (zerop x) x (/ x (abs x)))
```

For a rational number, signum will return one of -1, 0, or 1 according to whether the number is negative, zero, or positive. For a floating-point number, the result will be a floating-point number of the same format whose value is minus one, zero, or one. For a complex number z, (signum z) is a complex number of the same phase but with unit magnitude, unless z is a complex zero, in which case the result is z. For example:

```
(signum 0) ⇒ 0
(signum -3.7L5) ⇒ -1.0L0
(signum 4/5) ⇒ 1
(signum #C(7.5 10.0)) ⇒ #C(0.6 0.8)
(signum #C(0.0 -14.7)) ⇒ #C(0.0 -1.0)
```

For non-complex rational numbers, signum is a rational function, but it may be irrational for complex arguments.

sin *radians*   [*Function*]
cos *radians*   [*Function*]
tan *radians*   [*Function*]

sin returns the sine of the argument, cos the cosine, and tan the tangent. The argument is in radians. The argument may be complex.

cis *radians*   [*Function*]

This computes $e^{i \cdot radians}$. The name cis means "cos + i sin," because $e^{i\theta} = \cos \theta + i \sin \theta$. The argument is in radians and may be any non-complex number. The result is a complex number whose real part is the cosine of the argument and whose imaginary part is the sine. Put another way, the result is a complex number whose phase is the equal to the argument (mod 2π) and whose magnitude is unity.

Implementation note: Often it is cheaper to calculate the sine and cosine of a single angle together than to perform two disjoint calculations.

---

asin *number*   [*Function*]
acos *number*   [*Function*]

asin returns the arc sine of the argument, and acos the arc cosine. The result is in radians. The argument may be complex.

The arc sine and arc cosine functions may be defined mathematically for an argument x as follows:

Arc sine $-i \log (ix + \sqrt{1 - x^2})$
Arc cosine $-i \log (x + i\sqrt{1 - x^2})$

Note that the result of either asin or acos may be complex even if the argument is not complex; this occurs when the absolute value of the argument is greater than one.

Implementation note: These formulae are mathematically correct, assuming completely accurate computation. They may be terrible methods for floating-point computation! Implementors should consult a good text on numerical analysis. The formulas given above are not necessarily the simplest ones for real-valued computations, either; they are chosen to define the branch cuts in desirable ways for the complex case.

---

atan *y* &optional *x*   [*Function*]

An arc tangent is calculated and the result is returned in radians.

With two arguments y and x, neither argument may be complex. The result is the arc tangent of the quantity y/x. The signs of y and x are used to derive quadrant information; moreover, x may be zero provided y is not zero. The value of `atan` is always between $-\pi$ (exclusive) and π (inclusive). The following table details various special cases.

Condition		Cartesian locus	Range of result
$y = 0$	$x > 0$	Positive x-axis	0
$y > 0$	$x > 0$	Quadrant I	$0 < \text{result} < \pi/2$
$y > 0$	$x = 0$	Positive y-axis	$\pi/2$
$y > 0$	$x < 0$	Quadrant II	$\pi/2 < \text{result} < \pi$
$y = 0$	$x < 0$	Negative x-axis	π
$y < 0$	$x < 0$	Quadrant III	$-\pi < \text{result} < -\pi/2$
$y < 0$	$x = 0$	Negative y-axis	$-\pi/2$
$y < 0$	$x > 0$	Quadrant IV	$-\pi/2 < \text{result} < 0$
$y = 0$	$x = 0$	Origin	error

With only one argument y, the argument may be complex. The result is the arc tangent of y, which may be defined by the following formula:

Arc tangent
$$-i \log \left((1 + iy) \sqrt{1/(1 + y^2)}\right)$$

Implementation note: This formula is mathematically correct, assuming completely accurate computation. It may be a terrible method for floating-point computation! Implementors should consult a good text on numerical analysis. The formula given above is not necessarily the simplest one for real-valued computations, either; it is chosen to define the branch cuts in desirable ways for the complex case.

For a non-complex argument y, the result is non-complex and lies between $-\pi/2$ and $\pi/2$ (both exclusive).

Compatibility note: MACLISP has a function called `atan` whose range is from 0 to 2π. Almost every other programming language (ANSI FORTRAN, IBM PL/I, INTERLISP) has a two-argument arc tangent function with range $-\pi$ to π. ZETALISP provides two two-argument arc tangent functions, `atan` (compatible with MACLISP) and `atan2` (compatible with all others).

COMMON LISP makes two-argument atan the standard one with range $-\pi$ to π. Observe that this makes the one-argument and two-argument versions of atan compatible in the sense that the branch cuts do not fall in different places. The INTERLISP one-argument function arctan has a range from 0 to π, while nearly every other programming language provides the range $-\pi/2$ to $\pi/2$ for one-argument arc tangent! Nevertheless, since INTERLISP uses the standard two-argument version of arc tangent, its branch cuts are inconsistent anyway.

---

pi   *[Constant]*

This global variable has as its value the best possible approximation to π in *long* floating-point format. For example:

```
(defun sind (x)                ;The argument is in degrees.
  (sin (* x (/ (float pi x) 180)))))
```

An approximation to π in some other precision can be obtained by writing (float pi x), where x is a floating-point number of the desired precision, or by writing (coerce pi *type*), where *type* is the name of the desired type, such as short-float.

sinh *number*   *[Function]*
cosh *number*   *[Function]*
tanh *number*   *[Function]*
asinh *number*   *[Function]*
acosh *number*   *[Function]*
atanh *number*   *[Function]*

These functions compute the hyperbolic sine, cosine, tangent, arc sine, arc cosine, and arc tangent functions, which are mathematically defined for an argument x as follows:

Hyperbolic sine	$(e^x - e^{-x})/2$
Hyperbolic cosine	$(e^x + e^{-x})/2$
Hyperbolic tangent	$(e^x - e^{-x})/(e^x + e^{-x})$
Hyperbolic arc sine	$\log(x + \sqrt{1+x^2})$
Hyperbolic arc cosine	$\log(x + (x+1)\sqrt{(x-1)/(x+1)})$
Hyperbolic arc tangent	$\log((1+x)\sqrt{1-1/x^2})$

Note that the result of acosh may be complex even if the argument is not complex; this occurs when the argument is less than one. Also, the result of atanh may be complex even if the argument is not complex; this occurs when the absolute value of the argument is greater than one.

Implementation note: These formulae are mathematically correct, assuming completely accurate computation. They may be terrible methods for floating-point computation! Implementors should consult a good text on numerical analysis. The formulas given above are not necessarily the simplest ones for real-valued computations, either; they are chosen to define the branch cuts in desirable ways for the complex case.

12.5.3. Branch Cuts, Principal Values, and Boundary Conditions in the Complex Plane

Many of the irrational and transcendental functions are multiply defined in the complex domain; for example, there are in general an infinite number of complex values for the logarithm function. In each such case, a principal value must be chosen for the function to return. In general, such values cannot be chosen so as to make the range continuous; lines in the domain called *branch cuts* must be defined, which in turn define the discontinuities in the range.

COMMON LISP defines the branch cuts, principal values, and boundary conditions for the complex functions following a proposal for complex functions in APL[14]. The contents of this section are borrowed largely from that proposal.

Compatibility note: The branch cuts defined here differ in a few very minor respects from those advanced by W. Kahan, who considers not only the "usual" definitions but also the special modifications necessary for IEEE proposed floating-point arithmetic, which has infinities and minus zero as explicit computational objects. For example, he proposes that $\sqrt{-4+0i} = 2i$, but $\sqrt{-4-0i} = -2i$.

It may be that the differences between the APL proposal and Kahan's proposal will be ironed out. If so, COMMON LISP may be changed as necessary to be compatible with these other groups. Any changes from the specification below are likely to be quite minor, probably concerning primarily questions of which side of a branch cut is continuous with the cut itself.

`sqrt`

The branch cut for square root lies along the negative real axis, continuous with quadrant II. The range consists of the right half-plane, including the non-negative imaginary axis and excluding the negative imaginary axis.

`phase`

The branch cut for the phase function lies along the negative real axis, continuous with quadrant II. The range consists of that portion of the real axis between $-\pi$ (exclusive) and π (inclusive).

log

The branch cut for the logarithm function of one argument (natural logarithm) lies along the negative real axis, continuous with quadrant II. The domain excludes the origin. For a complex number z, log z is defined to be $(\log |z|) + i\ phase(z)$. Therefore the range of the one-argument logarithm function is that strip of the complex plane containing numbers with imaginary parts between $-\pi$ (exclusive) and π (inclusive).

The two-argument logarithm function is defined as $\log_b z = (\log z)/(\log b)$. This defines the principal values precisely. The range of the two-argument logarithm function is the entire complex plane. It is an error if z is zero. If z is non-zero and b is zero, the logarithm is taken to be zero.

exp

The simple exponential function has no branch cut.

expt

The two-argument exponential function is defined as $b^x = e^{x\ \log b}$. This defines the principal values precisely. The range of the two-argument exponential function is the entire complex plane. Regarded as a function of x, with b fixed, there is no branch cut. Regarded as a function of b, with x fixed, there is in general a branch cut along the negative real axis, continuous with quadrant II. The domain excludes the origin. By definition, $0^0 = 1$. If $b = 0$ and the real part of x is strictly positive, then $b^x = 0$. For all other values of x, 0^x is an error.

asin

The following definition for arc sine determines the range and branch cuts:

$$\arcsin z = -i\ \log (i\ z + \sqrt{1 - z^2})$$

The branch cut for the arc sine function is in two pieces: one along the negative real axis to the left of -1 (inclusive), continuous with quadrant II, and one along the positive real axis to the right of 1 (inclusive), continuous with quadrant IV. The range is that strip of the complex plane containing numbers whose real part is between $-\pi/2$ and $\pi/2$. A number with real part equal to $-\pi/2$ is in the range if and only if its imaginary part is non-negative; a number with real part equal to $\pi/2$ is in the range if and only if its imaginary part is non-positive.

acos

The following definition for arc cosine determines the range and branch cuts:

$$\arccos z = -i \log (z + i \sqrt{1 - z^2})$$

or, which is equivalent,

$$\arccos z = (\pi/2) - \arcsin z$$

The branch cut for the arc cosine function is in two pieces: one along the negative real axis to the left of -1 (inclusive), continuous with quadrant II, and one along the positive real axis to the right of 1 (inclusive), continuous with quadrant IV. This is the same branch cut as for arc sine. The range is that strip of the complex plane containing numbers whose real part is between 0 and π. A number with real part equal to 0 is in the range if and only if its imaginary part is non-negative; a number with real part equal to π is in the range if and only if its imaginary part is non-positive.

atan

The following definition for (one-argument) arc tangent determines the range and branch cuts:

$$\arctan z = -i \log ((1 + i z) \sqrt{1/(1 + z^2)})$$

Beware of simplifying this formula; "obvious" simplifications are likely to alter the branch cuts or the values on the branch cuts incorrectly. The branch cut for the arc tangent function is in two pieces: one along the positive imaginary axis above i (exclusive), continuous with quadrant II, and one along the negative imaginary axis below $-i$ (exclusive), continuous with quadrant IV. The points i and $-i$ are excluded from the domain. The range is that strip of the complex plane containing numbers whose real part is between $-\pi/2$ and $\pi/2$. A number with real part equal to $-\pi/2$ is in the range if and only if its imaginary part is strictly positive; a number with real part equal to $\pi/2$ is in the range if and only if its imaginary part is strictly negative. Thus the range of arc tangent is identical to that of arc sine with the points $-\pi/2$ and $\pi/2$ excluded.

asinh

The following definition for the inverse hyperbolic sine determines the range and branch cuts:

$$\operatorname{arcsinh} z = \log (z + \sqrt{1 + z^2})$$

The branch cut for the inverse hyperbolic sine function is in two pieces: one along
the positive imaginary axis above i (inclusive), continuous with quadrant I, and
one along the negative imaginary axis below $-i$ (inclusive), continuous with quadrant III. The range is that strip of the complex plane containing numbers whose
imaginary part is between $-\pi/2$ and $\pi/2$. A number with imaginary part equal to
$-\pi/2$ is in the range if and only if its real part is non-positive; a number with
imaginary part equal to $\pi/2$ is in the range if and only if its real part is non-negative.

acosh

The following definition for the inverse hyperbolic cosine determines the range and
branch cuts:

$$\operatorname{arccosh} z = \log\left(z + (z+1)\sqrt{(z-1)/(z+1)}\right)$$

The branch cut for the inverse hyperbolic cosine function lies along the real axis
to the left of 1 (inclusive), extending indefinitely along the negative real axis,
continuous with quadrant II and (between 0 and 1) with quadrant I. The range is
that half-strip of the complex plane containing numbers whose real part is non-negative
and whose imaginary part is between $-\pi$ (exclusive) and π (inclusive). A number
with real part zero is in the range if its imaginary part is between zero (inclusive)
and π (inclusive).

atanh

The following definition for the inverse hyperbolic tangent determines the range
and branch cuts:

$$\operatorname{arctanh} z = \log\left((1+z)\sqrt{1 - 1/z^2}\right)$$

Beware of simplifying this formula; "obvious" simplifications are likely to alter the
branch cuts or the values on the branch cuts incorrectly. The branch cut for the
inverse hyperbolic tangent function is in two pieces: one along the negative real
axis to the left of -1 (inclusive), continuous with quadrant III, and one along the
positive real axis to the right of 1 (inclusive), continuous with quadrant I. The
points -1 and 1 are excluded from the domain. The range is that strip of the
complex plane containing numbers whose imaginary part is between $-\pi/2$ and
$\pi/2$. A number with imaginary part equal to $-\pi/2$ is in the range if and only if
its real part is strictly negative; a number with imaginary part equal to $\pi/2$ is in
the range if and only if its real part is strictly positive. Thus the range of the inverse

hyperbolic tangent function is identical to that of the inverse hyperbolic sine function with the points $-\pi i/2$ and $\pi i/2$ excluded.

With these definitions, the following useful identities are obeyed throughout the applicable portion of the complex domain, even on the branch cuts:

$\sin i\,z = i\,\sinh z$	$\sinh i\,z = i\,\sin z$	$\arctan i\,z = i\,\mathrm{arctanh}\,z$
$\cos i\,z = \cosh z$	$\cosh i\,z = \cos z$	$\mathrm{arcsinh}\,i\,z = i\,\arcsin z$
$\tan i\,z = i\,\tanh z$	$\arcsin i\,z = i\,\mathrm{arcsinh}\,z$	$\mathrm{arctanh}\,i\,z = i\,\arctan z$

12.6. Type Conversions and Component Extractions on Numbers

While most arithmetic functions will operate on any kind of number, coercing types if necessary, the following functions are provided to allow specific conversions of data types to be forced when desired.

`float` *number* &optional *other*   [*Function*]

This converts any non-complex number to a floating-point number. With no second argument, if *number* is already a floating-point number, then *number* is returned; otherwise a `single-float` is produced. If the argument *other* is provided, then it must be a floating-point number, and *number* is converted to the same format as *other*. See also `coerce`.

`rational` *number*   [*Function*]
`rationalize` *number*   [*Function*]

Each of these functions converts any non-complex number to be a rational number. If the argument is already rational, it is returned. The two functions differ in their treatment of floating-point numbers.

`rational` assumes that the floating-point number is completely accurate and returns a rational number mathematically equal to the precise value of the floating-point number.

`rationalize` assumes that the floating-point number is accurate only to the precision of the floating-point representation, and may return any rational number for which the floating-point number is the best available approximation of its format; in doing this it attempts to keep both numerator and denominator small.

It is always the case that

```
(float (rational x) x) ≡ x
```

and

```
(float (rationalize x) x) ≡ x
```

That is, rationalizing a floating-point number by either method and then converting it back to a floating-point number of the same format produces the original number. What distinguishes the two functions is that `rational` typically has a simple, inexpensive implementation, whereas `rationalize` goes to more trouble to produce a result that is more pleasant to view and simpler for some purposes to compute with.

---

numerator *rational*   [*Function*]
denominator *rational*   [*Function*]

These functions take a rational number (an integer or ratio) and return as an integer the numerator or denominator of the canonical reduced form of the rational. The numerator of an integer is that integer; the denominator of an integer is 1. Note that

```
(gcd (numerator x) (denominator x)) ⇒ 1
```

The denominator will always be a strictly positive integer; the numerator may be any integer. For example:

```
(numerator (/ 8 -6)) ⇒ -4
(denominator (/ 8 -6)) ⇒ 3
```

There is no `fix` function in COMMON LISP because there are several interesting ways to convert non-integral values to integers. These are provided by the functions below, which perform not only type-conversion but also some non-trivial calculations as well.

---

floor *number* &optional *divisor*   [*Function*]
ceiling *number* &optional *divisor*   [*Function*]
truncate *number* &optional *divisor*   [*Function*]
round *number* &optional *divisor*   [*Function*]

In the simple one-argument case, each of these functions converts its argument *number* (which must not be complex) to be an integer. If the argument is already an integer, it is returned directly. If the argument is a ratio or floating-point number, the functions use different algorithms for the conversion.

floor converts its argument by truncating toward negative infinity; that is, the result is the largest integer that is not larger than the argument.

ceiling converts its argument by truncating toward positive infinity; that is, the result is the smallest integer that is not smaller than the argument.

truncate converts its argument by truncating toward zero; that is, the result is the integer of the same sign as the argument and which has the greatest integral magnitude not greater than that of the argument.

round converts its argument by rounding to the nearest integer; if *number* is exactly halfway between two integers (that is, of the form *integer* + 0.5), then it is rounded to the one that is even (divisible by two).

The following table shows what the four functions produce when given various arguments.

Argument	floor	ceiling	truncate	round
2.6	2	3	2	3
2.5	2	3	2	2
2.4	2	3	2	2
0.7	0	1	0	1
0.3	0	1	0	0
-0.3	-1	0	0	0
-0.7	-1	0	0	-1
-2.4	-3	-2	-2	-2
-2.5	-3	-2	-2	-2
-2.6	-3	-2	-2	-3

If a second argument *divisor* is supplied, then the result is the appropriate type of rounding or truncation applied to the result of dividing the *number* by the *divisor*. For example, (floor 5 2) ≡ (floor (/ 5 2)) but is potentially more efficient. The *divisor* may be any non-complex number. The one-argument case is exactly like the two-argument case where the second argument is 1.

Each of the functions actually returns *two* values, whether given one or two arguments. The second result is the remainder and may be obtained using multiple-value-bind and related constructs. If any of these functions is given two arguments x and y and produces results q and r, then $q \cdot y + r = x$. The first result q is always an integer. The remainder r is an integer if both arguments are integers, is rational if both arguments are rational, and is floating-point if either argument is floating-point. One consequence is that in the one-argument case the remainder is always a number of the same type as the argument.

When only one argument is given, the two results are exact; the mathematical sum of the two results is always equal to the mathematical value of the argument.

Compatibility note: The names of the functions floor, ceiling, truncate, and round are more accurate than names like fix that have heretofore been used in various LISP systems. The names used here are compatible with standard mathematical terminology (and with PL/1, as it happens). In FORTRAN ifix means truncate. ALGOL 68 provides round and uses entier to mean floor. In MACLISP, fix and ifix both mean floor (one is generic, the other flonum-in/fixnum-out). In INTERLISP, fix means truncate. In ZETALISP, fix means floor and fixr means round. STANDARD LISP provides a fix function but does not specify precisely what it does. The existing usage of the name fix is so confused that it seemed best to avoid it altogether.

The names and definitions given here have recently been adopted by ZETALISP, and MACLISP and NIL seem likely to follow suit.

---

mod *number divisor*   [*Function*]
rem *number divisor*   [*Function*]

mod performs the operation floor on its two arguments and returns the *second* result of floor as its only result. Similarly, rem performs the operation truncate on its arguments and returns the *second* result of truncate as its only result.

mod and rem are therefore the usual modulus and remainder functions when applied to two integer arguments. In general, however, the arguments may be integers or floating-point numbers.

```
(mod 13 4) ⇒ 1          (rem 13 4) ⇒ 1
(mod -13 4) ⇒ 3         (rem -13 4) ⇒ -1
(mod 13 -4) ⇒ -3        (rem 13 -4) ⇒ 1
(mod -13 -4) ⇒ -1       (rem -13 -4) ⇒ -1
(mod 13.4 1) ⇒ 0.4      (rem 13.4 1) ⇒ 0.4
(mod -13.4 1) ⇒ 0.6     (rem -13.4 1) ⇒ -0.4
```

Compatibility note: The INTERLISP function remainder is essentially equivalent to the COMMON LISP function rem. The MACLISP function remainder is like rem but accepts only integer arguments.

---

ffloor *number* &optional *divisor*   [*Function*]
fceiling *number* &optional *divisor*   [*Function*]
ftruncate *number* &optional *divisor*   [*Function*]
fround *number* &optional *divisor*   [*Function*]

These functions are just like floor, ceiling, truncate, and round, except that the result (the first result of two) is always a floating-point number rather than an integer. It is roughly as if `ffloor` gave its arguments to `floor`, and then applied `float` to the first result before passing them both back. In practice, however, `ffloor` may be implemented much more efficiently. Similar remarks apply to the other three functions. If the first argument is a floating-point number, and the second argument is not a floating-point number of longer format, then the first result will be a floating-point number of the same type as the first argument. For example:

```
(ffloor -4.7) ⇒ -5.0 and 0.3
(ffloor 3.5d0) ⇒ 3.0d0 and 0.5d0
```

`decode-float` *float*	[*Function*]
`scale-float` *float integer*	[*Function*]
`float-radix` *float*	[*Function*]
`float-sign` *float1* &optional *float2*	[*Function*]
`float-digits` *float*	[*Function*]
`float-precision` *float*	[*Function*]
`integer-decode-float` *float*	[*Function*]

The function `decode-float` takes a floating-point number and returns three values.

The first value is a new floating-point number of the same format representing the significand; the second value is an integer representing the exponent; and the third value is a floating-point number of the same format indicating the sign. Let b be the radix for the floating-point representation; then `decode-float` divides the argument by an integral power of b so as to bring its value between $1/b$ (inclusive) and 1 (exclusive), and returns the quotient as the first value. If the argument is zero, however, the result equals the absolute value of the argument (that is, if there is a negative zero, its significand is considered to be a positive zero).

The second value of `decode-float` is the integer exponent e to which b must be raised to produce the appropriate power for the division. If the argument is zero, any integer value may be returned, provided that the identity shown below for `scale-float` holds.

The third value of `decode-float` is a floating-point number, of the same format as the argument, whose absolute value is one and whose sign matches that of the argument.

The function `scale-float` takes a floating-point number f (not necessarily between $1/b$ and 1) and an integer k, and returns (`* `f` (expt (float `b` $f$`) `$k$`))`. (The use of `scale-float` may be much more efficient than using exponentiation and multiplication, and avoids intermediate overflow and underflow if the final result is representable.)

Note that

```
(multiple-value-bind (signif expon sign)
                     (decode-float f)
  (scale-float signif expon))
≡ (abs f)
```

and

```
(multiple-value-bind (signif expon sign)
                     (decode-float f)
  (* (scale-float signif expon) sign))
≡ f
```

The function `float-radix` returns (as an integer) the radix b of the floating-point argument.

The function `float-sign` returns a floating-point number z such that z and *float1* have the same sign and also such that z and *float2* have the same absolute value. The argument *float2* defaults to the value of (`float 1` *float1*); (`float-sign x`) therefore always produces a `1.0` or `-1.0` of appropriate format according to the sign of x. (Note that if an implementation has distinct representations for negative zero and positive zero, then (`float-sign -0.0`) $\Rightarrow$ `-1.0`.)

The function `float-digits` returns, as a non-negative integer, the number of radix-b digits used in the representation of its argument (including any implicit digits, such as a "hidden bit"). The function `float-precision` returns, as a non-negative integer, the number of significant radix-b digits present in the argument; if the argument is (a floating-point) zero, then the result is (an integer) zero. For normalized floating-point numbers, the results of `float-digits` and `float-precision` will be the same, but the precision will be less than the number of representation digits for a denormalized or zero number.

The function `integer-decode-float` is similar to `decode-float` but for its first value returns, as an `integer`, the significand scaled so as to be an integer. For an argument f, this integer will be strictly less than

```
(expt b (float-precision f))
```

but no less than

```
(expt b (- (float-precision f) 1))
```

except that if f is zero, then the integer value will be zero.

The second value bears the same relationship to the first value as for `decode-float`:

```
(multiple-value-bind (signif expon sign)
                     (integer-decode-float f)
  (scale-float (float signif f) expon))
≡ (abs f)
```

The third value of `integer-decode-float` will be 1 or -1.

Rationale: These functions allow the writing of machine-independent, or at least machine-parameterized, floating-point software of reasonable efficiency.

`complex` *realpart* &optional *imagpart*   [*Function*]

The arguments must be non-complex numbers; a number is returned that has *realpart* as its real part and *imagpart* as its imaginary part, possibly converted according to the rule of floating-point contagion (thus both components will be of the same type). If *imagpart* is not specified, then `(coerce 0 (type-of realpart))` is effectively used. Note that if both the *realpart* and *imagpart* are rational and the *imagpart* is zero, then the result is just the *realpart* because of the rule of canonical representation for complex rationals. It follows that the result of `complex` is not always a complex number; it may be simply a `rational`.

`realpart` *number*   [*Function*]
`imagpart` *number*   [*Function*]

These return the real and imaginary parts of a complex number. If *number* is a non-complex number, then `realpart` returns its argument *number* and `imagpart` returns (* 0 *number*), which has the effect that the imaginary part of a rational is 0 and that of a floating-point number is a floating-point zero of the same format.

12.7. Logical Operations on Numbers

The logical operations in this section require integers as arguments; it is an error to supply a non-integer as an argument. The functions all treat integers as if they were represented in two's-complement notation.

Implementation note: Internally, of course, an implementation of COMMON LISP may or may not use a two's-complement representation. All that is necessary is that the logical operations perform calculations so as to give this appearance to the user.

The logical operations provide a convenient way to represent an infinite vector of bits. Let such a conceptual vector be indexed by the non-negative integers. Then bit j is assigned a "weight" 2^j. Assume that only a finite number of bits are ones or only a finite number of bits are zeros. A vector with only a finite number of one-bits is represented as the sum of the weights of the one-bits, a positive integer. A vector with only a finite number of zero-bits is represented as -1 minus the sum of the weights of the zero-bits, a negative integer.

This method of using integers to represent bit-vectors can in turn be used to represent sets. Suppose that some (possibly countably infinite) universe of discourse for sets is mapped into the non-negative integers. Then a set can be represented as a bit vector; an element is in the set if the bit whose index corresponds to that element is a one-bit. In this way all finite sets can be represented (by positive integers), as well as all sets whose complements are finite (by negative integers). The functions `logior`, `logand`, and `logxor` defined below then compute the union, intersection, and symmetric difference operations on sets represented in this way.

`logior` &rest *integers*   [*Function*]

This returns the bit-wise logical *inclusive or* of its arguments. If no argument is given, then the result is zero, which is an identity for this operation.

`logxor` &rest *integers*   [*Function*]

This returns the bit-wise logical *exclusive or* of its arguments. If no argument is given, then the result is zero, which is an identity for this operation.

`logand` &rest *integers*   [*Function*]

This returns the bit-wise logical *and* of its arguments. If no argument is given, then the result is -1, which is an identity for this operation.

`logeqv` &rest *integers*   [*Function*]

This returns the bit-wise logical *equivalence* (also known as *exclusive nor*) of its arguments. If no argument is given, then the result is -1, which is an identity for this operation.

`lognand` *integer1 integer2*   [*Function*]
`lognor` *integer1 integer2*   [*Function*]
`logandc1` *integer1 integer2*   [*Function*]
`logandc2` *integer1 integer2*   [*Function*]
`logorc1` *integer1 integer2*   [*Function*]
`logorc2` *integer1 integer2*   [*Function*]

These are the other six non-trivial bit-wise logical operations on two arguments. Because they are not associative, they take exactly two arguments rather than any non-negative number of arguments.

```
(lognand n1 n2) ≡ (lognot (logand n1 n2))
 (lognor n1 n2) ≡ (lognot (logior n1 n2))
(logandc1 n1 n2) ≡ (logand (lognot n1) n2)
(logandc2 n1 n2) ≡ (logand n1 (lognot n2))
(logiorc1 n1 n2) ≡ (logior (lognot n1) n2)
(logiorc2 n1 n2) ≡ (logior n1 (lognot n2))
```

The ten bit-wise logical operations on two integers are summarized in this table:

Argument 1	0	0	1	1	
Argument 2	0	1	0	1	*Operation name*
logand	0	0	0	1	and
logior	0	1	1	1	inclusive or
logxor	0	1	1	0	exclusive or
logeqv	1	0	0	1	equivalence (exclusive nor)
lognand	1	1	1	0	not-and
lognor	1	0	0	0	not-or
logandc1	0	1	0	0	and complement of arg1 with arg2
logandc2	0	0	1	0	and arg1 with complement of arg2
logorc1	1	1	0	1	or complement of arg1 with arg2
logorc2	1	0	1	1	or arg1 with complement of arg2

boole *op integer1 integer2*	[*Function*]
boole-clr	[*Constant*]
boole-set	[*Constant*]
boole-1	[*Constant*]
boole-2	[*Constant*]
boole-c1	[*Constant*]
boole-c2	[*Constant*]
boole-and	[*Constant*]
boole-ior	[*Constant*]
boole-xor	[*Constant*]
boole-eqv	[*Constant*]
boole-nand	[*Constant*]
boole-nor	[*Constant*]
boole-andc1	[*Constant*]
boole-andc2	[*Constant*]
boole-orc1	[*Constant*]
boole-orc2	[*Constant*]

The function `boole` takes an operation *op* and two integers, and returns an integer produced by performing the logical operation specified by *op* on the two integers. The precise values of the sixteen constants are implementation-dependent, but they are suitable for use as the first argument to `boole`:

	integer1	0	0	1	1	
	integer2	0	1	0	1	*Operation performed*
`boole-clr`		0	0	0	0	always 0
`boole-set`		1	1	1	1	always 1
`boole-1`		0	0	1	1	*integer1*
`boole-2`		0	1	0	1	*integer2*
`boole-c1`		1	1	0	0	complement of *integer1*
`boole-c2`		1	0	1	0	complement of *integer2*
`boole-and`		0	0	0	1	and
`boole-ior`		0	1	1	1	inclusive or
`boole-xor`		0	1	1	0	exclusive or
`boole-eqv`		1	0	0	1	equivalence (exclusive nor)
`boole-nand`		1	1	1	0	not-and
`boole-nor`		1	0	0	0	not-or
`boole-andc1`		0	1	0	0	and complement of *integer1* with *integer2*
`boole-andc2`		0	0	1	0	and *integer1* with complement of *integer2*
`boole-orc1`		1	1	0	1	or complement of *integer1* with *integer2*
`boole-orc2`		1	0	1	1	or *integer1* with complement of *integer2*

`boole` can therefore compute all sixteen logical functions on two arguments. In general,

```
(boole boole-and x y) ≡ (logand x y)
```

and the latter is more perspicuous. However, `boole` is useful when it is necessary to parameterize a procedure so that it can use one of several logical operations.

`lognot` *integer*   [*Function*]

This returns the bit-wise logical *not* of its argument. Every bit of the result is the complement of the corresponding bit in the argument.

```
(logbitp j (lognot x)) ≡ (not (logbitp j x))
```

`logtest` *integer1 integer2*   [*Function*]

`logtest` is a predicate that is true if any of the bits designated by the 1's in *integer1* are 1's in *integer2*.

```
(logtest x y) ≡ (not (zerop (logand x y)))
```

logbitp *index integer*   [*Function*]

logbitp is true if the bit in *integer* whose index is *index* (that is, its weight is
2^{index}) is a one-bit; otherwise it is false. For example:

(logbitp 2 6) is true
(logbitp 0 6) is false
(logbitp *k n*) ≡ (ldb-test (byte 1 *k*) *n*)

ash *integer count*   [*Function*]

This function shifts *integer* arithmetically left by *count* bit positions if *count* is
positive, or right − *count* bit positions if *count* is negative. The sign of the result
is always the same as the sign of *integer*.

Mathematically speaking, this operation performs the computation
floor(*integer*·2^{count}).

Logically, this moves all of the bits in *integer* to the left, adding zero-bits at the
bottom, or moves them to the right, discarding bits. (In this context the question
of what gets shifted in on the left is irrelevant; integers, viewed as strings of bits,
are "half-infinite," that is, conceptually extend infinitely far to the left.) For
example:

(logbitp *j* (ash *n k*)) ≡ (and (>= *j k*) (logbitp (- *j k*) *n*))

logcount *integer*   [*Function*]

The number of bits in *integer* is determined and returned. If *integer* is positive,
then 1 bits in its binary representation are counted. If *integer* is negative, then the
0 bits in its two's-complement binary representation are counted. The result is
always a non-negative integer. For example:

(logcount 13) ⇒ 3   ;Binary representation is ...0001101
(logcount -13) ⇒ 2   ;Binary representation is ...1110011
(logcount 30) ⇒ 4   ;Binary representation is ...0011110
(logcount -30) ⇒ 4   ;Binary representation is ...1100010

The following identity always holds:

(logcount x) ≡ (logcount (- (+ x 1)))
           ≡ (logcount (lognot x))

integer-length *integer*   [*Function*]

This function performs the computation

ceiling(log₂(**if** *integer* < 0 **then** − *integer* **else** *integer* + 1))

This is useful in two different ways. First, if *integer* is non-negative, then its value can be represented in unsigned binary form in a field whose width in bits is no smaller than (integer-length *integer*). Second, regardless of the sign of *integer*, its value can be represented in signed binary two's-complement form in a field whose width in bits is no smaller than (+ (integer-length *integer*) 1). For example:

```
(integer-length 0) ⇒ 0
(integer-length 1) ⇒ 1
(integer-length 3) ⇒ 2
(integer-length 4) ⇒ 3
(integer-length 7) ⇒ 3
(integer-length -1) ⇒ 0
(integer-length -4) ⇒ 2
(integer-length -7) ⇒ 3
(integer-length -8) ⇒ 3
```

Compatibility note: This function is similar to the MacLisp function haulong. One may define haulong as

```
(haulong x) ≡ (integer-length (abs x))
```

12.8. Byte Manipulation Functions

Several functions are provided for dealing with an arbitrary-width field of contiguous bits appearing anywhere in an integer. Such a contiguous set of bits is called a *byte*. Here the term *byte* does not imply some fixed number of bits (such as eight), rather a field of arbitrary and user-specifiable width.

The byte-manipulation functions use objects called *byte specifiers* to designate a specific byte position within an integer. The representation of a byte specifier is implementation-dependent; in particular, it may or may not be a number. It is sufficient to know that the function byte will construct one, and that the byte-manipulation functions will accept them. The function byte accepts two integers representing the *position* and *size* of the byte and returns a byte specifier. Such a specifier designates a byte whose width is *size* and whose bits have weights $2^{position + size - 1}$ through $2^{position}$.

byte *size position*   [*Function*]

byte takes two integers representing the size and position of a byte and returns a byte specifier suitable for use as an argument to byte-manipulation functions.

byte-size *bytespec*   [*Function*]
byte-position *bytespec*   [*Function*]

Given a byte specifier, byte-size returns the size specified as an integer;
byte-position similarly returns the position. For example:

(byte-size (byte $j\,k$)) $\equiv j$
(byte-position (byte $j\,k$)) $\equiv k$

ldb *bytespec integer*   [*Function*]

bytespec specifies a byte of *integer* to be extracted. The result is returned as a non-negative integer.

(logbitp j (ldb (byte $s\,p$) n)) $\equiv$ (and (< $j\,s$) (logbitp (+ $j\,p$) n))

The name of the function ldb means "load byte."

Compatibility note: The MACLISP function haipart can be implemented in terms of ldb as follows:

```
(defun haipart (integer count)
  (let ((x (abs integer)))
    (if (minusp count)
        (ldb (byte (- count) 0) x)
        (ldb (byte count (max 0 (- (integer-length x) n)))
             x))))
```

If the argument *integer* is specified by a form that is a *place* form acceptable to
setf, then setf may be used with ldb to modify a byte within the integer that is
stored in that *place*. The effect is to perform a dpb operation and then store the
result back into the *place*.

ldb-test *bytespec integer*   [*Function*]

ldb-test is a predicate that is true if any of the bits designated by the byte specifier
bytespec are 1's in *integer*; that is, it is true if the designated field is non-zero.

(ldb-test *bytespec n*) $\equiv$ (not (zerop (ldb *bytespec n*)))

mask-field *bytespec integer*   [*Function*]

This is similar to ldb; however, the result contains the specified byte of *integer* in
the position specified by *bytespec*, rather than in position 0 as with ldb. The result
therefore agrees with *integer* in the byte specified but has zero-bits everywhere
else. For example:

```
(ldb bs (mask-field bs n)) ≡ (ldb bs n)

(logbitp j (mask-field (byte s p) n))
   ≡ (and (>= j p) (< j (+ p s)) (logbitp j n))

(mask-field bs n) ≡ (logand n (dpb -1 bs 0))
```

If the argument *integer* is specified by a form that is a *place* form acceptable to
setf, then setf may be used with mask-field to modify a byte within the integer
that is stored in that *place*. The effect is to perform a deposit-field operation
and then store the result back into the *place*.

dpb *newbyte bytespec integer*   [*Function*]

This returns a number that is the same as *integer* except in the bits specified by
bytespec. Let *s* be the size specified by *bytespec*; then the low *s* bits of *newbyte*
appear in the result in the byte specified by *bytespec*. The integer *newbyte* is
therefore interpreted as being right-justified, as if it were the result of ldb. For
example:

```
(logbitp j (dpb m (byte s p) n))
   ≡ (if (and (>= j p) (< j (+ p s)))
         (logbitp (- j p) m)
         (logbitp j n))
```

The name of the function dpb means "deposit byte."

deposit-field *newbyte bytespec integer*   [*Function*]

This function is to mask-field as dpb is to ldb. The result is an integer that
contains the bits of *newbyte* within the byte specified by *bytespec*, and elsewhere
contains the bits of *integer*. For example:

```
(logbitp j (dpb m (byte s p) n))
   ≡ (if (and (>= j p) (< j (+ p s)))
         (logbitp j m)
         (logbitp j n))
```

Implementation note: If the *bytespec* is a constant, one may of course construct, at compile
time, an equivalent mask *m*, for example by computing (deposit-field -1 *bytespec* 0).
Given this mask *m*, one may then compute

(deposit-field *newbyte bytespec integer*)

by computing

```
(logior (logand newbyte m) (logand integer (lognot m)))
```

where the result of (lognot m) can of course also be computed at compile time. However, the following expression may also be used and may require fewer temporary registers in some situations:

```
(logxor integer (logand m (logxor integer newbyte)))
```

A related, though possibly less useful, trick is that

```
(let ((z (logand (logxor x y) m)))
  (setq x (logxor z x))
  (setq y (logxor z y)))
```

interchanges those bits of x and y for which the mask m is 1, and leaves alone those bits of x and y for which m is 0.

12.9. Random Numbers

The COMMON LISP facility for generating pseudo-random numbers has been carefully defined to make its use reasonably portable. While two implementations may produce different series of pseudo-random numbers, the distribution of values should be relatively independent of such machine-dependent aspects as word size.

random *number* &optional *state*   [*Function*]

(random n) accepts a positive number n and returns a number of the same kind between zero (inclusive) and n (exclusive). The number n may be an integer or a floating-point number. An approximately uniform choice distribution is used. If n is an integer, each of the possible results occurs with (approximate) probability $1/n$. (The qualifier "approximate" is used because of implementation considerations; in practice, the deviation from uniformity should be quite small.)

The argument *state* must be an object of type random-state; it defaults to the value of the variable *random-state*. This object is used to maintain the state of the pseudo-random-number generator and is altered as a side effect of the random operation.

Compatibility note: random of zero arguments as defined in MACLISP has been omitted because its value is too implementation-dependent (limited by fixnum range).

Implementation note: In general, even if random of zero arguments were defined as in MACLISP, it is not adequate to define (random n) for integral n to be simply (mod (random) n); this fails to be uniformly distributed if n is larger than the largest number produced by random, or even if n merely approaches this number. This is another reason for omitting random of zero arguments in COMMON LISP. Assuming that the underlying mechanism produces "random bits" (possibly in chunks such as fixnums), the best approach is to produce enough random bits to construct an integer k some number d of bits larger than (integer-length n) (see integer-length), and then compute (mod k n). The quantity d should be at least 7, and preferably 10 or more.

To produce random floating-point numbers in the half-open range $[A, B)$, accepted practice (as determined by a look through the *Collected Algorithms from the ACM*, particularly algorithms 133, 266, 294, and 370) is to compute $X \cdot (B - A) + A$, where X is a floating-point number uniformly distributed over $[0.0, 1.0)$ and computed by calculating a random integer N in the range $[0, M)$ (typically by a multiplicative-congruential or linear-congruential method mod M) and then setting $X = N/M$. See also [10]. If one takes $M = 2^f$, where f is the length of the significand of a floating-point number (and it is in fact common to choose M to be a power of two), then this method is equivalent to the following assembly-language-level procedure. Assume the representation has no hidden bit. Take a floating-point 0.5, and clobber its entire significand with random bits. Normalize the result if necessary.

For example, on the DEC PDP-10, assume that accumulator T is completely random (all 36 bits are random). Then the code sequence

```
LSH  T,-9        ;Clear high 9 bits; low 27 are random.
FSC  T,128.      ;Install exponent and normalize.
```

will produce in T a random floating-point number uniformly distributed over $[0.0, 1.0)$. (Instead of the LSH instruction, one could do

```
TLZ  T,777000    ;That's 777000 octal.
```

but if the 36 random bits came from a congruential random-number generator, the high-order bits tend to be "more random" than the low-order ones, and so the LSH would be better for uniform distribution. Ideally all the bits would be the result of high-quality randomness.)

With a hidden-bit representation, normalization is not a problem, but dealing with the hidden bit is. The method can be adapted as follows. Take a floating-point 1.0 and clobber the explicit significand bits with random bits; this produces a random floating-point number in the range $[1.0, 2.0)$. Then simply subtract 1.0. In effect, we let the hidden bit creep in and then subtract it away again.

For example, on the DEC VAX, assume that register T is completely random (but a little less random than on the PDP-10, as it has only 32 random bits). Then the code sequence

```
INSV  #^X81,#7,#9,T   ;Install correct sign bit and exponent.
SUBF  #^F1.0,T        ;Subtract 1.0.
```

will produce in T a random floating-point number uniformly distributed over $[0.0, 1.0)$. Again, if the low-order bits are not random enough, then the instruction

```
ROTL  #7,T
```

should be performed first.

Implementors may wish to consult reference [17] for a discussion of some efficient methods of generating pseudo-random numbers.

random-state   [*Variable*]

This variable holds a data structure, an object of type random-state, that encodes the internal state of the random-number generator that random uses by default. The nature of this data structure is implementation-dependent. It may be printed out and successfully read back in, but may or may not function correctly as a random-number state object in another implementation. A call to random will perform a side effect on this data structure. Lambda-binding this variable to a different random-number state object will correctly save and restore the old state object, of course.

make-random-state &optional *state*   [*Function*]

This function returns a new object of type random-state, suitable for use as the value of the variable *random-state*. If *state* is nil or omitted, random-state returns a *copy* of the current random-number state object (the value of the variable *random-state*). If *state* is a state object, a copy of that state object is returned. If *state* is t, then a new state object is returned that has been "randomly" initialized by some means (such as by a time-of-day clock).

Rationale: COMMON LISP purposely provides no way to initialize a random-state object from a user-specified "seed." The reason for this is that the number of bits of state information in a random-state object may vary widely from one implementation to another, and there is no simple way to guarantee that any user-specified seed value will be "random enough." Instead, the initialization of random-state objects is left to the implementor in the case where the argument t is given to make-random-state.

To handle the common situation of executing the same program many times in a reproducible manner, where that program uses random, the following procedure may be used:

1. Evaluate (make-random-state t) to create a random-state object.

2. Write that object to a file, using print, for later use.

3. Whenever the program is to be run, first use read to create a copy of the random-state object from the printed representation in the file. Then use the random-state object newly created by the read operation to initialize the random-number generator for the program.

It is for the sake of this procedure for reproducible execution that implementations are required to provide a read/print syntax for objects of type random-state.

It is also possible to make copies of a random-state object directly without going through the print/read process, simply by using the make-random-state function to copy the object; this allows the same sequence of random numbers to be generated many times within a single program.

Implementation note: A recommended way to implement the type `random-state` is effectively to use the machinery for `defstruct`. The usual structure syntax may then be used for printing `random-state` objects; one might look something like

`#S(RANDOM-STATE DATA #(14 49 98436589 786345 8734658324 ...))`

where the components are of course completely implementation-dependent.

`random-state-p` *object*   [*Function*]

`random-state-p` is true if its argument is a random-state object, and otherwise is false.

`(random-state-p x)` ≡ `(typep x 'random-state)`

12.10. Implementation Parameters

The values of the named constants defined in this section are implementation-dependent. They may be useful for parameterizing code in some situations.

`most-positive-fixnum`   [*Constant*]
`most-negative-fixnum`   [*Constant*]

The value of `most-positive-fixnum` is that fixnum closest in value to positive infinity provided by the implementation.

The value of `most-negative-fixnum` is that fixnum closest in value to negative infinity provided by the implementation.

`most-positive-short-float`   [*Constant*]
`least-positive-short-float`   [*Constant*]
`least-negative-short-float`   [*Constant*]
`most-negative-short-float`   [*Constant*]

The value of `most-positive-short-float` is that short-format floating-point number closest in value to (but not equal to) positive infinity provided by the implementation.

The value of `least-positive-short-float` is that positive short-format floating-point number closest in value to (but not equal to) zero provided by the implementation.

The value of `least-negative-short-float` is that negative short-format floating-point number closest in value to (but not equal to) zero provided by the implementation. (Note that even if an implementation supports minus zero as a distinct short floating-point value, `least-negative-short-float` must not be minus zero.)

The value of `most-negative-short-float` is that short-format floating-point number closest in value to (but not equal to) negative infinity provided by the implementation.

`most-positive-single-float`	[*Constant*]
`least-positive-single-float`	[*Constant*]
`least-negative-single-float`	[*Constant*]
`most-negative-single-float`	[*Constant*]
`most-positive-double-float`	[*Constant*]
`least-positive-double-float`	[*Constant*]
`least-negative-double-float`	[*Constant*]
`most-negative-double-float`	[*Constant*]
`most-positive-long-float`	[*Constant*]
`least-positive-long-float`	[*Constant*]
`least-negative-long-float`	[*Constant*]
`most-negative-long-float`	[*Constant*]

These are analogous to the constants defined above for short-format floating-point numbers.

`short-float-epsilon`	[*Constant*]
`single-float-epsilon`	[*Constant*]
`double-float-epsilon`	[*Constant*]
`long-float-epsilon`	[*Constant*]

These constants have as value, for each floating-point format, the smallest positive floating-point number e of that format such that the expression

```
(not (= (float 1 e) (+ (float 1 e) e)))
```

is true when actually evaluated.

`short-float-negative-epsilon`	[*Constant*]
`single-float-negative-epsilon`	[*Constant*]
`double-float-negative-epsilon`	[*Constant*]
`long-float-negative-epsilon`	[*Constant*]

These constants have as value, for each floating-point format, the smallest positive floating-point number e of that format such that the expression

```
(not (= (float 1 e) (- (float 1 e) e)))
```

is true when actually evaluated.

13

Characters

COMMON LISP provides a character data type; objects of this type represent printed symbols such as letters.

In general, characters in COMMON LISP are not true objects; eq cannot be counted upon to operate on them reliably. In particular, it is possible that the expression

```
(let ((x z) (y z)) (eq x y))
```

may be false rather than true, if the value of z is a character.

Rationale: This odd breakdown of eq in the case of characters allows the implementor enough design freedom to produce exceptionally efficient code on conventional architectures. In this respect the treatment of characters exactly parallels that of numbers, as described in chapter 12.

If two objects are to be compared for "identity," but either might be a character, then the predicate eql is probably appropriate.

13.1. Character Attributes

Every character has three attributes: code, bits, and font. The code attribute is intended to distinguish among the printed glyphs and formatting functions for characters. The bits attribute allows extra flags to be associated with a character. The font attribute permits a specification of the style of the glyphs (such as italics).

---

char-code-limit   [Constant]

The value of char-code-limit is a non-negative integer that is the upper exclusive bound on values produced by the function char-code, which returns the *code* component of a given character; that is, the values returned by char-code are non-negative and strictly less than the value of char-code-limit.

char-font-limit   *[Constant]*

The value of char-font-limit is a non-negative integer that is the upper exclusive bound on values produced by the function char-font, which returns the *font* component of a given character; that is, the values returned by char-font are non-negative and strictly less than the value of char-font-limit.

Implementation note: No COMMON LISP implementation is required to support non-zero font attributes; if it does not, then char-font-limit should be 1.

char-bits-limit   *[Constant]*

The value of char-bits-limit is a non-negative integer that is the upper exclusive bound on values produced by the function char-bits, which returns the *bits* component of a given character; that is, the values returned by char-bits are non-negative and strictly less than the value of char-bits-limit. Note that the value of char-bits-limit will be a power of two.

Implementation note: No COMMON LISP implementation is required to support non-zero bits attributes; if it does not, then char-bits-limit should be 1.

13.2. Predicates on Characters

The predicate characterp may be used to determine whether any LISP object is a character object.

standard-char-p *char*   *[Function]*

The argument *char* must be a character object. standard-char-p is true if the argument is a "standard character," that is, an object of type standard-char.

Note that any character with a non-zero *bits* or *font* attribute is non-standard.

graphic-char-p *char*   *[Function]*

The argument *char* must be a character object. graphic-char-p is true if the argument is a "graphic" (printing) character, and false if it is a "non-graphic" (formatting or control) character. Graphic characters have a standard textual representation as a single glyph, such as A or * or =. By convention, the space character is considered to be graphic. Of the standard characters all but #\Newline are graphic. The semi-standard characters #\Backspace, #\Tab, #\Rubout, #\Linefeed, #\Return, and #\Page are not graphic.

Programs may assume that graphic characters of font 0 are all of the same width when printed, for example, for purposes of columnar formatting. (This does not prohibit the use of a variable-pitch font as font 0, but merely implies that every implementation of COMMON LISP must provide *some* mode of operation in which font 0 is a fixed-pitch font.) Portable programs should assume that, in general, non-graphic characters and characters of other fonts may be of varying widths.

Any character with a non-zero bits attribute is non-graphic.

---

string-char-p *char* [*Function*]

The argument *char* must be a character object. string-char-p is true if *char* can be stored into a string, and otherwise is false. Any character that satisfies standard-char-p also satisfies string-char-p; others may also.

---

alpha-char-p *char* [*Function*]

The argument *char* must be a character object. alpha-char-p is true if the argument is an alphabetic character, and otherwise is false.

If a character is alphabetic, then it is perforce graphic. Therefore any character with a non-zero bits attribute cannot be alphabetic. Whether a character is alphabetic may depend on its font number.

Of the standard characters (as defined by standard-char-p), the letters A through z and a through z are alphabetic.

---

upper-case-p *char* [*Function*]
lower-case-p *char* [*Function*]
both-case-p *char* [*Function*]

The argument *char* must be a character object.

upper-case-p is true if the argument is an uppercase character, and otherwise is false.

lower-case-p is true if the argument is a lowercase character, and otherwise is false.

both-case-p is true if the argument is an uppercase character and there is a corresponding lowercase character (which can be obtained using char-downcase), or if the argument is a lowercase character and there is a corresponding uppercase character (which can be obtained using char-upcase).

If a character is either uppercase or lowercase, it is necessarily alphabetic (and therefore is graphic, and therefore has a zero *bits* attribute). However, it is permissible in theory for an alphabetic character to be neither uppercase nor lowercase (in a non-Roman font, for example).

Of the standard characters (as defined by standard-char-p), the letters A through Z are uppercase and a through z are lowercase.

---

digit-char-p *char* &optional (*radix* 10)   [*Function*]

The argument *char* must be a character object, and *radix* must be a non-negative integer. If *char* is not a digit of the radix specified by *radix*, then digit-char-p is false; otherwise it returns a non-negative integer that is the "weight" of *char* in that radix.

Digits are necessarily graphic characters.

Of the standard characters (as defined by standard-char-p), the characters 0 through 9, A through Z, and a through z are digits. The weights of 0 through 9 are the integers 0 through 9, and of A through Z (and also a through z) are 10 through 35. digit-char-p returns the weight for one of these digits if and only if its weight is strictly less than *radix*. Thus, for example, the digits for radix 16 are

```
0 1 2 3 4 5 6 7 8 9 A B C D E F
```

Here is an example of the use of digit-char-p:

```
(defun convert-string-to-integer (str &optional (radix 10))
   "Given a digit string and optional radix, return an integer."
   (do ((j 0 (+ j 1))
        (n 0 (+ (* n radix)
                (or (digit-char-p (char str j) radix)
                    (error "Bad radix-~D digit: ~C"
                        radix
                        (char str j))))))
       ((= j (length str)) n)))
```

---

alphanumericp *char*   [*Function*]

The argument *char* must be a character object. alphanumericp is true if *char* is either alphabetic or numeric. By definition,

```
(alphanumericp x)
   ≡ (or (alpha-char-p x) (not (null (digit-char-p x))))
```

Alphanumeric characters are therefore necessarily graphic (as defined by graphic-char-p).

Of the standard characters (as defined by standard-char-p), the characters 0 through 9, A through Z, and a through z are alphanumeric.

char= *character* &rest *more-characters*	[*Function*]
char/= *character* &rest *more-characters*	[*Function*]
char< *character* &rest *more-characters*	[*Function*]
char> *character* &rest *more-characters*	[*Function*]
char<= *character* &rest *more-characters*	[*Function*]
char>= *character* &rest *more-characters*	[*Function*]

The arguments must all be character objects. These functions compare the objects using the implementation-dependent total ordering on characters, in a manner analogous to numeric comparisons by = and related functions.

The total ordering on characters is guaranteed to have the following properties:

• The standard alphanumeric characters obey the following partial ordering:

    A<B<C<D<E<F<G<H<I<J<K<L<M<N<O<P<Q<R<S<T<U<V<W<X<Y<Z
    a<b<c<d<e<f<g<h<i<j<k<l<m<n<o<p<q<r<s<t<u<v<w<x<y<z
    0<1<2<3<4<5<6<7<8<9
    either 9<A *or* Z<0
    either 9<a *or* z<0

This implies that alphabetic ordering holds within each case (upper and lower), and that the digits as a group are not interleaved with letters. However, the ordering or possible interleaving of uppercase letters and lowercase letters is unspecified. (Note that both the ASCII and the EBCDIC character sets conform to this specification. As it happens, neither ordering interleaves uppercase and lowercase letters: in the ASCII ordering, 9<A and Z<a, whereas in the EBCDIC ordering z<A and Z<0.)

• If two characters have the same bits and font attributes, then their ordering by char< is consistent with the numerical ordering by the predicate < on their code attributes.

• If two characters differ in any attribute (code, bits, or font), then they are different.

The total ordering is not necessarily the same as the total ordering on the integers produced by applying char-int to the characters (although it is a reasonable implementation technique to use that ordering).

While alphabetic characters of a given case must be properly ordered, they need not be contiguous; thus (char<= #\a x #\z) is *not* a valid way of determining whether or not x is a lowercase letter. That is why a separate lower-case-p predicate is provided.

```
(char= #\d #\d) is true.
(char/= #\d #\d) is false.
(char= #\d #\x) is false.
(char/= #\d #\x) is true.
(char= #\d #\D) is false.
(char/= #\d #\D) is true.
(char= #\d #\d #\d #\d) is true.
(char/= #\d #\d #\d #\d) is false.
(char= #\d #\d #\x #\d) is false.
(char/= #\d #\d #\x #\d) is false.
(char= #\d #\y #\x #\c) is false.
(char/= #\d #\y #\x #\c) is true.
(char= #\d #\c #\d) is false.
(char/= #\d #\c #\d) is false.
(char< #\d #\x) is true.
(char<= #\d #\x) is true.
(char< #\d #\d) is false.
(char<= #\d #\d) is true.
(char< #\a #\e #\y #\z) is true.
(char<= #\a #\e #\y #\z) is true.
(char< #\a #\e #\e #\y) is false.
(char<= #\a #\e #\e #\y) is true.
(char> #\e #\d) is true.
(char>= #\e #\d) is true.
(char> #\d #\c #\b #\a) is true.
(char>= #\d #\c #\b #\a) is true.
(char> #\d #\d #\c #\a) is false.
(char>= #\d #\d #\c #\a) is true.
(char> #\e #\d #\b #\c #\a) is false.
(char>= #\e #\d #\b #\c #\a) is false.
(char> #\z #\A) may be true or false.
(char> #\Z #\a) may be true or false.
```

There is no requirement that (eq c1 c2) be true merely because (char= c1 c2) is true. While eq may distinguish two character objects that char= does not, it is distinguishing them not as *characters*, but in some sense on the basis of a lower-level implementation characteristic. (Of course, if (eq c1 c2) is true, then one may expect (char= c1 c2) to be true.) However, eql and equal compare character objects in the same way that char= does.

char-equal *character* &rest *more-characters*	[*Function*]
char-not-equal *character* &rest *more-characters*	[*Function*]
char-lessp *character* &rest *more-characters*	[*Function*]
char-greaterp *character* &rest *more-characters*	[*Function*]
char-not-greaterp *character* &rest *more-characters*	[*Function*]
char-not-lessp *character* &rest *more-characters*	[*Function*]

The predicate char-equal is like char=, and similarly for the others, except according to a different ordering such that differences of bits attributes and case are ignored, and font information is taken into account in an implementation-dependent manner. For the standard characters, the ordering is such that A=a, B=b, and so on, up to Z=z, and furthermore either 9<A or Z<0. For example:

```
(char-equal #\A #\a) is true
(char= #\A #\a) is false
(char-equal #\A #\Control-A) is true
```

The ordering may depend on the font information. For example, an implementation might decree that (char-equal #\p #\p) be true, but that (char-equal #\p #\π) be false (where #\π is a lowercase p in some font). Assuming italics to be in font 1 and the Greek alphabet in font 2, this is the same as saying that (char-equal #0\p #1\p) may be true and at the same time (char-equal #0\p #2\p) may be false.

13.3. Character Construction and Selection

These functions may be used to extract attributes of a character and to construct new characters.

char-code *char*	[*Function*]

The argument *char* must be a character object. char-code returns the *code* attribute of the character object; this will be a non-negative integer less than the (normal) value of the variable char-code-limit.

char-bits *char*   [*Function*]

The argument *char* must be a character object. char-bits returns the *bits* attribute
of the character object; this will be a non-negative integer less than the (normal)
value of the variable char-bits-limit.

char-font *char*   [*Function*]

The argument *char* must be a character object. char-font returns the *font* attribute
of the character object; this will be a non-negative integer less than the (normal)
value of the variable char-font-limit.

code-char *code* &optional (*bits* 0) (*font* 0)   [*Function*]

All three arguments must be non-negative integers. If it is possible in the
implementation to construct a character object whose code attribute is *code*, whose
bits attribute is *bits*, and whose font attribute is *font*, then such an object is returned;
otherwise nil is returned.

For any integers *c*, *b*, and *f*, if (code-char *c* *b* *f*) is not nil then

```
(char-code (code-char c b f)) ⇒ c
(char-bits (code-char c b f)) ⇒ b
(char-font (code-char c b f)) ⇒ f
```

If the font and bits attributes of a character object c are zero, then it is the case
that

```
(char= (code-char (char-code c)) c)
```

is true.

make-char *char* &optional (*bits* 0) (*font* 0)   [*Function*]

The argument *char* must be a character, and *bits* and *font* must be non-negative
integers. If it is possible in the implementation to construct a character object whose
code attribute is the same as the code attribute of *char*, whose bits attribute is *bits*,
and whose font attribute is *font*, then such an object is returned; otherwise nil is
returned.

If *bits* and *font* are zero, then make-char cannot fail. This implies that for every
character object one can "turn off" its bits and font attributes.

13.4. Character Conversions

These functions perform various transformations on characters, including case conversions.

---

character *object*   [*Function*]

The function `character` coerces its argument to be a character if possible; see `coerce`.

```
(character x) ≡ (coerce x 'character)
```

---

char-upcase *char*   [*Function*]
char-downcase *char*   [*Function*]

The argument *char* must be a character object. `char-upcase` attempts to convert its argument to an uppercase equivalent; `char-downcase` attempts to convert its argument to a lowercase equivalent.

   `char-upcase` returns a character object with the same font and bits attributes as *char*, but with possibly a different code attribute. If the code is different from *char*'s, then the predicate `lower-case-p` is true of *char*, and `upper-case-p` is true of the result character. Moreover, if (`char=` (`char-upcase` x) x) is *not* true, then it is true that

```
(char= (char-downcase (char-upcase x)) x)
```

Similarly, `char-downcase` returns a character object with the same font and bits attributes as *char*, but with possibly a different code attribute. If the code is different from *char*'s, then the predicate `upper-case-p` is true of *char*, and `lower-case-p` is true of the result character. Moreover, if (`char=` (`char-downcase` x) x) is *not* true, then it is true that

```
(char= (char-upcase (char-downcase x)) x)
```

Note that the action of `char-upcase` and `char-downcase` may depend on the bits and font attribute of the character. In particular, they have no effect on a character with a non-zero bits attribute, because such characters are by definition not alphabetic. See `alpha-char-p`.

---

digit-char *weight* &optional (*radix* 10) (*font* 0)   [*Function*]

All arguments must be integers. `digit-char` determines whether or not it is possible to construct a character object whose font attribute is *font*, and whose *code* is such that the result character has the weight *weight* when considered as a digit of the radix *radix* (see the predicate `digit-char-p`). It returns such a character if that is possible, and otherwise returns `nil`.

`digit-char` cannot return `nil` if *font* is zero, *radix* is between 2 and 36 inclusive, and *weight* is non-negative and less than *radix*.

If more than one character object can encode such a weight in the given radix, one will be chosen consistently by any given implementation; moreover, among the standard characters, uppercase letters are preferred to lowercase letters. For example:

```
(digit-char 7) ⇒ #\7
(digit-char 12) ⇒ nil
(digit-char 12 16) ⇒ #\C        ;not #\c
(digit-char 6 2) ⇒ nil
(digit-char 1 2) ⇒ #\1
```

Note that no argument is provided for specifying the *bits* component of the returned character, because a digit cannot have a non-zero *bits* component. The reasoning is that every digit is graphic (see `digit-char-p`) and no graphic character has a non-zero *bits* component (see `graphic-char-p`).

`char-int` *char*   [*Function*]

The argument *char* must be a character object. `char-int` returns a non-negative integer encoding the character object.

If the font and bits attributes of *char* are zero, then `char-int` returns the same integer `char-code` would. Also,

```
(char= c1 c2) ≡ (= (char-int c1) (char-int c2))
```

for characters c1 and *c2*.

This function is provided primarily for the purpose of hashing characters.

`int-char` *integer*   [*Function*]

The argument must be a non-negative integer. `int-char` returns a character object c such that `(char-int c)` is equal to *integer*, if possible; otherwise `int-char` returns false.

`char-name` *char*   [*Function*]

The argument *char* must be a character object. If the character has a name, then that name (a string) is returned; otherwise `nil` is returned. All characters that have zero font and bits attributes and that are non-graphic (do not satisfy the predicate graphic-char-p) have names. Graphic characters may or may not have names.

The standard newline and space characters have the respective names Newline and Space. The semi-standard characters have the names Tab, Page, Rubout, Linefeed, Return, and Backspace.

Characters that have names can be notated as #\ followed by the name. (See section 22.1.4.) Although the name may be written in any case, it is stylish to capitalize it thus: #\Space.

char-name will only locate "simple" character names; it will not construct names such as Control-Space on the basis of the character's bits attribute.

---

name-char *name* [*Function*]

The argument name must be an object coerceable to a string as if by the function string. If the name is the same as the name of a character object (as determined by string-equal), that object is returned; otherwise nil is returned.

13.5. Character Control-Bit Functions

COMMON LISP provides explicit names for four bits of the bits attribute: *Control*, *Meta*, *Hyper*, and *Super*. The following definitions are provided for manipulating these. Each COMMON LISP implementation provides these functions for compatibility, even if it does not support any or all of the bits named below.

---

char-control-bit [*Constant*]
char-meta-bit [*Constant*]
char-super-bit [*Constant*]
char-hyper-bit [*Constant*]

The values of these named constants are the "weights" (as integers) for the four named control bits. The weight of the control bit is 1; of the meta bit, 2; of the super bit, 4; and of the hyper bit, 8.

If a given implementation of COMMON LISP does not support a particular bit, then the corresponding constant is zero instead.

---

char-bit *char name* [*Function*]

char-bit takes a character object *char* and the name of a bit, and returns non-nil if the bit of that name is set in *char*, or nil if the bit is not set in *char*. For example:

```
(char-bit #\Control-X :control) ⇒ true
```

Valid values for *name* are implementation-dependent, but typically are `:control`, `:meta`, `:hyper`, and `:super`. It is an error to give `char-bit` the name of a bit not supported by the implementation.

If the argument *char* is specified by a form that is a *place* form acceptable to `setf`, then `setf` may be used with `char-bit` to modify a bit of the character stored in that *place*. The effect is to perform a `set-char-bit` operation and then store the result back into the *place*.

`set-char-bit` *char name newvalue*   [*Function*]

`char-bit` takes a character object *char*, the name of a bit, and a flag. A character is returned that is just like *char* except that the named bit is set or reset according to whether *newvalue* is non-`nil` or `nil`. Valid values for *name* are implementation-dependent, but typically are `:control`, `:meta`, `:hyper`, and `:super`. For example:

```
(set-char-bit #\X :control t) ⇒ #\Control-X
(set-char-bit #\Control-X :control t) ⇒ #\Control-X
(set-char-bit #\Control-X :control nil) ⇒ #\X
```

14

Sequences

The type `sequence` encompasses both lists and vectors (one-dimensional arrays). While these are different data structures with different structural properties leading to different algorithmic uses, they do have a common property: each contains an ordered set of elements. Note that `nil` is considered to be a sequence, of length zero.

There are some operations that are useful on both lists and arrays because they deal with ordered sets of elements. One may ask the number of elements, reverse the ordering, extract a subsequence, and so on. For such purposes COMMON LISP provides a set of generic functions on sequences:

```
elt            reverse         map          remove
length         nreverse        some         remove-duplicates
subseq         concatenate     every        delete
copy-seq       position        notany       delete-duplicates
fill           find            notevery     substitute
replace        sort            reduce       nsubstitute
count          merge           search       mismatch
```

Some of these operations come in more than one version. Such versions are indicated by adding a suffix (or, occasionally, a prefix) to the basic name of the operation. In addition, many operations accept one or more optional keyword arguments that can modify the operation in various ways.

If the operation requires testing sequence elements according to some criterion, then the criterion may be specified in one of two ways. The basic operation accepts an item, and elements are tested for being `eql` to that item. (A test other than `eql` can be specified by the `:test` or `:test-not` keyword. It is an error to use both of these keywords in the same call.) The variants formed by adding `-if` and `-if-not` to the basic operation name do not take an item, but instead a one-argument predicate, and elements are tested for satisfying or not satisfying the predicate. As an example,

```
(remove item sequence)
```

returns a copy of *sequence* from which all elements `eql` to *item* have been removed;

```
(remove item sequence :test #'equal)
```

returns a copy of *sequence* from which all elements `equal` to *item* have been removed;

```
(remove-if #'numberp sequence)
```

returns a copy of *sequence* from which all numbers have been removed.

If an operation tests elements of a sequence in any manner, the keyword argument `:key`, if not `nil`, should be a function of one argument that will extract from an element the part to be tested in place of the whole element. For example, the effect of the MACLISP expression `(assq item seq)` could be obtained by

```
(find item sequence :test #'eq :key #'car)
```

This searches for the first element of *sequence* whose *car* is `eq` to *item*.

For some operations it can be useful to specify the direction in which the sequence is conceptually processed. In this case the basic operation normally processes the sequence in the forward direction, and processing in the reverse direction is indicated by a non-`nil` value for the keyword argument `:from-end`. (The processing order specified by the `:from-end` is purely conceptual. Depending on the object to be processed and on the implementation, the actual processing order may be different. For this reason a user-supplied *test* function should be free of side effects.)

Many operations allow the specification of a subsequence to be operated upon. Such operations have keyword arguments called `:start` and `:end`. These arguments should be integer indices into the sequence, with *start* ≤ *end* (it is an error if *start* > *end*). They indicate the subsequence starting with and *including* element *start* and up to but *excluding* element *end*. The length of the subsequence is therefore *end* − *start*. If *start* is omitted, it defaults to zero; and if *end* is omitted or `nil`, it defaults to the length of the sequence. Therefore if both *start* and *end* are omitted the entire sequence is processed by default. For the most part, subsequence specification is permitted purely for the sake of efficiency; one can simply call `subseq` instead to extract the subsequence before operating on it. Note, however, that operations that calculate indices return indices into the original sequence, not into the subsequence:

```
(position #\b "foobar" :start 2 :end 5) => 3
(position #\b (subseq "foobar" 2 5)) => 1
```

If two sequences are involved, then the keyword arguments :start1, :end1, :start2, and :end2 are used to specify separate subsequences for each sequence.

For some functions, notably remove and delete, the keyword argument :count is used to specify how many occurrences of the item should be affected. If this is nil or is not supplied, all matching items are affected.

In the following function descriptions, an element x of a sequence "satisfies the test" if any of the following holds:

- A basic function was called, *testfn* was specified by the keyword :test, and (funcall *testfn* *item* (*keyfn* x)) is true.

- A basic function was called, *testfn* was specified by the keyword :test-not, and (funcall *testfn* *item* (*keyfn* x)) is false.

- An -if function was called, and (funcall *predicate* (*keyfn* x)) is true.

- An -if-not function was called, and (funcall *predicate* (*keyfn* x)) is false.

In each case *keyfn* is the value of the :key keyword argument (the default being the identity function). See, for example, remove.

In the following function descriptions, two elements x and y taken from sequences "match" if either of the following holds:

- *testfn* was specified by the keyword :test, and (funcall *testfn* (*keyfn* x) (*keyfn* y)) is true.

- *testfn* was specified by the keyword :test-not, and (funcall *testfn* (*keyfn* x) (*keyfn* y)) is false.

See, for example, search.

You may depend on the order in which arguments are given to *testfn*; this permits the use of non-commutative test functions in a predictable manner. The order of the arguments to *testfn* corresponds to the order in which those arguments (or the sequences containing those arguments) were given to the sequence function in question. If a sequence function gives two elements from the same sequence argument to *testfn*, they are given in the same order in which they appear in the sequence.

Whenever a sequence function must construct and return a new vector, it always returns a *simple* vector (see section 2.5). Similarly, any strings constructed will be simple strings.

14.1. Simple Sequence Functions

Most of the following functions perform simple operations on a single sequence; make-sequence constructs a new sequence.

`elt` *sequence index*   [*Function*]

This returns the element of *sequence* specified by *index*, which must be a non-negative integer less than the length of the *sequence* as returned by `length`. The first element of a sequence has index `0`.

(Note that `elt` observes the fill pointer in those vectors that have fill pointers. The array-specific function `aref` may be used to access vector elements that are beyond the vector's fill pointer.)

`setf` may be used with `elt` to destructively replace a sequence element with a new value.

`subseq` *sequence start* &optional *end*   [*Function*]

This returns the subsequence of *sequence* specified by *start* and *end*. `subseq` *always* allocates a new sequence for a result; it never shares storage with an old sequence. The result subsequence is always of the same type as the argument *sequence*.

`setf` may be used with `subseq` to destructively replace a subsequence with a sequence of new values; see also `replace`.

`copy-seq` *sequence*   [*Function*]

A copy is made of the argument *sequence*; the result is `equalp` to the argument but not `eq` to it.

`(copy-seq x)` ≡ `(subseq x 0)`

but the name `copy-seq` is more perspicuous when applicable.

`length` *sequence*   [*Function*]

The number of elements in *sequence* is returned as a non-negative integer. If the sequence is a vector with a fill pointer, the "active length" as specified by the fill pointer is returned. See section 17.5.

`reverse` *sequence*   [*Function*]

The result is a new sequence of the same kind as *sequence*, containing the same elements but in reverse order. The argument is not modified.

`nreverse` *sequence*   [*Function*]

The result is a sequence containing the same elements as *sequence* but in reverse order. The argument may be destroyed and re-used to produce the result. The result may or may not be `eq` to the argument, so it is usually wise to say something like (setq x (nreverse x)), because simply (nreverse x) is not guaranteed to leave a reversed value in x.

make-sequence *type size* &key :initial-element   [*Function*]

This returns a sequence of type *type* and of length *size*, each of whose elements has been initialized to the :initial-element argument. If specified, the :initial-element argument must be an object that can be an element of a sequence of type *type*. For example:

```
(make-sequence '(vector double-float) 100
               :initial-element 1d0)
```

If an :initial-element argument is not specified, then the sequence will be initialized in an implementation-dependent way.

14.2. Concatenating, Mapping, and Reducing Sequences

The functions in this section each operate on an arbitrary number of sequence except for reduce, which is included here because of its conceptual relationship to the mapping functions.

concatenate *result-type* &rest *sequences*   [*Function*]

The result is a new sequence that contains all the elements of all the sequences in order. All of the sequences are copied from; the result does not share any structure with any of the argument sequences (in this concatenate differs from append). The type of the result is specified by *result-type*, which must be a subtype of sequence, as for the function coerce. It must be possible for every element of the argument sequences to be an element of a sequence of type *result-type*.

If only one *sequence* argument is provided and it has the type specified by *result-type*, concatenate is required to copy the argument rather than simply returning it. If a copy is not required, but only possible type-conversion, then the coerce function may be appropriate.

map *result-type function sequence* &rest *more-sequences*   [*Function*]

The *function* must take as many arguments as there are sequences provided; at least one sequence must be provided. The result of map is a sequence such that element *j* is the result of applying *function* to element *j* of each of the argument sequences. The result sequence is as long as the shortest of the input sequences.

If the *function* has side effects, it can count on being called first on all the elements numbered 0, then on all those numbered 1, and so on.

The type of the result sequence is specified by the argument *result-type* (which must be a subtype of the type `sequence`), as for the function `coerce`. In addition, one may specify `nil` for the result type, meaning that no result sequence is to be produced; in this case the *function* is invoked only for effect, and `map` returns `nil`. This gives an effect similar to that of `mapc`.

Compatibility note: In MacLISP, ZetaLISP, InterLISP, and indeed even LISP 1.5, the function `map` has always meant a non-value-returning version. However, standard computer science literature, including, in particular, the recent wave of papers on "functional programming," have come to use `map` to mean what in the past LISP implementations have called `mapcar`. To simplify things henceforth, COMMON LISP follows current usage, and what was formerly called `map` is named `map1` in COMMON LISP.

For example:

```
(map 'list #'- '(1 2 3 4)) ⇒ (-1 -2 -3 -4)
(map 'string
     #'(lambda (x) (if (oddp x) #\1 #\0))
     '(1 2 3 4))
  ⇒ "1010"
```

`some` *predicate sequence* &rest *more-sequences*	[*Function*]
`every` *predicate sequence* &rest *more-sequences*	[*Function*]
`notany` *predicate sequence* &rest *more-sequences*	[*Function*]
`notevery` *predicate sequence* &rest *more-sequences*	[*Function*]

These are all predicates. The *predicate* must take as many arguments as there are sequences provided. The *predicate* is first applied to the elements with index 0 in each of the sequences, and possibly then to the elements with index 1, and so on, until a termination criterion is met or the end of the shortest of the *sequences* is reached.

If the *predicate* has side effects, it can count on being called first on all the elements numbered 0, then on all those numbered 1, and so on.

`some` returns as soon as any invocation of *predicate* returns a non-nil value; `some` returns that value. If the end of a sequence is reached, `some` returns `nil`. Thus, considered as a predicate, it is true if *some* invocation of *predicate* is true.

`every` returns `nil` as soon as any invocation of *predicate* returns `nil`. If the end of a sequence is reached, `every` returns a non-`nil` value. Thus, considered as a predicate, it is true if *every* invocation of *predicate* is true.

`notany` returns `nil` as soon as any invocation of *predicate* returns a non-`nil` value. If the end of a sequence is reached, `notany` returns a non-`nil` value. Thus, considered as a predicate, it is true if *no* invocation of *predicate* is true.

notevery returns a non-nil value as soon as any invocation of *predicate* returns
nil. If the end of a sequence is reached, notevery returns nil. Thus, considered
as a predicate, it is true if *not every* invocation of *predicate* is true.

Compatibility note: The order of the arguments here is not compatible with INTERLISP and
ZETALISP. This is to stress the similarity of these functions to map. The functions are
therefore extended here to functions of more than one argument, and to multiple sequences.

---

reduce *function sequence* &key :from-end :start   [*Function*]
                                :end :initial-value

The reduce function combines all the elements of a sequence using a binary
operation; for example, using + one can add up all the elements.

The specified subsequence of the *sequence* is combined or "reduced" using the
function, which must accept two arguments. The reduction is left-associative, unless the :from-end argument is true (it defaults to nil), in which case it is
right-associative. If an :initial-value argument is given, it is logically placed
before the subsequence (after it if :from-end is true) and included in the reduction
operation.

If the specified subsequence contains exactly one element and no :initial-
value is given, then that element is returned and the *function* is not called. If the
specified subsequence is empty and an :initial-value is given, then the
:initial-value is returned and the *function* is not called.

If the specified subsequence is empty and no :initial-value is given, then
the *function* is called with zero arguments, and reduce returns whatever the function does. (This is the only case where the *function* is called with other than two
arguments.)

```
(reduce #'+ '(1 2 3 4)) ⇒ 10
(reduce #'- '(1 2 3 4)) ≡ (- (- (- 1 2) 3) 4) ⇒ -8
(reduce #'- '(1 2 3 4) :from-end t)       ;Alternating sum.
   ≡ (- 1 (- 2 (- 3 4))) ⇒ -2
(reduce #'+ '()) ⇒ 0
(reduce #'+ '(3)) ⇒ 3
(reduce #'+ '(foo)) ⇒ foo
(reduce #'list '(1 2 3 4)) ⇒ (((1 2) 3) 4)
(reduce #'list '(1 2 3 4) :from-end t) ⇒ (1 (2 (3 4)))
(reduce #'list '(1 2 3 4) :initial-value 'foo)
   ⇒ ((((foo 1) 2) 3) 4)
(reduce #'list '(1 2 3 4)
        :from-end t :initial-value 'foo)
   ⇒ (1 (2 (3 (4 foo))))
```

If the *function* produces side effects, the order of the calls to the *function* can be correctly predicted from the reduction ordering demonstrated above.

The name "reduce" for this function is borrowed from APL.

14.3. Modifying Sequences

Each of these functions alters the contents of a sequence or produces an altered copy of a given sequence.

fill *sequence item* &key :start :end   [*Function*]

The *sequence* is destructively modified by replacing each element of the subsequence specified by the :start and :end parameters with the *item*. The *item* may be any LISP object but must be a suitable element for the *sequence*. The *item* is stored into all specified components of the *sequence*, beginning at the one specified by the :start index (which defaults to zero), up to but not including the one specified by the :end index (which defaults to the length of the sequence). fill returns the modified *sequence*. For example:

```
(setq x (vector 'a 'b 'c 'd 'e)) ⇒ #(a b c d e)
(fill x 'z :start 1 :end 3) ⇒ #(a z z d e)
  and now x ⇒ #(a z z d e)
(fill x 'p) ⇒ #(p p p p p)
  and now x ⇒ #(p p p p p)
```

replace *sequence1 sequence2* &key :start1 :end1   [*Function*]
                                    :start2 :end2

The sequence *sequence1* is destructively modified by copying successive elements into it from *sequence2*. The elements of *sequence2* must be of a type that may be stored into *sequence1*. The subsequence of *sequence2* specified by :start2 and :end2 is copied into the subsequence of *sequence1* specified by :start1 and :end1. (The arguments :start1 and :start2 default to zero. The arguments :end1 and :end2 default to nil, meaning the end of the appropriate sequence.) If these subsequences are not of the same length, then the shorter length determines how many elements are copied; the extra elements near the end of the longer subsequence are not involved in the operation. The number of elements copied may be expressed as:

```
(min (- end1 start1) (- end2 start2))
```

The value returned by replace is the modified *sequence1*.

If *sequence1* and *sequence2* are the same (eq) object and the region being modified overlaps the region being copied from, then it is as if the entire source region were copied to another place and only then copied back into the target region. However, if *sequence1* and *sequence2* are *not* the same, but the region being modified overlaps the region being copied from (perhaps because of shared list structure or displaced arrays), then after the replace operation the subsequence of *sequence1* being modified will have unpredictable contents.

remove *item sequence* &key :from-end :test :test-not   [*Function*]
        :start :end :count :key

remove-if *test sequence* &key :from-end :start   [*Function*]
        :end :count :key

remove-if-not *test sequence* &key :from-end :start   [*Function*]
        :end :count :key

The result is a sequence of the same kind as the argument *sequence* that has the same elements except that those in the subsequence delimited by :start and :end and satisfying the test (see above) have been removed. This is a non-destructive operation; the result is a copy of the input *sequence*, save that some elements are not copied. Elements not removed occur in the same order in the result that they did in the argument.

The :count argument, if supplied, limits the number of elements removed; if more than :count elements satisfy the test, then of these elements only the leftmost are removed, as many as specified by :count.

A non-nil :from-end specification matters only when the :count argument is provided; in that case only the rightmost :count elements satisfying the test are removed. For example:

```
(remove 4 '(1 2 4 1 3 4 5)) ⇒ (1 2 1 3 5)
(remove 4 '(1 2 4 1 3 4 5) :count 1) ⇒ (1 2 1 3 4 5)
(remove 4 '(1 2 4 1 3 4 5) :count 1 :from-end t)
  ⇒ (1 2 4 1 3 5)
(remove 3 '(1 2 4 1 3 4 5) :test #'>) ⇒ (4 3 4 5)
(remove-if #'oddp '(1 2 4 1 3 4 5)) ⇒ (2 4 4)
(remove-if #'evenp '(1 2 4 1 3 4 5) :count 1 :from-end t)
  ⇒ (1 2 4 1 3 5)
```

The result of remove may share with the argument *sequence*; a list result may share a tail with an input list, and the result may be eq to the input *sequence* if no elements need to be removed.

```
delete item sequence &key :from-end :test :test-not        [Function]
                          :start :end :count :key
delete-if test sequence &key :from-end :start              [Function]
                          :end :count :key
delete-if-not test sequence &key :from-end :start          [Function]
                          :end :count :key
```

This is the destructive counterpart to `remove`. The result is a sequence of the same kind as the argument *sequence* that has the same elements except that those in the subsequence delimited by `:start` and `:end` and satisfying the test (see above) have been deleted. This is a destructive operation. The argument *sequence* may be destroyed and used to construct the result; however, the result may or may not be `eq` to *sequence*. Elements not deleted occur in the same order in the result that they did in the argument.

The `:count` argument, if supplied, limits the number of elements deleted; if more than `:count` elements satisfy the test, then of these elements only the leftmost are deleted, as many as specified by `:count`.

A non-nil `:from-end` specification matters only when the `:count` argument is provided; in that case only the rightmost `:count` elements satisfying the test are deleted. For example:

```
(delete 4 '(1 2 4 1 3 4 5)) => (1 2 1 3 5)
(delete 4 '(1 2 4 1 3 4 5) :count 1) => (1 2 1 3 4 5)
(delete 4 '(1 2 4 1 3 4 5) :count 1 :from-end t)
   => (1 2 4 1 3 5)
(delete 3 '(1 2 4 1 3 4 5) :test #'>) => (4 3 4 5)
(delete-if #'oddp '(1 2 4 1 3 4 5)) => (2 4 4)
(delete-if #'evenp '(1 2 4 1 3 4 5) :count 1 :from-end t)
   => (1 2 4 1 3 5)
```

Compatibility note: In MACLISP, the `delete` function uses an `equal` comparison rather than `eql`, which is the default test for `delete` in COMMON LISP. Where in MACLISP one would write `(delete x y)`, one must in COMMON LISP write `(delete x y :test #'equal)` to get the completely identical effect. Similarly, one can get the precise effect, and no more, of the MACLISP `(delq x y)` by writing in COMMON LISP `(delete x y :test #'eq)`.

```
remove-duplicates sequence &key :from-end :test :test-not   [Function]
                          :start :end :key
delete-duplicates sequence &key :from-end :test :test-not   [Function]
                          :start :end :key
```

The elements of *sequence* are compared pairwise, and if any two match, then the one occurring earlier in the sequence is discarded (but if the :from-end argument is true, then the one later in the sequence is discarded). The result is a sequence of the same kind as the argument sequence with enough elements removed so that no two of the remaining elements match. The order of the elements remaining in the result is the same as the order in which they appear in *sequence*.

remove-duplicates is the non-destructive version of this operation. The result of remove-duplicates may share with the argument *sequence*; a list result may share a tail with an input list, and the result may be eq to the input *sequence* if no elements need to be removed.

delete-duplicates may destroy the argument *sequence*.

Some examples:

```
(remove-duplicates '(a b c b d d e)) ⇒ (a c b d e)
(remove-duplicates '(a b c b d d e) :from-end t) ⇒ (a b c d e)
(remove-duplicates '((foo #\a) (bar #\%) (baz #\A))
                   :test #'char-equal :key #'cadr)
 ⇒ ((bar #\%) (baz #\A))
(remove-duplicates '((foo #\a) (bar #\%) (baz #\A))
                   :test #'char-equal :key #'cadr :from-end t)
 ⇒ ((foo #\a) (bar #\%))
```

These functions are useful for converting a sequence into a canonical form suitable for representing a set.

substitute *newitem olditem sequence* &key :from-end :test   [*Function*]
                                           :test-not :start
                                           :end :count :key
substitute-if *newitem test sequence* &key :from-end   [*Function*]
                                           :start :end
                                           :count :key
substitute-if-not *newitem test sequence* &key :from-end   [*Function*]
                                               :start :end
                                               :count :key

The result is a sequence of the same kind as the argument *sequence* that has the same elements except that those in the subsequence delimited by :start and :end and satisfying the test (see above) have been replaced by *newitem*. This is a non-destructive operation; the result is a copy of the input *sequence*, save that some elements are changed.

The :count argument, if supplied, limits the number of elements altered; if more than :count elements satisfy the test, then of these elements only the leftmost are replaced, as many as specified by :count.

A non-nil :from-end specification matters only when the :count argument is provided; in that case only the rightmost :count elements satisfying the test are replaced. For example:

```
(substitute 9 4 '(1 2 4 1 3 4 5)) ⇒ (1 2 9 1 3 9 5)
(substitute 9 4 '(1 2 4 1 3 4 5) :count 1) ⇒ (1 2 9 1 3 4 5)
(substitute 9 4 '(1 2 4 1 3 4 5) :count 1 :from-end t)
  ⇒ (1 2 4 1 3 9 5)
(substitute 9 3 '(1 2 4 1 3 4 5) :test #'>) ⇒ (9 9 4 9 3 4 5)
(substitute-if 9 #'oddp '(1 2 4 1 3 4 5)) ⇒ (9 2 4 9 9 4 9)
(substitute-if 9 #'evenp '(1 2 4 1 3 4 5) :count 1 :from-end t)
  ⇒ (1 2 4 1 3 9 5)
```

The result of substitute may share with the argument *sequence*; a list result may share a tail with an input list, and the result may be eq to the input *sequence* if no elements need to be changed.

See also subst, which performs substitutions throughout a tree.

---

nsubstitute *newitem olditem sequence* &key :from-end :test   [*Function*]
                                             :test-not :start
                                             :end :count :key
nsubstitute-if *newitem test sequence* &key :from-end   [*Function*]
                                             :start :end
                                             :count :key
nsubstitute-if-not *newitem test sequence* &key :from-end   [*Function*]
                                                 :start :end
                                                 :count :key

This is the destructive counterpart to substitute. The result is a sequence of the same kind as the argument *sequence* that has the same elements except that those in the subsequence delimited by :start and :end and satisfying the test (see above) have been replaced by *newitem*. This is a destructive operation. The argument *sequence* may be destroyed and used to construct the result; however, the result may or may not be eq to *sequence*.

See also nsubst, which performs destructive substitutions throughout a tree.

14.4. Searching Sequences for Items

Each of these functions searches a sequence to locate one or more elements satisfying some test.

```
find item sequence &key :from-end :test :test-not          [Function]
                         :start :end :key
find-if test sequence &key :from-end :start :end :key      [Function]
find-if-not test sequence &key :from-end :start :end :key  [Function]
```

If the *sequence* contains an element satisfying the test, then the leftmost such element is returned; otherwise nil is returned.

If :start and :end keyword arguments are given, only the specified subsequence of *sequence* is searched.

If a non-nil :from-end keyword argument is specified, then the result is the *rightmost* element satisfying the test.

```
position item sequence &key :from-end :test :test-not      [Function]
                            :start :end :key
position-if test sequence &key :from-end :start :end :key  [Function]
position-if-not test sequence &key :from-end               [Function]
                               :start :end :key
```

If the *sequence* contains an element satisfying the test, then the index within the sequence of the leftmost such element is returned as a non-negative integer; otherwise nil is returned.

If :start and :end keyword arguments are given, only the specified subsequence of *sequence* is searched. However, the index returned is relative to the entire sequence, not to the subsequence.

If a non-nil :from-end keyword argument is specified, then the result is the index of the *rightmost* element satisfying the test. (The index returned, however, is an index from the left-hand end, as usual.)

```
count item sequence &key :from-end :test :test-not         [Function]
                         :start :end :key
count-if test sequence &key :from-end :start :end :key     [Function]
count-if-not test sequence &key :from-end :start :end :key [Function]
```

The result is always a non-negative integer, the number of elements in the specified subsequence of *sequence* satisfying the test.

The :from-end argument does not affect the result returned; it is accepted purely for compatibility with other sequence functions.

```
mismatch sequence1 sequence2 &key :from-end :test :test-not [Function]
                                  :key :start1 :start2
                                  :end1 :end2
```

The specified subsequences of *sequence1* and *sequence2* are compared element-wise. If they are of equal length and match in every element, the result is nil. Otherwise, the result is a non-negative integer. This result is the index within *sequence1* of the leftmost position at which the two subsequences fail to match; or, if one subsequence is shorter than and a matching prefix of the other, the result is the index relative to *sequence1* beyond the last position tested.

If a non-nil :from-end keyword argument is given, then *one plus* the index of the *rightmost* position in which the sequences differ is returned. In effect, the (sub)sequences are aligned at their right-hand ends; then, the last elements are compared, the penultimate elements, and so on. The index returned is again an index relative to *sequence1*.

search *sequence1 sequence2* &key :from-end :test :test-not   [*Function*]
                               :key :start1 :start2 :end1 :end2

A search is conducted for a subsequence of *sequence2* that element-wise matches *sequence1*. If there is no such subsequence, the result is nil; if there is, the result is the index into *sequence2* of the leftmost element of the leftmost such matching subsequence.

If a non-nil :from-end keyword argument is given, the index of the leftmost element of the *rightmost* matching subsequence is returned.

The implementation may choose to search the sequence in any order; there is no guarantee on the number of times the test is made. For example, search with a non-nil :from-end argument might actually search a list from left to right instead of from right to left (but in either case would return the rightmost matching subsequence, of course). Therefore it is a good idea for a user-supplied predicate to be free of side effects.

14.5. Sorting and Merging

These functions may destructively modify argument sequences in order to put a sequence into sorted order or to merge two already sorted sequences.

sort *sequence predicate* &key :key   [*Function*]
stable-sort *sequence predicate* &key :key   [*Function*]

The *sequence* is destructively sorted according to an order determined by the *predicate*. The *predicate* should take two arguments, and return non-nil if and only if the first argument is strictly less than the second (in some appropriate sense). If the first argument is greater than or equal to the second (in the appropriate sense), then the *predicate* should return nil.

The sort function determines the relationship between two elements by giving keys extracted from the elements to the *predicate*. The :key argument, when applied to an element, should return the key for that element. The :key argument defaults to the identity function, thereby making the element itself be the key.

The :key function should not have any side effects. A useful example of a :key function would be a component selector function for a defstruct structure, used in sorting a sequence of structures.

```
(sort a p :key s) ≡ (sort a #'(lambda (x y) (p (s x) (s y))))
```

While the above two expressions are equivalent, the first may be more efficient in some implementations for certain types of arguments. For example, an implementation may choose to apply *s* to each item just once, putting the resulting keys into a separate table, and then sort the parallel tables, as opposed to applying *s* to an item every time just before applying the *predicate*.

If the :key and *predicate* functions always return, then the sorting operation will always terminate, producing a sequence containing the same elements as the original sequence (that is, the result is a permutation of *sequence*). This is guaranteed even if the *predicate* does not really consistently represent a total order (in which case the elements will be scrambled in some unpredictable way, but no element will be lost). If the :key function consistently returns meaningful keys, and the *predicate* does reflect some total ordering criterion on those keys, then the elements of the result sequence will be properly sorted according to that ordering.

The sorting operation performed by sort is not guaranteed *stable*. Elements considered equal by the *predicate* may or may not stay in their original order. (The *predicate* is assumed to consider two elements *x* and *y* to be equal if (funcall *predicate x y*) and (funcall *predicate y x*) are both false.) The function stable-sort guarantees stability, but may be slower than sort in some situations.

The sorting operation may be destructive in all cases. In the case of an array argument, this is accomplished by permuting the elements in place. In the case of a list, the list is destructively reordered in the same manner as for nreverse. Thus if the argument should not be destroyed, the user must sort a copy of the argument.

Should execution of the :key function or the *predicate* cause an error, the state of the list or array being sorted is undefined. However, if the error is corrected, the sort will, of course, proceed correctly.

Note that since sorting requires many comparisons, and thus many calls to the *predicate*, sorting will be much faster if the *predicate* is a compiled function rather than interpreted.

An example:

```
(setq foovector (sort foovector #'string-lessp :key #'car))
```

If `foovector` contained these items before the sort

```
("Tokens" "The Lion Sleeps Tonight")
("Carpenters" "Close to You")
("Rolling Stones" "Brown Sugar")
("Beach Boys" "I Get Around")
("Mozart" "Eine Kleine Nachtmusik" (K 525))
("Beatles" "I Want to Hold Your Hand")
```

then after the sort `foovector` would contain

```
("Beach Boys" "I Get Around")
("Beatles" "I Want to Hold Your Hand")
("Carpenters" "Close to You")
("Mozart" "Eine Kleine Nachtmusik" (K 525))
("Rolling Stones" "Brown Sugar")
("Tokens" "The Lion Sleeps Tonight")
```

`merge` *result-type sequence1 sequence2 predicate* &key :key   [*Function*]

The sequences *sequence1* and *sequence2* are destructively merged according to an order determined by the *predicate*. The result is a sequence of type *result-type*, which must be a subtype of `sequence`, as for the function `coerce`. The *predicate* should take two arguments and return non-`nil` if and only if the first argument is strictly less than the second (in some appropriate sense). If the first argument is greater than or equal to the second (in the appropriate sense), then the *predicate* should return `nil`.

The `merge` function determines the relationship between two elements by giving keys extracted from the elements to the *predicate*. The `:key` function, when applied to an element, should return the key for that element; the `:key` function defaults to the identity function, thereby making the element itself be the key.

The `:key` function should not have any side effects. A useful example of a `:key` function would be a component selector function for a `defstruct` structure, used to merge a sequence of structures.

If the `:key` and *predicate* functions always return, then the merging operation will always terminate. The result of merging two sequences x and y is a new sequence z, such that the length of z is the sum of the lengths of x and y, and z contains the all the elements of x and y. If $x1$ and $x2$ are two elements of x, and $x1$ precedes $x2$ in x, then $x1$ precedes $x2$ in z, and similarly for elements of y. In short, z is an *interleaving* of x and y.

Moreover, if x and y were correctly sorted according to the *predicate*, then z will also be correctly sorted as shown in this example.

```
(merge 'list '(1 3 4 6 7) '(2 5 8) #'<) ⇒ (1 2 3 4 5 6 7 8)
```

If *x* or *y* is not so sorted, then *z* will not be sorted, but will nevertheless be an interleaving of *x* and *y*.

The merging operation is guaranteed *stable*; if two or more elements are considered equal by the *predicate*, then the elements from *sequence1* will precede those from *sequence2* in the result. (The *predicate* is assumed to consider two elements *x* and *y* to be equal if (funcall *predicate x y*) and (funcall *predicate y x*) are both false.) For example:

```
(merge 'string "BOY" "nosy" #'char-lessp) ⇒ "BnOosYy"
```

The result can *not* be "BnoOsYy", "BnOosyY", or "BnoOsyY". The function char-lessp ignores case, and so considers the characters Y and y to be equal, for example; the stability property then guarantees that the character from the first argument (Y) must precede the one from the second argument (y).

15

Lists

A *cons*, or dotted pair, is a compound data object having two components called the *car* and *cdr*. Each component may be any LISP object. A *list* is a chain of conses linked by *cdr* fields; the chain is terminated by some atom (a non-cons object). An ordinary list is terminated by nil, the empty list (also written ()). A list whose *cdr* chain is terminated by some non-nil atom is called a *dotted list*.

The recommended predicate for testing for the end of a list is endp.

15.1. Conses

These are the basic operations on conses viewed as pairs rather than as the constituents of a list.

---

car *list*   [*Function*]

This returns the *car* of *list*, which must be a cons or (); that is, *list* must satisfy the predicate listp. By definition, the *car* of () is (). If the cons is regarded as the first cons of a list, then car returns the first element of the list. For example:

(car '(a b c)) ⇒ a

See first. The *car* of a cons may be altered by using rplaca or setf.

---

cdr *list*   [*Function*]

This returns the *cdr* of *list*, which must be a cons or (); that is, *list* must satisfy the predicate listp. By definition, the *cdr* of () is (). If the cons is regarded as the first cons of a list, then cdr returns the rest of the list, which is a list with all elements but the first of the original list. For example:

(cdr '(a b c)) ⇒ (b c)

See rest. The *cdr* of a cons may be altered by using rplacd or setf.

caar *list*	[*Function*]
cadr *list*	[*Function*]
cdar *list*	[*Function*]
cddr *list*	[*Function*]
caaar *list*	[*Function*]
caadr *list*	[*Function*]
cadar *list*	[*Function*]
caddr *list*	[*Function*]
cdaar *list*	[*Function*]
cdadr *list*	[*Function*]
cddar *list*	[*Function*]
cdddr *list*	[*Function*]
caaaar *list*	[*Function*]
caaadr *list*	[*Function*]
caadar *list*	[*Function*]
caaddr *list*	[*Function*]
cadaar *list*	[*Function*]
cadadr *list*	[*Function*]
caddar *list*	[*Function*]
cadddr *list*	[*Function*]
cdaaar *list*	[*Function*]
cdaadr *list*	[*Function*]
cdadar *list*	[*Function*]
cdaddr *list*	[*Function*]
cddaar *list*	[*Function*]
cddadr *list*	[*Function*]
cdddar *list*	[*Function*]
cddddr *list*	[*Function*]

All of the compositions of up to four car and cdr operations are defined as separate COMMON LISP functions. The names of these functions begin with c and end with r, and in between is a sequence of a and d letters corresponding to the composition performed by the function. For example:

(cddadr x) is the same as (cdr (cdr (car (cdr x))))

If the argument is regarded as a list, then cadr returns the second element of the list, caddr the third, and cadddr the fourth. If the first element of a list is a list, then caar is the first element of the sublist, cdar is the rest of that sublist, and cadar is the second element of the sublist, and so on.

As a matter of style, it is often preferable to define a function or macro to access part of a complicated data structure, rather than to use a long car/cdr string. For example, one might define a macro to extract the list of parameter variables from a lambda-expression:

```
(defmacro lambda-vars (lambda-exp) `(cadr ,lambda-exp))
```

and then use lambda-vars for this purpose instead of cadr. See also defstruct, which will automatically define new record data types and access functions for instances of them.

Any of these functions may be used to specify a *place* for setf.

---

cons *x y*   [*Function*]

cons is the primitive function to create a new *cons* whose *car* is *x* and whose *cdr* is *y*. For example:

```
(cons 'a 'b) ⇒ (a . b)
(cons 'a (cons 'b (cons 'c '()))) ⇒ (a b c)
(cons 'a '(b c d)) ⇒ (a b c d)
```

cons may be thought of as creating a *cons*, or as adding a new element to the front of a list.

---

tree-equal *x y* &key :test :test-not   [*Function*]

This is a predicate that is true if *x* and *y* are isomorphic trees with identical leaves, that is, if *x* and *y* are atoms that satisfy the test (by default eql), or if they are both conses and their *car*'s are tree-equal and their *cdr*'s are tree-equal. Thus tree-equal recursively compares conses (but not any other objects that have components). See equal, which does recursively compare certain other structured objects, such as strings.

15.2. Lists

The following functions perform various operations on lists.

---

endp *object*   [*Function*]

The predicate endp is the recommended way to test for the end of a list. It is false of conses, true of nil, and an error for all other arguments.

Implementation note: Implementations are encouraged to signal an error, especially in the interpreter, for a non-list argument. The `endp` function is defined so as to allow compiled code to perform simply an atom check or a null check if speed is more important than safety.

`list-length` *list*   [*Function*]

`list-length` returns, as an integer, the length of *list*. `list-length` differs from `length` when the *list* is circular; `length` may fail to return, whereas `list-length` will return `nil`. For example:

```
(list-length '()) ⇒ 0
(list-length '(a b c d)) ⇒ 4
(list-length '(a (b c) d)) ⇒ 3
(let ((x (list 'a b c)))
  (rplacd (last x) x)
  (list-length x)) ⇒ nil
```

`list-length` could be implemented as follows:

```
(defun list-length (x)
  (do ((n 0 (+ n 2))              ;Counter.
       (fast x (cddr fast))       ;Fast pointer: leaps by 2.
       (slow x (cdr slow)))       ;Slow pointer: leaps by 1.
      (nil)
    ;; If fast pointer hits the end, return the count.
    (when (endp fast) (return n))
    (when (endp (cdr fast)) (return (+ n 1)))
    ;; If fast pointer eventually equals slow pointer,
    ;;   then we must be stuck in a circular list.
    ;; (A deeper property is the converse: if we are
    ;;   stuck in a circular list, then eventually the
    ;;   fast pointer will equal the slow pointer.
    ;;   That fact justifies this implementation.)
    (when (and (eq fast slow) (> n 0)) (return nil))))
```

See `length`, which will return the length of any sequence.

`nth` *n list*   [*Function*]

(`nth` *n list*) returns the *n*th element of *list*, where the *car* of the list is the "zeroth" element. The argument *n* must be a non-negative integer. If the length of the list is not greater than *n*, then the result is ( ), that is, nil. (This is consistent with the idea that the *car* and *cdr* of ( ) are each ( ).) For example:

```
(nth 0 '(foo bar gack)) ⇒ foo
(nth 1 '(foo bar gack)) ⇒ bar
(nth 3 '(foo bar gack)) ⇒ ()
```

Compatibility note: This is not the same as the INTERLISP function called nth, which is similar to but not exactly the same as the COMMON LISP function nthcdr. This definition of nth is compatible with ZETALISP and NIL. Also, some people have used macros and functions called nth of their own in their old MACLISP programs, which may not work the same way.

---

nth may be used to specify a *place* to setf; when nth is used in this way, the argument *n* must be less than the length of the *list*.

Note that the arguments to nth are reversed from the order used by most other sequence selector functions such as elt.

first *list*	[*Function*]
second *list*	[*Function*]
third *list*	[*Function*]
fourth *list*	[*Function*]
fifth *list*	[*Function*]
sixth *list*	[*Function*]
seventh *list*	[*Function*]
eighth *list*	[*Function*]
ninth *list*	[*Function*]
tenth *list*	[*Function*]

These functions are sometimes convenient for accessing particular elements of a list. first is the same as car, second is the same as cadr, third is the same as caddr, and so on. Note that the ordinal numbering used here is one-origin, as opposed to the zero-origin numbering used by nth:

```
(fifth x) ≡ (nth 4 x)
```

setf may be used with each of these functions to store into the indicated position of a list.

rest *list*	[*Function*]

rest means the same as cdr but mnemonically complements first. setf may be used with rest to replace the *cdr* of a list with a new value.

nthcdr *n list*   [*Function*]

(nthcdr *n list*) performs the cdr operation *n* times on *list*, and returns the result. For example:

```
(nthcdr 0 '(a b c)) ⇒ (a b c)
(nthcdr 2 '(a b c)) ⇒ (c)
(nthcdr 4 '(a b c)) ⇒ ()
```

In other words, it returns the *n*th *cdr* of the list.

Compatibility note: This is similar to the INTERLISP function nth, except that the INTERLISP function is one-based instead of zero-based.

```
(car (nthcdr n x)) ≡ (nth n x)
```

last *list*   [*Function*]

last returns the last cons (*not* the last element!) of *list*. If *list* is (), it returns (). For example:

```
(setq x '(a b c d))
(last x) ⇒ (d)
(rplacd (last x) '(e f))
x ⇒ '(a b c d e f)
(last '(a b c . d)) ⇒ (c . d)
```

list &rest *args*   [*Function*]

list constructs and returns a list of its arguments. For example:

```
(list 3 4 'a (car '(b . c)) (+ 6 -2)) ⇒ (3 4 a b 4)
```

list* *arg* &rest *others*   [*Function*]

list* is like list except that the last *cons* of the constructed list is "dotted." The last argument to list* is used as the *cdr* of the last cons constructed; this need not be an atom. If it is not an atom, then the effect is to add several new elements to the front of a list. For example:

```
(list* 'a 'b 'c 'd) ⇒ (a b c . d)
```

This is like

```
(cons 'a (cons 'b (cons 'c 'd)))
```

Also:

```
(list* 'a 'b 'c '(d e f)) ⇒ (a b c d e f)
(list* x) ≡ x
```

make-list *size* &key :initial-element   [*Function*]

This creates and returns a list containing *size* elements, each of which is initialized to the :initial-element argument (which defaults to nil). *size* should be a non-negative integer. For example:

```
(make-list 5) ⇒ (nil nil nil nil nil)
(make-list 3 :initial-element 'rah) ⇒ (rah rah rah)
```

append &rest *lists*   [*Function*]

The arguments to append are lists. The result is a list that is the concatenation of the arguments. The arguments are not destroyed. For example:

```
(append '(a b c) '(d e f) '() '(g)) ⇒ (a b c d e f g)
```

Note that append copies the top-level list structure of each of its arguments *except* the last. The function concatenate can perform a similar operation, but always copies all its arguments. See also nconc, which is like append but destroys all arguments but the last.

The last argument actually need not be a list but may be any LISP object, which becomes the tail end of the constructed list. For example, (append '(a b c) 'd) ⇒ (a b c . d).

(append *x* '()) is an idiom once frequently used to copy the list *x*, but the copy-list function is more appropriate to this task.

copy-list *list*   [*Function*]

This returns a list that is equal to *list*, but not eq. Only the top level of list structure is copied; that is, copy-list copies in the *cdr* direction but not in the *car* direction. If the list is "dotted," that is, (cdr (last *list*)) is a non-nil atom, this will be true of the returned list also. See also copy-seq and copy-tree.

copy-alist *list*   [*Function*]

copy-alist is for copying association lists. The top level of list structure of *list* is copied, just as for copy-list. In addition, each element of *list* that is a cons is replaced in the copy by a new cons with the same *car* and *cdr*.

copy-tree *object* [*Function*]

copy-tree is for copying trees of conses. The argument *object* may be any LISP object. If it is not a cons, it is returned; otherwise the result is a new cons of the results of calling copy-tree on the *car* and *cdr* of the argument. In other words, all conses in the tree are copied recursively, stopping only when non-conses are encountered. Circularities and the sharing of substructure are *not* preserved.

Compatibility note: This function is called copy in INTERLISP.

---

revappend *x y* [*Function*]

(revappend *x y*) is exactly the same as (append (reverse *x*) *y*) except that it is potentially more efficient. Both *x* and *y* should be lists. The argument *x* is copied, not destroyed. Compare this with nreconc, which destroys its first argument.

nconc &rest *lists* [*Function*]

nconc takes lists as arguments. It returns a list that is the arguments concatenated together. The arguments are changed, rather than copied. (Compare this with append, which copies arguments rather than destroying them.) For example:

```
(setq x '(a b c))
(setq y '(d e f))
(nconc x y) ⇒ (a b c d e f)
x ⇒ (a b c d e f)
```

Note, in the example, that the value of x is now different, since its last cons has been rplacd'd to the value of y. If one were then to evaluate (nconc x y) again, it would yield a piece of "circular" list structure, whose printed representation would be (a b c d e f d e f d e f ...), repeating forever; if the *print-circle* switch were non-nil, it would be printed as (a b c . #1=(d e f . #1#)).

nreconc *x y* [*Function*]

(nreconc *x y*) is exactly the same as (nconc (nreverse *x*) *y*) except that it is potentially more efficient. Both *x* and *y* should be lists. The argument *x* is destroyed. Compare this with revappend.

push *item place* [*Macro*]

The form *place* should be the name of a generalized variable containing a list; *item* may refer to any LISP object. The *item* is consed onto the front of the list, and the augmented list is stored back into *place* and returned. The form *place* may be any form acceptable as a generalized variable to setf. If the list held in *place* is viewed as a push-down stack, then push pushes an element onto the top of the stack. For example:

```
(setq x '(a (b c) d))
(push 5 (cadr x)) ⇒ (5 b c) and now x ⇒ (a (5 b c) d)
```

The effect of (push *item place*) is roughly equivalent to

```
(setf place (cons item place))
```

except that the latter would evaluate any subforms of *place* twice, while push takes care to evaluate them only once. Moreover, for certain *place* forms push may be significantly more efficient than the setf version.

---

pushnew *item place* &key :test :test-not :key   [*Macro*]

The form *place* should be the name of a generalized variable containing a list; *item* may refer to any LISP object. If the *item* is not already a member of the list (as determined by comparisons using the :test predicate, which defaults to eql), then the *item* is consed onto the front of the list, and the augmented list is stored back into *place* and returned; otherwise the unaugmented list is returned. The form *place* may be any form acceptable as a generalized variable to setf. If the list held in *place* is viewed as a set, then pushnew adjoins an element to the set; see adjoin.

The keyword arguments to pushnew follow the conventions for the generic sequence functions. See chapter 14. In effect, these keywords are simply passed on to the adjoin function.

pushnew returns the new contents of the *place*. For example:

```
(setq x '(a (b c) d))
(pushnew 5 (cadr x)) ⇒ (5 b c)    and now x ⇒ (a (5 b c) d)
(pushnew 'b (cadr x)) ⇒ (5 b c)   and x is unchanged
```

The effect of

```
(pushnew item place :test p)
```

is roughly equivalent to

```
(setf place (adjoin item place :test p))
```

except that the latter would evaluate any subforms of *place* twice, while pushnew takes care to evaluate them only once. Moreover, for certain *place* forms pushnew may be significantly more efficient than the setf version.

pop *place*   [*Macro*]

The form *place* should be the name of a generalized variable containing a list. The result of pop is the car of the contents of *place*, and as a side effect the cdr of the contents is stored back into *place*. The form *place* may be any form acceptable as a generalized variable to setf. If the list held in *place* is viewed as a push-down stack, then pop pops an element from the top of the stack and returns it. For example:

```
(setq stack '(a b c))
(pop stack) ⇒ a and now stack ⇒ (b c)
```

The effect of (pop *place*) is roughly equivalent to

```
(prog1 (car place) (setf place (cdr place)))
```

except that the latter would evaluate any subforms of *place* three times, while pop takes care to evaluate them only once. Moreover, for certain *place* forms pop may be significantly more efficient than the setf version.

butlast *list* &optional *n*   [*Function*]

This creates and returns a list with the same elements as *list*, excepting the last *n* elements. *n* defaults to 1. The argument is not destroyed. If the *list* has fewer than *n* elements, then () is returned. For example:

```
(butlast '(a b c d)) ⇒ (a b c)
(butlast '((a b) (c d))) ⇒ ((a b))
(butlast '(a)) ⇒ ()
(butlast nil) ⇒ ()
```

The name is from the phrase "all elements but the last."

nbutlast *list* &optional *n*   [*Function*]

This is the destructive version of butlast; it changes the *cdr* of the cons $n + 1$ from the end of the *list* to nil. *n* defaults to 1. If the *list* has fewer than *n* elements, then nbutlast returns (), and the argument is not modified. (Therefore one normally writes (setq a (nbutlast a)) rather than simply (nbutlast a).) For example:

```
(setq foo '(a b c d))
(nbutlast foo) ⇒ (a b c)
foo ⇒ (a b c)
(nbutlast '(a)) ⇒ ()
(nbutlast 'nil) ⇒ ()
```

`ldiff` *list sublist*   [*Function*]

list should be a list, and *sublist* should be a sublist of *list*, that is, one of the conses that make up *list*. `ldiff` (meaning "list difference") will return a new (freshly consed) list, whose elements are those elements of *list* that appear before *sublist*. If *sublist* is not a tail of *list* (and in particular if *sublist* is `nil`), then a copy of the entire *list* is returned. The argument *list* is not destroyed. For example:

```
(setq x '(a b c d e))
(setq y (cdddr x)) ⇒ (d e)
(ldiff x y) ⇒ (a b c)
```
but
```
(ldiff '(a b c d) '(c d)) ⇒ (a b c d)
```
since the sublist was not `eq` to any part of the list.

15.3. Alteration of List Structure

The functions `rplaca` and `rplacd` may be used to make alterations in already existing list structure, that is, to change the *car* or *cdr* of an existing cons. One may also use `setf` in conjunction with `car` and `cdr`.

The structure is not copied but is destructively altered; hence caution should be exercised when using these functions, as strange side effects can occur if portions of list structure become shared. The `nconc`, `nreverse`, `nreconc`, and `nbutlast` functions, already described, have the same property, as do certain of the generic sequence functions such as `delete`. However, they are normally not used for this side effect; rather, the list-structure modification is purely for efficiency, and compatible non-modifying functions are provided.

`rplaca` *x y*   [*Function*]

(`rplaca` *x y*) changes the *car* of *x* to *y* and returns (the modified) *x*. *x* must be a cons, but *y* may be any LISP object. For example:

```
(setq g '(a b c))
(rplaca (cdr g) 'd) ⇒ (d c)
Now g ⇒ (a d c)
```


`rplacd` *x y*   [*Function*]

(`rplacd` *x y*) changes the *cdr* of *x* to *y* and returns (the modified) *x*. *x* must be a cons, but *y* may be any LISP object. For example:

```
(setq x '(a b c))
(rplacd x 'd) ⇒ (a . d)
Now x ⇒ (a . d)
```

15.4. Substitution of Expressions

A number of functions are provided for performing substitutions within a tree. All take a tree and a description of old subexpressions to be replaced by new ones. They come in non-destructive and destructive varieties and specify substitution either by two arguments or by an association list.

The naming conventions for these functions and for their keyword arguments generally follow the conventions for the generic sequence functions. See chapter 14.

subst *new old tree* &key :test :test-not :key	[*Function*]
subst-if *new test tree* &key :key	[*Function*]
subst-if-not *new test tree* &key :key	[*Function*]

(subst *new old tree*) makes a copy of *tree*, substituting *new* for every subtree or leaf of *tree* (whether the subtree or leaf is a *car* or a *cdr* of its parent) such that *old* and the subtree or leaf satisfy the test. It returns the modified copy of *tree*. The original *tree* is unchanged, but the result tree may share with parts of the argument *tree*.

Compatibility note: In MacLisp, subst is guaranteed *not* to share with the *tree* argument, and the idiom (subst nil nil x) was used to copy a tree x. In Common Lisp, the function copy-tree should be used to copy a tree, as the subst idiom will not work.

For example:

```
(subst 'tempest 'hurricane
       '(shakespeare wrote (the hurricane)))
   ⇒ (shakespeare wrote (the tempest))
(subst 'foo 'nil '(shakespeare wrote (twelfth night)))
   ⇒ (shakespeare wrote (twelfth night . foo) . foo)
(subst '(a . cons) '(old . pair)
       '((old . spice) ((old . shoes) old . pair) (old . pair))
       :test #'equal)
   ⇒ ((old . spice) ((old . shoes) a . cons) (a . cons))
```

This function is not destructive; that is, it does not change the *car* or *cdr* of any already existing list structure. One possible definition of subst:

```
(defun subst (old new tree &rest x &key test test-not key)
  (cond ((satisfies-the-test old tree :test test
                                     :test-not test-not :key key)
         new)
        ((atom tree) tree)
        (t (let ((a (apply #'subst old new (car tree) x))
                 (d (apply #'subst old new (cdr tree) x)))
             (if (and (eql a (car tree))
                      (eql d (cdr tree)))
                 tree
                 (cons a d))))))
```

See also substitute, which substitutes for top-level elements of a sequence.

nsubst *new old tree* &key :test :test-not :key   [*Function*]
nsubst-if *new test tree* &key :key   [*Function*]
nsubst-if-not *new test tree* &key :key   [*Function*]

nsubst is a destructive version of subst. The list structure of *tree* is altered by destructively replacing with *new* each leaf or subtree of the *tree* such that *old* and the leaf or subtree satisfy the test.

sublis *alist tree* &key :test :test-not :key   [*Function*]

sublis makes substitutions for objects in a tree (a structure of conses). The first argument to sublis is an association list. The second argument is the tree in which substitutions are to be made, as for subst. sublis looks at all subtrees and leaves of the tree; if a subtree or leaf appears as a key in the association list (that is, the key and the subtree or leaf satisfy the test), it is replaced by the object it is associated with. This operation is non-destructive. In effect, sublis can perform several subst operations simultaneously. For example:

```
(sublis '((x . 100) (z . zprime))
        '(plus x (minus g z x p) 4 . x))
   => (plus 100 (minus g zprime 100 p) 4 . 100)

(sublis '(((+ x y) . (- x y)) ((- x y) . (+ x y)))
        '(* (/ (+ x y) (+ x p)) (- x y))
        :test #'equal)
   => (* (/ (- x y) (+ x p)) (+ x y))
```

nsublis *alist tree* &key :test :test-not :key   [*Function*]

nsublis is like sublis but destructively modifies the relevant parts of the *tree*.

15.5. Using Lists as Sets

COMMON LISP includes functions that allow a list of items to be treated as a *set*. There are functions to add, remove, and search for items in a list, based on various criteria. There are also set union, intersection, and difference functions.

The naming conventions for these functions and for their keyword arguments generally follow the conventions for the generic sequence functions. See chapter 14.

member *item list* &key :test :test-not :key   [*Function*]
member-if *predicate list* &key :key   [*Function*]
member-if-not *predicate list* &key :key   [*Function*]

The *list* is searched for an element that satisfies the test. If none is found, nil is returned; otherwise, the tail of *list* beginning with the first element that satisfied the test is returned. The *list* is searched on the top level only. These functions are suitable for use as predicates. For example:

```
(member 'snerd '(a b c d)) ⇒ nil
(member-if #'numberp '(a #\Space 5/3 foo)) ⇒ (5/3 foo)
(member 'a '(g (a y) c a d e a f)) ⇒ (a d e a f)
```

Note, in the last example, that the value returned by member is eq to the portion of the list beginning with a. Thus rplaca on the result of member may be used to alter the found list element, if a check is first made that member did not return nil.

See also find and position.

Compatibility note: In MACLISP, the member function uses an equal comparison rather than eql, which is the default test for member in COMMON LISP. Where in MACLISP one would write (member x y), in COMMON LISP one must write (member x y :test #'equal) to get a completely identical effect. Similarly, one can get the precise effect, and no more, of the MACLISP (memq x y) by writing in COMMON LISP (member x y :test #'eq).

---

tailp *sublist list*   [*Function*]

This predicate is true if *sublist* is a sublist of *list* (i.e., one of the conses that makes up *list*); otherwise it is false. Another way to look at this is that tailp is true if (nthcdr *n* *list*) is *sublist*, for some value of *n*. See ldiff.

`adjoin` *item list* &key :test :test-not :key   [*Function*]

`adjoin` is used to add an element to a set, provided that it is not already a member. The equality test defaults to `eql`.

(adjoin *item list*) ≡ (if (member *item list*) *list* (cons *item list*))

In general, the test may be any predicate; the *item* is added to the list only if there is no element of the list that "satisfies the test."

   `adjoin` deviates from the usual rules described in chapter 14 for the treatment of arguments named *item* and *key*. If a *key* function is specified, it is applied to *item* as well as to each element of the list. The rationale is that if the *item* is not yet in the list, it soon will be, and so the test is more properly viewed as being between two elements rather than between a separate *item* and an element.

(adjoin *item list* :key *fn*)
   ≡ (if (member (*fn item*) *list* :key *fn*) *list* (cons *item list*))

See `pushnew`.

`union` *list1 list2* &key :test :test-not :key   [*Function*]
`nunion` *list1 list2* &key :test :test-not :key   [*Function*]

`union` takes two lists and returns a new list containing everything that is an element of either of the *lists*. If there is a duplication between two lists, only one of the duplicate instances will be in the result. If either of the arguments has duplicate entries within it, the redundant entries may or may not appear in the result. For example:

(union '(a b c) '(f a d))
   ⇒ (a b c f d) or (b c f a d) or (d f a b c) or ...

(union '((x 5) (y 6)) '((z 2) (x 4)) :key #'car)
   ⇒ ((x 5) (y 6) (z 2)) or ((x 4) (y 6) (z 2)) or ...

   There is no guarantee that the order of elements in the result will reflect the ordering of the arguments in any particular way. The implementation is therefore free to use any of a variety of strategies. The result list may share cells with, or be `eq` to, either of the arguments if appropriate.

   In general, the test may be any predicate, and the union operation may be described as follows. For all possible ordered pairs consisting of one element from *list1* and one element from *list2*, the test is used to determine whether they "match." For every matching pair, at least one of the two elements of the pair will be in the result. Moreover, any element from either list that matches no element of the other will appear in the result. All this is very general, but probably not particularly useful unless the test is an equivalence relation.

The :test-not argument can be useful when the test function is the logical negation of an equivalence test. A good example of this is the function mismatch, which is logically inverted so that possibly useful information can be returned if the arguments do not match. This additional "useful information" is discarded in the following example; mismatch is used purely as a predicate.

```
(union '(#(a b) #(5 0 6) #(f 3))
       '(#(5 0 6) (a b) #(g h))
       :test-not
       #'mismatch)
  ⇒ (#(a b) #(5 0 6) #(f 3) #(g h))   ;One possible result
  ⇒ ((a b) #(f 3) #(5 0 6) #(g h))    ;Another possible result
```

Using :test-not #'mismatch differs from using :test #'equalp, for example, because mismatch will determine that #(a b) and (a b) are the same, while equalp would regard them as not the same.

nunion is the destructive version of union. It performs the same operation but may destroy the argument lists, using their cells to construct the result.

intersection *list1* *list2* &key :test :test-not :key	[*Function*]
nintersection *list1* *list2* &key :test :test-not :key	[*Function*]

intersection takes two lists and returns a new list containing everything that is an element of both argument lists. If either list has duplicate entries, the redundant entries may or may not appear in the result. For example:

```
(intersection '(a b c) '(f a d)) ⇒ (a)
```

There is no guarantee that the order of elements in the result will reflect the ordering of the arguments in any particular way. The implementation is therefore free to use any of a variety of strategies. The result list may share cells with, or be eq to, either of the arguments if appropriate.

In general, the test may be any predicate, and the intersection operation may be described as follows. For all possible ordered pairs consisting of one element from *list1* and one element from *list2*, the test is used to determine whether they "match." For every matching pair, exactly one of the two elements of the pair will be put in the result. No element from either list appears in the result that does not match an element from the other list. All this is very general, but probably not particularly useful unless the test is an equivalence relation.

`nintersection` is the destructive version of `intersection`. It performs the same operation, but may destroy *list1* using its cells to construct the result. (The argument *list2* is *not* destroyed.)

`set-difference` *list1* *list2* &key :test :test-not :key   [*Function*]
`nset-difference` *list1* *list2* &key :test :test-not :key   [*Function*]

`set-difference` returns a list of elements of *list1* that do not appear in *list2*. This operation is not destructive.

There is no guarantee that the order of elements in the result will reflect the ordering of the arguments in any particular way. The implementation is therefore free to use any of a variety of strategies. The result list may share cells with, or be `eq` to, either of the arguments if appropriate.

In general, the test may be any predicate, and the set difference operation may be described as follows. For all possible ordered pairs consisting of one element from *list1* and one element from *list2*, the test is used to determine whether they "match." An element of *list1* appears in the result if and only if it does not match any element of *list2*. This is very general and permits interesting applications. For example, one can remove from a list of strings all those strings containing one of a given list of characters:

```
;; Remove all flavor names that contain "c" or "w".
(set-difference '("strawberry" "chocolate" "banana"
                  "lemon" "pistachio" "rhubarb")
                '(#\c #\w)
                :test
                #'(lambda (s c) (find c s)))
⇒ ("banana" "rhubarb" "lemon")  ;One possible ordering.
```

`nset-difference` is the destructive version of `set-difference`. This operation may destroy *list1*.

Compatibility note: An approximately equivalent INTERLISP function is `ldifference`.

`set-exclusive-or` *list1* *list2* &key :test :test-not :key   [*Function*]
`nset-exclusive-or` *list1* *list2* &key :test :test-not :key   [*Function*]

`set-exclusive-or` returns a list of elements that appear in exactly one of *list1* and *list2*. This operation is not destructive.

There is no guarantee that the order of elements in the result will reflect the ordering of the arguments in any particular way. The implementation is therefore free to use any of a variety of strategies. The result list may share cells with, or be `eq` to, either of the arguments if appropriate.

In general, the test may be any predicate, and the set-exclusive-or operation may be described as follows. For all possible ordered pairs consisting of one element from *list1* and one element from *list2*, the test is used to determine whether they "match." The result contains precisely those elements of *list1* and *list2* that appear in no matching pair.

`nset-exclusive-or` is the destructive version of `set-exclusive-or`. Both lists may be destroyed in producing the result.

`subsetp` *list1* *list2* `&key` `:test` `:test-not` `:key`   [*Function*]

`subsetp` is a predicate that is true if every element of *list1* appears in ("matches" some element of) *list2*, and false otherwise.

15.6. Association Lists

An *association list*, or *a-list*, is a data structure used very frequently in LISP. An a-list is a list of pairs (conses); each pair is an association. The *car* of a pair is called the *key*, and the *cdr* is called the *datum*.

An advantage of the a-list representation is that an a-list can be incrementally augmented simply by adding new entries to the front. Moreover, because the searching function `assoc` searches the a-list in order, new entries can "shadow" old entries. If an a-list is viewed as a mapping from keys to data, then the mapping can be not only augmented but also altered in a non-destructive manner by adding new entries to the front of the a-list.

Sometimes an a-list represents a bijective mapping, and it is desirable to retrieve a key given a datum. For this purpose, the "reverse" searching function `rassoc` is provided. Other variants of a-list searches can be constructed using the function `find` or `member`.

It is permissible to let `nil` be an element of an a-list in place of a pair. Such an element is not considered to be a pair but is simply passed over when the a-list is searched by `assoc`.

`acons` *key datum a-list*   [*Function*]

`acons` constructs a new association list by adding the pair *(key . datum)* to the old *a-list*.

```
(acons x y a) ≡ (cons (cons x y) a)
```

pairlis *keys data* &optional *a-list*   [*Function*]

`pairlis` takes two lists and makes an association list that associates elements of the first list to corresponding elements of the second list. It is an error if the two lists *keys* and *data* are not of the same length. If the optional argument *a-list* is provided, then the new pairs are added to the front of it.

The new pairs may appear in the resulting a-list in any order; in particular, either forward or backward order is permitted. Therefore the result of the call

```
(pairlis '(one two) '(1 2) '((three . 3) (four . 19)))
```

might be

```
((one . 1) (two . 2) (three . 3) (four . 19))
```

but could equally well be

```
((two . 2) (one . 1) (three . 3) (four . 19))
```

assoc *item a-list* &key :test :test-not :key   [*Function*]
assoc-if *predicate a-list*   [*Function*]
assoc-if-not *predicate a-list*   [*Function*]

Each of these searches the association list *a-list*. The value is the first pair in the a-list such that the *car* of the pair satisfies the test, or `nil` if there is no such pair in the a-list. For example:

```
(assoc 'r '((a . b) (c . d) (r . x) (s . y) (r . z)))
       ⇒ (r . x)
(assoc 'goo '((foo . bar) (zoo . goo))) ⇒ nil
(assoc '2 '((1 a b c) (2 b c d) (-7 x y z))) ⇒ (2 b c d)
```

It is possible to `rplacd` the result of `assoc` *provided* that it is not `nil`, in order to "update" the "table" that was `assoc`'s second argument. (However, it is often better to update an a-list by adding new pairs to the front, rather than altering old pairs.) For example:

```
(setq values '((x . 100) (y . 200) (z . 50)))
(assoc 'y values) ⇒ (y . 200)
(rplacd (assoc 'y values) 201)
(assoc 'y values) ⇒ (y . 201) now
```

A typical trick is to say `(cdr (assoc x y))`. Because the *cdr* of `nil` is guaranteed to be `nil`, this yields `nil` if no pair is found *or* if a pair is found whose *cdr* is `nil`. This is useful if `nil` serves its usual role as a "default value."

The two expressions

(assoc *item* *list* :test *fn*)

and

(find *item* *list* :test *fn* :key #'car)

are equivalent in meaning with one important exception: if nil appears in the a-list in place of a pair, and the *item* being searched for is nil, find will blithely compute the *car* of the nil in the a-list, find that it is equal to the *item*, and return nil, whereas assoc will ignore the nil in the a-list and continue to search for an actual pair (cons) whose *car* is nil. See find and position.

Compatibility note: In MACLISP, the assoc function uses an equal comparison rather than eql, which is the default test for assoc in COMMON LISP. Where in MACLISP one would write (assoc x y), in COMMON LISP one must write (assoc x y :test #'equal) to get the completely identical effect. Similarly, one can get the precise effect, and no more, of the MACLISP (assq x y) by writing in COMMON LISP (assoc x y :test #'eq).

In INTERLISP, assoc uses an eq test, and sassoc uses an INTERLISP equal test.

---

rassoc *item* *a-list* &key :test :test-not :key   [*Function*]
rassoc-if *predicate* *a-list*   [*Function*]
rassoc-if-not *predicate* *a-list*   [*Function*]

rassoc is the reverse form of assoc; it searches for a pair whose *cdr* satisfies the test, rather than the *car*. If the *a-list* is considered to be a mapping, then rassoc treats the *a-list* as representing the inverse mapping. For example:

(rassoc 'a '((a . b) (b . c) (c . a) (z . a))) ⇒ (c . a)

The expressions

(rassoc *item* *list* :test *fn*)

and·

(find *item* *list* :test *fn* :key #'cdr)

are equivalent in meaning, except when the *item* is nil and nil appears in place of a pair in the a-list. See the discussion of the function assoc.

16

Hash Tables

A hash table is a LISP object that can efficiently map a given LISP object to another LISP object. Each hash table has a set of *entries*, each of which associates a particular *key* with a particular *value*. The basic functions that deal with hash tables can create entries, delete entries, and find the value that is associated with a given key. Finding the value is very fast, even if there are many entries, because hashing is used; this is an important advantage of hash tables over property lists.

A given hash table can only associate one *value* with a given *key*; if you try to add a second *value*, it will replace the first. Also, adding a value to a hash table is a destructive operation; the hash table is modified. By contrast, association lists can be augmented non-destructively.

Hash tables come in three kinds, the difference being whether the keys are compared with eq, eql, or equal. In other words, there are hash tables that hash on Lisp *objects* (using eq or eql) and there are hash tables that hash on *tree structure* (using equal).

Hash tables are created with the function make-hash-table, which takes various options, including which kind of hash table to make (the default being the eql kind). To look up a key and find the associated value, use gethash. New entries are added to hash tables using setf with gethash. To remove an entry, use remhash. Here is a simple example.

```
(setq a (make-hash-table))
(setf (gethash 'color a) 'brown)
(setf (gethash 'name a) 'fred)
(gethash 'color a) ⇒ brown
(gethash 'name a) ⇒ fred
(gethash 'pointy a) ⇒ nil
```

In this example, the symbols color and name are being used as keys, and the symbols brown and fred are being used as the associated values. The hash table has two items in it, one of which associates from `color` to `brown`, and the other of which associates from `name` to `fred`.

Keys do not have to be symbols; they can be any LISP object. Likewise, values can be any LISP object.

When a hash table is first created, it has a *size*, which is the maximum number of entries it can hold. Usually the actual capacity of the table is somewhat less, since the hashing is not perfectly collision-free. With the maximum possible bad luck, the capacity could be very much less, but this rarely happens. If so many entries are added that the capacity is exceeded, the hash table will automatically grow, and the entries will be *rehashed* (new hash values will be recomputed, and everything will be rearranged so that the fast hash lookup still works). This is transparent to the caller; it all happens automatically.

Compatibility note: This hash table facility is compatible with ZETALISP. It is similar to the hasharray facility of INTERLISP, and some of the function names are the same. However, it is *not* compatible with INTERLISP. The exact details and the order of arguments are designed to be consistent with the rest of MACLISP rather than with INTERLISP. For instance, the order of arguments to `maphash` is different, there is no "system hash table," and there is not the INTERLISP restriction that keys and values may not be `nil`.

16.1. Hash Table Functions

This section documents the functions for hash tables, which use *objects* as keys and associate other objects with them.

```
make-hash-table &key :test :size
                     :rehash-size :rehash-threshold          [Function]
```

This function creates and returns a new hash table. The `:test` argument determines how keys are compared; it must be one of the three values `#'eq`, `#'eql`, or `#'equal`, or one of the three symbols `eq`, `eql`, or `equal`. If no test is specified, `eql` is assumed.

The `:size` argument sets the initial size of the hash table, in entries. (The actual size may be rounded up from the size you specify to the next "good" size, for example to make it a prime number.) You won't necessarily be able to store precisely this many entries into the table before it overflows and becomes bigger, but this argument does serve as a hint to the implementation of approximately how many entries you intend to store.

The `:rehash-size` argument specifies how much to increase the size of the hash table when it becomes full. This can be an integer greater than zero, which is the number of entries to add, or it can be a floating-point number greater than one, which is the ratio of the new size to the old size. The default value for this argument is implementation-dependent.

The `:rehash-threshold` argument specifies how full the hash table can get before it must grow. This can be an integer greater than zero and less than the `:rehash-size` (in which case it will be scaled whenever the table is grown), or it can be a floating-point number between zero and one. The default value for this argument is implementation-dependent.

An example of the use of `make-hash-table`:

```
(make-hash-table :rehash-size 1.5
                 :size (* number-of-widgets 43))
```

`hash-table-p` *object* [*Function*]

`hash-table-p` is true if its argument is a hash table, and otherwise is false.

```
(hash-table-p x) ≡ (typep x 'hash-table)
```

`gethash` *key hash-table* &optional *default* [*Function*]

`gethash` finds the entry in *hash-table* whose key is *key* and returns the associated value. If there is no such entry, `gethash` returns *default*, which is `nil` if not specified.

`gethash` actually returns two values, the second being a predicate value that is true if an entry was found, and false if no entry was found.

`setf` may be used with `gethash` to make new entries in a hash table. If an entry with the specified *key* already exists, it is removed before the new entry is added. The *default* argument may be specified to `gethash` in this context; it is ignored by `setf`, but may be useful in such macros as `incf` that are related to `setf`:

```
(incf (gethash a-key table 0))
```

means the approximately the same as

```
(setf (gethash a-key table 0) (+ (gethash a-key table 0) 1))
```

which in turn would be treated as simply

```
(setf (gethash a-key table) (+ (gethash a-key table 0) 1))
```

`remhash` *key hash-table* [*Function*]

`remhash` removes any entry for *key* in *hash-table*. This is a predicate that is true if there was an entry or false if there was not.

maphash *function hash-table* [*Function*]

For each entry in *hash-table*, maphash calls *function* on two arguments: the key of
the entry and the value of the entry. If entries are added to or deleted from the
hash table while a maphash is in progress, the results are unpredictable, with one
exception: if the *function* calls remhash to remove the entry currently being processed
by the *function*, or performs a setf of gethash on that entry to change the associated
value, then those operations will have the intended effect. For example:

```
;; Alter every entry in MY-HASH-TABLE, replacing the value with
;; its square root. Entries with negative values are removed.
(maphash #'(lambda (key val)
             (if (minusp val)
                 (remhash key my-hash-table)
                 (setf (gethash key my-hash-table)
                       (sqrt val)))))
          my-hash-table)
```

maphash returns nil.

clrhash *hash-table* [*Function*]

This removes all the entries from *hash-table* and returns the hash table itself.

hash-table-count *hash-table* [*Function*]

This returns the number of entries in the *hash-table*. When a hash table is first
created or has been cleared, the number of entries is zero.

16.2. Primitive Hash Function

The function sxhash is a convenient tool for the user who needs to create more
complicated hashed data structures than are provided by hash-table objects.

sxhash *object* [*Function*]

sxhash computes a hash code for an object and returns the hash code as a non-negative
fixnum. A property of sxhash is that (equal *x y*) implies (= (sxhash *x*)
(sxhash *y*)).

The manner in which the hash code is computed is implementation-dependent,
but is independent of the particular "incarnation" or "core image." Hash values
produced by sxhash may be written out to files, for example, and meaningfully
read in again into an instance of the same implementation.

17

Arrays

An array is an object with components arranged according to a rectilinear coordinate system. In principle, an array in COMMON LISP may have any number of dimensions, including zero. (A zero-dimensional array has exactly one element.) In practice, an implementation may limit the number of dimensions supported, but every COMMON LISP implementation must support arrays of up to seven dimensions. Each dimension is a non-negative integer; if any dimension of an array is zero, the array has no elements.

An array may be a *general array*, meaning each element may be any LISP object, or it may be a *specialized array*, meaning that each element must be of a given restricted type.

One-dimensional arrays are called vectors. General vectors may contain any LISP object. Vectors whose elements are restricted to type `string-char` are called *strings*. Vectors whose elements are restricted to type `bit` are called *bit-vectors*.

17.1. Array Creation

Do not be daunted by the many options of the function `make-array`! All that is required to construct an array is a list of the dimensions; most of the options are for relatively esoteric applications.

```
make-array dimensions &key :element-type :initial-element    [Function]
                           :initial-contents :adjustable
                           :fill-pointer :displaced-to
                           :displaced-index-offset
```

This is the primitive function for making arrays. The *dimensions* argument should be a list of non-negative integers that are to be the dimensions of the array; the length of the list will be the dimensionality of the array. Each dimension must be smaller than `array-dimension-limit`, and the product of all the dimensions must be smaller than `array-total-size-limit`. Note that if *dimensions* is `nil` then a zero-dimensional array is created. For convenience when making a one-dimensional array, the single dimension may be provided as an integer rather than a list of one integer.

An implementation of COMMON LISP may impose a limit on the rank of an array, but this limit may not be smaller than 7. Therefore, any COMMON LISP program may assume the use of arrays of rank 7 or less. The implementation-dependent limit on array rank is reflected in `array-rank-limit`.

The keyword arguments for `make-array` are as follows:

`:element-type`

This argument should be the name of the type of the elements of the array; an array is constructed of the most specialized type that can nevertheless accommodate elements of the given type. The type t specifies a general array, one whose elements may be any LISP object; this is the default type.

`:initial-element`

This argument may be used to initialize each element of the array. The value must be of the type specified by the `:element-type` argument. If the `:initial-element` option is omitted, the initial values of the array elements are undefined (unless the `:initial-contents` or `:displaced-to` option is used). The `:initial- element` option may not be used with the `:initial-contents` or `:displaced-to` option.

`:initial-contents`

This argument may be used to initialize the contents of the array. The value is a nested structure of sequences. If the array is zero-dimensional, then the value specifies the single element. Otherwise, the value must be a sequence whose length is equal to the first dimension; each element must be a nested structure for an array whose dimensions are the remaining dimensions, and so on. For example:

```
(make-array '(4 2 3) :initial-contents
            '(((a b c) (1 2 3))
             ((d e f) (3 1 2))
             ((g h i) (2 3 1))
             ((j k l) (0 0 0))))
```

The numbers of levels in the structure must equal the rank of the array. Each leaf of the nested structure must be of the type specified by the `:type` option. If the

:initial-contents option is omitted, the initial values of the array elements are undefined (unless the :initial-element or :displaced-to option is used). The :initial-contents option may not be used with the :initial-element or :displaced-to option.

:adjustable

This argument, if specified and not nil, indicates that it must be possible to alter the array's size dynamically after it is created. This argument defaults to nil.

:fill-pointer

This argument specifies that the array should have a fill pointer. If this option is specified and not nil, the array must be one-dimensional. The value is used to initialize the fill pointer for the array. If the value t is specified, the length of the array is used; otherwise the value must be an integer between 0 (inclusive) and the length of the array (inclusive). This argument defaults to nil.

:displaced-to

This argument, if specified and not nil, specifies that the array will be a *displaced* array. The argument must then be an array; make-array will create an *indirect* or *shared* array that shares its contents with the specified array. In this case the :displaced-index-offset option may be useful. It is an error if the array specified as the :displaced-to argument does not have the same :element-type as the array being created. The :displaced-to option may not be used with the :initial-element or :initial-contents option. This argument defaults to nil.

:displaced-index-offset

This argument may be used only in conjunction with the displaced-to option. It must be a non-negative integer (it defaults to zero); it is made to be the index-offset of the created shared array.

When an array A is given as the :displaced-to argument to make-array when creating array B, then array B is said to be *displaced* to array A. Now the total number of elements in an array, called the *total size* of the array, is calculated as the product of all the dimensions (see array-total-size). It is required that the total size of A be no smaller than the sum of the total size of B plus the offset n specified by the :displaced-index-offset argument. The effect of displacing is that array B does not have any elements of its own, but instead maps accesses to itself into accesses to array A. The mapping treats both arrays as if they were

one-dimensional by taking the elements in row-major order, and then maps an
access to element k of array B to an access to element $k + n$ of array A.

If `make-array` is called with the `:adjustable`, `:fill-pointer`, and
`:displaced-to` arguments each either unspecified or `nil`, then the resulting array
is guaranteed to be a *simple* array. (See section 2.5.)

Here are some examples of the use of `make-array`:

```
;; Create a one-dimensional array of five elements.
(make-array 5)
```

```
;; Create a two-dimensional array, 3 by 4, with four-bit elements.
(make-array '(3 4) :element-type '(mod 16))
```

```
;; Create an array of single-floats.
(make-array 5 :element-type 'single-float))
```

```
;; Making a shared array.
(setq a (make-array '(4 3)))
(setq b (make-array 8 :displaced-to a
                      :displaced-index-offset 2))
```

```
;; Now it is the case that:
        (aref b 0) ≡ (aref a 0 2)
        (aref b 1) ≡ (aref a 1 0)
        (aref b 2) ≡ (aref a 1 1)
        (aref b 3) ≡ (aref a 1 2)
        (aref b 4) ≡ (aref a 2 0)
        (aref b 5) ≡ (aref a 2 1)
        (aref b 6) ≡ (aref a 2 2)
        (aref b 7) ≡ (aref a 3 0)
```

The last example depends on the fact that arrays are, in effect, stored in row-major
order for purposes of sharing. Put another way, the indices for the elements of an
array are ordered lexicographically.

Compatibility note: Both ZETALISP, as described in reference [21], and FORTRAN [1, 2]
store arrays in column-major order.

`array-rank-limit`   *[Constant]*

The value of `array-rank-limit` is a positive integer that is the upper exclusive
bound on the rank of an array. This bound depends on the implementation but will

not be smaller than 8; therefore every COMMON LISP implementation supports arrays whose rank is between 0 and 7 (inclusive). (Implementors are encouraged to make this limit as large as practicable without sacrificing performance.)

---

array-dimension-limit   [*Constant*]

The value of array-dimension-limit is a positive integer that is the upper exclusive bound on each individual dimension of an array. This bound depends on the implementation but will not be smaller than 1024. (Implementors are encouraged to make this limit as large as practicable without sacrificing performance.)

---

array-total-size-limit   [*Constant*]

The value of array-total-size-limit is a positive integer that is the upper exclusive bound on the total number of elements in an array. This bound depends on the implementation but will not be smaller than 1024. (Implementors are encouraged to make this limit as large as practicable without sacrificing performance.)

The actual limit on array size imposed by the implementation may vary according to the :element-type of the array; in this case the value of array-total-size-limit will be the smallest of these individual limits.

---

vector &rest *objects*   [*Function*]

The function vector is a convenient means for creating a simple general vector with specified initial contents. It is analogous to the function list.

```
(vector a_1 a_2 ... a_n)
  ≡ (make-array (list n) :element-type t
          :initial-contents (list a_1 a_2 ... a_n))
```

17.2. Array Access

The function aref is normally used for accessing an element of an array. Other access functions, such as svref, char, and bit may be more efficient in specialized circumstances.

---

aref *array* &rest *subscripts*   [*Function*]

This accesses and returns the element of *array* specified by the *subscripts*. The number of subscripts must equal the rank of the array, and each subscript must be a non-negative integer less than the corresponding array dimension.

aref is unusual among the functions that operate on arrays in that it completely ignores fill pointers. aref can access without error any array element, whether active or not. The generic sequence function elt, however, observes the fill pointer; accessing an element beyond the fill pointer with elt is an error.

setf may be used with aref to destructively replace an array element with a new value.

Under some circumstances it is desirable to write code that will extract an element from an array a given a list z of the indices, in such a way that the code works regardless of the rank of the array. This is easy using apply:

```
(apply #'aref a z)
```

(The length of the list must of course equal the rank of the array.) This construction may be used with setf to alter the element so selected to some new value w:

```
(setf (apply #'aref a z) w)
```

svref *simple-vector index*   [*Function*]

The first argument must be a simple general vector, that is, an object of type simple-vector. The element of the *simple-vector* specified by the integer *index* is returned. The *index* must be non-negative and less than the length of the vector.

setf may be used with svref to destructively replace a simple-vector element with a new value.

svref is identical to aref except that it requires its first argument to be a simple vector. In some implementations of COMMON LISP, svref may be faster than aref in situations where it is applicable. See also schar and sbit.

17.3. Array Information

The following functions extract from an array interesting information other than the elements.

array-element-type *array*   [*Function*]

array-element-type returns a type specifier for the set of objects that can be stored in the *array*. This set may be larger than the set requested when the array was created; for example, the result of

```
(array-element-type (make-array 5 :element-type '(mod 5)))
```

could be (mod 5), (mod 8), fixnum, t, or any other type of which (mod 5) is a subtype. See subtypep.

array-rank *array* [*Function*]

This returns the number of dimensions (axes) of *array*. This will be a non-negative integer. See array-rank-limit.

Compatibility note: In ZETALISP, this is called array-#-dims. This name causes problems in other LISP dialects because of the # character.

---

array-dimension *array axis-number* [*Function*]

The length of dimension number *axis-number* of the *array* is returned. *array* may be any kind of array, and *axis-number* should be a non-negative integer less than the rank of *array*. If the *array* is a vector with a fill pointer, array-dimension returns the total size of the vector, including inactive elements, not the size indicated by the fill pointer. (The function length will return the size indicated by the fill pointer.)

Compatibility note: This is similar to the ZETALISP function array-dimension-n, but takes its arguments in the other order, and is zero-origin for consistency instead of one-origin. In ZETALISP (array-dimension-n 0) returns the length of the array leader.

---

array-dimensions *array* [*Function*]

array-dimensions returns a list whose elements are the dimensions of *array*.

array-total-size *array* [*Function*]

array-total-size returns the total number of elements in the *array*, calculated as the product of all the dimensions.

```
(array-total-size x)
   ≡ (apply #'* (array-dimensions x))
   ≡ (reduce #'* (array-dimensions x))
```

Note that the total size of a zero-dimensional array is 1. The total size of a one-dimensional array is calculated without regard for any fill pointer.

array-in-bounds-p *array* &rest *subscripts* [*Function*]

This predicate checks whether the *subscripts* are all legal subscripts for *array*. The predicate is true if they are all legal; otherwise it is false. The *subscripts* must be integers. The number of *subscripts* supplied must equal the rank of the array. Like aref, array-in-bounds-p ignores fill pointers.

`array-row-major-index` *array* &rest *subscripts*   [*Function*]

This function takes an array and valid subscripts for the array and returns a single non-negative integer less than the total size of the array that identifies the accessed element in the row-major ordering of the elements. The number of *subscripts* supplied must equal the rank of the array. Each subscript must be a non-negative integer less than the corresponding array dimension. Like `aref`, `array-row-major-index` ignores fill pointers.

A possible definition of `array-row-major-index`, with no error-checking, would be

```
(defun array-row-major-index (a &rest subscripts)
  (apply #'+ (maplist #'(lambda (x y)
                          (* (car x) (apply #'* (cdr y))))
                      subscripts
                      (array-dimensions a))))
```

For a one-dimensional array, the result of `array-row-major-index` always equals the supplied subscript.

`adjustable-array-p` *array*   [*Function*]

This predicate is true if the argument (which must be an array) is adjustable, and otherwise is false.

17.4. Functions on Arrays of Bits

The functions described in this section operate only on arrays of bits, that is, specialized arrays whose elements are all `0` or `1`.

`bit` *bit-array* &rest *subscripts*   [*Function*]
`sbit` *simple-bit-array* &rest *subscripts*   [*Function*]

`bit` is exactly like `aref` but requires an array of bits, that is, one of type (`array bit`). The result will always be `0` or `1`.

`sbit` is like `bit` but additionally requires that the first argument be a *simple* array (see section 2.5).

Note that `bit` and `sbit`, unlike `char` and `schar`, allow the first argument to be an array of any rank.

`setf` may be used with `bit` or `sbit` to destructively replace a bit-array element with a new value.

`bit` and `sbit` are identical to `aref` except for the more specific type requirements on the first argument. In some implementations of COMMON LISP, `bit` may be faster than `aref` in situations where it is applicable, and `sbit` may similarly be faster than `bit`.

`bit-and` *bit-array1 bit-array-2* &optional *result-bit-array*	[*Function*]
`bit-ior` *bit-array1 bit-array-2* &optional *result-bit-array*	[*Function*]
`bit-xor` *bit-array1 bit-array-2* &optional *result-bit-array*	[*Function*]
`bit-eqv` *bit-array1 bit-array-2* &optional *result-bit-array*	[*Function*]
`bit-nand` *bit-array1 bit-array2* &optional *result-bit-array*	[*Function*]
`bit-nor` *bit-array1 bit-array2* &optional *result-bit-array*	[*Function*]
`bit-andc1` *bit-array1 bit-array2* &optional *result-bit-array*	[*Function*]
`bit-andc2` *bit-array1 bit-array2* &optional *result-bit-array*	[*Function*]
`bit-orc1` *bit-array1 bit-array2* &optional *result-bit-array*	[*Function*]
`bit-orc2` *bit-array1 bit-array2* &optional *result-bit-array*	[*Function*]

These functions perform bit-wise logical operations on bit-arrays. All of the arguments to any of these functions must be bit-arrays of the same rank and dimensions. The result is a bit-array of matching rank and dimensions, such that any given bit of the result is produced by operating on corresponding bits from each of the arguments.

If the third argument is `nil` or omitted, a new array is created to contain the result. If the third argument is a bit-array, the result is destructively placed into that array. If the third argument is `t`, then the first argument is also used as the third argument; that is, the result is placed back in the first array.

The following table indicates what the result bit is for each operation as a function of the two corresponding argument bits.

argument1 *argument2*	0 0	0 1	1 0	1 1	*Operation name*
`bit-and`	0	0	0	1	and
`bit-ior`	0	1	1	1	inclusive or
`bit-xor`	0	1	1	0	exclusive or
`bit-eqv`	1	0	0	1	equivalence (exclusive nor)
`bit-nand`	1	1	1	0	not-and
`bit-nor`	1	0	0	0	not-or
`bit-andc1`	0	1	0	0	and complement of *argument1* with *argument2*
`bit-andc2`	0	0	1	0	and *argument1* with complement of *argument2*
`bit-orc1`	1	1	0	1	or complement of *argument1* with *argument2*
`bit-orc2`	1	0	1	1	or *argument1* with complement of *argument2*

For example:

```
(bit-and #*1100 #*1010) ⇒ #*1000
(bit-xor #*1100 #*1010) ⇒ #*0110
(bit-andc1 #*1100 #*1010) ⇒ #*0100
```

See `logand` and related functions.

`bit-not` *bit-array* &optional *result-bit-array* [*Function*]

The first argument must be an array of bits. A bit-array of matching rank and dimensions is returned that contains a copy of the argument with all the bits inverted. See `lognot`.

If the second argument is `nil` or omitted, a new array is created to contain the result. If the second argument is a bit-array, the result is destructively placed into that array. If the second argument is `t`, then the first argument is also used as the second argument; that is, the result is placed back in the first array.

17.5. Fill Pointers

Several functions for manipulating a *fill pointer* are provided in COMMON LISP to make it easy to incrementally fill in the contents of a vector and, more generally, to allow efficient varying of the length of a vector. For example, a string with a fill pointer has most of the characteristics of a PL/I varying string.

The fill pointer is a non-negative integer no larger than the total number of elements in the vector (as returned by `array-dimension`); it is the number of "active" or "filled-in" elements in the vector. The fill pointer constitutes the "active length" of the vector; all vector elements whose index is less than the fill pointer are active, and the others are inactive. Nearly all functions that operate on the contents of a vector will operate only on the active elements. An important exception is `aref`, which can be used to access any vector element whether in the active region of the vector or not. It is important to note that vector elements not in the active region are still considered part of the vector.

Implementation note: An implication of this rule is that vector elements outside the active region may not be garbage-collected.

Only vectors (one-dimensional arrays) may have fill pointers; multidimensional arrays may not. (Note, however, that one can create a multidimensional array that is *displaced* to a vector that has a fill pointer.)

`array-has-fill-pointer-p` *array*   [*Function*]

The argument must be an array. `array-has-fill-pointer-p` returns t if the array has a fill pointer, and otherwise returns `nil`. Note that `array-has-fill- pointer-p` always returns `nil` if the *array* is not one-dimensional.

`fill-pointer` *vector*   [*Function*]

The fill pointer of *vector* is returned. It is an error if the *vector* does not have a fill pointer.

   `setf` may be used with `fill-pointer` to change the fill pointer of a vector. The fill pointer of a vector must always be an integer between zero and the size of the vector (inclusive).

`vector-push` *new-element vector*   [*Function*]

vector must be a one-dimensional array that has a fill pointer, and *new-element* may be any object. `vector-push` attempts to store *new-element* in the element of the vector designated by the fill pointer, and to increase the fill pointer by one. If the fill pointer does not designate an element of the vector (specifically, when it gets too big), it is unaffected and `vector-push` returns `nil`. Otherwise, the store and increment take place and `vector-push` returns the *former* value of the fill pointer (one less than the one it leaves in the vector); thus the value of `vector-push` is the index of the new element pushed.

`vector-push-extend` *new-element vector* &optional *extension*   [*Function*]

`vector-push-extend` is just like `vector-push` except that if the fill pointer gets too large, the vector is extended (using `adjust-array`) so that it can contain more elements. If, however, the vector is not adjustable, then `vector-push-extend` signals an error. The optional argument *extension*, which must be a positive integer, is the minimum number of elements to be added to the vector if it must be extended; it defaults to a "reasonable" implementation-dependent value.

`vector-pop` *vector*   [*Function*]

vector must be a one-dimensional array that has a fill pointer. If the fill pointer is zero, `vector-pop` signals an error. Otherwise the fill pointer is decreased by one, and the vector element designated by the new value of the fill pointer is returned.

17.6. Changing the Dimensions of an Array

This function may be used to resize or reshape an array. Its options are similar to those of `make-array`.

`adjust-array` *array new-dimensions* &key   [*Function*]
                          `:element-type`
                          `:initial-element`
                          `:initial-contents`
                          `:fill-pointer`
                          `:displaced-to`
                          `:displaced-index-offset`

`adjust-array` takes an array and a number of other arguments as for `make-array`. The number of dimensions specified by *new-dimensions* must equal the rank of *array*.

`adjust-array` returns an array of the same type and rank as *array*, with the specified *new-dimensions*. In effect, the *array* argument itself is modified to conform to the new specifications, but this may be achieved either by modifying the *array* or by creating a new array and modifying the *array* argument to be *displaced* to the new array.

In the simplest case, one specifies only the *new-dimensions* and possibly an `:initial-element` argument. Those elements of *array* that are still in bounds appear in the new array. The elements of the new array that are not in the bounds of *array* are initialized to the `:initial-element`; if this argument is not provided, then the initial contents of any new elements are undefined.

If `:element-type` is specified, then *array* must be such that it could have been originally created with that type; otherwise an error is signalled. Specifying `:element-type` to `adjust-array` serves only to require such an error check.

If `:initial-contents` or `:displaced-to` is specified, then it is treated as for `make-array`. In this case none of the original contents of *array* appears in the new array.

If `:fill-pointer` is specified, the fill pointer of the *array* is reset as specified. An error is signalled if *array* had no fill pointer already.

`adjust-array` may, depending on the implementation and the arguments, simply alter the given array or create and return a new one. In the latter case the given array will be altered so as to be displaced to the new array and have the given new dimensions.

It is not permitted to call `adjust-array` on an array that was not created with the :adjustable option. The predicate adjustable-array-p may be used to determine whether or not an array is adjustable.

If adjust-array is applied to an *array* that is displaced to another array x, then afterwards neither *array* nor the returned result is displaced to x unless such displacement is explicitly re-specified in the call to adjust-array.

For example, suppose that the 4-by-4 array m looks like this:

```
#2A( ( alpha      beta      gamma      delta    )
     ( epsilon    zeta      eta        theta    )
     ( iota       kappa     lambda     mu       )
     ( nu         xi        omicron    pi       ) )
```

Then the result of

```
(adjust-array m '(3 5) :initial-element 'baz)
```

is a 3-by-5 array with contents

```
#2A( ( alpha      beta      gamma      delta      baz    )
     ( epsilon    zeta      eta        theta      baz    )
     ( iota       kappa     lambda     mu         baz    ) )
```

Note that if array a is created displaced to array b and subsequently array b is given to adjust-array, array a will still be displaced to array b; the effects of this displacement and the rule of row-major storage order must be taken into account.

18

Strings

A string is a specialized vector (one-dimensional array) whose elements are characters. Specifically, the type `string` is identical to the type `(vector string-char)`, which in turn is the same as `(array string-char (*))`.

Any string-specific function defined in this chapter whose name begins with the prefix `string` will accept a symbol instead of a string as an argument *provided* that the operation never modifies that argument; the print name of the symbol is used. In this respect the string-specific sequence operations are not simply specializations of generic versions; the generic sequence operations described in chapter 14 never accept symbols as sequences. This slight inelegance is permitted in COMMON LISP in the name of pragmatic utility. One may get the effect of having a generic sequence function operate on either symbols or strings by applying the coercion function `string` to any argument whose data type is in doubt.

Also, there is a slight non-parallelism in the names of string functions. Where the suffixes `equalp` and `eql` would be more appropriate, for historical compatibility the suffixes `equal` and `=` are used instead to indicate case-insensitive and case-sensitive character comparison, respectively.

Any LISP object may be tested for being a string by the predicate `stringp`.

Note that strings, like all vectors, may have fill pointers (though such strings are not necessarily *simple*). String operations generally operate only on the active portion of the string (below the fill pointer). See `fill-pointer` and related functions.

18.1. String Access

The following functions access a single character element of a string.

char *string index*   [*Function*]
schar *simple-string index*   [*Function*]

The given *index* must be a non-negative integer less than the length of *string*, which must be a string. The character at position *index* of the string is returned as a character object. (This character will necessarily satisfy the predicate `string-char-p`.) As with all sequences in COMMON LISP, indexing is zero-origin. For example:

```
(char "Floob-Boober-Bab-Boober-Bubs" 0) ⇒ #\F
(char "Floob-Boober-Bab-Boober-Bubs" 1) ⇒ #\l
```

See `aref` and `elt`. In effect,

```
(char s j) ≡ (aref (the string s) j)
```

`setf` may be used with `char` to destructively replace a character within a string.

For `char`, the string may be any string; for `schar`, it must be a simple string. In some implementations of COMMON LISP, the function `schar` may be faster than `char` when it is applicable.

18.2. String Comparison

The naming conventions for these functions and for their keyword arguments generally follow the conventions for the generic sequence functions. See chapter 14.

string= *string1 string2* &key :start1 :end1 :start2 :end2   [*Function*]

`string=` compares two strings and is true if they are the same (corresponding characters are identical) but is false if they are not. The function `equal` calls `string=` if applied to two strings.

The keyword arguments `:start1` and `:start2` are the places in the strings to start the comparison. The arguments `:end1` and `:end2` are the places in the strings to stop comparing; comparison stops just *before* the position specified by a limit. The start arguments default to zero (beginning of string), and the end arguments (if either omitted or `nil`) default to the lengths of the strings (end of string), so that by default the entirety of each string is examined. These arguments are provided so that substrings can be compared efficiently.

`string=` is necessarily false if the (sub)strings being compared are of unequal length; that is, if

```
(not (= (- end1 start1) (- end2 start2)))
```

is true, then `string=` is false.

```
(string= "foo" "foo") is true
(string= "foo" "Foo") is false
(string= "foo" "bar") is false
(string= "together" "frog" :start1 1 :end1 3 :start2 2)
    is true
```

Compatibility note: `string=` is called `strequal` in INTERLISP.

`string-equal` *string1* *string2* &key :start1 :end1 :start2 :end2 [*Function*]

`string-equal` is just like `string=` except that differences in case are ignored; two characters are considered to be the same if `char-equal` is true of them. For example:

```
(string-equal "foo" "Foo") is true
```

`string<` *string1* *string2* &key :start1 :end1 :start2 :end2   [*Function*]
`string>` *string1* *string2* &key :start1 :end1 :start2 :end2   [*Function*]
`string<=` *string1* *string2* &key :start1 :end1 :start2 :end2   [*Function*]
`string>=` *string1* *string2* &key :start1 :end1 :start2 :end2   [*Function*]
`string/=` *string1* *string2* &key :start1 :end1 :start2 :end2   [*Function*]

These functions compare the two string arguments lexicographically, and the result is `nil` unless *string1* is respectively less than, greater than, less than or equal to, greater than or equal to, or not equal to *string2*. If the condition is satisfied, however, then the result is the index within the strings of the first character position at which the strings fail to match; put another way, the result is the length of the longest common prefix of the strings.

A string *a* is less than a string *b* if in the first position in which they differ the character of *a* is less than the corresponding character of *b* according to the function `char<` , or if string *a* is a proper prefix of string *b* (of shorter length and matching in all the characters of *a*).

The keyword arguments :start1 and :start2 are the places in the strings to start the comparison. The keyword arguments :end1 and :end2 are the places in the strings to stop comparing; comparison stops just *before* the position specified by a limit. The "start" arguments default to zero (beginning of string), and the "end" arguments (if either omitted or `nil`) default to the lengths of the strings (end of string), so that by default the entirety of each string is examined. These arguments are provided so that substrings can be compared efficiently. The index returned in case of a mismatch is an index into *string1*.

string-lessp *string1* *string2* &key :start1 :end1   [*Function*]
                                       :start2 :end2
string-greaterp *string1* *string2* &key :start1 :end1   [*Function*]
                                       :start2 :end2
string-not-greaterp *string1* *string2* &key :start1 :end1   [*Function*]
                                       :start2 :end2
string-not-lessp *string1* *string2* &key :start1 :end1   [*Function*]
                                       :start2 :end2
string-not-equal *string1* *string2* &key :start1 :end1   [*Function*]
                                       :start2 :end2

These are exactly like string<, string>, string<=, string>=, and string/=,
respectively, except that distinctions between uppercase and lowercase letters are
ignored. It is as if char-lessp were used instead of char< for comparing characters.

18.3. String Construction and Manipulation

Most of the interesting operations on strings may be performed with the generic
sequence functions described in chapter 14. The following functions perform additional
operations that are specific to strings.

make-string *size* &key :initial-element   [*Function*]

This returns a string (in fact a simple string) of length *size*, each of whose characters
has been initialized to the :initial-element argument. If an :initial-element
argument is not specified, then the string will be initialized in an implementation-dependent way.

Implementation note: It may be convenient to initialize the string to null characters, or to
spaces, or to garbage ("whatever was there").

A string is really just a one-dimensional array of "string characters" (that is,
those characters that are members of type string-char). More complex character
arrays may be constructed using the function make-array.

string-trim *character-bag string*   [*Function*]
string-left-trim *character-bag string*   [*Function*]
string-right-trim *character-bag string*   [*Function*]

string-trim returns a substring of *string*, with all characters in *character-bag*
stripped off the beginning and end. The function string-left-trim is similar but

strips characters off only the beginning; `string-right-trim` strips off only the end. The argument *character-bag* may be any sequence containing characters. For example:

```
(string-trim '(#\Space #\Tab #\Newline) " garbanzo beans
       ") ⇒ "garbanzo beans"
(string-trim " (*)" " ( *three (silly) words* ) ")
   ⇒ "three (silly) words"
(string-left-trim " (*)" " ( *three (silly) words* ) ")
   ⇒ "three (silly) words* ) "
(string-right-trim " (*)" " ( *three (silly) words* ) ")
   ⇒ " ( *three (silly) words"
```

If no characters need to be trimmed from the *string*, then either the argument *string* itself or a copy of it may be returned, at the discretion of the implementation.

`string-upcase` *string* &key :start :end	[*Function*]
`string-downcase` *string* &key :start :end	[*Function*]
`string-capitalize` *string* &key :start :end	[*Function*]

`string-upcase` returns a string just like *string* with all lowercase characters replaced by the corresponding uppercase characters. More precisely, each character of the result string is produced by applying the function `char-upcase` to the corresponding character of *string*.

`string-downcase` is similar, except that uppercase characters are converted to lowercase characters (using `char-downcase`).

The keyword arguments `:start` and `:end` delimit the portion of the string to be affected. The result is always of the same length as *string*, however.

The argument is not destroyed. However, if no characters in the argument require conversion, the result may be either the argument or a copy of it, at the implementation's discretion. For example:

```
(string-upcase "Dr. Livingston, I presume?")
   ⇒ "DR. LIVINGSTON, I PRESUME?"
(string-downcase "Dr. Livingston, I presume?")
   ⇒ "dr. livingston, i presume?"
(string-upcase "Dr. Livingston, I presume?" :start 6 :end 10)
   ⇒ "Dr. LiVINGston, I presume?"
```

`string-capitalize` produces a copy of *string* such that, for every word in the copy, the first character of the word, if case-modifiable, is uppercase and any other case-modifiable characters in the word are lowercase. For the purposes of `string-capitalize`, a word is defined to be a consecutive subsequence consisting of alphanumeric characters or digits, delimited at each end either by a non-alphanumeric character or by an end of the string. For example:

```
(string-capitalize " hello ") ⇒ " Hello "
(string-capitalize
    "occlUDeD cASEmenTs FOreSTAll iNADVertent DEFenestraTION")
⇒  "Occluded Casements Forestall Inadvertent Defenestration"
(string-capitalize 'kludgy-hash-search) ⇒ "Kludgy-Hash-Search"
(string-capitalize "DON'T!") ⇒ "Don'T!"    ;not "Don't!"
(string-capitalize "pipe 13a, foo1bc") ⇒ "Pipe 13a, Foo1bc"
```

Compatibility note: Very approximate INTERLISP equivalents to `string-upcase`, `string-downcase`, and `string-capitalize` are u-case, l-case with second argument nil, and l-case with second argument t.

`nstring-upcase` *string* &key :start :end	[*Function*]
`nstring-downcase` *string* &key :start :end	[*Function*]
`nstring-capitalize` *string* &key :start :end	[*Function*]

These functions are just like `string-upcase`, `string-downcase`, and `string-capitalize` but destructively modify the argument *string* by altering case-modifiable characters as necessary.

The keyword arguments `:start` and `:end` delimit the portion of the string to be affected. The argument *string* is returned as the result.

`string` *x*	[*Function*]

Most of the string functions effectively apply `string` to such of their arguments as are supposed to be strings. If *x* is a string, it is returned. If *x* is a symbol, its print name is returned. If *x* is a string character (a character of type `string-char`), then a string containing that one character is returned. In any other situation, an error is signalled.

To convert a sequence of characters to a string, use coerce. (Note that `(coerce x 'string)` will not succeed if x is a symbol. Conversely, `string` will not convert a list or other sequence to be a string.)

To get the string representation of a number or any other LISP object, use `prin1-to-string`, `princ-to-string`, or format.

19

Structures

COMMON LISP provides a facility for creating named record structures with named components. In effect, the user can define a new data type; every data structure of that type has components with specified names. Constructor, access, and assignment constructs are automatically defined when the data type is defined.

This chapter is divided into two parts. The first part discusses the basics of the structure facility, which is very simple and allows the user to take advantage of the type-checking, modularity, and convenience of user-defined record data types. The second part, beginning with section 19.5, discusses a number of specialized features of the facility that have advanced applications. These features are completely optional, and you needn't even know they exist in order to take advantage of the basics.

19.1. Introduction to Structures

The structure facility is embodied in the defstruct macro, which allows the user to create and use aggregate data types with named elements. These are like "structures" in PL/I, or "records" in PASCAL.

As an example, assume you are writing a LISP program that deals with space ships in a two-dimensional plane. In your program, you need to represent a space ship by a LISP object of some kind. The interesting things about a space ship, as far as your program is concerned, are its position (represented as x and y coordinates), velocity (represented as components along the x and y axes), and mass.

A ship might therefore be represented as a record structure with five components: x-position, y-position, x-velocity, y-velocity, and mass. This structure could in turn be implemented as a LISP object in a number of ways. It could be a list of five elements; the x-position could be the *car*, the y-position the *cadr*, and so on. Equally well it could be a vector of five elements: the x-position could be element 0, the y-position element 1, and so on. The problem with either of these representations is that the components occupy places in the object that are quite arbitrary and hard to remember. Someone looking at (cadddr ship1) or (aref ship1 3) in a piece of code might find it difficult to determine that this is accessing the y-velocity component of ship1. Moreover, if the representation of a ship should have to be changed, it would be very difficult to find all the places in the code to be changed to match (not all occurrences of cadddr are intended to extract the y-velocity from a ship).

Ideally components of record structures should have names. One would like to write something like (ship-y-velocity ship1) instead of (cadddr ship1). One would also like a more mnemonic way to create a ship than this:

```
(list 0 0 0 0 0)
```

Indeed, one would like ship to be a new data type, just like other LISP data types, that one could test with typep, for example. The defstruct facility provides all of this.

defstruct itself is a macro that defines a structure. For the space ship example, one might define the structure by saying:

```
(defstruct ship
  x-position
  y-position
  x-velocity
  y-velocity
  mass)
```

This declares that every ship is an object with five named components. The evaluation of this form does several things:

- It defines ship-x-position to be a function of one argument, a ship, that returns the x-position of the ship; ship-y-position and the other components are given similar function definitions. These functions are called the *access functions*, as they are used to access elements of the structure.

- The symbol ship becomes the name of a data type of which instances of ships are elements. This name becomes acceptable to typep, for example; (typep x 'ship) is true if x is a ship and false if x is any object other than a ship.

- A function named ship-p of one argument is defined; it is a predicate that is true if its argument is a ship and is false otherwise.

- A function called make-ship is defined that, when invoked, will create a data structure with five components, suitable for use with the access functions. Thus executing

```
(setq ship2 (make-ship))
```

sets `ship2` to a newly created `ship` object. One can specify the initial values of any desired component in the call to `make-ship` by using keyword arguments in this way:

```
(setq ship2 (make-ship   :mass *default-ship-mass*
                         :x-position 0
                         :y-position 0))
```

This constructs a new ship and initializes three of its components. This function is called the *constructor function* because it constructs a new structure.

- The `#s` syntax can be used to read instances of `ship` structures, and a printer function is provided for printing out ship structures. For example, the value of the variable `ship2` shown above might be printed as

```
#S(ship   x-position 0   y-position 0   x-velocity nil
          y-velocity nil   mass 170000.0)
```

- A function called `copy-ship` of one argument is defined that, when given a `ship` object, will create a new `ship` object that is a copy of the given one. This function is called the *copier function*.

- One may use `setf` to alter the components of a `ship`:

```
(setf (ship-x-position ship2) 100)
```

This alters the *x*-position of *ship2* to be `100`. This works because `defstruct` behaves as if it generates an appropriate `defsetf` form for each access function.

This simple example illustrates the power of `defstruct` to provide abstract record structures in a convenient manner. `defstruct` has many other features as well for specialized purposes.

19.2. How to Use Defstruct

All structures are defined through the `defstruct` construct.

`defstruct` *name-and-options* [*doc-string*] {*slot-description*}⁺   [*Macro*]

This defines a record-structure data type. A general call to `defstruct` looks like the following example.

```
(defstruct (name option-1 option-2 ...)
           doc-string
           slot-description-1
           slot-description-2
           ...)
```

The *name* must be a symbol; it becomes the name of a new data type consisting of all instances of the structure. The function `typep` will accept and use this name as appropriate. The *name* is returned as the value of the *defstruct* form.

Usually no options are needed at all. If no options are specified, then one may write simply *name* instead of (*name*) after the word `defstruct`. The syntax of options and the options provided are discussed in section 19.5.

If the optional documentation string *doc-string* is present, then it is attached to the *name* as a documentation string of type `structure`; see `documentation`.

Each *slot-description-j* is of the form

```
(slot-name  default-init
            slot-option-name-1  slot-option-value-1
            slot-option-name-2  slot-option-value-2
            ...)
```

Each *slot-name* must be a symbol; an access function is defined for each slot. If no options and no *default-init* are specified, then one may write simply *slot-name* instead of (*slot-name*) as the slot description. The *default-init* is a form that is evaluated *each time* a structure is to be constructed; the value is used as the initial value of the slot. If no *default-init* is specified, then the initial contents of the slot are undefined and implementation-dependent. The available slot-options are described in section 19.4.

Compatibility note: Slot-options are not currently provided in ZETALISP, but this is an upward-compatible extension.

`defstruct` not only defines an access function for each slot, but also arranges for `setf` to work properly on such access functions, defines a predicate named *name*-p, defines a constructor function named `make-`*name*, and defines a copier function named `copy-`*name*. All names of automatically created functions are interned in whatever package is current at the time the `defstruct` form is processed (see `*package*`). Also, all such functions may be declared `inline` at the discretion of the implementation to improve efficiency; if you do not want some function declared `inline`, follow the `defstruct` form with a `notinline` declaration to override any automatic `inline` declaration.

19.3. Using the Automatically Defined Constructor Function

After you have defined a new structure with `defstruct`, you can create instances
of this structure by using the constructor function. By default, `defstruct` defines
this function automatically. For a structure named `foo`, the constructor function is
normally named `make-foo`; you can specify a different name by giving it as the
argument to the `:constructor` option, or specify that you don't want a normal
constructor function at all by using `nil` as the argument (in which case one or
more "by-position" constructors should be requested; see section 19.6.

A call to a constructor function, in general, has the form

(*name-of-constructor-function*
   slot-keyword-1 form-1
   slot-keyword-2 form-2
   ...)

All arguments are keyword arguments. Each *slot-keyword* should be a keyword
whose name matches the name of a slot of the structure (`defstruct` determines
the possible keywords simply by interning each slot-name in the keyword package).
All the *keyword*s and *forms* are evaluated. In short, it is just as if the constructor
function took all its arguments as `&key` parameters. For example, the `ship` structure
shown in section 19.1 has a constructor function that takes arguments roughly as
if its definition were

```
(defun make-ship (&key x-position y-position
                       x-velocity y-velocity mass)
  ...)
```

If *slot-keyword-j* names a slot, then that element of the created structure will be
initialized to the value of *form-j*. If no pair *slot-keyword-j* and *form-j* is present for
a given slot, then the slot will be initialized by evaluating the *default-init* form
specified for that slot in the call to `defstruct`. (In other words, the initialization
specified in the `defstruct` defers to any specified in a call to the constructor
function.) If the default initialization form is used, it is evaluated at construction
time, but in the lexical environment of the `defstruct` form in which it appeared.
If the `defstruct` itself also did not specify any initialization, the element's initial
value is undefined. You should always specify the initialization, either in the
`defstruct` or in the call to the constructor function, if you care about the initial
value of the slot.

Each initialization form specified for a `defstruct` component, when used by
the constructor function for an otherwise unspecified component, is re-evaluated
on every call to the constructor function. It is as if the initialization forms were

used as *init* forms for the keyword parameters of the constructor function. For example, if the form (gensym) were used as an initialization form, either in the constructor-function call or as the default initialization form in the defstruct form, then every call to the constructor function would call gensym once to generate a new symbol.

19.4. Defstruct Slot-Options

Each *slot-description* in a defstruct form may specify one or more slot-options. A slot-option consists of a pair of a keyword and a value (which is not a form to be evaluated, but the value itself). For example:

```
(defstruct ship
  (x-position 0.0 :type short-float)
  (y-position 0.0 :type short-float)
  (x-velocity 0.0 :type short-float)
  (y-velocity 0.0 :type short-float)
  (mass *default-ship-mass* :type short-float :read-only t))
```

This specifies that each slot will always contain a short-format floating-point number, and that the last slot may not be altered once a ship is constructed.

The available slot-options are:

:type

The option :type *type* specifies that the contents of the slot will always be of the specified data type. This is entirely analogous to the declaration of a variable or function; indeed, it effectively declares the result type of the access function. An implementation may or may not choose to check the type of the new object when initializing or assigning to a slot. Note that the argument form *type* is not evaluated; it must be a valid type specifier.

:read-only

The option :read-only *x*, where *x* is not nil, specifies that this slot may not be altered; it will always contain the value specified at construction time. setf will not accept the access function for this slot. If *x* is nil, this slot-option has no effect. Note that the argument form *x* is not evaluated.

Note that it is impossible to specify a slot-option unless a default value is specified first.

19.5. Defstruct Options

The preceding description of defstruct is all that the average user will need (or want) to know in order to use structures. The remainder of this chapter discusses more complex features of the defstruct facility.

This section explains each of the options that can be given to defstruct. A defstruct option may be either a keyword or a list of a keyword and arguments for that keyword. (Note that the syntax for defstruct options differs from the pair syntax used for slot-options. No part of any of these options is evaluated.)

:conc-name

This provides for automatic prefixing of names of access functions. It is conventional to begin the names of all the access functions of a structure with a specific prefix, the name of the structure followed by a hyphen. This is the default behavior.

The argument to the :conc-name option specifies an alternate prefix to be used. (If a hyphen is to be used as a separator, it must be specified as part of the prefix.) If nil is specified as an argument, then *no* prefix is used; then the names of the access functions are the same as the slot names, and it is up to the user to name the slots reasonably.

Note that no matter what is specified for :conc-name, with a constructor function one uses slot keywords that match the slot names, with no prefix attached. On the other hand, one uses the access-function name when using setf. Here is an example:

```
(defstruct door knob-color width material)
(setq my-door (make-door :knob-color 'red :width 5.0))
(door-width my-door) ⇒ 5.0
(setf (door-width my-door) 43.7)
(door-width my-door) ⇒ 43.7
(door-knob-color my-door) ⇒ red
```

:constructor

This option takes one argument, a symbol, which specifies the name of the constructor function. If the argument is not provided or if the option itself is not provided, the name of the constructor is produced by concatenating the string "MAKE-" and the name of the structure, putting the name in whatever package is current at the time the defstruct form is processed (see *package*). If the argument is provided and is nil, no constructor function is defined.

This option actually has a more general syntax that is explained in section 19.6.

`:copier`

This option takes one argument, a symbol, which specifies the name of the copier function. If the argument is not provided or if the option itself is not provided, the name of the copier is produced by concatenating the string "COPY-" and the name of the structure, putting the name in whatever package is current at the time the `defstruct` form is processed (see `*package*`). If the argument is provided and is `nil`, no copier function is defined.

The automatically defined copier function simply makes a new structure and transfers all components verbatim from the argument into the newly created structure. No attempt is made to make copies of the components. Corresponding components of the old and new structures will therefore be `eql`.

`:predicate`

This option takes one argument, which specifies the name of the type predicate. If the argument is not provided or if the option itself is not provided, the name of the predicate is made by concatenating the name of the structure to the string "-P", putting the name in whatever package is current at the time the `defstruct` form is processed (see `*package*`). If the argument is provided and is `nil`, no predicate is defined. A predicate can be defined only if the structure is "named"; if the `:type` option is specified and the `:named` option is not specified, then the `:predicate` option must either be unspecified or have the value `nil`.

`:include`

This option is used for building a new structure definition as an extension of an old structure definition. As an example, suppose you have a structure called `person` that looks like this:

```
(defstruct person name age sex)
```

Now suppose you want to make a new structure to represent an astronaut. Since astronauts are people too, you would like them to also have the attributes of name, age, and sex, and you would like LISP functions that operate on `person` structures to operate just as well on `astronaut` structures. You can do this by defining `astronaut` with the `:include` option, as follows:

```
(defstruct (astronaut (:include person)
                      (:conc-name astro-))
  helmet-size
  (favorite-beverage 'tang))
```

The `:include` option causes the structure being defined to have the same slots

as the included structure. This is done in such a way that the access functions for
the included structure will also work on the structure being defined. In this example,
an `astronaut` will therefore have five slots: the three defined in `person` and the
two defined in `astronaut` itself. The access functions defined by the `person`
structure can be applied to instances of the `astronaut` structure, and they will
work correctly. Moreover, `astronaut` will have its own access functions for components defined by the `person` structure. The following examples illustrate how
you can use `astronaut` structures:

```
(setq x (make-astronaut :name 'buzz
                        :age 45.
                        :sex t
                        :helmet-size 17.5))
```

```
(person-name x) ⇒ buzz
(astro-name x) ⇒ buzz
(astro-favorite-beverage x) ⇒ tang
```

The difference between the access functions `person-name` and `astro-name` is
that `person-name` may be correctly applied to any `person`, including an `astronaut`,
while `astro-name` may be correctly applied only to an `astronaut`. (An implementation may or may not check for incorrect use of access functions.)

At most one `:include` option may be specified in a single `defstruct` form.
The argument to the `:include` option is required and must be the name of some
previously defined structure. If the structure being defined has no `:type` option,
then the included structure must also have had no `:type` option specified for it. If
the structure being defined has a `:type` option, then the included structure must
have been declared with a `:type` option specifying the same representation type.

If no `:type` option is involved, then the structure name of the including structure
definition becomes the name of a data type, of course, and therefore a valid type
specifier recognizable by `typep`; moreover, it becomes a subtype of the included
structure. In the above example, `astronaut` is a subtype of `person`; hence

```
(typep (make-astronaut) 'person)
```

is true, indicating that all operations on persons will also work on astronauts.

The following is an advanced feature of the `:include` option. Sometimes, when
one structure includes another, the default values or slot-options for the slots that
came from the included structure are not what you want. The new structure can
specify default values or slot-options for the included slots different from those the
included structure specifies, by giving the `:include` option as:

```
(:include name slot-description-1 slot-description-2 ...)
```

Each *slot-description-j* must have a *slot-name* or *slot-keyword* that is the same as that of some slot in the included structure. If *slot-description-j* has no *default-init*, then in the new structure the slot will have no initial value. Otherwise its initial value form will be replaced by the *default-init* in *slot-description-j*. A normally writable slot may be made read-only. If a slot is read-only in the included structure, then it must also be so in the including structure. If a type is specified for a slot, it must be the same as, or a subtype of, the type specified in the included structure. If it is a strict subtype, the implementation may or may not choose to error-check assignments.

For example, if we had wanted to define astronaut so that the default age for an astronaut is 45, then we could have said:

```
(defstruct (astronaut (:include person (age 45)))
   helmet-size
   (favorite-beverage 'tang))
```

:print-function

This option may be used only if the :type option is not specified. The argument to the :print-function option should be a function of three arguments, in a form acceptable to the function special form, to be used to print structures of this type. When a structure of this type is to be printed, the function is called on three arguments: the structure to be printed, a stream to print to, and an integer indicating the current depth (to be compared against *print-level*). The printing function should observe the values of such printer-control variables as *print-escape* and *print-pretty*.

If the :print-function option is not specified and the :type option also not specified, then a default printing function is provided for the structure that will print out all its slots using #s syntax (see section 22.1.4).

:type

The :type option explicitly specifies the representation to be used for the structure. It takes one argument, which must be one of the types enumerated below.

Specifying this option has the effect of forcing a specific representation and of forcing the components to be stored in the order specified in the defstruct form in corresponding successive elements of the specified representation. It also *prevents* the structure name from becoming a valid type specifier recognizable by typep. See section 19.7 for details.

Normally this option is not specified, in which case the structure is represented in an implementation-dependent manner.

vector

This produces the same result as specifying (vector t). The structure is represented as a general vector, storing components as vector elements. The first component is vector element 1 if the structure is :named, and element 0 otherwise.

(vector *element-type*)

The structure is represented as a (possibly specialized) vector, storing components as vector elements. Every component must be of a type that can be stored in a vector of the type specified. The first component is vector element 1 if the structure is :named, and element 0 otherwise. The structure may be :named only if the type symbol is a subtype of the specified element-type.

list

The structure is represented as a list. The first component is the *cadr* if the structure is :named, and the *car* if it is :unnamed.

:named

The :named option specifies that the structure is "named"; this option takes no argument. If no :type option is specified, then the structure is always named; so this option is useful only in conjunction with the :type option. See section 19.7 for a further description of this option.

:initial-offset

This allows you to tell defstruct to skip over a certain number of slots before it starts allocating the slots described in the body. This option requires an argument, a non-negative integer, which is the number of slots you want defstruct to skip. The :initial-offset option may be used only if the :type option is also specified. See section 19.7.3 for a further description of this option.

19.6. By-position Constructor Functions

If the :constructor option is given as (:constructor *name arglist*), then instead of making a keyword-driven constructor function, defstruct defines a "positional" constructor function, taking arguments whose meaning is determined by the argument's position rather than by a keyword. The *arglist* is used to describe what the arguments to the constructor will be. In the simplest case something like

`(:constructor make-foo (a b c))` defines `make-foo` to be a three-argument constructor function whose arguments are used to initialize the slots named `a`, `b`, and `c`.

In addition, the keywords `&optional`, `&rest`, and `&aux` are recognized in the argument list. They work in the way you might expect, but there are a few fine points worthy of explanation. Consider this example:

```
(:constructor create-foo
        (a &optional b (c 'sea) &rest d &aux e (f 'eff)))
```

This defines `create-foo` to be a constructor of one or more arguments. The first argument is used to initialize the `a` slot. The second argument is used to initialize the `b` slot. If there isn't any second argument, then the default value given in the body of the `defstruct` (if given) is used instead. The third argument is used to initialize the `c` slot. If there isn't any third argument, then the symbol `sea` is used instead. Any arguments following the third argument are collected into a list and used to initialize the `d` slot. If there are three or fewer arguments, then `nil` is placed in the `d` slot. The `e` slot *is not initialized*; its initial value is undefined. Finally, the `f` slot is initialized to contain the symbol `eff`.

The actions taken in the `b` and `e` cases were carefully chosen to allow the user to specify all possible behaviors. Note that the `&aux` "variables" can be used to completely override the default initializations given in the body.

With this definition, one can write

```
(create-foo 1 2)
```

instead of

```
(make-foo :a 1 :b 2)
```

and of course `create-foo` provides defaulting different from that of `make-foo`.

It is permissible to use the `:constructor` option more than once, so that you can define several different constructor functions, each taking different parameters.

Because a constructor of this type operates By Order of Arguments, it is sometimes known as a BOA constructor.

19.7. Structures of Explicitly Specified Representational Type

Sometimes it is important to have explicit control over the representation of a structure. The `:type` option allows one to specify that a structure must be implemented in a particular way, using a list or a specific kind of vector, and to specify the exact allocation of structure slots to components of the representation. A structure may also be "unnamed" or "named," according to whether the structure name is stored in (and thus recoverable from) the structure.

19.7.1. Unnamed Structures

Sometimes a particular data representation is imposed by external requirements, and yet it is desirable to document the data format as a defstruct-style structure. For example, consider expressions built up from numbers, symbols, and binary operations such as + and *. An operation might be represented as it is in LISP, as a list of the operator and the two operands. This fact can be expressed succinctly with defstruct in this manner:

```
(defstruct (binop (:type list))
  (operator '? :type symbol)
  operand-1
  operand-2)
```

This will define a constructor function make-binop and three selector functions, namely binop-operator, binop-operand-1, and binop-operand-2. (It will *not*, however, define a predicate binop-p, for reasons explained below.)

The effect of make-binop is simply to construct a list of length three:

```
(make-binop :operator '+ :operand-1 'x :operand-2 5)
  ⇒ (+ x 5)
(make-binop :operand-2 4 :operator '*)
  ⇒ (* nil 4)
```

It is just like the function list except that it takes keyword arguments and performs slot defaulting appropriate to the binop conceptual data type. Similarly, the selector functions binop-operator, binop-operand-1, and binop-operand-2 are essentially equivalent to car, cadr, and caddr, respectively. (They might not be completely equivalent because, for example, an implementation would be justified in adding error-checking code to ensure that the argument to each selector function is a length-3 list.)

We speak of binop as being a "conceptual" data type because binop is not made a part of the COMMON LISP type system. The predicate typep will not recognize binop as a type specifier, and type-of will return list when given a binop structure. Indeed, there is no way to distinguish a data structure constructed by make-binop from any other list that happens to have the correct structure.

There is not even any way to recover the structure name binop from a structure created by make-binop. This can be done, however, if the structure is "named."

19.7.2. Named Structures

A "named" structure has the property that, given an instance of the structure, the structure name (that names the type) can be reliably recovered. For structures defined with no :type option, the structure name actually becomes part of the COMMON LISP data-type system. The function type-of, when applied to such a structure, will return the structure name as the type of the object; the predicate typep will recognize the structure name as a valid type specifier.

For structures defined with a :type option, type-of will return a type specifier such as list or (vector t), depending on the type specified to the :type option. The structure name does not become a valid type specifier. However, if the :named option is also specified, then the first component of the structure (as created by a defstruct constructor function) will always contain the structure name. This allows the structure name to be recovered from an instance of the structure and allows a reasonable predicate for the conceptual type to be defined: the automatically defined *name*-p predicate for the structure operates by first checking that its argument is of the proper type (list, (vector t), or whatever) and then checking whether the first component contains the appropriate type name.

Consider the binop example shown above, modified only to include the :named option:

```
(defstruct (binop (:type list) :named)
  (operator '? :type symbol)
  operand-1
  operand-2)
```

As before, this will define a constructor function make-binop and three selector functions binop-operator, binop-operand-1, and binop-operand-2. It will also define a predicate binop-p.

The effect of make-binop is now to construct a list of length four:

```
(make-binop :operator '+ :operand-1 'x :operand-2 5)
   ⇒ (binop + x 5)
(make-binop :operand-2 4 :operator '*)
   ⇒ (binop * nil 4)
```

The structure has the same layout as before except that the structure name binop is included as the first list element. The selector functions binop-operator, binop-operand-1, and binop-operand-2 are essentially equivalent to cadr, caddr, and cadddr, respectively. The predicate binop-p is more or less equivalent to the following definition.

```
(defun binop-p (x)
  (and (consp x) (eq (car x) 'binop)))
```

The name `binop` is still not a valid type specifier recognizable to `typep`, but at least there is a way of distinguishing `binop` structures from other similarly defined structures.

19.7.3. Other Aspects of Explicitly Specified Structures

The `:initial-offset` option allows one to specify that slots be allocated beginning at a representational element other than the first. For example, the form

```
(defstruct (binop (:type list) (:initial-offset 2))
  (operator '? :type symbol)
  operand-1
  operand-2)
```

would result in the following behavior for `make-binop`:

```
(make-binop :operator '+ :operand-1 'x :operand-2 5)
   ⇒ (nil nil + x 5)
(make-binop :operand-2 4 :operator '*)
   ⇒ (nil nil * nil 4)
```

The selector functions `binop-operator`, `binop-operand-1`, and `binop-operand-2` would be essentially equivalent to `caddr`, `cadddr`, and `car` of `cddddr`, respectively. Similarly, the form

```
(defstruct (binop (:type list) :named (:initial-offset 2))
  (operator '? :type symbol)
  operand-1
  operand-2)
```

would result in the following behavior for `make-binop`:

```
(make-binop :operator '+ :operand-1 'x :operand-2 5)
  ⇒ (nil nil binop + x 5)
(make-binop :operand-2 4 :operator '*)
  ⇒ (nil nil binop * nil 4)
```

If the `:include` is used with the `:type` option, then the effect is first to skip over as many representation elements as needed to represent the included structure, then to skip over any additional elements specified by the :initial-offset option, and then to begin allocation of elements from that point. For example:

```
(defstruct (binop (:type list) :named (:initial-offset 2))
  (operator '? :type symbol)
  operand-1
  operand-2)

(defstruct (annotated-binop (:type list)
                            (:initial-offset 3)
                            (:include binop))
  commutative associative identity)

(make-annotated-binop :operator '*
                      :operand-1 'x
                      :operand-2 5
                      :commutative t
                      :associative t
                      :identity 1)
  ⇒ (nil nil binop * x 5 nil nil nil t t 1)
```

The first two `nil` elements stem from the :initial-offset of 2 in the definition of `binop`. The next four elements contain the structure name and three slots for `binop`. The next three `nil` elements stem from the :initial-offset of 3 in the definition of `annotated-binop`. The last three list elements contain the additional slots for an `annotated-binop`.

20

The Evaluator

The mechanism that executes LISP programs is called the evaluator. More precisely, the evaluator accepts a form and performs the computation specified by the form. This mechanism is made available to the user through the function `eval`.

The evaluator is typically implemented as an interpreter that traverses the given form recursively, performing each step of the computation as it goes. An interpretive implementation is not required, however. A permissible alternative approach is for the evaluator first to completely compile the form into machine-executable code and then invoke the resulting code. This technique virtually eliminates incompatibilities between interpreted and compiled code, but also renders the `evalhook` mechanism relatively useless. Various mixed strategies are also possible. All of these approaches should produce the same results when executing a correct program, but may produce different results for incorrect programs. For example, the approaches may differ as to when macro calls are expanded; macro definitions should not depend on the time at which they are expanded. Implementors should document the evaluation strategy for each implementation.

20.1. Run-Time Evaluation of Forms

The function `eval` is the main user interface to the evaluator. Hooks are provided for user-supplied debugging routines to obtain control during the execution of an interpretive evaluator. The functions `evalhook` and `applyhook` provide alternative interfaces to the evaluator mechanism for use by these debugging routines.

`eval` *form* [*Function*]

The *form* is evaluated in the current dynamic environment and a null lexical environment. Whatever results from the evaluation is returned from the call to `eval`.

Note that when you write a call to `eval` *two* levels of evaluation occur on the argument form you write. First the argument form is evaluated, as for arguments to any function, by the usual argument evaluation mechanism (which involves an implicit use of `eval`). Then the argument is passed to the `eval` function, where another evaluation occurs. For example:

```
(eval (list 'cdr (car '((quote (a . b)) c)))) ⇒ b
```

The argument form `(list 'cdr (car '((quote (a . b)) c)))` is evaluated in the usual way to produce the argument `(cdr (quote (a . b)))`; this is then given to `eval` because `eval` is being called explicitly, and `eval` evaluates its argument `(cdr (quote (a . b)))` to produce `b`.

If all that is required for some application is to obtain the current dynamic value of a given symbol, the function `symbol-value` may be more efficient than `eval`.

`*evalhook*`   [*Variable*]

`*applyhook*`   [*Variable*]

If the value of `*evalhook*` is not `nil`, then `eval` behaves in a special way. The non-`nil` value of `*evalhook*` should be a function that takes two arguments, a form and an environment; this is called the *eval hook function*. When a form is to be evaluated (any form at all, even a number or a symbol), whether implicitly or via an explicit call to `eval`, no attempt is made to evaluate the form. Instead, the hook function is invoked and is passed the form to be evaluated as its first argument. The hook function is then responsible for evaluating the form; whatever is returned by the hook function is assumed to be the result of evaluating the form.

The variable `*applyhook*` is similar to `*evalhook*` but is used when a function is about to be applied to arguments. If the value of `*applyhook*` is not `nil`, then `eval` behaves in a special way. The non-`nil` value of `*applyhook*` should be a function that takes three arguments, a function, a list of arguments, and an environment; this is called the *apply hook function*. When a function is about to be applied to a list of arguments, no attempt is made to apply the function. Instead, the hook function is invoked and is passed the function and the list of arguments as its first and second arguments. The hook function is then responsible for evaluating the form; whatever is returned by the hook function is assumed to be the result of evaluating the form. The apply hook function is used only for application of ordinary functions within `eval`. It is not used for applications via `apply` or `funcall`, for applications by such functions as `map` or `reduce`, or for invocation of macro-expansion functions by either `eval` or `macroexpand`.

The last argument passed to either kind of hook function contains information about the lexical environment in an implementation-dependent format. These arguments are suitable for the functions `evalhook`, `applyhook`, and `macroexpand`.

When either kind of hook function is invoked, both `*evalhook*` and `*applyhook*` are rebound to the value `nil` around the invocation of the hook function. This is so that the hook function will not be invoked recursively on evaluations and applications that occur in the course of executing the code of the hook function. The functions `evalhook` and `applyhook` are useful for performing recursive evaluations and applications within the hook function.

The hook feature is provided as an aid to debugging. The `step` facility is implemented using this hook.

If a non-local exit causes a throw back to the top level of LISP, perhaps because an error could not be corrected, then `*evalhook*` and `*applyhook*` are automatically reset to `nil` as a safety feature.

---

evalhook *form evalhookfn applyhookfn* &optional *env*   [*Function*]
applyhook *function args evalhookfn applyhookfn* &optional *env*   [*Function*]

The functions `evalhook` and `applyhook` are provided to make it easier to exploit the hook feature.

In the case of `evalhook`, the *form* is evaluated. In the case of `applyhook`, the *function* is applied to the list of arguments *args*. In either case, for the duration of the operation the variable `*evalhook*` is bound to *evalhookfn*, and `*applyhook*` is bound to *applyhookfn*. Furthermore, the *env* argument is used as the lexical environment for the operation; *env* defaults to the null environment. The check for a hook function is *bypassed* for the evaluation of the *form* itself (for `evalhook`) or for the application of the *function* to the *args* itself (for `applyhook`), but not for subsidiary evaluations and applications. such as evaluations of subforms. It is this one-shot bypass that makes `evalhook` and `applyhook` so useful.

Here is an example of a very simple tracing routine that uses just the `evalhook` feature.

```
(defvar *hooklevel* 0)

(defun hook (x)
  (let ((*evalhook* 'eval-hook-function))
    (eval x)))

(defun eval-hook-function (form &optional env)
  (let ((*hooklevel* (+ *hooklevel* 1)))
    (format *trace-output* "~%~V@TForm:   ~S"
            (* *hooklevel* 2) form)
    (let ((values (multiple-value-list
                    (evalhook form
                              #'eval-hook-function
                              nil
                              env))))
      (format *trace-output* "~%~V@TValue:~{~ S~}"
              (* *hooklevel* 2) values)
      (values-list values))))
```

Using these routines, one might see the following interaction:

```
(hook '(cons (floor *print-base* 2) 'b))
  Form: (CONS (FLOOR *PRINT-BASE* 2) (QUOTE B))
    Form: (FLOOR *PRINT-BASE* 3)
      Form: *PRINT-BASE*
      Value: 10
      Form: 3
      Value: 3
    Value: 3 1
    Form: (QUOTE B)
    Value: B
  Value: (3 . B)
(3 . B)
```

constantp *object* [*Function*]

If the predicate constantp is true of an object, then that object, when considered as a form to be evaluated, always evaluates to the same thing; it is a constant. This includes self-evaluating objects such as numbers, characters, strings, bit-vectors, and keywords, as well as all constant symbols declared by defconstant, such as nil, t, and pi. In addition, a list whose *car* is quote, such as (quote foo), is considered to be a constant.

If constantp is false of an object, then that object, considered as a form, might or might not always evaluate to the same thing.

20.2. The Top-Level Loop

Normally one interacts with LISP through a "top-level read-eval-print loop," so called because it is the highest level of control and consists of an endless loop that reads an expression, evaluates it, and prints the results. One has an effect on the state of the LISP system only by invoking actions that have side effects.

The precise nature of the top-level loop for COMMON LISP is purposely not rigorously specified here so that implementors can experiment to improve the user interface. For example, an implementor may choose to require line-at-a-time input, or may provide a fancy editor or complex graphics-display interface. An implementor may choose to provide explicit prompts for input, or may choose (as MACLISP does) not to clutter up the transcript with prompts.

The top-level loop is required to trap all throws and recover gracefully. It is also required to print all values resulting from evaluation of a form, perhaps on separate lines. If a form returns zero values, as little as possible should be printed.

The following variables are maintained by the top-level loop as a limited safety net, in case the user forgets to save an interesting input expression or output value. (Note that the names of some of these variables violate the convention that names of global variables begin and end with an asterisk.) These are intended primarily for user interaction, which is why they have short names. Use of these variables should be avoided in programs.

+	[*Variable*]
+ +	[*Variable*]
+ + +	[*Variable*]

While a form is being evaluated by the top-level loop, the variable + is bound to the previous form read by the loop. The variable + + holds the previous value of + (that is, the form evaluated two interactions ago), and + + + holds the previous value of + +.

	[*Variable*]

While a form is being evaluated by the top-level loop, the variable - is bound to the form itself; that is, it is the value about to be given to + once this interaction is done.

*	[*Variable*]
* *	[*Variable*]
* * *	[*Variable*]

While a form is being evaluated by the top-level loop, the variable * is bound to the result printed at the end of the last time through the loop; that is, it is the value produced by evaluating the form in +. If several values were produced, * contains the first value only; * contains nil if zero values were produced. The variable * * holds the previous value of * (that is, the result printed two interactions ago), and * * * holds the previous value of * *.

If the evaluation of + is aborted for some reason, then the values associated with *, * *, and * * * are not updated; they are updated only if the printing of values is at least begun (though not necessarily completed).

/	[*Variable*]
/ /	[*Variable*]
/ / /	[*Variable*]

While a form is being evaluated by the top-level loop, the variable / is bound to a list of the results printed at the end of the last time through the loop; that is, it is a list of all values produced by evaluating the form in +. The value of * should always be the same as the *car* of the value of /. The variable // holds the previous value of / (that is, the results printed two interactions ago), and /// holds the previous value of //. Therefore the value of ** should always be the same as the *car* of //, and similarly for *** and ///.

If the evaluation of + is aborted for some reason, then the values associated with /, //, and /// are not updated; they are updated only if the printing of values is at least begun (though not necessarily completed).

As an example of the processing of these variables, consider the following possible transcript, where › is a prompt by the top-level loop for user input:

```
>(cons - -)                    ;Interaction 1
((CONS - -) CONS - -)          ; Cute, huh?

>(values)                      ;Interaction 2
                               ; There is nothing to print.

>(cons 'a 'b)                  ;Interaction 3
(A . B)                        ; There is a single value.

>(hairy-loop)^G                ;Interaction 4
### QUIT to top level.         ; (User aborts the computation.)

>(floor 13 4)                  ;Interaction 5
3                              ; There are two values.
1
```

At this point we have:

```
+++ ⇒ (cons 'a 'b)      *** ⇒ NIL        /// ⇒ ()
++  ⇒ (hairy-loop)      **  ⇒ (A . B)    //  ⇒ ((A . B))
+   ⇒ (floor 13 4)      *   ⇒ 3          /   ⇒ (3 1)
```

21

Streams

Streams are objects that serve as sources or sinks of data. Character streams produce or absorb characters; binary streams produce or absorb integers. The normal action of a COMMON LISP system is to read characters from a character input stream, parse the characters as representations of COMMON LISP data objects, evaluate each object (as a form) as it is read, and print representations of the results of evaluation to an output character stream.

Typically streams are connected to files or to an interactive terminal. Streams, being LISP objects, serve as the ambassadors of external devices by which input/output is accomplished.

A stream, whether a character stream or a binary stream, may be input-only, output-only, or bidirectional. What operations may be performed on a stream depends on which of the six types of stream it is.

21.1. Standard Streams

There are several variables whose values are streams used by many functions in the LISP system. These variables and their uses are listed here. By convention, variables that are expected to hold a stream capable of input have names ending with -input, and similarly -output for output streams. Those expected to hold a bidirectional stream have names ending with -io.

standard-input   [*Variable*]

In the normal LISP top-level loop, input is read from *standard-input* (that is, whatever stream is the value of the global variable *standard-input*). Many input functions, including read and read-char, take a stream argument that defaults to *standard-input*.

standard-output   [*Variable*]

In the normal LISP top-level loop, output is sent to *standard-output* (that is, whatever stream is the value of the global variable *standard-output*). Many output functions, including `print` and `write-char`, take a stream argument that defaults to `*standard-output*`.

`*error-output*`   [*Variable*]

The value of `*error-output*` is a stream to which error messages should be sent. Normally this is the same as `*standard-output*`, but `*standard-output*` might be bound to a file and `*error-output*` left going to the terminal or a separate file of error messages.

`*query-io*`   [*Variable*]

The value of `*query-io*` is a stream to be used when asking questions of the user. The question should be output to this stream, and the answer read from it. When the normal input to a program may be coming from a file, questions such as "Do you really want to delete all of the files in your directory?" should nevertheless be sent directly to the user; and the answer should come from the user, not from the data file. For such purposes `*query-io*` should be used instead of `*standard-input*` and `*standard-output*`. `*query-io*` is used by such functions as `yes-or-no-p`.

`*debug-io*`   [*Variable*]

The value of `*debug-io*` is a stream to be used for interactive debugging purposes. This is often the same as the value of `*query-io*`, but need not be.

`*terminal-io*`   [*Variable*]

The value of `*terminal-io*` is ordinarily the stream that connects to the user's console. Typically, writing to this stream would cause the output to appear on a display screen, for example, and reading from the stream would accept input from a keyboard. It is intended that standard input functions such as `read` and `read-char`, when used with this stream, would cause "echoing" of the input into the output side of the stream. (The means by which this is accomplished are of course highly implementation-dependent.)

`*trace-output*`   [*Variable*]

The value of `*trace-output*` is the stream on which the `trace` function prints its output.

`*standard-input*`, `*standard-output*`, `*error-output*`, `*trace-output*`, `*query-io*`, and `*debug-io*` are initially bound to synonym streams that pass all operations on to the stream that is the value of *terminal-io*. (See make-synonym-stream.) Thus any operations performed on those streams will go to the terminal.

No user program should ever change the value of *terminal-io*. A program that wants (for example) to divert output to a file should do so by binding the value of *standard-output*; that way error messages sent to *error-output* can still get to the user by going through *terminal-io*, which is usually what is desired.

21.2. Creating New Streams

Perhaps the most important constructs for creating new streams are those that open files; see with-open-file and open. The following functions construct streams without reference to a file system.

---

make-synonym-stream *symbol*   [*Function*]

make-synonym-stream creates and returns a "synonym stream." Any operations on the new stream will be performed on the stream that is then the value of the dynamic variable named by the *symbol*. If the value of the variable should change or be bound, then the synonym stream will operate on the new stream.

---

make-broadcast-stream &rest *streams*   [*Function*]

This returns a stream that only works in the output direction. Any output sent to this stream will be sent to all of the *streams* given. The set of operations that may be performed on the new stream is the intersection of those for the given streams. The results returned by a stream operation are the values resulting from performing the operation on the last stream in *streams*; the results of performing the operation on all preceding streams are discarded. If no *streams* are given as arguments, then the result is a "bit sink"; all output to the resulting stream is discarded.

---

make-concatenated-stream &rest *streams*   [*Function*]

This returns a stream that only works in the input direction. Input is taken from the first of the *streams* until it reaches end-of-file; then that stream is discarded, and input is taken from the next of the *streams*, and so on. If no arguments are given, the result is a stream with no content; any input attempt will result in end-of-file.

---

make-two-way-stream *input-stream output-stream*   [*Function*]

This returns a bidirectional stream that gets its input from *input-stream* and sends its output to *output-stream*.

`make-echo-stream` *input-stream output-stream*   [*Function*]

This returns a bidirectional stream that gets its input from *input-stream* and sends its output to *output-stream*. In addition, all input taken from *input-stream* is echoed to *output-stream*.

`make-string-input-stream` *string &optional start end*   [*Function*]

This returns an input stream. The input stream will supply, in order, the characters in the substring of *string* delimited by *start* and *end*; after the last character has been supplied, the stream will then be at end-of-file.

`make-string-output-stream`   [*Function*]

This returns an output stream that will accumulate all output given it for the benefit of the function `get-output-stream-string`.

`get-output-stream-string` *string-output-stream*   [*Function*]

Given a stream produced by `make-string-output-stream`, this returns a string containing all the characters output to the stream so far. The stream is then reset; thus each call to `get-output-stream-string` gets only the characters since the last such call (or the creation of the stream, if no such previous call has been made).

`with-open-stream` (*var stream*) {*declaration*}* {*form*}*   [*Macro*]

The form *stream* is evaluated and must produce a stream. The variable *var* is bound with the stream as its value, and then the forms of the body are executed as an implicit `progn`; the results of evaluating the last form are returned as the value of the `with-open-stream` form. The stream is automatically closed on exit from the `with-open-stream` form, no matter whether the exit is normal or abnormal; see `close`. The stream should be regarded as having dynamic extent.

`with-input-from-string` (*var string* {*keyword value*}*)   [*Macro*]
                              {*declaration*}* {*form*}*

The body is executed as an implicit `progn` with the variable *var* bound to a character input stream that supplies successive characters from the value of the form *string*. `with-input-from-string` returns the results from the last *form* of the body.

The input stream is automatically closed on exit from the `with-input-from-string` form, no matter whether the exit is normal or abnormal.

The stream should be regarded as having dynamic extent.

The following keyword options may be used:

:index

The form after the :index keyword should be a *place* acceptable to setf. If the with-input-from-string form is exited normally, then the *place* will have stored into it the index into the *string* indicating the first character not read (the length of the string if all characters were used). The *place* is not updated as reading progresses, but only at the end of the operation.

:start

The :start keyword takes an argument indicating, in the manner usual for sequence functions, the beginning of a substring of *string* to be used.

:end

The :end keyword takes an argument indicating, in the manner usual for sequence functions, the end of a substring of *string* to be used.

Here is an example of the use of with-input-from-string:

```
(with-input-from-string (s "Animal Crackers" :index j :start 6)
  (read s)) ⇒ crackers
```

As a side effect, the variable j is set to 15.

The :start and :index keywords may both specify the same variable, which is a pointer within the string to be advanced, perhaps repeatedly by some containing loop.

with-output-to-string (*var* [*string*]) {*declaration*}* {*form*}*   [*Macro*]

The body is executed as an implicit progn with the variable *var* bound to a character output stream. All output to that stream is saved in a string. This may be done in one of two ways.

If no *string* argument is provided, then the value of with-output-from-string is a string containing all the collected output.

If *string* is specified, it must be a string with a fill pointer; the output is incrementally appended to the string, as if using vector-push-extend if the string is adjustable, and otherwise as if using vector-push. In this case with-output-to-string returns the results from the last *form* of the body.

In either case, the output stream is automatically closed on exit from the with-output-from-string form, no matter whether the exit is normal or abnormal. The stream should be regarded as having dynamic extent.

21.3. Operations on Streams

This section contains discussion of only those operations that are common to all streams. Input and output is rather complicated and is discussed separately in chapter 22. The interface between streams and the file system is discussed in chapter 23.

`streamp` *object*   [*Function*]

`streamp` is true if its argument is a stream, and otherwise is false.

`(streamp x)` ≡ `(typep x 'stream)`

`input-stream-p` *stream*   [*Function*]

This predicate is true if its argument (which must be a stream) can handle input operations, and otherwise is false.

`output-stream-p` *stream*   [*Function*]

This predicate is true if its argument (which must be a stream) can handle output operations, and otherwise is false.

`stream-element-type` *stream*   [*Function*]

A type specifier is returned to indicate what objects may be read from or written to the argument *stream*, which must be a stream. Streams created by `open` will have an element type restricted to a subset of `character` or `integer`, but in principle a stream may conduct transactions using any LISP objects.

`close` *stream* &key `:abort`   [*Function*]

The argument must be a stream. The stream is closed. No further input/output operations may be performed on it. However, certain inquiry operations may still be performed, and it is permissible to close an already closed stream.

If the `:abort` parameter is not `nil` (it defaults to `nil`), it indicates an abnormal termination of the use of the stream. An attempt is made to clean up any side effects of having created the stream in the first place. For example, if the stream performs output to a file that was newly created when the stream was created, then if possible the file is deleted and any previously existing file is not superseded.

22

Input/Output

COMMON LISP provides a rich set of facilities for performing input/output. All input/output operations are performed on streams of various kinds. This chapter is devoted to stream data transfer operations. Streams are discussed in chapter 21, and ways of manipulating files through streams are discussed in chapter 23.

While there is provision for reading and writing binary data, most of the I/O operations in COMMON LISP read or write characters. There are simple primitives for reading and writing single characters or lines of data. The format function can perform complex formatting of output data, directed by a control string in manner similar to a FORTRAN FORMAT statement or a PL/I PUT EDIT statement. The most useful I/O operations, however, read and write printed representations of arbitrary LISP objects.

22.1. Printed Representation of LISP Objects

LISP objects in general are not text strings, but complex data structures. They have very different properties from text strings as a consequence of their internal representation. However, to make it possible to get at and talk about LISP objects, LISP provides a representation of most objects in the form of printed text; this is called the *printed representation*, which is used for input/output purposes and in the examples throughout this manual. Functions such as print take a LISP object and send the characters of its printed representation to a stream. The collection of routines that does this is known as the (LISP) *printer*. The read function takes characters from a stream, interprets them as a printed representation of a LISP object, builds that object, and returns it; the collection of routines that does this is called the (LISP) *reader*.

Ideally, one could print a LISP object and then read the printed representation back in, and so obtain the same identical object. In practice this is difficult and for some purposes not even desirable. Instead, reading a printed representation produces an object that is (with obscure technical exceptions) equal to the originally printed object.

Most LISP objects have more than one possible printed representation. For example, the integer twenty-seven can be written in any of these ways:

```
27      27.      #o33      #x1B      #b11011      #.(* 3 3 3)      81/3
```

A list of two symbols A and B can be printed in many ways:

```
(A B)      (a b)      ( a b )      (\A |B|)
   (|\A|
  B
)
```

The last example, which is spread over three lines, may be ugly, but it is legitimate. In general, wherever whitespace is permissible in a printed representation, any number of spaces and newlines may appear.

When `print` produces a printed representation, it must choose arbitrarily from among many possible printed representations. It attempts to choose one that is readable. There are a number of global variables that can be used to control the actions of `print`, and a number of different printing functions.

This section describes in detail what is the standard printed representation for any Lisp object, and also describes how `read` operates.

22.1.1. What the Read Function Accepts

The purpose of the LISP reader is to accept characters, interpret them as the printed representation of a LISP object, and construct and return such an object. The reader cannot accept everything that the printer produces; for example, the printed representations of compiled code objects cannot be read in. However, the reader has many features that are not used by the output of the printer at all, such as comments, alternative representations, and convenient abbreviations for frequently used but unwieldy constructs. The reader is also parameterized in such a way that it can be used as a lexical analyzer for a more general user-written parser.

The reader is organized as a recursive-descent parser. Broadly speaking, the reader operates by reading a character from the input stream and treating it in one of three ways. Whitespace characters serve as separators but are otherwise ignored. Constituent and escape characters are accumulated to make a *token*, which is then interpreted as a number or symbol. Macro characters trigger the invocation of functions (possibly user-supplied) that can perform arbitrary parsing actions, including recursive invocation of the reader.

More precisely, when the reader is invoked, it reads a single character from the input stream and dispatches according to the syntactic type of that character. Every character that can appear in the input stream must be of exactly one of the following kinds: *illegal, whitespace, constituent, single escape, multiple escape*, or *macro*. Macro characters are further divided into the types *terminating* and *non-terminating* (of tokens). (Note that macro characters have nothing whatever to do with macros in their operation. There is a superficial similarity in that macros allow the user to extend the syntax of COMMON LISP at the level of forms, while macro characters allow the user to extend the syntax at the level of characters.) Constituents additionally have one or more attributes, the most important of which is *alphabetic*; these attributes are discussed further in section 22.1.2.

The parsing of COMMON LISP expressions is discussed in terms of these syntactic character types because the types of individual characters are not fixed but may be altered by the user (see `set-syntax-from-char` and `set-macro-character`). The characters of the standard character set initially have the syntactic types shown in Table 22-1. Note that the brackets, braces, question mark, and exclamation point (that is, [,], {, }, ?, and !) are normally defined to be constituents, but they are not used for any purpose in standard COMMON LISP syntax and do not occur in the names of built-in COMMON LISP functions or variables. These characters are explicitly reserved to the user. The primary intent is that they be used as macro characters; but a user might choose, for example, to make ! be a *single escape* character (as it is in PORTABLE STANDARD LISP).

The algorithm performed by the COMMON LISP reader is roughly as follows:

1. If at end of file, perform end-of-file processing (as specified by the caller of the `read` function). Otherwise, read one character from the input stream, call it *x*, and dispatch according to the syntactic type of *x* to one of steps 2 to 7.

2. If *x* is an *illegal* character, signal an error.

3. If *x* is a *whitespace* character, then discard it and go back to step 1.

4. If *x* is a *macro* character (at this point the distinction between *terminating* and *non-terminating* macro characters does not matter), then execute the function associated with that character. The function may return zero values or one value (see `values`).

   The macro-character function may of course read characters from the input stream; if it does, it will see those characters following the macro character. The function may even invoke the reader recursively. This is how the macro character (constructs a list: by invoking the reader recursively to read the elements of the list.

   If one value is returned, then return that value as the result of the read operation; the algorithm is done. If zero values are returned, then go back to step 1.

5. If *x* is a *single escape* character (normally \), then read the next character and

Table 22-1: Standard Character Syntax Types

\<tab\>	*whitespace*	\<page\>	*whitespace*	\<newline\>	*whitespace*
\<space\>	*whitespace*	@	*constituent*	`	*terminating macro*
!	*constituent**	A	*constituent*	a	*constituent*
"	*terminating macro*	B	*constituent*	b	*constituent*
#	*non-terminating macro*	C	*constituent*	c	*constituent*
$	*constituent*	D	*constituent*	d	*constituent*
%	*constituent*	E	*constituent*	e	*constituent*
&	*constituent*	F	*constituent*	f	*constituent*
'	*terminating macro*	G	*constituent*	g	*constituent*
(	*terminating macro*	H	*constituent*	h	*constituent*
)	*terminating macro*	I	*constituent*	i	*constituent*
*	*constituent*	J	*constituent*	j	*constituent*
+	*constituent*	K	*constituent*	k	*constituent*
,	*terminating macro*	L	*constituent*	l	*constituent*
-	*constituent*	M	*constituent*	m	*constituent*
.	*constituent*	N	*constituent*	n	*constituent*
/	*constituent*	O	*constituent*	o	*constituent*
0	*constituent*	P	*constituent*	p	*constituent*
1	*constituent*	Q	*constituent*	q	*constituent*
2	*constituent*	R	*constituent*	r	*constituent*
3	*constituent*	S	*constituent*	s	*constituent*
4	*constituent*	T	*constituent*	t	*constituent*
5	*constituent*	U	*constituent*	u	*constituent*
6	*constituent*	V	*constituent*	v	*constituent*
7	*constituent*	W	*constituent*	w	*constituent*
8	*constituent*	X	*constituent*	x	*constituent*
9	*constituent*	Y	*constituent*	y	*constituent*
:	*constituent*	Z	*constituent*	z	*constituent*
;	*terminating macro*	[	*constituent**	{	*constituent**
<	*constituent*	\	*single escape*	|	*multiple escape*
=	*constituent*	]	*constituent**	}	*constituent**
>	*constituent*	^	*constituent*	~	*constituent*
?	*constituent**	_	*constituent*	\<rubout\>	*constituent*
\<backspace\>	*constituent*	\<return\>	*whitespace*	\<linefeed\>	*whitespace*

*The characters marked with an asterisk are initially constituents, but are reserved to the user for use as macro characters or for any other desired purpose.

call it *y* (but if at end of file, signal an error instead). Ignore the usual syntax of *y* and pretend it is a *constituent* whose only attribute is *alphabetic*. (If *y* is a lowercase character, leave it alone; do not replace it with the corresponding uppercase character.) Use *y* to begin a token, and go to step 8.

6. If *x* is a *multiple escape* character (normally ¦), then begin a token (initially containing no characters) and go to step 9.

7. If *x* is a *constituent* character, then it begins an extended token. After the entire token is read in, it will be interpreted either as representing a LISP object such as a symbol or number (in which case that object is returned as the result of the read operation), or as being of illegal syntax (in which case an error is signalled). If *x* is a lowercase character, replace it with the corresponding uppercase character. Use *x* to begin a token, and go on to step 8.

8. (At this point a token is being accumulated, and an even number of *multiple escape* characters have been encountered.) If at end of file, go to step 10. Otherwise, read a character (call it *y*), and perform one of the following actions according to its syntactic type:

   • If *y* is a *constituent* or *non-terminating macro* then do the following. If *y* is a lowercase character, replace it with the corresponding uppercase character. Append *y* to the token being built, and repeat step 8.

   • If *y* is a *single escape* character, then read the next character and call it *z* (but if at end of file, signal an error instead). Ignore the usual syntax of *z* and pretend it is a *constituent* whose only attribute is *alphabetic*. (If *z* is a lowercase character, leave it alone; do not replace it with the corresponding uppercase character.) Append *z* to the token being built, and repeat step 8.

   • If *y* is a *multiple escape* character, then go to step 9.

   • If *y* is an *illegal* character, signal an error.

   • If *y* is a *terminating macro* character, then it terminates the token. First ''unread'' the character *y* (see `unread-char`), and then go to step 10.

   • If *y* is a *whitespace* character, then it terminates the token. First ''unread'' the character *y* if appropriate (see `read-preserving-whitespace`), and then go to step 10.

9. (At this point a token is being accumulated, and an odd number of *multiple escape* characters have been encountered.) If at end of file, signal an error. Otherwise, read a character (call it *y*), and perform one of the following actions according to its syntactic type:

   • If *y* is a *constituent, macro,* or *whitespace* character, then ignore the usual syntax of that character and pretend it is a *constituent* whose only attribute is *alphabetic*. (If *y* is a lowercase character, leave it alone; do not replace it with the corresponding uppercase character.) Append *y* to the token being built, and repeat step 9.

   • If *y* is a *single escape* character, then read the next character and call it *z* (but if at end of file, signal an error instead). Ignore the usual syntax of *z* and pretend it is a *constituent* whose only attribute is *alphabetic*. (If z is a lowercase character, leave it alone; do not replace it with the corresponding uppercase character.) Append z to the token being built, and repeat step 9.

- If y is a *multiple escape* character, then go to step 8.
- If y is an *illegal* character, signal an error.

10. An entire token has been accumulated. Interpret it as representing a LISP object and return that object as the result of the read operation, or signal an error if the token is not of legal syntax.

As a rule, a *single escape* character never stands for itself but always serves to cause the following character to be treated as a simple alphabetic character. A *single escape* character can be included in a token only if preceded by another *single escape* character.

A *multiple escape* character also never stands for itself. The characters between a pair of *multiple escape* characters are all treated as simple alphabetic characters, except that *single escape* and *multiple escape* characters must nevertheless be preceded by a *single escape* character to be included.

Compatibility note: In MACLISP, the | character is implemented as a macro character that reads characters up to the next unescaped | and then makes a token; no characters are ever read beyond the second | of a matching pair. In COMMON LISP, the second | does not terminate the token being read but merely reverts to the ordinary (rather than multiple-escape) mode of token accumulation. This results in some differences in the way certain character sequences are interpreted. For example, the sequence |foo||bar| would be read in MACLISP as two distinct tokens |foo| and |bar|, whereas in COMMON LISP it would be treated as a single token equivalent to |foobar|. The sequence |foo|bar|baz| would be read in MACLISP as three distinct tokens |foo|, bar, and |baz|, whereas in COMMON LISP it would be treated as a single token equivalent to |fooBARbaz|; note that the middle three lowercase letters are converted to uppercase letters as they do not fall within a matching pair of vertical bars.

One reason for the different treatment of | in COMMON LISP lies in the syntax for package-qualified symbol names. A sequence such as |foo:bar| ought to be interpreted as a symbol whose name is foo:bar; the colon should be treated as a simple alphabetic character because it lies within a pair of vertical bars. The symbol |bar| within the package |foo| can be notated, not as |foo:bar|, but as |foo|:|bar|; the colon can serve as a package marker because it falls outside the vertical bars, and yet the notation is treated as a single token thanks to the new rules adopted in COMMON LISP.

In MACLISP, the parentheses are treated as additional character types. In COMMON LISP they are simply *macro* characters, as described in section 22.1.3.

What MACLISP calls a "single character object" (tokens of type *single*) are not provided for explicitly in COMMON LISP. They can be viewed as simply a kind of macro character. That is, the effect of

```
(setsyntax '$ 'single nil)
(setsyntax '% 'single nil)
```

in MacLisp can be achieved in Common Lisp by

```
(defun single-macro-character (stream char)
  (declare (ignore stream))
  (intern (string char)))
```

```
(set-macro-character '$ #'single-macro-character)
(set-macro-character '% #'single-macro-character)
```

22.1.2. Parsing of Numbers and Symbols

When an extended token is read, it is interpreted as a number or symbol. In general, the token is interpreted as a number if it satisfies the syntax for numbers specified in Table 22-2; this is discussed in more detail below.

The characters of the extended token may serve various syntactic functions as shown in Table 22-3, but it must be remembered that any character included in a token under the control of an escape character is treated as *alphabetic* rather than according to the attributes shown in the table. One consequence of this rule is that a whitespace, macro, or escape character will always be treated as alphabetic within an extended token because such a character cannot be included in an extended token except under the control of an escape character.

To allow for extensions to the syntax of numbers, a syntax for *potential numbers* is defined in Common Lisp that is more general than the actual syntax for numbers. Any token that is not a potential number and does not consist entirely of dots will

---

Table 22-2: Actual Syntax of Numbers

number ::= *integer* | *ratio* | *floating-point-number*
integer ::= [*sign*] {*digit*}$^+$ [*decimal-point*]
ratio ::= [*sign*] {*digit*}$^+$ / {*digit*}$^+$
floating-point-number ::= [*sign*] {*digit*}* *decimal-point* {*digit*}$^+$ [*exponent*]
                          | [*sign*] {*digit*}$^+$ [*decimal-point* {*digit*}*] *exponent*
sign ::= + | -
decimal-point ::= .
digit ::= 0 | 1 | 2 | 3 | 4 | 5 | 6 | 7 | 8 | 9
exponent ::= *exponent-marker* [*sign*] {*digit*}$^+$
exponent-marker ::= e | s | f | d | l | E | S | F | D | L

The notation {*x*}* means zero or more occurrences of *x*, the notation {*x*}$^+$ means one or more occurrences of *x*, and the notation [*x*] means zero or one occurrences of *x*.

Table 22-3: Standard Constituent Character Attributes

!	*alphabetic*	\<backspace\>	*illegal*	
"	*alphabetic* *	\<tab\>	*illegal* *	
#	*alphabetic* *	\<newline\>	*illegal* *	
$	*alphabetic*	\<linefeed\>	*illegal* *	
%	*alphabetic*	\<page\>	*illegal*	
&	*alphabetic*	\<return\>	*illegal* *	
'	*alphabetic* *	\<space\>	*illegal* *	
(	*alphabetic* *	+	*alphabetic, plus sign*	
)	*alphabetic* *	-	*alphabetic, minus sign*	
*	*alphabetic*	.	*alphabetic, dot, decimal point*	
,	*alphabetic* *	/	*alphabetic, ratio marker*	
0	*alphadigit*	A, a	*alphadigit*	
1	*alphadigit*	B, b	*alphadigit*	
2	*alphadigit*	C, c	*alphadigit*	
3	*alphadigit*	D, d	*alphadigit, double-float exponent marker*	
4	*alphadigit*	E, e	*alphadigit, float exponent marker*	
5	*alphadigit*	F, f	*alphadigit, single-float exponent marker*	
6	*alphadigit*	G, g	*alphadigit*	
7	*alphadigit*	H, h	*alphadigit*	
8	*alphadigit*	I, i	*alphadigit*	
9	*alphadigit*	J, j	*alphadigit*	
:	*package marker*	K, k	*alphadigit*	
;	*alphabetic* *	L, l	*alphadigit, long-float exponent marker*	
<	*alphabetic*	M, m	*alphadigit*	
=	*alphabetic*	N, n	*alphadigit*	
>	*alphabetic*	O, o	*alphadigit*	
?	*alphabetic*	P, p	*alphadigit*	
@	*alphabetic*	Q, q	*alphadigit*	
[	*alphabetic*	R, r	*alphadigit*	
\	*alphabetic* *	S, s	*alphadigit, short-float exponent marker*	
]	*alphabetic*	T, t	*alphadigit*	
^	*alphabetic*	U, u	*alphadigit*	
_	*alphabetic*	V, v	*alphadigit*	
`	*alphabetic* *	W, w	*alphadigit*	
{	*alphabetic*	X, x	*alphadigit*	
		alphabetic *	Y, y	*alphadigit*	
}	*alphabetic*	Z, z	*alphadigit*	
~	*alphabetic*	\<rubout\>	*illegal*	

The interpretations in this table apply only to characters whose syntactic type is *constituent*. Entries marked with an asterisk are normally shadowed because the indicated characters are of syntactic type *whitespace, macro, single escape,* or *multiple escape*. Characters with the *alphadigit* attribute are interpreted as having the digit or alphabetic attribute according to whether or not the character is a valid digit in the radix specified by *read-base*. Characters with the *illegal* attribute cannot ever appear in a token except under the control of an escape character.

always be taken to be a symbol, now and in the future; programs may rely on this fact. Any token that is a potential number but does not fit the actual number syntax defined below is a *reserved token* and has an implementation-dependent interpretation; an implementation may signal an error, quietly treat the token as a symbol, or take some other action. Programmers should avoid the use of such reserved tokens. (A symbol whose name looks like a reserved token can always be written using one or more escape characters.)

A token is a potential number if it satisfies the following requirements:

- It consists entirely of digits, signs (+ or -), ratio markers (/), decimal points (.), extension characters (^ or _), and number markers. (A number marker is a letter. Whether a letter may be treated as a number marker depends on context, but no letter that is adjacent to another letter may ever be treated as a number marker. Floating-point exponent markers are instances of number markers.)
- It contains at least one digit. (Letters may be considered to be digits, depending on the value of *read-base*, but only in tokens containing no decimal points.)
- It begins with a digit, sign, decimal point, or extension character.
- It does not end with a sign.

As examples, the following tokens are potential numbers, but they are *not* actually numbers as defined below, and so are reserved tokens. (They do indicate some interesting possibilities for future extensions.)

```
1b5000          ??????q         1.7J            -3/4+6.7J       12/25/83
27^19           3^4/5           6//7            3.1.2.6         ^-43^
3.141_592_653_589_793_238_4 -3.7+2.6i-6.17j+19.6k
```

The following tokens are *not* potential numbers but are always treated as symbols:

```
/               /5              +               1+              1-
foo+            ab.cd           _               ^               ^/-
```

The following tokens are potential numbers if the value of *read-base* is 16 (an abnormal situation), but they are always treated as symbols if the value of *read-base* is 10 (the usual value):

```
bad-face        25-dec-83       a/b             fad_cafe        f^
```

It is possible for there to be an ambiguity as to whether a letter should be treated as a digit or as a number marker. In such a case, the letter is always treated as a digit rather than as a number marker.

Note that the printed representation for a potential number may not contain any escape characters. An escape character robs the following character of all syntactic qualities, forcing it to be strictly alphabetic and therefore unsuitable for use in a potential number. For example, all of the following representations are interpreted as symbols, not numbers:

\256   25\64   1.0\E6   !100!   3\.14159   !3/4!   3\/4   5!!

In each case, removing the escape character(s) would allow the token to be treated as a number.

If a potential number can in fact be interpreted as a number according to the BNF syntax in Table 22-2, then a number object of the appropriate type is constructed and returned. It should be noted that in a given implementation it may be that not all tokens conforming to the actual syntax for numbers can actually be converted into number objects. For example, specifying too large or too small an exponent for a floating-point number may make the number impossible to represent in the implementation. Similarly, a ratio with denominator zero (such as -35/000) cannot be represented in *any* implementation. In any such circumstance where a token with the syntax of a number cannot be converted to an internal number object, an error is signalled. (On the other hand, an error must not be signalled for specifying too many significant digits for a floating-point number; an appropriately truncated or rounded value should be produced.)

There is an omission in the syntax of numbers, as described in Table 22-2, in that the syntax does not account for the possible use of letters as digits. The radix used for reading integers and ratios is normally decimal. However, this radix is actually determined by the value of the variable *read-base*, whose initial value is 10. *read-base* may take on any integral value between 2 and 36; let this value be n. Then a token x is interpreted as an integer or ratio in base n if it could be properly so interpreted in the syntax #nRx (see section 22.1.4). So, for example, if the value of *read-base* is 16, then the printed representation

(a small face in a bad place)

would be interpreted as if the following representation had been read with *read-base* set to 10:

(10 small 64206 in 10 2989 place)

because four of the seven tokens in the list can be interpreted as hexadecimal numbers. This facility is intended to be used in reading files of data that for some reason contain numbers not in decimal radix; it may also be used for reading programs written in LISP dialects (such as MACLISP) whose default number radix is not decimal. Non-decimal constants in COMMON LISP programs or portable COMMON LISP data files should be written using #O, #X, #B, or #nR syntax.

When *read-base* has a value greater than ten, an ambiguity is introduced into the actual syntax for numbers because a letter can serve as either a digit or an exponent marker; a simple example is 1E0 when the value of *read-base* is 16. The ambiguity is resolved in accordance with the general principle that interpretation as a digit is preferred to interpretation as a number marker. The consequence in this case is that if a token can be interpreted as either an integer or a floating-point number, then it is taken to be an integer.

If a token consists solely of dots (with no escape characters), then an error is signalled, except in one circumstance: if the token is a single dot and occurs in a situation appropriate to "dotted list" syntax, then it is accepted as a part of such syntax. Signalling an error catches not only misplaced dots in dotted list syntax, but also lists that were truncated by *print-length* cutoff, because such lists end with a three-dot sequence (...). Examples:

`(a . b)`	;A dotted pair of a and b
`(a.b)`	;A list of one element, the symbol named a.b
`(a. b)`	;A list of two elements a. and b
`(a .b)`	;A list of two elements a and .b
`(a \. b)`	;A list of three elements a, ., and b
`(a !.! b)`	;A list of three elements a, ., and b
`(a \... b)`	;A list of three elements a, ..., and b
`(a !...! b)`	;A list of three elements a, ..., and b
`(a b . c)`	;A dotted list of a and b with c at the end
`.iot`	;The symbol whose name is .iot
`(. b)`	;Illegal; an error is signalled.
`(a .)`	;Illegal; an error is signalled.
`(a .. b)`	;Illegal; an error is signalled.
`(a . . b)`	;Illegal; an error is signalled.
`(a b c ...)`	;Illegal; an error is signalled.

In all other cases, the token is construed to be the name of a symbol. If there are any package markers (colons) in the token, they divide the token into pieces used to control the lookup and creation of the symbol.

If there is a single package marker, and it occurs at the beginning of the token, then the token is interpreted as a keyword, that is, a symbol in the :keyword package. The part of the token after the package marker must not have the syntax of a number.

If there is a single package marker not at the beginning or end of the token, then it divides the token into two parts. The first part specifies a package; the second part is the name of an external symbol available in that package. Neither of the two parts may have the syntax of a number.

If there are two adjacent package markers not at the beginning or end of the token, then they divide the token into two parts. The first part specifies a package;

the second part is the name of a symbol within that package (possibly an internal symbol). Neither of the two parts may have the syntax of a number.

If a symbol token contains no package markers, then the entire token is the name of the symbol. The symbol is looked up in the default package; see *package*.

All other patterns of package markers, including the cases where there are more than two package markers or where a package marker appears at the end of the token, presently do not mean anything in COMMON LISP; see chapter 11. It is therefore currently an error to use such patterns in a COMMON LISP program. The valid patterns for tokens may be summarized as follows:

nnnnn	a number
xxxxx	a symbol in the current package
:*xxxxx*	a symbol in the keyword package
ppppp:*xxxxx*	an external symbol in the *ppppp* package
ppppp::*xxxxx*	a (possibly internal) symbol in the *ppppp* package

where *nnnnn* has the syntax of a number, and *xxxxx* and *ppppp* do not have the syntax of a number.

---

read-base   [*Variable*]

The value of *read-base* controls the interpretation of tokens by read as being integers or ratios. Its value is the radix in which integers and ratios are to be read; the value may be any integer from 2 to 36 (inclusive) and is normally 10 (decimal radix). Its value affects only the reading of integers and ratios. In particular, floating-point numbers are always read in decimal radix. The value of *read-base* does not affect the radix for rational numbers whose radix is explicitly indicated by #O, #X, #B, or #nR syntax or by a trailing decimal point.

Care should be taken when setting *read-base* to a value larger than 10, because tokens that would normally be interpreted as symbols may be interpreted as numbers instead. For example, with *read-base* set to 16 (hexadecimal radix), variables with names such as a, b, f, bad, and face will be treated by the reader as numbers (with decimal values 10, 11, 15, 2989, and 64206, respectively). The ability to alter the input radix is provided in COMMON LISP primarily for the purpose of reading data files in special formats, rather than for the purpose of altering the default radix in which to read programs. The user is strongly encouraged to use #O, #X, #B, or #nR syntax when notating non-decimal constants in programs.

Compatibility note: This variable corresponds to the variable called ibase in MACLISP and to the function called radix in INTERLISP.

read-suppress'   [*Variable*]

When the value of *read-suppress* is nil, the LISP reader operates normally. When it is not nil, then most of the interesting operations of the reader are suppressed; input characters are parsed, but much of what is read is not interpreted.

The primary purpose of *read-suppress* is to support the operation of the read-time conditional constructs #+ and #- (see section 22.1.4). It is important for these constructs to be able to skip over the printed representation of a LISP expression despite the possibility that the syntax of the skipped expression may not be entirely legal for the current implementation; this is because a primary application of #+ and #- is to allow the same program to be shared among several LISP implementations despite small incompatibilities of syntax.

A non-nil value of *read-suppress* has the following specific effects on the COMMON LISP reader:

- All extended tokens are completely uninterpreted. It matters not whether the token looks like a number, much less like a valid number; the pattern of package markers also does not matter. An extended token is simply discarded and treated as if it were nil; that is, reading an extended token when *read-suppress* is non-nil simply returns nil. (One consequence of this is that the error concerning improper dotted-list syntax will not be signalled.)

- Any standard # macro-character construction that requires, permits, or disallows an infix numerical argument, such as #nR, will not enforce any constraint on the presence, absence, or value of such an argument.

- The #\ construction always produces the value nil. It will not signal an error even if an unknown character name is seen.

- Each of the #B, #O, #X, and #R constructions always scans over a following token and produces the value nil. It will not signal an error even if the token does not have the syntax of a rational number.

- The #* construction always scans over a following token and produces the value nil. It will not signal an error even if the token does not consist solely of the characters 0 and 1.

- Each of the #. and #, constructions reads the following form (in suppressed mode, of course) but does not evaluate it. The form is discarded and nil is produced.

- Each of the #A, #S, and #: constructions reads the following form (in suppressed mode, of course) but does not interpret it in any way; it need not even be a list in the case of #S, or a symbol in the case of #:. The form is discarded and nil is produced.

- The #= construction is totally ignored. It does not read a following form. It produces no object, but is treated as whitespace.

• The `##` construction always produces `nil`.

Note that, no matter what the value of `*read-suppress*`, parentheses still continue to delimit (and construct) lists; the `#(` construction continues to delimit vectors; and comments, strings, and the quote and backquote constructions continue to be interpreted properly. Furthermore, such situations as `')`, `#<`, `#)`, and `#<space>` continue to signal errors.

In some cases, it may be appropriate for a user-written macro-character definition to check the value of `*read-suppress*` and avoid certain computations or side effects if its value is not `nil`.

22.1.3. Macro Characters

If the reader encounters a macro character, then the function associated with that macro character is invoked and may produce an object to be returned. This function may read following characters in the stream in whatever syntax it likes (it may even call `read` recursively) and return the object represented by that syntax. Macro characters may or may not be recognized, of course, when read as part of other special syntaxes (such as for strings).

The reader is therefore organized into two parts: the basic dispatch loop, which also distinguishes symbols and numbers, and the collection of macro characters. Any character can be reprogrammed as a macro character; this is a means by which the reader can be extended. The macro characters normally defined are as follows:

`(`

The left-parenthesis character initiates reading of a pair or list. The function `read` is called recursively to read successive objects until a right parenthesis is found to be next in the input stream. A list of the objects read is returned. Thus

```
(a b c)
```

is read as a list of three objects (the symbols `a`, `b`, and `c`). The right parenthesis need not immediately follow the printed representation of the last object; whitespace characters and comments may precede it. This can be useful for putting one object on each line and making it easy to add new objects:

```
(defun traffic-light (color)
  (case color
    (green)
    (red (stop))
    (amber (accelerate))      ;Insert more colors after this line.
    ))
```

It may be that *no* objects precede the right parenthesis, as in ( ) or ( ); this reads as a list of zero objects (the empty list).

If a token that is just a dot, not preceded by an escape character, is read after some object then exactly one more object must follow the dot, possibly followed by whitespace, followed by the right parenthesis:

(a b c . d)

This means that the *cdr* of the last pair in the list is not nil, but rather the object whose representation followed the dot. The above example might have been the result of evaluating

(cons 'a (cons 'b (cons 'c 'd))) ⇒ (a b c . d)

Similarly, we have

(cons 'znets 'wolq-zorbitan) ⇒ (znets . wolq-zorbitan)

It is permissible for the object following the dot to be a list:

(a b c d . (e f . (g))) is the same as (a b c d e f g)

but this is a non-standard form that print will never produce.

)

The right-parenthesis character is part of various constructs (such as the syntax for lists) using the left-parenthesis character and is invalid except when used in such a construct.

'

The single-quote (accent acute) character provides an abbreviation to make it easier to put constants in programs. *'foo* reads the same as (quote *foo*): a list of the symbol quote and *foo*.

;

Semicolon is used to write comments. The semicolon and all characters up to and including the next newline are ignored. Thus a comment can be put at the end of any line without affecting the reader. (A comment will terminate a token, but a newline would terminate the token anyway.)

"

The double quote character begins the printed representation of a string. Characters are read from the input stream and accumulated until another double quote is encountered. An exception to this occurs if a *single escape* character is seen; the

```
;;;; COMMENT-EXAMPLE function.
;;; This function is useless except to demonstrate comments.
;;; (Actually, this example is much too cluttered with them.)
;;; Notice that there are several kinds of comments.

(defun comment-example (x y)      ;X is anything; Y is an a-list.
  (cond ((listp x) x)             ;If X is a list, use that.
        ;; X is now not a list.  There are two other cases.
        ((symbolp x)
         ;; Look up a symbol in the a-list.
         (cdr (assoc x y)))       ;Remember, (cdr nil) is nil.
        ;; Do this when all else fails:
        (t (cons x                ;Add x to a default list.
                 '((lisp t)       ;LISP is okay.
                   (fortran nil)     ;FORTRAN is not.
                   (pl/i -500)   ;You can put comments in "data"
                   (ada .001)    ; as well as in "programs".
                   ;; COBOL??
                   (teco -1.0e9)))))))
```

This example illustrates a few conventions for comments in common use. Comments may begin with one to four semicolons.

- Single-semicolon comments are all aligned to the same column at the right; usually each comments about only the line it is on. Occasionally two or three contain a single sentence together; this is indicated by indenting all but the first by a space (after the semicolon).

- Double-semicolon comments are aligned to the level of indentation of the code. A space follows the two semicolons. Usually each describes the state of the program at that point or describes the section that follows.

- Triple-semicolon comments are aligned to the left margin. Usually they are not used within function definitions but precede them in large blocks.

- Quadruple-semicolon comments are interpreted as subheadings.

Compatibility note: These conventions arose among users of MacLisp and have been found to be very useful. The conventions are conveniently exploited by certain software tools, such as the EMACS editor and the ATSIGN listing program developed at MIT.

escape character is discarded, the next character is accumulated, and accumulation continues. When a matching double quote is seen, all the accumulated characters up to but not including the matching double quote are made into a simple string and returned.

The backquote (accent grave) character makes it easier to write programs to construct complex data structures by using a template. As an example, writing

```
`(cond ((numberp ,x) ,@y) (t (print ,x) ,@y))
```

is roughly equivalent to writing

```
(list 'cond
      (cons (list 'numberp x) y)
      (list* 't (list 'print x) y))
```

The general idea is that the backquote is followed by a template, a picture of a data structure to be built. This template is copied, except that within the template commas can appear. Where a comma occurs, the form following the comma is to be evaluated to produce an object to be inserted at that point. Assume b has the value 3, for example, then evaluating the form denoted by `` `(a b ,b ,(+ b 1) b) `` produces the result (a b 3 4 b).

If a comma is immediately followed by an at-sign (@), then the form following the at-sign is evaluated to produce a *list* of objects. These objects are then "spliced" into place in the template. For example, if x has the value (a b c), then

```
`(x ,x ,@x foo ,(cadr x) bar ,(cdr x) baz ,@(cdr x))
   ⇒ (x (a b c) a b c foo b bar (b c) baz b c)
```

The backquote syntax can be summarized formally as follows. For each of several situations in which backquote can be used, a possible interpretation of that situation as an equivalent form is given. Note that the form is equivalent only in the sense that when it is evaluated it will calculate the correct result. An implementation is quite free to interpret backquote in any way such that a backquoted form, when evaluated, will produce a result `equal` to that produced by the interpretation shown here.

- `` `basic `` is the same as `'basic`, that is, (`quote` *basic*), for any form *basic* that is not a list or a general vector.
- `` `,form `` is the same as *form*, for any *form*, provided that the representation of *form* does not begin with "@" or ".". (A similar caveat holds for all occurrences of a form after a comma.)
- `` `,@form `` is an error.

- `` `(x1 x2 x3 ... xn . atom) `` may be interpreted to mean

  (append [x1] [x2] [x3] ... [xn] (quote atom))

  where the brackets are used to indicate a transformation of an xj as follows:

  - [form] is interpreted as (list `form), which contains a backquoted form that must then be further interpreted.

  - [,form] is interpreted as (list form).

  - [,@form] is interpreted simply as form.

- `` `(x1 x2 x3 ... xn) `` may be interpreted to mean the same as the backquoted form `` `(x1 x2 x3 ... xn . nil) ``, thereby reducing it to the previous case.

- `` `(x1 x2 x3 ... xn . ,form) `` may be interpreted to mean

  (append [x1] [x2] [x3] ... [xn] form)

  where the brackets indicate a transformation of an xj as described above.

- `` `(x1 x2 x3 ... xn . ,@form) `` is an error.

- `` `#(x1 x2 x3 ... xn) `` may be interpreted to mean

  (apply #'vector `(x1 x2 x3 ... xn))

No other uses of comma are permitted; in particular, it may not appear within the #A or #S syntax.

Anywhere ",@" may be used, the syntax ",." may be used instead to indicate that it is permissible to destroy the list produced by the form following the ",."; this may permit more efficient code, using nconc instead of append, for example.

If the backquote syntax is nested, the innermost backquoted form should be expanded first. This means that if several commas occur in a row, the leftmost one belongs to the innermost backquote.

Once again, it is emphasized that an implementation is free to interpret a backquoted form as any form that, when evaluated, will produce a result that is equal to the result implied by the above definition. In particular, no guarantees are made as to whether the constructed copy of the template will or will not share list structure with the template itself. As an example, the above definition implies that

`((,a b) ,c ,@d)

will be interpreted as if it were

(append (list (append (list a) (list 'b) 'nil)) (list c) d 'nil)

but it could also be legitimately interpreted to mean any of the following.

```
(append (list (append (list a) (list 'b))) (list c) d)
(append (list (append (list a) '(b))) (list c) d)
(append (list (cons a '(b))) (list c) d)
(list* (cons a '(b)) c d)
(list* (cons a (list 'b)) c d)
(list* (cons a '(b)) c (copy-list d))
```

(There is no good reason why `copy-list` should be performed, but it is not prohibited.)

,

The comma character is part of the backquote syntax and is invalid if used other than inside the body of a backquote construction as described above.

#

This is a *dispatching* macro character. It reads an optional digit string and then one more character, and uses that character to select a function to run as a macro-character function.

The # character also happens to be a non-terminating macro character. This is completely independent of the fact that it is a dispatching macro character; it is a coincidence that the only standard dispatching macro character in COMMON LISP is also the only standard non-terminating macro character.

See the next section for predefined # macro-character constructions.

22.1.4. Standard Dispatching Macro Character Syntax

The standard syntax includes forms introduced by the # character. These take the general form of a #, a second character that identifies the syntax, and following arguments in some form. If the second character is a letter, then case is not important; #O and #o are considered to be equivalent, for example.

Certain # forms allow an unsigned decimal number to appear between the # and the second character; some other forms even require it. Those forms that do not explicitly permit such a number to appear forbid it.

The currently-defined # constructs are described below and summarized in Table 22-4; more are likely to be added in the future. However, the constructs #!, #?, #[, #], #{, and #} are explicitly reserved for the user and will never be defined by the COMMON LISP standard.

Table 22-4: Standard # Macro Character Syntax

#!	*undefined**	#\<backspace\>	*signals error*
#"	*undefined*	#\<tab\>	*signals error*
##	*reference to* #= *label*	#\<newline\>	*signals error*
#$	*undefined*	#\<linefeed\>	*signals error*
#%	*undefined*	#\<page\>	*signals error*
#&	*undefined*	#\<return\>	*signals error*
#'	`function` *abbreviation*	#\<space\>	*signals error*
#(	*simple vector*	#+	*read-time conditional*
#)	*signals error*	#-	*read-time conditional*
#*	*bit-vector*	#.	*read-time evaluation*
#,	*load-time evaluation*	#/	*undefined*
#0	*used for infix arguments*	#A, #a	*array*
#1	*used for infix arguments*	#B, #b	*binary rational*
#2	*used for infix arguments*	#C, #c	*complex number*
#3	*used for infix arguments*	#D, #d	*undefined*
#4	*used for infix arguments*	#E, #e	*undefined*
#5	*used for infix arguments*	#F, #f	*undefined*
#6	*used for infix arguments*	#G, #g	*undefined*
#7	*used for infix arguments*	#H, #h	*undefined*
#8	*used for infix arguments*	#I, #i	*undefined*
#9	*used for infix arguments*	#J, #j	*undefined*
#:	*uninterned symbol*	#K, #k	*undefined*
#;	*undefined*	#L, #l	*undefined*
#<	*signals error*	#M, #m	*undefined*
#=	*label following object*	#N, #n	*undefined*
#>	*undefined*	#O, #o	*octal rational*
#?	*undefined**	#P, #p	*undefined*
#@	*undefined*	#Q, #q	*undefined*
#[	*undefined**	#R, #r	*radix-n rational*
#\	*character object*	#S, #s	*structure*
#]	*undefined**	#T, #t	*undefined*
#^	*undefined*	#U, #u	*undefined*
#_	*undefined*	#V, #v	*undefined*
#`	*undefined*	#W, #w	*undefined*
#{	*undefined**	#X, #x	*hexadecimal rational*
#¦	*balanced comment*	#Y, #y	*undefined*
#}	*undefined**	#Z, #z	*undefined*
#~	*undefined*	#\<rubout\>	*undefined*

* The combinations marked by an asterisk are explicitly reserved to the user and will never be defined by COMMON LISP.

#\

#*x* reads in as a character object that represents the character *x*. Also, #*name* reads in as the character object whose name is *name*. Note that the backslash \ allows this construct to be parsed easily by EMACS-like editors.

In the single-character case, the character *x* must be followed by a non-constituent character, lest a *name* appear to follow the #\. A good model of what happens is that after #\ is read, the reader backs up over the \ and then reads an extended token, treating the initial \ as an escape character (whether it really is or not in the current readtable).

Uppercase and lowercase letters are distinguished after #\; #\A and #\a denote different character objects. Any character works after #\, even those that are normally special to read, such as parentheses. Non-printing characters may be used after #\, although for them names are generally preferred.

#*name* reads in as a character object whose name is *name* (actually, whose name is (string-upcase *name*); therefore the syntax is case-insensitive). The *name* should have the syntax of a symbol. The following names are standard across all implementations:

newline
The character that represents the division between lines

space
The space or blank character

The following names are semi-standard; if an implementation supports them, they should be used for the described characters and no others.

rubout
The rubout or delete character

page
The form-feed or page-separator character

tab
The tabulate character

backspace
The backspace character

return
The carriage return character

linefeed
The line-feed character

In some implementations, one or more of these characters might be a synonym for a standard character; #\Linefeed might be the same as #\Newline for example.

When the LISP printer types out the name of a special character, it uses the same table as the #\ reader; therefore any character name you see typed out is acceptable as input (in that implementation). Standard names are always preferred over non-standard names for printing.

The following convention is used in implementations that support non-zero bits attributes for character objects. If a name after #\ is longer than one character and has a hyphen in it, then it may be split into the two parts preceding and following the first hyphen; the first part (actually, string-upcase of the first part) may then be interpreted as the name or initial of a bit, and the second part as the name of the character (which may in turn contain a hyphen and be subject to further splitting). For example:

```
#\Control-Space        #\Control-Meta-Tab
#\C-M-Return           #\H-S-M-C-Rubout
```

If the character name consists of a single character, then that character is used. Another \ may be necessary to quote the character.

```
#\Control-%            #\Control-Meta-\"
#\Control-\a           #\Meta->
```

If an unsigned decimal integer appears between the # and \, it is interpreted as a font number, to become the font attribute of the character object (see char-font).

#'

#'*foo* is an abbreviation for (function *foo*). *foo* may be the printed representation of any LISP object. This abbreviation may be remembered by analogy with the ' macro-character, since the function and quote special forms are similar in form.

#(

A series of representations of objects enclosed by #(and) is read as a simple vector of those objects. This is analogous to the notation for lists.

If an unsigned decimal integer appears between the # and (, it specifies explicitly the length of the vector. In that case, it is an error if too many objects are specified before the closing), and if too few are specified, the last object (it is an error if there are none in this case) is used to fill all remaining elements of the vector. For example,

```
#(a b c c c c)
#6(a b c c c c)
#6(a b c)
#6(a b c c)
```

all mean the same thing: a vector of length 6 with elements a, b, and four instances of c. The notation #( ) denotes an empty vector, as does #0( ) (which is legitimate because it is not the case that too few elements are specified).

#*

A series of binary digits (0 and 1) preceded by #* is read as a simple bit-vector containing those bits, the leftmost bit in the series being bit 0 of the bit-vector.

If an unsigned decimal integer appears between the # and *, it specifies explicitly the length of the vector. In that case, it is an error if too many bits are specified, and if too few are specified the last one (it is an error if there are none in this case) is used to fill all remaining elements of the bit-vector. For example,

```
#*101111
#6*101111
#6*101
#6*1011
```

all mean the same thing: a vector of length 6 with elements 1, 0, 1, 1, 1, and 1. The notation #* denotes an empty bit-vector, as does #0* (which is legitimate because it is not the case that too few elements are specified).

#:

#:*foo* requires *foo* to have the syntax of an unqualified symbol name (no embedded colons). It denotes an *uninterned* symbol whose name is *foo*. Every time this syntax is encountered, a different uninterned symbol is created. If it is necessary to refer to the same uninterned symbol more than once in the same expression, the #= syntax may be useful.

#.

#.*foo* is read as the object resulting from the evaluation of the LISP object represented by *foo*, which may be the printed representation of any LISP object. The evaluation is done during the read process, when the #. construct is encountered. The #. syntax therefore performs a read-time evaluation of *foo*. By contrast, #, (see below) performs a load-time evaluation.

Both #. and #, allow you to include, in an expression being read, an object that does not have a convenient printed representation; instead of writing a representation for the object, you write an expression that will *compute* the object.

#,

#,*foo* is read as the object resulting from the evaluation of the LISP object represented by *foo*, which may be the printed representation of any LISP object. The evaluation is done during the read process, unless the compiler is doing the reading, in which case it is arranged that *foo* will be evaluated when the file of compiled code is loaded. The #, syntax therefore performs a load-time evaluation of *foo*. By contrast, #. (see above) performs a read-time evaluation. In a sense, #, is like specifying (eval load) to eval-when, whereas #. is more like specifying (eval compile). It makes no difference when loading interpreted code; when code is to be compiled, however, #. specifies compile-time evaluation and #, specifies load-time evaluation.

#B

#b*rational* reads *rational* in binary (radix 2). For example, #B1101 ≡ 13, and #b101/11 ≡ 5/3.

#O

#o*rational* reads *rational* in octal (radix 8). For example, #o37/15 ≡ 31/13, and #o777 ≡ 511.

#X

#x*rational* reads *rational* in hexadecimal (radix 16). The digits above 9 are the letters A through F (the lowercase letters a through f are also acceptable). For example, #xFOO ≡ 3840.

#*n*R

#*radix*r*rational* reads *rational* in radix *radix*. *radix* must consist of only digits, and it is read in decimal; its value must be between 2 and 36 (inclusive).

For example, #3r102 is another way of writing 11, and #11R32 is another way of writing 35. For radices larger than 10, letters of the alphabet are used in order for the digits after 9.

#*n*A

The syntax #*n*A*object* constructs an *n*-dimensional array, using *object* as the value of the :initial-contents argument to make-array.

The value of *n* makes a difference: #2A((0 1 5) (foo 2 (hot dog))), for example, represents a 2-by-3 matrix:

```
0        1        5
foo      2        (hot dog)
```

In contrast, #1A((0 1 5) (foo 2 (hot dog))) represents a length-2 array whose elements are lists:

```
(0 1 5)      (foo 2 (hot dog))
```

Furthermore, #0A((0 1 5) (foo 2 (hot dog))) represents a zero-dimensional array whose sole element is a list:

```
((0 1 5) (foo 2 (hot dog)))
```

Similarly, #0Afoo (or, more readably, #0A foo) represents a zero-dimensional array whose sole element is the symbol foo. The expression #1Afoo would not be legal because foo is not a sequence.

#S

The syntax #s(*name slot1 value1 slot2 value2* ...) denotes a structure. This is legal only if *name* is the name of a structure already defined by defstruct and if the structure has a standard constructor macro, which it normally will. Let *cm* stand for the name of this constructor macro; then this syntax is equivalent to

#.(*cm keyword1* '*value1 keyword2* '*value2* ...)

where each *keywordj* is the result of computing

(intern (string *slotj*) 'keyword)

(This computation is made so that one need not write a colon in front of every slot name.) The net effect is that the constructor macro is called with the specified slots having the specified values (note that one does not write quote marks in the #s syntax). Whatever object the constructor macro returns is returned by the #s syntax.

#*n*=

The syntax #*n*=*object* reads as whatever LISP object has *object* as its printed representation. However, that object is labelled by *n*, a required unsigned decimal

integer, for possible reference by the syntax *#n#* (below). The scope of the label
is the expression being read by the outermost call to `read`. Within this expression
the same label may not appear twice.

#n#

The syntax *#n#*, where *n* is a required unsigned decimal integer, serves as a reference to some object labelled by *#n=*; that is, *#n#* represents a pointer to the same
identical (`eq`) object labelled by *#n=*. This permits notation of structures with shared
or circular substructure. For example, a structure created in the variable `y` by this
code:

```
(setq x (list 'p 'q))
(setq y (list (list 'a 'b) x 'foo x))
(rplacd (last y) (cdr y))
```

could be represented in this way:

```
((a b) . #1=(#2=(p q) foo #2# . #1#))
```

Without this notation, but with `*print-length*` set to `10`, the structure would
print in this way:

```
((a b) (p q) foo (p q) (p q) foo (p q) (p q) foo (p q) ...)
```

A reference *#n#* may occur only after a label *#n=*; forward references are not
permitted. In addition, the reference may not appear as the labelled object itself
(that is, one may not write *#n= #n#*), because the object labelled by *#n=* is not
well defined in this case.

#+

The *#+* syntax provides a read-time conditionalization facility; the syntax is

#+*feature form*

If *feature* is "true," then this syntax represents a LISP object whose printed
representation is *form*. If *feature* is "false," then this syntax is effectively whitespace;
it is as if it did not appear.

The *feature* should be the printed representation of a symbol or list. If *feature*
is a symbol, then it is true if and only if it is a member of the list that is the value
of the global variable `*features*`.

Compatibility note: MacLisp uses the status special form for this purpose, and ZetaLisp duplicates status essentially only for the sake of (status features). The use of a variable allows one to bind the features list, when compiling, for example.

Otherwise, *feature* should be a Boolean expression composed of and, or, and not operators on (recursive) *feature* expressions.

For example, suppose that in implementation A the features spice and perq are true, and in implementation B the feature lispm is true. Then the expressions on the left below are read the same as those on the right in implementation A:

```
(cons #+spice "Spice" #+lispm "Lispm" x)        (cons "Spice" x)
(setq a '(1 2 #+perq 43 #+(not perq) 27))       (setq a '(1 2 43))
(let ((a 3) #+(or spice lispm) (b 3))           (let ((a 3) (b 3))
   (foo a))                                         (foo a))
```

In implementation B, however, they are read in this way:

```
(cons #+spice "Spice" #+lispm "Lispm" x)        (cons "Lispm" x)
(setq a '(1 2 #+perq 43 #+(not perq) 27))       (setq a '(1 2 27))
(let ((a 3) #+(or spice lispm) (b 3))           (let ((a 3) (b 3))
   (foo a))                                         (foo a))
```

The #+ construction must be used judiciously if unreadable code is not to result. The user should make a careful choice between read-time conditionalization and run-time conditionalization.

The #+ syntax operates by first reading the *feature* specification and then skipping over the *form* if the *feature* is "false." This skipping of a form is a bit tricky because of the possibility of user-defined macro characters and side effects caused by the #. and #, constructions. It is accomplished by binding the variable *read-suppress* to a non-nil value and then calling the read function. See the description of *read-suppress* for the details of this operation.

#-

#-*feature form* is equivalent to #+(not *feature*) *form*.

#|

#|...|# is treated as a comment by the reader, just as everything from a semicolon to the next newline is treated as a comment. Anything may appear in the comment, except that it must be balanced with respect to other occurrences of #| and |#. Except for this nesting rule, the comment may contain any characters whatsoever.

The main purpose of this construct is to allow "commenting out" of blocks of code or data. The balancing rule allows such blocks to contain pieces already so commented out. In this respect the *#|...|#* syntax of COMMON LISP differs from the */*...*/* comment syntax used by PL/I and C.

#‹

This is not legal reader syntax. It is used in the printed representation of objects that cannot be read back in. Attempting to read a *#‹* will cause an error. (More precisely, it *is* legal syntax, but the macro-character function for it signals an error.)

#<space>, #<tab>, #<newline>, #<page>, #<return>

A *#* followed by a whitespace character is not legal reader syntax. This prevents abbreviated forms produced via *print-level* cutoff from reading in again, as a safeguard against losing information. (More precisely, this *is* legal syntax, but the macro-character function for it signals an error.)

#)

This is not legal reader syntax. This prevents abbreviated forms produced via *print-level* cutoff from reading in again, as a safeguard against losing information. (More precisely, this *is* legal syntax, but the macro-character function for it signals an error.)

22.1.5. The Readtable

Previous sections describe the standard syntax accepted by the read function. This section discusses the advanced topic of altering the standard syntax either to provide extended syntax for LISP objects or to aid the writing of other parsers.

There is a data structure called the *readtable* that is used to control the reader. It contains information about the syntax of each character equivalent to that in Table 22-1. It is set up exactly as in Table 22-1 to give the standard COMMON LISP meanings to all the characters, but the user can change the meanings of characters to alter and customize the syntax of characters. It is also possible to have several readtables describing different syntaxes and to switch from one to another by binding the variable *readtable*.

Even if an implementation supports characters with non-zero *bits* and *font* attributes, it need not (but may) allow for such characters to have syntax descriptions in the readtable. However, every character of type string-char must be represented in the readtable.

`*readtable*`   [*Variable*]

The value of `*readtable*` is the current readtable. The initial value of this is a
readtable set up for standard COMMON LISP syntax. You can bind this variable to
temporarily change the readtable being used.

To program the reader for a different syntax, a set of functions are provided for
manipulating readtables. Normally, you should begin with a copy of the standard
COMMON LISP readtable and then customize the individual characters within that
copy.

`copy-readtable` &optional *from-readtable to-readtable*   [*Function*]

A copy is made of *from-readtable*, which defaults to the current readtable (the
value of the global variable `*readtable*`). If *from-readtable* is `nil`, then a copy
of a standard COMMON LISP readtable is made. For example,

```
(setq *readtable* (copy-readtable nil))
```

will restore the input syntax to standard COMMON LISP syntax, even if the original
readtable has been clobbered (assuming it is not so badly clobbered that you cannot
type in the above expression!). On the other hand,

```
(setq *readtable* (copy-readtable))
```

will merely replace the current readtable with a copy of itself.

If *to-readtable* is unsupplied or `nil`, a fresh copy is made. Otherwise, *to-readtable*
must be a readtable, which is destructively copied into.

`readtablep` *object*   [*Function*]

`readtablep` is true if its argument is a readtable, and otherwise is false.

```
(readtablep x) ≡ (typep x 'readtable)
```

`set-syntax-from-char` *to-char from-char*   [*Function*]
                    &optional *to-readtable from-readtable*

This makes the syntax of *to-char* in *to-readtable* be the same as the syntax of
from-char in *from-readtable*. The *to-readtable* defaults to the current readtable (the
value of the global variable `*readtable*`), and *from-readtable* defaults to `nil`,
meaning to use the syntaxes from the standard LISP readtable.

Only attributes as shown in Table 22-1 are copied; moreover, if a *macro char-*
acter is copied, the macro definition function is copied also. However, attributes

as shown in Table 22-3 are not copied; they are "hard-wired" into the extended-token parser. For example, if the definition of s is copied to *, then * will become a *constituent* that is *alphabetic* but cannot be used as an exponent indicator for short-format floating-point number syntax.

It "works" to copy a macro definition from a character such as " to another character; the standard definition for " looks for another character that is the same as the character that invoked it. It doesn't "work" to copy the definition of (to {, for example; it can be done, but it lets one write lists in the form {a b c), not {a b c}, because the definition always looks for a closing parenthesis, not a closing brace. See the function read-delimited-list, which is useful in this connection.

---

set-macro-character *char function*   [*Function*]
&optional *non-terminating-p readtable*

get-macro-character *char* &optional *readtable*   [*Function*]

set-macro-character causes *char* to be a macro character that when seen by read causes *function* to be called. If *non-terminating-p* is not nil (it defaults to nil), then it will be a non-terminating macro character: it may be embedded within extended tokens. set-macro-character returns t.

get-macro-character returns the function associated with *char* and, as a second value, returns the *non-terminating-p* flag; it returns nil if *char* does not have macro-character syntax. In each case, *readtable* defaults to the current readtable.

The *function* is called with two arguments, *stream* and *char*. The *stream* is the input stream, and *char* is the macro character itself. In the simplest case, *function* may return a LISP object. This object is taken to be that whose printed representation was the macro character and any following characters read by the *function*. As an example, a plausible definition of the standard single quote character is:

```
(defun single-quote-reader (stream char)
  (declare (ignore char))
  (list 'quote (read stream t nil t)))

(set-macro-character #\' #'single-quote-reader)
```

(Note that t is specified for the *recursive-p* argument to read; see section 22.2.1.) The function reads an object following the single-quote and returns a list of the symbol quote and that object. The *char* argument is ignored.

The function may choose instead to return *zero* values (for example, by using (values) as the return expression). In this case, the macro character and whatever it may have read contribute nothing to the object being read. As an example, here is a plausible definition for the standard semicolon (comment) character:

```
(defun semicolon-reader (stream char)
  (declare (ignore char))
  ;; First swallow the rest of the current input line.
  ;; End-of-file is acceptable for terminating the comment.
  (do () ((char= (read-char stream nil #\Newline t) #\Newline)))
  ;; Return zero values.
  (values))

(set-macro-character #\; #'semicolon-reader)
```

(Note that t is specified for the *recursive-p* argument to read-char; see section 22.2.1.)

The *function* should not have any side effects other than on the *stream*. Because of backtracking and restarting of the read operation, front ends (such as editors and rubout handlers) to the reader may cause *function* to be called repeatedly during the reading of a single expression in which the macro character only appears once.

Compatibility note: The ability to return either zero or one value is the closest COMMON LISP macro characters come to the splicing macro characters of MACLISP or the splice macro characters of INTERLISP. The COMMON LISP definition does not allow the splicing of arbitrarily many values, but it does allow a macro-character function to decide after it is invoked whether or not to yield a value, an option not possible in MACLISP or INTERLISP.

MACLISP has nothing equivalent to non-terminating macro characters. The INTERLISP equivalents of terminating and non-terminating macro characters are macro characters with the ALWAYS or FIRST option, respectively. COMMON LISP has nothing equivalent to the INTERLISP ALONE macro-character option.

---

make-dispatch-macro-character *char* &optional   [*Function*]
                        non-terminating-p readtable

This causes the character *char* to be a dispatching macro character in *readtable* (which defaults to the current readtable). If *non-terminating-p* is not nil (it defaults to nil), then it will be a non-terminating macro character: it may be embedded within extended tokens. make-dispatch-macro-character returns t.

Initially every character in the dispatch table has a character-macro function that signals an error. Use set-dispatch-macro-character to define entries in the dispatch table.

set-dispatch-macro-character *disp-char sub-char function*   [*Function*]
&optional *readtable*

get-dispatch-macro-character *disp-char sub-char*   [*Function*]
&optional *readtable*

set-dispatch-macro-character causes *function* to be called when the *disp-char* followed by *sub-char* is read. The *readtable* defaults to the current readtable. The arguments and return values for *function* are the same as for normal macro characters except that *function* gets *sub-char*, not *disp-char*, as its second argument and also receives a third argument that is the non-negative integer whose decimal representation appeared between *disp-char* and *sub-char*, or nil if no decimal integer appeared there.

The *sub-char* may not be one of the ten decimal digits; they are always reserved for specifying an infix integer argument. Moreover, if *sub-char* is a lowercase character (see lower-case-p), its uppercase equivalent is used instead. (This is how the rule is enforced that the case of a dispatch sub-character doesn't matter.)

set-dispatch-macro-character returns t.

get-dispatch-macro-character returns the macro-character function for *sub-char* under *disp-char*, or nil if there is no function associated with *sub-char*.

If the *sub-char* is one of the ten decimal digits, get-dispatch-macro-character always returns nil. If *sub-char* is a lowercase character, its uppercase equivalent is used instead.

For either function, an error is signalled if the specified *disp-char* is not in fact a dispatch character in the specified readtable. It is necessary to use make-dispatch-macro-character to set up the dispatch character before specifying its sub-characters.

As an example, suppose one would like *#$foo* to be read as if it were (dollars *foo*). One might say:

```
(defun !#$-reader! (stream subchar arg)
  (declare (ignore subchar arg))
  (list 'dollars (read stream t nil t)))

(set-dispatch-macro-character #\# #\$ #'!#$-reader!)
```

Compatibility note: This macro-character mechanism is different from those in MacLisp, InterLisp, and ZetaLisp. Recently Lisp systems have implemented very general readers, even readers so programmable that they can parse arbitrary compiled BNF grammars. Unfortunately, these readers can be complicated to use. This design is an attempt to make the reader as simple as possible to understand, use, and implement. Splicing macros have been eliminated; a recent informal poll indicates that no one uses them to produce other than zero or one value. The ability to access parts of the object preceding the macro character has been eliminated. The MacLisp single-character-object feature has been eliminated because it is seldom used and trivially obtainable by defining a macro.

The user is encouraged to turn off most macro characters, turn others into single-character-object macros, and then use read purely as a lexical analyzer on top of which to build a parser. It is unnecessary, however, to cater to more complex lexical analysis or parsing than that needed for COMMON LISP.

22.1.6. What the Print Function Produces

The COMMON LISP printer is controlled by a number of special variables. These are referred to in the following discussion and are fully documented at the end of this section.

How an expression is printed depends on its data type, as described in the following paragraphs.

Integers

If appropriate, a radix specifier may be printed; see the variable *print-radix*. If an integer is negative, a minus sign is printed and then the absolute value of the integer is printed. Integers are printed in the radix specified by the variable *print-base* in the usual positional notation, most significant digit first. The number zero is represented by the single digit 0 and never has a sign. A decimal point may then be printed, depending on the value of *print-radix*.

Ratios

If appropriate, a radix specifier may be printed; see the variable *print-radix*. If the ratio is negative, a minus sign is printed. Then the absolute value of the numerator is printed, as for an integer; then a /; then the denominator. The numerator and denominator are both printed in the radix specified by the variable *print-base*; they are obtained as if by the numerator and denominator functions, and so ratios are always printed in reduced form (lowest terms).

Floating-point numbers

If the sign of the number (as determined by the function float-sign) is negative, then a minus sign is printed. Then the magnitude is printed in one of two ways. If the magnitude of the floating-point number is either zero or between 10^{-3} (inclusive) and 10^7 (exclusive), it may be printed as the integer part of the number, then a decimal point, followed by the fractional part of the number; there is always at least one digit on each side of the decimal point. If the format of the number does not match that specified by the variable *read-default-float-format*, then the exponent marker for that format and the digit 0 are also printed. For example, the base of the natural logarithms as a short-format floating-point number might be printed as 2.71828S0.

For non-zero magnitudes outside of the range 10^{-3} to 10^7, a floating-point number will be printed in "computerized scientific notation." The representation of the number is scaled to be between 1 (inclusive) and 10 (exclusive) and then printed, with one digit before the decimal point and at least one digit after the decimal point. Next the exponent marker for the format is printed, except that if the format of the number matches that specified by the variable *read-default-float-format*, then the exponent marker E is used. Finally, the power of ten by which the fraction must be multiplied to equal the original number is printed as a decimal integer. For example, Avogadro's number as a short-format floating-point number might be printed as 6.02S23.

Complex numbers

A complex number is printed as #C, an open parenthesis, the printed representation of its real part, a space, the printed representation of its imaginary part, and finally a close parenthesis.

Characters

When *print-escape* is nil, a character prints as itself; it is sent directly to the output stream. When *print-escape* is not nil, then #\ syntax is used. For example, the printed representation of the character #\A with control and meta bits on would be #\CONTROL-META-A, and that of #\a with control and meta bits on would be #\CONTROL-META-\a.

Symbols

When *print-escape* is nil, only the characters of the print name of the symbol are output (but the case in which to print any uppercase characters in the print name is controlled by the variable *print-case*).

The remaining paragraphs describing the printing of symbols cover the situation when *print-escape* is not nil.

Backslashes \ and vertical bars ¦ are included as required. In particular, backslash or vertical-bar syntax is used when the name of the symbol would be otherwise treated by the reader as a potential number (see section 22.1.2). In making this decision, it is assumed that the value of *print-base* being used for printing would be used as the value of *read-base* used for reading; the value of *read-base* at the time of printing is irrelevant. For example, if the value of *print-base* were 16 when printing the symbol face, it would have to be printed as \FACE or \Face or ¡FACE¡, because the token face would be read as a hexadecimal number (decimal value 64206) if *read-base* were 16.

The case in which to print any uppercase characters in the print name is controlled by the variable *print-case*. As a special case, nil may sometimes be printed as () instead, when *print-escape* and *print-pretty* are both not nil.

Package prefixes may be printed (using colon syntax) if necessary. The rules for package qualifiers are as follows. When the symbol is printed, if it is in the keyword package, then it is printed with a preceding colon; otherwise, if it is accessible in the current package, it is printed without any qualification; otherwise, it is printed with qualification. See chapter 11.

A symbol that is uninterned (has no home package) is printed preceded by #: if the variables *print-gensym* and *print-escape* are both non-nil; if either is nil, then the symbol is printed without a prefix, as if it were in the current package.

Implementation note: Because the #: syntax does not intern the following symbol, it is necessary to use circular-list syntax if *print-circle* is not nil and the same uninterned symbol appears several times in an expression to be printed. For example, the result of

```
(let ((x (make-symbol "FOO"))) (list x x))
```

would be printed as (#:foo #:foo) if *print-circle* were nil, but as (#1=#:foo #1#) if *print-circle* were not nil.

The case in which symbols are printed is controlled by the variable *print-case*.

Strings

The characters of the string are output in order. If *print-escape* is not nil, a double quote is output before and after, and all double quotes and single escape characters are preceded by backslash. The printing of strings is not affected by *print-array*. If the string has a fill pointer, then only those characters below the fill pointer are printed.

Conses

Wherever possible, list notation is preferred over dot notation. Therefore the following algorithm is used:

1. Print an open parenthesis, (.
2. Print the *car* of the cons.
3. If the *cdr* is a cons, make it the current cons, print a space, and go to step 2.
4. If the *cdr* is not null, print a space, a dot, a space, and the *cdr*.
5. Print a close parenthesis,).

This form of printing is clearer than showing each individual cons cell. Although the two expressions below are equivalent, and the reader will accept either one and produce the same data structure, the printer will always print such a data structure in the second form.

```
(a . (b . ((c . (d . nil)) . (e . nil))))
(a b (c d) e)
```

The printing of conses is affected by the variables *print-level* and *print-length*.

Bit-vectors

A bit-vector is printed as #* followed by the bits of the bit-vector in order. If *print-array* is nil, however, then the bit-vector is printed in a format (using #<) that is concise but not readable. If the bit-vector has a fill pointer, then only those bits below the fill pointer are printed.

Vectors

Any vector other than a string or bit-vector is printed using general-vector syntax; this means that information about specialized vector representations will be lost. The printed representation of a zero-length vector is #(). The printed representation of a non-zero-length vector begins with #(. Following that, the first element of the vector is printed. If there are any other elements, they are printed in turn, with a space printed before each additional element. A close parenthesis after the last element terminates the printed representation of the vector. The printing of vectors is affected by the variables *print-level* and *print-length*. If the vector has a fill pointer, then only those elements below the fill pointer are printed.

If *print-array* is nil, however, then the vector is not printed as described above, but in a format (using #<) that is concise but not readable.

Arrays

Normally any array other than a vector is printed using #*n*A format. Let *n* be the rank of the array. Then # is printed, then *n* as a decimal integer, then A, then *n* open parentheses. Next the elements are scanned in row-major order. Imagine the array indices being enumerated in odometer fashion, recalling that the dimensions are numbered from 0 to *n* − 1. Every time the index for dimension *j* is incremented, the following actions are taken:

1. If *j* < *n* − 1, then print a close parenthesis.
2. If incrementing the index for dimension *j* caused it to equal dimension *j*, reset that index to zero and increment dimension *j* − 1 (thereby performing these three steps recursively), unless *j* = 0, in which case simply terminate the entire algorithm. If incrementing the index for dimension *j* did not cause it to equal dimension *j*, then print a space.
3. If *j* < *n* − 1, then print an open parenthesis.

This causes the contents to be printed in a format suitable for the `:initial-contents` argument to `make-array`. The lists effectively printed by this procedure are subject to truncation by `*print-level*` and `*print-length*`.

If the array is of a specialized type, containing bits or string-characters, then the innermost lists generated by the algorithm given above may instead be printed using bit-vector or string syntax, provided that these innermost lists would not be subject to truncation by `*print-length*`. For example, a 3-by-2-by-4 array of string-characters that would ordinarily be printed as

```
#3A(((#\s #\t #\o #\p) (#\s #\p #\o #\t))
    ((#\p #\o #\s #\t) (#\p #\o #\t #\s))
    ((#\t #\o #\p #\s) (#\o #\p #\t #\s)))
```

may instead be printed more concisely as

```
#3A(("stop" "spot") ("post" "pots") ("tops" "opts"))
```

If `*print-array*` is `nil`, then the array is printed in a format (using #<) that is concise but not readable.

Random-states

COMMON LISP does not specify a specific syntax for printing objects of type `random-state`. However, every implementation must arrange to print a random-state object in such a way that, within the same implementation of COMMON LISP, the function read can construct from the printed representation a copy of the random-state object as if the copy had been made by make-random-state.

Pathnames

COMMON LISP does not specify a specific syntax for printing objects of type pathname. However, every implementation must arrange to print a pathname in such a way that, within the same implementation of COMMON LISP, the function read can construct from the printed representation an equivalent instance of the pathname object.

Structures defined by defstruct are printed under the control of the :print-function option to defstruct. If the user does not provide a printing function explicitly, then a default printing function is supplied that prints the structure using #S syntax (see section 22.1.4.)

Any other types are printed in an implementation-dependent manner. It is recommended that printed representations of all such objects begin with the characters #< and end with > so that the reader will catch such objects and not permit them to be read under normal circumstances. It is specifically and purposely *not* required that a COMMON LISP implementation be able to print an object of type hash-table, readtable, package, stream, or function in a way that can be read back in successfully by read; the use of #< syntax is especially recommended for the printing of such objects.

When debugging or when frequently dealing with large or deep objects at top level, the user may wish to restrict the printer from printing large amounts of information. The variables *print-level* and *print-length* allow the user to control how deep the printer will print and how many elements at a given level the printer will print. Thus the user can see enough of the object to identify it without having to wade through the entire expression.

---

print-escape   [*Variable*]

When this flag is nil, then escape characters are not output when an expression is printed. In particular, a symbol is printed by simply printing the characters of its print name. The function princ effectively binds *print-escape* to nil.

When this flag is not nil, then an attempt is made to print an expression in such a way that it can be read again to produce an equal structure. The function prin1 effectively binds *print-escape* to t. The initial value of this variable is t.

Compatibility note: *print-escape* controls what was called *slashification* in MACLISP.

print-pretty [*Variable*]

When this flag is nil, then only a small amount of whitespace is output when printing an expression.

When this flag is not nil, then the printer will endeavor to insert extra whitespace where appropriate to make the expression more readable. A few other simple changes may be made, such as printing 'foo instead of (quote foo).

The initial value of *print-pretty* is implementation-dependent.

print-circle [*Variable*]

When this flag is nil (the default), then the printing process proceeds by recursive descent; an attempt to print a circular structure may lead to looping behavior and failure to terminate.

When this flag is not nil, then the printer will endeavor to detect cycles in the structure to be printed, and to use #*n*= and #*n*# syntax to indicate the circularities.

print-base [*Variable*]

The value of *print-base* determines in what radix the printer will print rationals. This may be any integer from 2 to 36, inclusive; the default value is 10 (decimal radix). For radices above 10, letters of the alphabet are used to represent digits above 9.

Compatibility note: MacLisp calls this variable base, and its default value is 8, not 10.

In both MacLisp and Common Lisp, floating-point numbers are always printed in decimal, no matter what the value of *print-base*.

---

print-radix [*Variable*]

If the variable *print-radix* is non-nil, the printer will print a radix specifier to indicate the radix in which it is printing a rational number. To prevent confusion of the letter o with the digit 0, and of the letter B with the digit 8, the radix specifier is always printed using a lowercase letter. For example, if the current base is twenty-four (decimal), the decimal integer twenty-three would print as #24rN. If *print-base* is 2, 8, or 16, then the radix specifier used is #b, #o, or #x. For integers, base ten is indicated by a trailing decimal point instead of a leading radix specifier; for ratios, however, `#1Or` is used. The default value of `*print-radix*` is `nil`.

`*print-case*` *[Variable]*

The `read` function normally converts lowercase characters appearing in symbols to corresponding uppercase characters, so that internally print names normally contain only uppercase characters. However, users may prefer to see output using lowercase letters or letters of mixed case. This variable controls the case (upper, lower, or mixed) in which to print any uppercase characters in the names of symbols when vertical-bar syntax is not used. The value of `*print-case*` should be one of the keywords `:upcase`, `:downcase`, or `:capitalize`; the initial value is `:upcase`.

Lowercase characters in the internal print name are always printed in lowercase, and are preceded by a single escape character or enclosed by multiple escape characters. Uppercase characters in the internal print name are printed in upper case, in lower case, or in mixed case so as to capitalize words, according to the value of `*print-case*`. The convention for what constitutes a "word" is the same as for the function `string-capitalize`.

`*print-gensym*` *[Variable]*

The `*print-gensym*` variable controls whether the prefix `#:` is printed before symbols that have no home package. The prefix is printed if the variable is not `nil`. The initial value of `*print-gensym*` is `t`.

`*print-level*` *[Variable]*
`*print-length*` *[Variable]*

The `*print-level*` variable controls how many levels deep a nested data object will print. If `*print-level*` is `nil` (the initial value), then no control is exercised. Otherwise, the value should be an integer, indicating the maximum level to be printed. An object to be printed is at level `O`; its components (as of a list or vector) are at level `1`; and so on. If an object to be recursively printed has components and is at a level equal to or greater than the value of `*print-level*`, then the object is printed as simply `#`.

The `*print-length*` variable controls how many elements at a given level are printed. A value of `nil` (the initial value) indicates that there be no limit to the number of components printed. Otherwise, the value of `*print-length*` should be an integer. Should the number of elements of a data object exceed the value *print-length*, the printer will print three dots, ..., in place of those elements beyond the number specified by *print-length*. (In the case of a dotted list, if the list contains exactly as many elements as the value of *print-length*, and in addition has the non-null atom terminating it, that terminating atom is printed rather than printing three dots.)

print-level and *print-length* affect the printing not only of lists, but also of vectors, arrays, and any other object printed with a list-like syntax. They do not affect the printing of symbols, strings, and bit-vectors.

The LISP reader will normally signal an error when reading an expression that has been abbreviated because of level or length limits. This signal is given because the # dispatch character normally signals an error when followed by whitespace or), and because ... is defined to be an illegal token, as are all tokens consisting entirely of periods (other than the single dot used in dot notation).

As an example, here are the ways the object

```
(if (member x y) (+ (car x) 3) '(foo . #(a b c d "Baz")))
```

would be printed for various values of *print-level* $=v$ and *print-length* $=n$.

v	n	output
0	1	#
1	1	(if ...)
1	2	(if # ...)
1	3	(if # # ...)
1	4	(if # # #)
2	1	(if ...)
2	2	(if (member x ...) ...)
2	3	(if (member x y) (+ # 3) ...)
3	2	(if (member x ...) ...)
3	3	(if (member x y) (+ (car x) 3) ...)
3	4	(if (member x y) (+ (car x) 3) '(foo . #(a b c d ...)))

print-array [*Variable*]

If print-array is nil, then the contents of arrays other than strings are never printed. Instead, arrays are printed in a concise form using #< that gives enough information for the user to be able to identify the array, but does not include the entire array contents. If print-array is not nil, non-string arrays are printed using #(, #*, or #nA syntax. The initial value of *print-array* is implementation-dependent.

22.2. Input Functions

The input functions are divided into two groups: those that operate on streams of characters and those that operate on streams of binary data.

22.2.1. Input from Character Streams

Many character input functions take optional arguments called *input-stream*, *eof-error-p*, and *eof-value*. The *input-stream* argument is the stream from which to obtain input; if unsupplied or `nil` it defaults to the value of the special variable `*standard-input*`. One may also specify `t` as a stream, meaning the value of the special variable `*terminal-io*`.

The *eof-error-p* argument controls what happens if input is from a file (or any other input source that has a definite end) and the end of the file is reached. If *eof-error-p* is true (the default), an error will be signalled at end of file. If it is false, then no error is signalled, and instead the function returns *eof-value*.

Functions such as `read` that read the representation of an object rather than a single character will always signal an error, regardless of *eof-error-p*, if the file ends in the middle of an object representation. For example, if a file does not contain enough right parentheses to balance the left parentheses in it, `read` will complain. If a file ends in a symbol or a number immediately followed by end-of-file, `read` will read the symbol or number successfully and when called again will see the end-of-file and only then act according to *eof-error-p*. Similarly, the function `read-line` will successfully read the last line of a file even if that line is terminated by end-of-file rather than the newline character. If a file contains ignorable text at the end, such as blank lines and comments, `read` will not consider it to end in the middle of an object. Thus an *eof-error-p* argument controls what happens when the file ends *between* objects.

Many input functions also take an argument called *recursive-p*. If specified and not `nil`, this argument specifies that this call is not a "top-level" call to `read` but an imbedded call, typically from the function for a macro character. It is important to distinguish such recursive calls for three reasons.

First, a top-level call establishes the context within which the `#n=` and `#n#` syntax is scoped. Consider, for example, the expression

```
(cons '#3=(p q r) '(x y . #3#))
```

If the single quote macro character were defined in this way:

```
(set-macro-character
   #\'
   #'(lambda (stream char)
       (declare (ignore char))
       (list 'quote (read stream))))
```

then the expression could not be read properly, because there would be no way to know when `read` is called recursively by the first occurrence of `'` that the label `#3=` would be referred to later in the containing expression. There would be no way to know because `read` could not determine that it was called by a macro-character function rather than from "top level." The correct way to define the single quote macro character uses the *recursive-p* argument:

```
(set-macro-character
  #\'
  #'(lambda (stream char)
      (declare (ignore char))
      (list 'quote (read stream t nil t))))
```

Second, a recursive call does not alter whether the reading process is to preserve whitespace or not (as determined by whether the top-level call was to `read` or `read-preserving-whitespace`). Suppose again that single-quote had the first, incorrect, macro-character definition shown above. Then a call to `read-preserving-whitespace` that read the expression `'foo` would fail to preserve the space character following the symbol `foo` because the single-quote macro character function calls `read`, not `read-preserving-whitespace`, to read the following expression (in this case `foo`). The correct definition, which passes the value `t` for the *recursive-p* argument to `read`, allows the top-level call to determine whether whitespace is preserved.

Third, when end-of-file is encountered and the *eof-error-p* argument is not `nil`, the kind of error that is signalled may depend on the value of *recursive-p*. If *recursive-p* is not `nil`, then the end-of-file is deemed to have occurred within the middle of a printed representation; if *recursive-p* is `nil`, then the end-of-file may be deemed to have occurred between objects rather than within the middle of one.

`read` &optional *input-stream eof-error-p eof-value recursive-p*   [*Function*]

`read` reads in the printed representation of a Lisp object from *input-stream*, builds a corresponding Lisp object, and returns the object.

Note that when the variable `*read-suppress*` is not `nil`, then `read` reads in a printed representation as best it can, but most of the work of interpreting the representation is avoided (the intent being that the result is to be discarded anyway). For example, all extended tokens produce the result `nil` regardless of their syntax.

`*read-default-float-format*`   [*Variable*]

The value of this variable must be a type specifier symbol for a specific floating-point format; these include `short-float`, `single-float`, `double-float`, `long-float`, and may include implementation-specific types as well. The default value is `single-float`.

`*read-default-float-format*` indicates the floating-point format to be used for reading floating-point numbers that have no exponent marker or have e or E for an exponent marker. (Other exponent markers explicitly prescribe the floating-point format to be used.) The printer also uses this variable to guide the choice of exponent markers when printing floating-point numbers.

---

read-preserving-whitespace &optional   [*Function*]
                          in-stream eof-error-p
                          eof-value recursive-p

Certain printed representations given to read, notably those of symbols and numbers, require a delimiting character after them. (Lists do not, because the close parenthesis marks the end of the list.) Normally read will throw away the delimiting character if it is a whitespace character; but read will preserve the character (using `unread-char`) if it is syntactically meaningful, because it may be the start of the next expression.

The function `read-preserving-whitespace` is provided for some specialized situations where it is desirable to determine precisely what character terminated the extended token.

As an example, consider this macro-character definition:

```
(defun slash-reader (stream char)
  (declare (ignore char))
  (do ((path (list (read-preserving-whitespace stream))
             (cons (progn (read-char stream nil nil t)
                          (read-preserving-whitespace
                            stream))
                   path)))
      ((not (char= (peek-char nil stream nil nil t) #\/))
       (cons 'path (nreverse path)))))
(set-macro-character #\/ #'slash-reader)
```

(This is actually a rather dangerous definition to make because expressions such as (/ x 3) will no longer be read properly. The ability to reprogram the reader syntax is very powerful and must be used with caution. This redefinition of / is shown here purely for the sake of example.)

Consider now calling read on this expression:

```
(zyedh /usr/games/zork /usr/games/boggle)
```

The / macro reads objects separated by more / characters; thus `/usr/games/zork` is intended to read as `(path usr games zork)`. The entire example expression should therefore be read as

```
(zyedh (path usr games zork) (path usr games boggle))
```

However, if `read` had been used instead of `read-preserving-whitespace`, then after the reading of the symbol `zork`, the following space would be discarded; the next call to `peek-char` would see the following `/`, and the loop would continue, producing this interpretation:

```
(zyedh (path usr games zork usr games boggle))
```

On the other hand, there are times when whitespace *should* be discarded. If a command interpreter takes single-character commands, but occasionally reads a LISP object, then if the whitespace after a symbol is not discarded it might be interpreted as a command some time later after the symbol had been read.

Note that `read-preserving-whitespace` behaves *exactly* like `read` when the *recursive-p* argument is not `nil`. The distinction is established only by calls with *recursive-p* equal to `nil` or omitted.

`read-delimited-list` *char* &optional *input-stream recursive-p*   [*Function*]

This reads objects from *stream* until the next character after an object's representation (ignoring whitespace characters and comments) is *char*. (The *char* should not have whitespace syntax in the current readtable.) A list of the objects read is returned.

To be more precise, `read-delimited-list` looks ahead at each step for the next non-whitespace character and peeks at it as if with `peek-char`. If it is *char*, then the character is consumed and the list of objects is returned. If it is a constituent or escape character, then `read` is used to read an object, which is added to the end of the list. If it is a macro character, the associated macro function is called; if the function returns a value, that value is added to the list. The peek-ahead process is then repeated.

This function is particularly useful for defining new macro characters. Usually it is desirable for the terminating character *char* to be a terminating macro character so that it may be used to delimit tokens; however, `read-delimited-list` makes no attempt to alter the syntax specified for *char* by the current readtable. The user must make any necessary changes to the readtable syntax explicitly. The following example illustrates this.

Suppose you wanted #{*a b c* ... *z*} to read as a list of all pairs of the elements $a, b, c, \ldots, z$; for example:

`#{p q z a}` reads as `((p q) (p z) (p a) (q z) (q a) (z a))`

This can be done by specifying a macro-character definition for `#{` that does two things: read in all the items up to the `}`, and construct the pairs. `read-delimited-list` performs the first task.

```
(defun !#{-reader! (stream char arg)
  (declare (ignore char arg))
  (mapcon #'(lambda (x)
              (mapcar #'(lambda (y) (list (car x) y)) (cdr x)))
          (read-delimited-list #\} stream t)))

(set-dispatch-macro-character #\# #\{ #'!#{-reader!)

(set-macro-character #\} (get-macro-character #\) nil))
```

(Note that `t` is specified for the *recursive-p* argument.)

It is necessary here to give a definition to the character `}` as well to prevent it from being a constituent. If the line

```
(set-macro-character #\} (get-macro-character #\) nil))
```

shown above were not included, then the `}` in

```
#{p q z a}
```

would be considered a constituent character, part of the symbol named `a}`. One could correct for this by putting a space before the `}`, but it is better simply to use the call to `set-macro-character`.

Giving `}` the same definition as the standard definition of the character `)` has the twin benefit of making it terminate tokens for use with `read-delimited-list` and also making it illegal for use in any other context (that is, attempting to read a stray `}` will signal an error).

Note that `read-delimited-list` does not take an *eof-error-p* (or *eof-value*) argument. The reason is that it is always an error to hit end-of-file during the operation of `read-delimited-list`.

`read-line` &optional *input-stream eof-error-p eof-value recursive-p* [*Function*]

`read-line` reads in a line of text terminated by a newline. It returns the line as a character string (*without* the newline character). This function is usually used to get a line of input from the user. A second returned value is a flag that is false if the line was terminated normally, or true if end-of-file terminated the (non-empty) line. If end-of-file is encountered immediately (that is, appears to terminate an empty line), then end-of-file processing is controlled in the usual way by the *eof-error-p*, *eof-value*, and *recursive-p* arguments.

The corresponding output function is `write-line`.

`read-char` &optional *input-stream eof-error-p eof-value recursive-p* [*Function*]

`read-char` inputs one character from *input-stream* and returns it as a character object.

The corresponding output function is `write-char`.

`unread-char` *character* &optional *input-stream*   [*Function*]

`unread-char` puts the *character* onto the front of *input-stream*. The *character* must be the same character that was most recently read from the *input-stream*. The *input-stream* "backs up" over this character; when a character is next read from *input-stream*, it will be the specified character followed by the previous contents of *input-stream*. `unread-char` returns `nil`.

One may apply `unread-char` only to the character most recently read from *input-stream*. Moreover, one may not invoke `unread-char` twice consecutively without an intervening `read-char` operation. The result is that one may back up only by one character, and one may not insert any characters into the input stream that were not already there.

Rationale: This is not intended to be a general mechanism, but rather an efficient mechanism for allowing the LISP reader and other parsers to perform one-character lookahead in the input stream. This protocol admits a wide variety of efficient implementations, such as simply decrementing a buffer pointer. To have to specify the character in the call to `unread-char` is admittedly redundant, since at any given time there is only one character that may be legally specified. The redundancy is intentional, again to give the implementation latitude.

`peek-char` &optional *peek-type input-stream*   [*Function*]
                   eof-error-p eof-value recursive-p

What `peek-char` does depends on the *peek-type*, which defaults to `nil`. With a *peek-type* of `nil`, `peek-char` returns the next character to be read from *input-stream*, without actually removing it from the input stream. The next time input is done from *input-stream*, the character will still be there. It is as if one had called `read-char` and then `unread-char` in succession.

If *peek-type* is `t`, then `peek-char` skips over whitespace characters (but not comments!), and then performs the peeking operation on the next character. This is useful for finding the (possible) beginning of the next printed representation of a LISP object. The last character examined (the one that starts an object) is not removed from the input stream.

If *peek-type* is a character object, then peek-char skips over input characters until a character that is char= to that object is found; that character is left in the input stream.

---

listen &optional *input-stream*   [*Function*]

The predicate listen is true if there is a character immediately available from *input-stream*, and is false if not. This is particularly useful when the stream obtains characters from an interactive device such as a keyboard. A call to read-char would simply wait until a character was available, but listen can sense whether or not input is available and allow the program to decide whether or not to attempt input. On a non-interactive stream, the general rule is that listen is true except when at end-of-file.

---

read-char-no-hang &optional *input-stream eof-error-p*   [*Function*]
                          eof-value recursive-p

This function is exactly like read-char, except that if it would be necessary to wait in order to get a character (as from a keyboard), nil is immediately returned without waiting. This allows one to efficiently check for input availability and get the input if it is available. This is different from the listen operation in two ways. First, read-char-no-hang potentially actually reads a character, whereas listen never inputs a character. Second, listen does not distinguish between end-of-file and no input being available, whereas read-char-no-hang does make that distinction, returning *eof-value* at end-of-file (or signalling an error if no *eof-error-p* is true) but always returning nil if no input is available.

---

clear-input &optional *input-stream*   [*Function*]

This clears any buffered input associated with *input-stream*. It is primarily useful for clearing type-ahead from keyboards when some kind of asynchronous error has occurred. If this operation doesn't make sense for the stream involved, then clear-input does nothing. clear-input returns nil.

---

read-from-string *string* &optional *eof-error-p eof-value* [*Function*]
                          &key :start :end
                             :preserve-whitespace

The characters of *string* are given successively to the LISP reader, and the LISP object built by the reader is returned. Macro characters and so on will all take effect.

The arguments :start and :end delimit a substring of *string* beginning at the character indexed by :start and up to but not including the character indexed by :end. By default :start is 0 (the beginning of the string) and :end is (length *string*). This is the same as for other string functions.

The flag :preserve-whitespace, if provided and not nil, indicates that the operation should preserve whitespace as for read-preserving-whitespace. It defaults to nil.

As with other reading functions, the arguments *eof-error-p* and *eof-value* control the action if the end of the (sub)string is reached before the operation is completed; reaching the end of the string is treated as any other end-of-file event.

read-from-string returns two values; the first is the object read, and the second is the index of the first character in the string not read. If the entire string was read, the second result will be either the length of the string or one greater than the length of the string. The parameter :preserve-whitespace may affect this second value.

(read-from-string "(a b c)") ⇒ (a b c) and 7

parse-integer *string* &key :start :end :radix   [*Function*]
                            :junk-allowed

This function examines the substring of *string* delimited by :start and :end (which default to the beginning and end of the string). It skips over whitespace characters and then attempts to parse an integer. The :radix parameter defaults to 10 and must be an integer between 2 and 36.

If :junk-allowed is not nil, then the first value returned is the value of the number parsed as an integer or nil if no syntactically correct integer was seen.

If :junk-allowed is nil (the default), then the entire substring is scanned. The returned value is the value of the number parsed as an integer. An error is signalled if the substring does not consist entirely of the representation of an integer, possibly surrounded on either side by whitespace characters.

In either case, the second value is the index into the string of the delimiter that terminated the parse, or it is the index beyond the substring if the parse terminated at the end of the substring (as will always be the case if *junk-allowed* is false).

Note that parse-integer does not recognize the syntactic radix-specifier prefixes #O, #B, #X, and #nR, nor does it recognize a trailing decimal point. It permits only an optional sign (+ or -) followed by a non-empty sequence of digits in the specified radix.

22.2.2. Input from Binary Streams

COMMON LISP currently specifies only a very simple facility for binary input: the reading of a single byte as an integer.

read-byte *binary-input-stream* &optional *eof-error-p eof-value*   [*Function*]

read-byte reads one byte from the *binary-input-stream* and returns it in the form of an integer.

22.3. Output Functions

The output functions are divided into two groups: those that operate on streams of characters and those that operate on streams of binary data. The function format operates on streams of characters but is described in a section separate from the other character-output functions because of its great complexity.

22.3.1. Output to Character Streams

These functions all take an optional argument called *output-stream*, which is where to send the output. If unsupplied or nil, *output-stream* defaults to the value of the variable *standard-output*. If it is t, the value of the variable *terminal-io* is used.

```
write object &key :stream :escape :radix :base          [Function]
               :circle :pretty :level :length
               :case :gensym :array
```

The printed representation of *object* is written to the output stream specified by :stream, which defaults to the value of *standard-output*.

The other keyword arguments specify values used to control the generation of the printed representation. Each defaults to the value of the corresponding global variable: see *print-escape*, *print-radix*, *print-base*, *print-circle*, *print-pretty*, *print-level*, *print-length*, *print-case*, *print-gensym*, and *print-array*. (This is the means by which these variables affect printing operations: supplying default values for the write function.) Note that the printing of symbols is also affected by the value of the variable *package*.

write returns *object*.

prin1 *object* &optional *output-stream*   [*Function*]
print *object* &optional *output-stream*   [*Function*]
pprint *object* &optional *output-stream*   [*Function*]
princ *object* &optional *output-stream*   [*Function*]

prin1 outputs the printed representation of *object* to *output-stream*. Escape characters are used as appropriate. Roughly speaking, the output from prin1 is suitable for input to the function read. prin1 returns *object*.

(prin1 *object* *output-stream*)
    ≡ (write *object* :stream *output-stream* :escape t)

print is just like prin1 except that the printed representation of *object* is preceded by a newline (see terpri) and followed by a space. print returns *object*.

pprint is just like print except that the trailing space is omitted and the *object* is printed with the *print-pretty* flag non-nil to produce "pretty" output. pprint returns no values (that is, it returns what the expression (values) returns: zero values).

princ is just like prin1 except that the output has no escape characters. A symbol is printed as simply the characters of its print name; a string is printed without surrounding double quotes; and there may be differences for other data types as well. The general rule is that output from princ is intended to look good to people, while output from prin1 is intended to be acceptable to the function read. princ returns *object*.

(princ *object* *output-stream*)
    ≡ (write *object* :stream *output-stream* :escape nil)

Compatibility note: In MACLISP, the functions prin1, print, and princ return t, not the argument *object*.

---

write-to-string *object* &key :escape :radix :base   [*Function*]
                             :circle :pretty :level :length
                             :case :gensym :array
prin1-to-string *object*   [*Function*]
princ-to-string *object*   [*Function*]

The object is effectively printed as if by write, prin1, or princ, respectively, and the characters that would be output are made into a string, which is returned.

Compatibility note: The INTERLISP function `mkstring` corresponds to the COMMON LISP function `princ-to-string`.

`write-char` *character* &optional *output-stream*   [*Function*]

`write-char` outputs the *character* to *output-stream*, and returns *character*.

`write-string` *string* &optional *output-stream* &key :start :end   [*Function*]
`write-line` *string* &optional *output-stream* &key :start :end   [*Function*]

`write-string` writes the characters of the specified substring of *string* to the *output-stream*. The `:start` and `:end` parameters delimit a substring of *string* in the usual manner (see chapter 14). `write-line` does the same thing, but then outputs a newline afterwards. (See `read-line`.) In either case, the *string* is returned (*not* the substring delimited by `:start` and `:end`).

In some implementations these may be significantly more efficient than an explicit loop using `write-char`.

`terpri` &optional *output-stream*   [*Function*]
`fresh-line` &optional *output-stream*   [*Function*]

`terpri` outputs a newline to *output-stream*. It is identical in effect to

`(write-char #\Newline output-stream)`

`terpri` returns `nil`.

`fresh-line` is similar to `terpri` but outputs a newline only if the stream is not already at the start of a line. (If for some reason this cannot be determined, then a newline is output anyway.) This guarantees that the stream will be on a "fresh line" while consuming as little vertical distance as possible. `fresh-line` is a predicate that is true if it output a newline, and otherwise false.

`finish-output` &optional *output-stream*   [*Function*]
`force-output` &optional *output-stream*   [*Function*]
`clear-output` &optional *output-stream*   [*Function*]

Some streams may be implemented in an asynchronous or buffered manner. The function `finish-output` attempts to ensure that all output sent to *output-stream* has reached its destination, and only then returns `nil`. `force-output` initiates the emptying of any internal buffers but returns `nil` without waiting for completion or acknowledgment.

The function `clear-output`, on the other hand, attempts to abort any outstanding output operation in progress in order to allow as little output as possible to continue to the destination. This is useful, for example, to abort a lengthy output to the terminal when an asynchronous error occurs. `clear-output` returns `nil`.

The precise actions of all three of these operations are implementation-dependent.

22.3.2. Output to Binary Streams

COMMON LISP currently specifies only a very simple facility for binary output: the writing of a single byte as an integer.

`write-byte` *integer binary-output-stream*   [*Function*]

`write-byte` writes one byte, the value of *integer*. It is an error if *integer* is not of the type specified as the `:element-type` argument to `open` when the stream was created. The value *integer* is returned.

22.3.3. Formatted Output to Character Streams

The function `format` is very useful for producing nicely formatted text, producing good-looking messages, and so on. `format` can generate a string or output to a stream.

Formatted output is performed not only by the `format` function itself, but by certain other functions that accept a control string "the way `format` does." For example, error-signalling functions such as `cerror` accept `format` control strings.

`format` *destination control-string* &rest *arguments*   [*Function*]

`format` is used to produce formatted output. `format` outputs the characters of *control-string*, except that a tilde (~) introduces a directive. The character after the tilde, possibly preceded by prefix parameters and modifiers, specifies what kind of formatting is desired. Most directives use one or more elements of *arguments* to create their output; the typical directive puts the next element of *arguments* into the output, formatted in some special way. It is an error if no argument remains for a directive requiring an argument, but it is not an error if one or more arguments remain unprocessed by a directive.

The output is sent to *destination*. If *destination* is `nil`, a string is created that contains the output; this string is returned as the value of the call to `format`. In all other cases `format` returns `nil`, performing output to *destination* as a side effect.

If *destination* is a stream, the output is sent to it. If *destination* is t, the output is sent to the stream that is the value of the variable *standard-output*. If *destination* is a string with a fill pointer, then in effect the output characters are added to the end of the string (as if by use of vector-push-extend).

The format function includes some extremely complicated and specialized features. It is not necessary to understand all or even most of its features to use format effectively. The beginner should skip over anything in the following documentation that is not immediately useful or clear. The more sophisticated features are there for the convenience of programs with complicated formatting requirements.

A format directive consists of a tilde (~), optional prefix parameters separated by commas, optional colon (:) and at-sign (@) modifiers, and a single character indicating what kind of directive this is. The alphabetic case of the directive character is ignored. The prefix parameters are generally integers, notated as optionally signed decimal numbers. Examples of control strings:

`"~s"`	;This is an s directive with no parameters or modifiers.
`"~3,-4:@s"`	;This is an s directive with two parameters, 3 and −4,
	; and both the colon and at-sign flags.
`"~,+4s"`	;Here the first prefix parameter is omitted and takes
	; on its default value, while the second parameter is 4.

Sometimes a prefix parameter is used to specify a character, for instance the padding character in a right- or left-justifying operation. In this case a single quote (') followed by the desired character may be used as a prefix parameter, to mean the character object that is the character following the single quote. For example, you can use ~5,'0d to print an integer in decimal radix in five columns with leading zeros, or ~5,'*d to get leading asterisks.

In place of a prefix parameter to a directive, you can put the letter v (or v), which takes an argument from *arguments* as a parameter to the directive. Normally this should be an integer or character object, as appropriate. This feature allows variable-width fields and the like. If the argument used by a v parameter is nil, the effect is as if the parameter had been omitted. You may also use the character # in place of a parameter; it represents the number of arguments remaining to be processed.

It is an error to give a format directive more parameters than it is described here as accepting. It is also an error to give colon or at-sign modifiers to a directive in a combination not specifically described here as being meaningful.

Here are some relatively simple examples to give you the general flavor of how format is used.

```
(format nil "foo") ⇒ "foo"

(setq x 5)
```

```
(format nil "The answer is ~D." x) ⇒ "The answer is 5."

(format nil "The answer is ~3D." x) ⇒ "The answer is   5."

(format nil "The answer is ~3,'0D." x) ⇒ "The answer is 005."

(format nil "The answer is ~:D." (expt 47 x))
                                  ⇒ "The answer is 229,345,007."
(setq y "elephant")

(format nil "Look at the ~A!" y) ⇒ "Look at the elephant!"

(format nil "Type ~:C to ~A."
        (set-char-bit #\D :control t)
        "delete all your files")
  ⇒ "Type Control-D to delete all your files."

(setq n 3)

(format nil "~D item~:P found." n) ⇒ "3 items found."

(format nil "~R dog~:[s are~; is~] here." n (= n 1))
      ⇒ "three dogs are here."

(format nil "~R dog~:*~[s are~; is~:;s are~] here." n)
      ⇒ "three dogs are here."

(format nil "Here ~[are~;is~:;are~] ~:*~R pupp~:@p." n)
      ⇒ "Here are three puppies."
```

In the descriptions of the directives which follows, the term *arg* in general refers to the next item of the set of *arguments* to be processed. The word or phrase at the beginning of each description is a mnemonic (not necessarily an accurate one!) for the directive.

~A

Ascii. An *arg*, any LISP object, is printed without escape characters (as by princ). In particular, if *arg* is a string, its characters will be output verbatim. If *arg* is nil it will be printed as nil; the colon modifier (~:A) will cause an *arg* of nil to be printed as (), but if *arg* is a composite structure, such as a list or vector, any contained occurrences of nil will still be printed as nil.

~*mincol*A inserts spaces on the right, if necessary, to make the width at least *mincol* columns. The @ modifier causes the spaces to be inserted on the left rather than the right.

~*mincol,colinc,minpad,padchar*A is the full form of ~A, which allows elaborate control of the padding. The string is padded on the right (or on the left if the @

modifier is used) with at least *minpad* copies of *padchar*; padding characters are then inserted *colinc* characters at a time until the total width is at least *mincol*. The defaults are 0 for *mincol* and *minpad*, 1 for *colinc*, and the space character for *padchar*.

~S

S-expression. This is just like ~A, but *arg* is printed *with* escape characters (as by prin1 rather than princ). The output is therefore suitable for input to read. ~S accepts all the arguments and modifiers that ~A does.

~D

Decimal. An *arg*, which should be an integer, is printed in decimal radix. ~D will never put a decimal point after the number.

~*mincol*D uses a column width of *mincol*; spaces are inserted on the left if the number requires fewer than *mincol* columns for its digits and sign. If the number doesn't fit in *mincol* columns, additional columns are used as needed.

~*mincol,padchar*D uses *padchar* as the pad character instead of space.

If *arg* is not an integer, it is printed in ~A format and decimal base.

The @ modifier causes the number's sign to be printed always; the default is to print it only if the number is negative. The : modifier causes commas to be printed between groups of three digits; the third prefix parameter may be used to change the character used as the comma. Thus the most general form of ~D is ~*mincol, padchar,commachar*D.

~B

Binary. This is just like ~D but prints in binary radix (radix 2) instead of decimal. The full form is therefore ~*mincol,padchar,commachar*B.

~O

Octal. This is just like ~D but prints in octal radix (radix 8) instead of decimal. The full form is therefore ~*mincol,padchar,commachar*O.

~X

Hexadecimal. This is just like ~D but prints in hexadecimal radix (radix 16) instead of decimal. The full form is therefore ~*mincol,padchar,commachar*X.

Compatibility note: In MacLisp and ZetaLisp the ~x directive outputs a space, and ~*n*x outputs *n* spaces, in a manner analogous to FORTRAN x format. In COMMON LISP the directive ~@T is used for that purpose.

~R

Radix. ~*n*R prints *arg* in radix *n*. The modifier flags and any remaining parameters are used as for the ~D directive. Indeed, ~D is the same as ~10R. The full form here is therefore ~*radix,mincol,padchar,commachar*R.

If no arguments are given to ~R, then an entirely different interpretation is given. The argument should be an integer; suppose it is 4.

- ~R prints *arg* as a cardinal English number: four.
- ~:R prints *arg* as an ordinal English number: fourth.
- ~@R prints *arg* as a Roman numeral: IV.
- ~:@R prints *arg* as an old Roman numeral: IIII.

~P

Plural. If *arg* is not eql to the integer 1, a lowercase s is printed; if *arg* is eql to 1, nothing is printed. (Notice that if *arg* is a floating-point 1.0, the s *is* printed.)

~:P does the same thing, after doing a ~:* to back up one argument; that is, it prints a lowercase s if the *last* argument was not 1. This is useful after printing a number using ~D.

~@p prints y if the argument is 1, or ies if it is not. ~:@p does the same thing, but backs up first.

```
(format nil "~D tr~:@p/~D win~:P" 7 1) ⇒ "7 tries/1 win"
(format nil "~D tr~:@p/~D win~:P" 1 0) ⇒ "1 try/0 wins"
(format nil "~D tr~:@p/~D win~:P" 1 3) ⇒ "1 try/3 wins"
```

~C

Character. The next *arg* should be a character; it is printed according to the modifier flags.

~C prints the character in an implementation-dependent abbreviated format. This format should be culturally compatible with the host environment.

~:C spells out the names of the control bits and represents non-printing characters by their names: Control-Meta-F, Control-Return, Space. This is a "pretty" format for printing characters.

~:@c prints what ~:c would, and then if the character requires unusual shift keys on the keyboard to type it, this fact is mentioned: Control-∂ (Top-F). This is the format used for telling the user about a key he is expected to type, in prompts, for instance. The precise output may depend not only on the implementation, but on the particular I/O devices in use.

~@c prints the character in a way that the LISP reader can understand, using #\ syntax.

Rationale: In some implementations the ~s directive would accomplish what ~c does, but the ~c directive is compatible with LISP dialects such as MACLISP that do not have a character data type.

~F

Fixed-format floating-point. The next *arg* is printed as a floating-point number.

The full form is ~*w*,*d*,*k*,*overflowchar*,*padchar*F. The parameter *w* is the width of the field to be printed; *d* is the number of digits to print after the decimal point; *k* is a scale factor that defaults to zero.

Exactly *w* characters will be output. First, leading copies of the character *padchar* (which defaults to a space) are printed, if necessary, to pad the field on the left. If the *arg* is negative, then a minus sign is printed; if the *arg* is not negative, then a plus sign is printed if and only if the @ modifier was specified. Then a sequence of digits, containing a single embedded decimal point, is printed; this represents the magnitude of the value of *arg* times 10^k, rounded to *d* fractional digits. (When rounding up and rounding down would produce printed values equidistant from the scaled value of *arg*, then the implementation is free to use either one. For example, printing the argument 6.375 using the format ~4,2F may correctly produce either 6.37 or 6.38.) Leading zeros are not permitted, except that a single zero digit is output before the decimal point if the printed value is less than one, and this single zero digit is not output after all if $w = d + 1$.

If it is impossible to print the value in the required format in a field of width *w*, then one of two actions is taken. If the parameter *overflowchar* is specified, then *w* copies of that parameter are printed instead of the scaled value of *arg*. If the *overflowchar* parameter is omitted, then the scaled value is printed using more than *w* characters, as many more as may be needed.

If the *w* parameter is omitted, then the field is of variable width. In effect, a value is chosen for *w* in such a way that no leading pad characters need to be printed and exactly *d* characters will follow the decimal point. For example, the directive ~,2F will print exactly two digits after the decimal point and as many as necessary before the decimal point.

If the parameter *d* is omitted, then there is no constraint on the number of digits to appear after the decimal point. A value is chosen for *d* in such a way that as many digits as possible may be printed subject to the width constraint imposed by the parameter *w* and the constraint that no trailing zero digits may appear in the fraction, except that if the fraction to be printed is zero, then a single zero digit should appear after the decimal point if permitted by the width constraint.

If both *w* and *d* are omitted, then the effect is to print the value using ordinary free-format output; prin1 uses this format for any number whose magnitude is either zero or between 10^{-3} (inclusive) and 10^7 (exclusive).

If *w* is omitted, then if the magnitude of *arg* is so large (or, if *d* is also omitted, so small) that more than 100 digits would have to be printed, then an implementation is free, at its discretion, to print the number using exponential notation instead, as if by the directive ~E (with all parameters to ~E defaulted, not taking their values from the ~F directive).

If *arg* is a rational number, then it is coerced to be a single-float and then printed. (Alternatively, an implementation is permitted to process a rational number by any other method that has essentially the same behavior but avoids such hazards as loss of precision or overflow because of the coercion. However, note that if *w* and *d* are unspecified and the number has no exact decimal representation, for example 1/3, some precision cutoff must be chosen by the implementation: only a finite number of digits may be printed.)

If *arg* is a complex number or some non-numeric object, then it is printed using the format directive ~wD, thereby printing it in decimal radix and a minimum field width of *w*. (If it is desired to print each of the real part and imaginary part of a complex number using a ~F directive, then this must be done explicitly with two ~F directives and code to extract the two parts of the complex number.)

Examples:

```
(defun foo (x)
  (format nil "~6,2F!~6,2,1,'*F!~6,2,,'?F!~6F!~,2F!~F"
          x x x x x x))

(foo 3.14159)  ⇒ "  3.14! 31.42!   3.14!3.1416!3.14!3.14159"
(foo -3.14159) ⇒ " -3.14!-31.42! -3.14!-3.142!-3.14!-3.14159"
(foo 100.0)    ⇒ "100.00!******!100.00! 100.0!100.00!100.0"
(foo 1234.0)   ⇒ "1234.00!******!??????!1234.0!1234.00!1234.0"
(foo 0.006)    ⇒ "  0.01!  0.06!  0.01! 0.006!0.01!0.006"
```

Compatibility note: The ~F directive is similar to the Fw.d edit descriptor in FORTRAN.

The presence or absence of the @ modifier corresponds to the effect of the FORTRAN SS or SP edit descriptor; nothing in COMMON LISP corresponds to the FORTRAN S edit descriptor.

The scale factor specified by the parameter k corresponds to the scale factor k specified by the FORTRAN kP edit descriptor.

In FORTRAN, the leading zero that precedes the decimal point when the printed value is less than one is optional; in COMMON LISP, the implementation is required to print that zero digit.

In COMMON LISP, the w and d parameters are optional; in FORTRAN, they are required.

In COMMON LISP, the pad character and overflow character are user-specifiable; in FORTRAN, they are always space and asterisk, respectively.

A FORTRAN implementation is prohibited from printing a representation of negative zero; COMMON LISP permits the printing of such a representation when appropriate.

In MACLISP and ZETALISP, the ~F format directive takes a single parameter: the number of digits to use in the printed representation. This incompatibility between COMMON LISP and MACLISP was introduced for the sake of cultural compatibility with FORTRAN.

~E

Exponential floating-point. The next *arg* is printed as a floating-point number in exponential notation.

The full form is ~w,d,e,k,*overflowchar*,*padchar*,*exponentchar*E. The parameter w is the width of the field to be printed; d is the number of digits to print after the decimal point; e is the number of digits to use when printing the exponent; k is a scale factor that defaults to one (not zero).

Exactly w characters will be output. First, leading copies of the character *padchar* (which defaults to a space) are printed, if necessary, to pad the field on the left. If the *arg* is negative, then a minus sign is printed; if the *arg* is not negative, then a plus sign is printed if and only if the @ modifier was specified. Then a sequence of digits, containing a single embedded decimal point, is printed. The form of this sequence of digits depends on the scale factor k. If k is zero, then d digits are printed after the decimal point, and a single zero digit appears before the decimal point if the total field width will permit it. If k is positive, then it must be strictly less than $d + 2$; k significant digits are printed before the decimal point, and $d - k + 1$ digits are printed after the decimal point. If k is negative, then it must be strictly greater than $-d$; a single zero digit appears before the decimal point if the total field width will permit it, and after the decimal point are printed first $-k$ zeros and then $d + k$ significant digits. The printed fraction must be properly rounded. (When rounding up and rounding down would produce printed values equidistant from the scaled value of *arg*, then the implementation is free to use either one.

For example, printing the argument ᏸᏅᏆ.Ꮥ using the format ~ᏸ,ᏄᎬ may correctly produce either Ꮄ.ᏥᏆᎬ+ᏐᏅ or Ꮄ.ᏥᏸᎬ+ᏐᏄ)

Following the digit sequence, the exponent is printed. First the character parameter *exponentchar* is printed; if this parameter is omitted, then the exponent marker that prin1 would use is printed, as determined from the type of the floating-point number and the current value of *read-default-float-format*. Next, either a plus sign or a minus sign is printed, followed by *e* digits representing the power of ten by which the printed fraction must be multiplied to properly represent the rounded value of *arg*.

If it is impossible to print the value in the required format in a field of width *w*, possibly because *k* is too large or too small or because the exponent cannot be printed in *e* character positions, then one of two actions is taken. If the parameter *overflowchar* is specified, then *w* copies of that parameter are printed instead of the scaled value of *arg*. If the *overflowchar* parameter is omitted, then the scaled value is printed using more than *w* characters, as many more as may be needed; if the problem is that *d* is too small for the specified *k* or that *e* is too small, then a larger value is used for *d* or *e* as may be needed.

If the *w* parameter is omitted, then the field is of variable width. In effect a value is chosen for *w* in such a way that no leading pad characters need to be printed.

If the parameter *d* is omitted, then there is no constraint on the number of digits to appear. A value is chosen for *d* in such a way that as many digits as possible may be printed subject to the width constraint imposed by the parameter *w*, the constraint of the scale factor *k*, and the constraint that no trailing zero digits may appear in the fraction, except that if the fraction to be printed is zero then a single zero digit should appear after the decimal point if permitted by the width constraint.

If the parameter *e* is omitted, then the exponent is printed using the smallest number of digits necessary to represent its value.

If all of *w*, *d*, and *e* are omitted, then the effect is to print the value using ordinary free-format exponential-notation output; prin1 uses this format for any non-zero number whose magnitude is less than 10^{-3} or greater than or equal to 10^7.

If *arg* is a rational number, then it is coerced to be a single-float and then printed. (Alternatively, an implementation is permitted to process a rational number by any other method that has essentially the same behavior but avoids such hazards as loss of precision or overflow because of the coercion. However, note that if *w* and *d* are unspecified and the number has no exact decimal representation, for example 1/3, some precision cutoff must be chosen by the implementation: only a finite number of digits may be printed.)

If *arg* is a complex number or some non-numeric object, then it is printed using the format directive ~wD, thereby printing it in decimal radix and a minimum field width of *w*. (If it is desired to print each of the real part and imaginary part of a complex number using a ~E directive, then this must be done explicitly with two ~E directives and code to extract the two parts of the complex number.)

Examples:

```
(defun foo (x)
  (format nil
          "~9,2,1,,'*E!~10,3,2,2,'?,,'$E!~9,3,2,-2,'%@e!~9,2E"
          x x x x))

(foo 3.14159)  ⇒ "  3.14E+0! 31.42$-01!+.003E+03!  3.14E+0"
(foo -3.14159) ⇒ " -3.14E+0!-31.42$-01!-.003E+03! -3.14E+0"
(foo 1100.0)   ⇒ "  1.10E+3! 11.00$+02!+.001E+06!  1.10E+3"
(foo 1100.0L0) ⇒ "  1.10L+3! 11.00$+02!+.001L+06!  1.10L+3"
(foo 1.1E13)   ⇒ "*********! 11.00$+12!+.001E+16! 1.10E+13"
(foo 1.1L120)  ⇒ "*********!??????????!%%%%%%%%%!1.10L+120"
(foo 1.1L1200) ⇒ "*********!??????????!%%%%%%%%%!1.10L+1200"
```

As an example of the effects of varying the scale factor, the code

```
(dotimes (k 13)
  (format t "~Scale factor ~2D: !~13,6,2,VE!"
          (- k 5) 3.14159))
```

produces the following output:

```
Scale factor -5: ! 0.000003E+06!
Scale factor -4: ! 0.000031E+05!
Scale factor -3: ! 0.000314E+04!
Scale factor -2: ! 0.003142E+03!
Scale factor -1: ! 0.031416E+02!
Scale factor  0: ! 0.314159E+01!
Scale factor  1: ! 3.141590E+00!
Scale factor  2: ! 31.41590E-01!
Scale factor  3: ! 314.1590E-02!
Scale factor  4: ! 3141.590E-03!
Scale factor  5: ! 31415.90E-04!
Scale factor  6: ! 314159.0E-05!
Scale factor  7: ! 3141590.E-06!
```

Compatibility note: The ~E directive is similar to the E*w.d* and E*w.dEe* edit descriptors in FORTRAN.

The presence or absence of the @ modifier corresponds to the effect of the FORTRAN SS or SP edit descriptor; nothing in COMMON LISP corresponds to the FORTRAN S edit descriptor.

The scale factor specified by the parameter k corresponds to the scale factor k specified by the FORTRAN kP edit descriptor; note, however, that the default value for k is one in COMMON LISP, as opposed to the default value of zero in FORTRAN. (On the other hand, note that a scale factor of one is used for FORTRAN list-directed output, which is roughly equivalent to using ~E with the w, d, e, and *overflowchar* parameters omitted.)

In COMMON LISP, the w and d parameters are optional; in FORTRAN, they are required.

In FORTRAN, omitting e causes the exponent to be printed using either two or three digits; if three digits are required, then the exponent marker is omitted. In COMMON LISP, omitting e causes the exponent to be printed using as few digits as possible; the exponent marker is never omitted.

In COMMON LISP, the pad character and overflow character are user-specifiable; in FORTRAN they are always space and asterisk, respectively.

A FORTRAN implementation is prohibited from printing a representation of negative zero; COMMON LISP permits the printing of such a representation when appropriate.

In MACLISP and ZETALISP, the ~E format directive takes a single parameter: the number of digits to use in the printed representation. This incompatibility between COMMON LISP and MACLISP was introduced for the sake of cultural compatibility with FORTRAN.

~G

General floating-point. The next *arg* is printed as a floating-point number in either fixed-format or exponential notation as appropriate.

The full form is ~w, d, e, k, *overflowchar, padchar, exponentchar*G. The format in which to print *arg* depends on the magnitude (absolute value) of the *arg*. Let n be an integer such that $10^{n-1} \le arg < 10^n$. (If *arg* is zero, let n be 0.) Let *ee* equal $e+2$, or 4 if e is omitted. Let *ww* equal $w - ee$, or nil if w is omitted. If d is omitted, first let q be the number of digits needed to print *arg* with no loss of information and without leading or trailing zeros; then let d equal (max q (min n ?)). Let *dd* equal $d - n$.

If $0 \le dd \le d$, then *arg* is printed as if by the format directives

~*ww*,*dd*,,*overflowchar*,*padchar*F~*ee*@T

Note that the scale factor k is not passed to the ~F directive. For all other values of *dd*, *arg* is printed as if by the format directive

~w,d,e,k,*overflowchar*,*padchar*,*exponentchar*E

In either case, an @ modifier is specified to the ~F or ~E directive if and only if one was specified to the ~G directive.

Examples:

```
(defun foo (x)
  (format nil "~9,2,1,,'*G!~9,3,2,3,'?,,'$G!~9,3,2,0,'%G!~9,2G"
          x x x))

(foo 0.0314159) ⇒ "   3.14E-2!314.2$-04!0.314E-01!  3.14E-2"
(foo 0.314159)  ⇒ "   0.31   !0.314  !0.314  ! 0.31    "
(foo 3.14159)   ⇒ "   3.1  ! 3.14  ! 3.14  ! 3.1    "
(foo 31.4159)   ⇒ "   31.  ! 31.4  ! 31.4  ! 31.    "
(foo 314.159)   ⇒ "   3.14E+2! 314.  ! 314.  !  3.14E+2"
(foo 3141.59)   ⇒ "   3.14E+3!314.2$+01!0.314E+04!  3.14E+3"
(foo 3141.59L0) ⇒ "   3.14L+3!314.2$+01!0.314L+04!  3.14L+3"
(foo 3.14E12)   ⇒ "**********!314.2$+10!0.314E+13!  3.14L+12"
(foo 3.14L120)  ⇒ "**********!??????????!%%%%%%%%%%!3.14L+120"
(foo 3.14L1200) ⇒ "**********!??????????!%%%%%%%%%%!3.14L+1200"
```

Compatibility note: The ~G directive is similar to the G*w.d* edit descriptor in FORTRAN.

The COMMON LISP rules for deciding between the use of ~F and ~E are compatible with the rules used by FORTRAN but have been extended to cover the cases where *w* or *d* is omitted or where *e* is specified.

In MACLISP and ZETALISP, the ~G format directive is equivalent to the COMMON LISP ~@* directive. This incompatibility between COMMON LISP and MACLISP was introduced for the sake of cultural compatibility with FORTRAN.

~$

Dollars floating-point. The next *arg* is printed as a floating-point number in fixed-format notation. This format is particularly convenient for printing a value as dollars and cents.

The full form is ~*d*,*n*,*w*,*padchar*$. The parameter *d* is the number of digits to print after the decimal point (default value 2); *n* is the minimum number of digits to print before the decimal point (default value 1); *w* is the minimum total width of the field to be printed (default value 0).

First padding and the sign are output. If the *arg* is negative, then a minus sign is printed; if the *arg* is not negative, then a plus sign is printed if and only if the @ modifier was specified. If the : modifier is used, the sign appears before any padding, and otherwise after the padding. If *w* is specified and the number of other characters to be output is less than *w*, then copies of *padchar* (which defaults to a space) are output to make the total field width equal *w*. Then *n* digits are printed for the integer part of *arg*, with leading zeros if necessary; then a decimal point; then *d* digits of fraction, properly rounded.

If the magnitude of *arg* is so large that more than *m* digits would have to be printed, where *m* is the larger of *w* and 100, then an implementation is free, at its discretion, to print the number using exponential notation instead, as if by the directive `~w,q,,,,padcharE`, where *w* and *padchar* are present or omitted according to whether they were present or omitted in the `~$` directive, and where $q = d + n - 1$, where *d* and *n* are the (possibly default) values given to the `~$` directive.

If *arg* is a rational number, then it is coerced to be a `single-float` and then printed. (Alternatively, an implementation is permitted to process a rational number by any other method that has essentially the same behavior but avoids such hazards as loss of precision or overflow because of the coercion.)

If *arg* is a complex number or some non-numeric object, then it is printed using the format directive `~wD`, thereby printing it in decimal radix and a minimum field width of *w*. (If it is desired to print each of the real part and imaginary part of a complex number using a `~$` directive, then this must be done explicitly with two `~$` directives and code to extract the two parts of the complex number.)

`~%`

This outputs a `#\Newline` character, thereby terminating the current output line and beginning a new one (see `terpri`). `~n%` outputs *n* newlines. No *arg* is used. Simply putting a newline in the control string would work, but `~%` is often used because it makes the control string look nicer in the middle of a LISP program.

`~&`

Unless it can be determined that the output stream is already at the beginning of a line, this outputs a newline (see `fresh-line`). `~n&` calls `fresh-line` and then outputs $n - 1$ newlines. `~0&` does nothing.

`~|`

This outputs a page separator character, if possible. `~n|` does this *n* times. | is vertical bar, not capital I.

`~~`

Tilde. This outputs a tilde. `~n~` outputs *n* tildes.

~<newline>

Tilde immediately followed by a newline ignores the newline and any following non-newline whitespace characters. With a :, the newline is ignored, but any following whitespace is left in place. With an @, the newline is left in place, but any following whitespace is ignored. This directive is typically used when a format control string is too long to fit nicely into one line of the program:

```
(defun type-clash-error (fn nargs argnum right-type wrong-type)
  (format *error-output*
          "~&~S requires its ~:[~:R~;~*~] ~
          argument to be of type ~S,~%but it was called ~
          with an argument of type ~S.~%"
          fn (eql nargs 1) argnum right-type wrong-type))
```

(type-clash-error 'aref nil 2 'integer 'vector) prints:
AREF requires its second argument to be of type INTEGER,
but it was called with an argument of type VECTOR.

(type-clash-error 'car 1 1 'list 'short-float) prints:
CAR requires its argument to be of type LIST,
but it was called with an argument of type SHORT-FLOAT.

Note that in this example newlines appear in the output only as specified by the ~& and ~% directives; the actual newline characters in the control string are suppressed because each is preceded by a tilde.

~T

Tabulate. This spaces over to a given column. ~*colnum,colinc*T will output sufficient spaces to move the cursor to column *colnum*. If the cursor is already at or beyond column *colnum*, it will output spaces to move it to column *colnum + k*colinc* for the smallest positive integer *k* possible, unless *colinc* is zero, in which case no spaces are output if the cursor is already at or beyond column *colnum*. *colnum* and *colinc* default to 1.

   Ideally, the current column position is determined by examination of the destination, whether a stream or string. (Although no user-level operation for determining the column position of a stream is defined by COMMON LISP, such a facility may exist at the implementation level.) If for some reason the current absolute column position cannot be determined by direct inquiry, format may be able to deduce the current column position by noting that certain directives (such as ~%, or ~&, or ~A with the argument being a string containing a newline) cause the column position to be reset to zero, and counting the number of characters emitted since that point. If that fails, format may attempt a similar deduction on the riskier assumption that the destination was at column zero when format was invoked. If even this heuristic fails or is implementationally inconvenient, at worst the ~T operation will simply output two spaces. (All this implies that code that uses format is more likely to be portable if all format control strings that use the ~T directive either begin with ~% or ~&, or are designed to be used only when the destination is known from other considerations to be at column zero.)

~@T performs *relative* tabulation. ~*colrel,colinc*@T outputs *colrel* spaces and then outputs the smallest non-negative number of additional spaces necessary to move the cursor to a column that is a multiple of *colinc*. For example, the directive ~3,8@T outputs three spaces and then moves the cursor to a "standard multiple-of-eight tab stop" if not at one already. If the current output column cannot be determined, however, then *colinc* is ignored, and exactly *colrel* spaces are output.

~*

The next *arg* is ignored. ~n* ignores the next *n* arguments.

~:* "ignores backwards"; that is, it backs up in the list of arguments so that the argument last processed will be processed again. ~n:* backs up *n* arguments.

When within a ~{ construct (see below), the ignoring (in either direction) is relative to the list of arguments being processed by the iteration.

~n@* is an "absolute goto" rather than a "relative goto": it goes to the *n*th *arg*, where 0 means the first one; *n* defaults to 0, so ~@* goes back to the first *arg*. Directives after a ~n@* will take arguments in sequence beginning with the one gone to. When within a ~{ construct, the "goto" is relative to the list of arguments being processed by the iteration.

~?

Indirection. The next *arg* must be a string, and the one after it a list; both are consumed by the ~? directive. The string is processed as a format control string, with the elements of the list as the arguments. Once the recursive processing of the control string has been finished, then processing of the control string containing the ~? directive is resumed. Example:

```
(format nil "~? ~D" "<~A ~D>" '("Foo" 5) 7) ⇒ "<Foo 5> 7"
(format nil "~? ~D" "<~A ~D>" '("Foo" 5 14) 7) ⇒ "<Foo 5> 7"
```

Note that in the second example three arguments are supplied to the control string "<~A ~D>", but only two are processed and the third is therefore ignored.

With the @ modifier, only one *arg* is directly consumed. The *arg* must be a string; it is processed as part of the control string as if it had appeared in place of the ~@? construct, and any directives in the recursively processed control string may consume arguments of the control string containing the ~@? directive. Example:

```
(format nil "~@? ~D" "<~A ~D>" "Foo" 5 7) ⇒ "<Foo 5> 7"
(format nil "~@? ~D" "<~A ~D>" "Foo" 5 14 7) ⇒ "<Foo 5> 14"
```

Here is a rather sophisticated example. The format function itself, as implemented at one time in ZETALISP, used a routine internal to the format package called format-error to signal error messages; format-error in turn used error, which used format recursively. Now format-error took a string and arguments, just like format, but also printed the control string to format (which at this point was available in the global variable *ctl-string*) and a little arrow showing where in the processing of the control string the error occurred. The variable *ctl-index* pointed one character after the place of the error.

```
(defun format-error (string &rest args)      ;Example
   (error nil "~?~%~V@T ↓ ~%~3@T\"~A\"~%"
            string args (+ *ctl-index* 3) *ctl-string*))
```

(The character set used in the ZETALISP implementation contains a down-arrow character ↓ , which is not a standard COMMON LISP character.) This first processed the given string and arguments using ~?, then output a newline, tabbed a variable amount for printing the down-arrow, and printed the control string between double quotes (note the use of \" to include double quotes within the control string). The effect was something like this:

```
(format t "The item is a ~[Foo~;Bar~;Loser~]." 'quux)
>>ERROR: The argument to the FORMAT "~[" command
          must be a number.
                    ↓
    "The item is a ~[Foo~;Bar~;Loser~]."
 . . .
```

Implementation note: Implementors may wish to report errors occurring within format control strings in the manner outlined here. It looks pretty flashy when done properly.

The format directives after this point are much more complicated than the foregoing; they constitute control structures that can perform case conversion, conditional selection, iteration, justification, and non-local exits. Used with restraint, they can perform powerful tasks. Used with abandon, they can produce completely unreadable and unmaintainable code.

The case-conversion, conditional, iteration, and justification constructs can contain other formatting constructs by bracketing them. These constructs must nest properly with respect to each other. For example, it is not legitimate to put the start of a case-conversion construct in each arm of a conditional and the end of the case-conversion construct outside the conditional:

```
(format nil "~:[abc~:@(def~;ghi~:@(jkl~]mno~)" x)        ;Illegal!
```

One might expect this to produce either `"abcDEFMNO"` or `"ghiJKLMNO"`, depending on whether x is false or true; but in fact the construction is illegal because the `~[...~;...~]` and `~(...~)` constructs are not properly nested.

The processing indirection caused by the `~?` directive is also a kind of nesting for the purposes of this rule of proper nesting. It is not permitted to start a bracketing construct within a string processed under control of a `~?` directive and end the construct at some point after the `~?` construct in the string containing that construct, or vice versa. For example, this situation is illegal:

```
(format nil "~?ghi~)" "abc~@(def")        ;Illegal!
```

One might expect it to produce `"abcDEFGHI"`, but in fact the construction is illegal because the `~?` and `~(...~)` constructs are not properly nested.

$\sim$(*str*$\sim$)

Case conversion. The contained control string *str* is processed, and what it produces is subject to case conversion.

With no flags, every uppercase character are converted to the corresponding lowercase character.

`~:(` capitalizes all words, as if by `string-capitalize`.

`~@(` capitalizes just the first word and forces the rest to lower case.

`~:@(` converts every lowercase character to the corresponding uppercase character.

In this example `~@(` is used to cause the first word produced by `~@R` to be capitalized:

```
(format nil "~@R ~(~@R~)" 14 14) ⇒ "XIV xiv"
(defun f (n) (format nil "~@(~R~) error~:P detected." n))
(f 0) ⇒ "Zero errors detected."
(f 1) ⇒ "One error detected."
(f 23) ⇒ "Twenty-three errors detected."
```

~[str0~;str1~;...~;strn~]

Conditional expression. This is a set of control strings, called *clauses*, one of which is chosen and used. The clauses are separated by ~; and the construct is terminated by ~]. For example,

```
"~[Siamese~;Manx~;Persian~] Cat"
```

The *arg*th clause is selected, where the first clause is number 0. If a prefix parameter is given (as ~n[), then the parameter is used instead of an argument. (This is useful only if the parameter is specified by #, to dispatch on the number of arguments remaining to be processed.) If *arg* is out of range then no clause is selected (and no error is signalled.). After the selected alternative has been processed, the control string continues after the ~].

~[str0~;str1~;...~;strn~:;default~] has a default case. If the *last* ~; used to separate clauses is ~:; instead, then the last clause is an "else" clause that is performed if no other clause is selected. For example:

```
"~[Siamese~;Manx~;Persian~:;Alley~] Cat"
```

~:[false~;true~] selects the *false* control string if *arg* is nil, and selects the *true* control string otherwise.

~@[true~] tests the argument. If it is not nil, then the argument is not used up by the ~[command but remains as the next one to be processed, and the one clause *true* is processed. If the *arg* is nil, then the argument is used up, and the clause is not processed. The clause therefore should normally use exactly one argument, and may expect it to be non-nil. For example:

```
(setq *print-level* nil *print-length* 5)
(format nil
        "~@[ print level = ~D~]~@[ print length = ~D~]"
        *print-level* *print-length*)
 ⇒ " print length = 5"
```

The combination of ~[and # is useful, for example, for dealing with English conventions for printing lists:

```
(setq foo "Items:~#[none~; ~S~; ~S and ~S~
          ~:;~@{~#[~; and~] ~S~^,~}~].")
(format nil foo)
      ⇒ "Items: none."
(format nil foo 'foo)
      ⇒ "Items: FOO."
```

```
(format nil foo 'foo 'bar)
        ⇒ "Items: FOO and BAR."
(format nil foo 'foo 'bar 'baz)
        ⇒ "Items: FOO, BAR, and BAZ."
(format nil foo 'foo 'bar 'baz 'quux)
        ⇒ "Items: FOO, BAR, BAZ, and QUUX."
```

~;

This separates clauses in ~[and ~< constructions. It is an error elsewhere.

~]

This terminates a ~[. It is an error elsewhere.

~{*str*~}

Iteration. This is an iteration construct. The argument should be a list, which is used as a set of arguments as if for a recursive call to format. The string *str* is used repeatedly as the control string. Each iteration can absorb as many elements of the list as it likes as arguments; if *str* uses up two arguments by itself, then two elements of the list will get used up each time around the loop. If before any iteration step the list is empty, then the iteration is terminated. Also, if a prefix parameter *n* is given, then there will be at most *n* repetitions of processing of *str*. Finally, the ~^ directive can be used to terminate the iteration prematurely.

Here are some simple examples:

```
(format nil "The winners are:~{ ~S~}."
        '(fred harry jill))
      ⇒ "The winners are: FRED HARRY JILL."
(format nil "Pairs:~{ <~S,~S>~}." '(a 1 b 2 c 3))
      ⇒ "Pairs: <A,1> <B,2> <C,3>."
```

~:{*str*~} is similar, but the argument should be a list of sublists. At each repetition step, one sublist is used as the set of arguments for processing *str*; on the next repetition, a new sublist is used, whether or not all of the last sublist had been processed. Example:

```
(format nil "Pairs:~:{ <~S,~S>~}."
        '((a 1) (b 2) (c 3)))
      ⇒ "Pairs: <A,1> <B,2> <C,3>."
```

~@{*str*~} is similar to ~{*str*~}, but instead of using one argument that is a list, all the remaining arguments are used as the list of arguments for the iteration. Example:

```
(format nil "Pairs:~@{ <~S,~S>~}."
            'a 1 'b 2 'c 3)
  ⇒ "Pairs: <A,1> <B,2> <C,3>."
```

If the iteration is terminated before all the remaining arguments are consumed, then any arguments not processed by the iteration remain to be processed by any directives following the iteration construct.

~:@{*str*~} combines the features of ~:{*str*~} and ~@{*str*~}. All the remaining arguments are used, and each one must be a list. On each iteration, the next argument is used as a list of arguments to *str*. Example:

```
(format nil "Pairs:~:@{ <~S,~S>~}."
            '(a 1) '(b 2) '(c 3))
  ⇒ "Pairs: <A,1> <B,2> <C,3>."
```

Terminating the repetition construct with ~:} instead of ~} forces *str* to be processed at least once, even if the initial list of arguments is null (however, it will not override an explicit prefix parameter of zero).

If *str* is empty, then an argument is used as *str*. It must be a string and precede any arguments processed by the iteration. As an example, the following are equivalent:

```
(apply #'format stream string arguments)
(format stream "~1{~:}" string arguments)
```

This will use string as a formatting string. The ~1{ says it will be processed at most once, and the ~:} says it will be processed at least once. Therefore it is processed exactly once, using arguments as the arguments. This case may be handled more clearly by the ~? directive, but this general feature of ~{ is more powerful than ~?.

~}

This terminates a ~{. It is an error elsewhere.

~*mincol,colinc,minpad,padchar*<*str*~>

Justification. This justifies the text produced by processing *str* within a field at least *mincol* columns wide. *str* may be divided up into segments with ~;, in which case the spacing is evenly divided between the text segments.

With no modifiers, the leftmost text segment is left justified in the field, and the rightmost text segment right justified; if there is only one text element, as a special case, it is right justified. The : modifier causes spacing to be introduced before the first text segment; the @ modifier causes spacing to be added after the last. The *minpad* parameter (default 0) is the minimum number of padding characters to be output between each segment. The padding character is specified by *padchar*, which defaults to the space character. If the total width needed to satisfy these constraints is greater than *mincol*, then the width used is *mincol* + *k*colinc* for the smallest possible non-negative integer value *k*; *colinc* defaults to 1, and *mincol* defaults to 0.

Examples:

```
(format nil "~10<foo~;bar~>")     ⇒  "foo    bar"
(format nil "~10:<foo~;bar~>")    ⇒  "  foo bar"
(format nil "~10:@<foo~;bar~>")   ⇒  " foo bar "
(format nil "~10<foobar~>")       ⇒  "    foobar"
(format nil "~10:<foobar~>")      ⇒  "    foobar"
(format nil "~10@<foobar~>")      ⇒  "foobar    "
(format nil "~10:@<foobar~>")     ⇒  " foobar   "
```

Note that *str* may include format directives. All the clauses in *str* are processed in order; it is the resulting pieces of text that are justified.

The ~^ directive may be used to terminate processing of the clauses prematurely, in which case only the completely processed clauses are justified.

If the first clause of a ~< is terminated with ~:; instead of ~;, then it is used in a special way. All of the clauses are processed (subject to ~^, of course), but the first one is not used in performing the spacing and padding. When the padded result has been determined, then if it will fit on the current line of output, it is output, and the text for the first clause is discarded. If, however, the padded text will not fit on the current line, then the text segment for the first clause is output before the padded text. The first clause ought to contain a newline (such as a ~% directive). The first clause is always processed, and so any arguments it refers to will be used; the decision is whether to use the resulting segment of text, not whether to process the first clause. If the ~:; has a prefix parameter *n*, then the padded text must fit on the current line with *n* character positions to spare to avoid outputting the first clause's text. For example, the control string

```
"~%;; ~{~<~%;; ~1:; ~S~>~^,~}.~%"
```

can be used to print a list of items separated by commas without breaking items over line boundaries, beginning each line with ;; . The prefix parameter 1 in ~1:;

accounts for the width of the comma that will follow the justified item if it is not the last element in the list, or the period if it is. If ~:; has a second prefix parameter, then it is used as the width of the line, thus overriding the natural line width of the output stream. To make the preceding example use a line width of 50, one would write

```
"~%;; ~{~<~%;; ~1,50:; ~S~>~^,~}.~%"
```

If the second argument is not specified, then format uses the line width of the output stream. If this cannot be determined (for example, when producing a string result), then format uses 72 as the line length.

~>

Terminates a ~<. It is an error elsewhere.

~^

Up and out. This is an escape construct. If there are no more arguments remaining to be processed, then the immediately enclosing ~{ or ~< construct is terminated. If there is no such enclosing construct, then the entire formatting operation is terminated. In the ~< case, the formatting *is* performed, but no more segments are processed before doing the justification. The ~^ should appear only at the *beginning* of a ~< clause, because it aborts the entire clause it appears in (as well as all following clauses). ~^ may appear anywhere in a ~{ construct.

```
(setq donestr "Done.~^ ~D warning~:P.~^ ~D error~:P.")
(format nil donestr) ⇒ "Done."
(format nil donestr 3) ⇒ "Done. 3 warnings."
(format nil donestr 1 5) ⇒ "Done. 1 warning. 5 errors."
```

If a prefix parameter is given, then termination occurs if the parameter is zero. (Hence ~^ is equivalent to ~#^.) If two parameters are given, termination occurs if they are equal. If three parameters are given, termination occurs if the first is less than or equal to the second and the second is less than or equal to the third. Of course, this is useless if all the prefix parameters are constants; at least one of them should be a # or a V parameter.

If ~^ is used within a ~:{ construct, then it merely terminates the current iteration step (because in the standard case it tests for remaining arguments of the current step only); the next iteration step commences immediately. To terminate the entire iteration process, use ~:^.

If ~^ appears within a control string being processed under the control of a ~? directive, but not within any ~{ or ~< construct within that string, then the string being processed will be terminated, thereby ending processing of the ~? directive.

Processing then continues within the string containing the ~? directive at the point following that directive.

If ~^ appears within a ~[or ~(construct, then all the commands up to the ~^ are properly selected or case-converted, the ~[or ~(processing is terminated, and the outward search continues for a ~{ or ~< construct to be terminated. For example:

```
(setq tellstr "~@(~@[~R~]~^ ~A.~)")
(format nil tellstr 23) ⇒ "Twenty-three."
(format nil tellstr nil "losers") ⇒ "Losers."
(format nil tellstr 23 "losers") ⇒ "Twenty-three losers."
```

Here are some examples of the use of ~^ within a ~< construct.

```
(format nil "~15<~S~;~^~S~;~^~S~>" 'foo)
        ⇒ "          FOO"
(format nil "~15<~S~;~^~S~;~^~S~>" 'foo 'bar)
        ⇒ "FOO          BAR"
(format nil "~15<~S~;~^~S~;~^~S~>" 'foo 'bar 'baz)
        ⇒ "FOO    BAR    BAZ"
```

Compatibility note: The ~Q directive and user-defined directives of ZETALISP have been omitted here, as well as control lists (as opposed to strings), which are rumored to be changing in meaning.

22.4. Querying the User

The following functions provide a convenient and consistent interface for asking questions of the user. Questions are printed and the answers are read using the stream *query-io*, which normally is synonymous with *terminal-io* but can be rebound to another stream for special applications.

---

y-or-n-p &optional *format-string* &rest *arguments*   [*Function*]

This predicate is for asking the user a question whose answer is either "yes" or "no." It types out a message (if supplied), reads an answer in some implementation-dependent manner (intended to be short and simple, like reading a single character such as Y or N), and is true if the answer was "yes" or false if the answer was "no."

If the *format-string* argument is supplied and not nil, then a fresh-line operation is performed; then a message is printed as if the *format-string* and *arguments* were given to format. Otherwise it is assumed that any message has already been printed by other means. If you want a question mark at the end of the message, you must put it there yourself; y-or-n-p will not add it. However, the message should not contain an explanatory note such as (Y or N), because the nature of the interface provided for y-or-n-p by a given implementation might not involve typing a character on a keyboard; y-or-n-p will provide such a note if appropriate.

All input and output are performed using the stream in the global variable *query-io*.

Here are some examples of the use of y-or-n-p:

```
(y-or-n-p "Produce listing file?")
(y-or-n-p "Cannot connect to network host ~S. Retry?" host)
```

y-or-n-p should only be used for questions that the user knows are coming or in situations where the user is known to be waiting for a response of some kind. If the user is unlikely to anticipate the question, or if the consequences of the answer might be grave and irreparable, then y-or-n-p should not be used because the user might type ahead and thereby accidentally answer the question. For such questions as "Shall I delete all of your files?" it is better to use yes-or-no-p.

---

yes-or-no-p &optional *format-string* &rest *arguments*   [*Function*]

This predicate, like y-or-n-p, is for asking the user a question whose answer is either "Yes" or "No." It types out a message (if supplied), attracts the user's attention (for example, by ringing the terminal's bell), and reads a reply in some implementation-dependent manner. It is intended that the reply require the user to take more action than just a single keystroke, such as typing the full word yes or no followed by a newline.

If the *format-string* argument is supplied and not nil, then a fresh-line operation is performed; then a message is printed as if the *format-string* and *arguments* were given to format. Otherwise it is assumed that any message has already been printed by other means. If you want a question mark at the end of the message, you must put it there yourself; yes-or-no-p will not add it. However, the message should not contain an explanatory note such as (Yes or No) because the nature of the interface provided for yes-or-no-p by a given implementation might not involve typing the reply on a keyboard; yes-or-no-p will provide such a note if appropriate.

All input and output are performed using the stream in the global variable *query-io*.

To allow the user to answer a yes-or-no question with a single character, use y-or-n-p. yes-or-no-p should be used for unanticipated or momentous questions; this is why it attracts attention and why it requires a multiple-action sequence to answer it.

23

File System Interface

A frequent use of streams is to communicate with a *file system* to which groups of data (files) can be written and from which files can be retrieved.

COMMON LISP defines a standard interface for dealing with such a file system. This interface is designed to be simple and general enough to accommodate the facilities provided by "typical" operating system environments within which COMMON LISP is likely to be implemented. The goal is to make COMMON LISP programs that perform only simple operations on files reasonably portable.

To this end, COMMON LISP assumes that files are named, that given a name one can construct a stream connected to a file of that name, and that the names can be fit into a certain canonical, implementation-independent form called a *pathname*.

Facilities are provided for manipulating pathnames, for creating streams connected to files, and for manipulating the file system through pathnames and streams.

23.1. File Names

COMMON LISP programs need to use names to designate files. The main difficulty in dealing with names of files is that different file systems have different naming formats for files. For example, here is a table of several file systems (actually, operating systems that provide file systems) and what equivalent file names might look like for each one:

System	File name
TOPS-20	`<LISPIO>FORMAT.FASL.13`
TOPS-10	`FORMAT.FAS[1,4]`
ITS	`LISPIO;FORMAT FASL`
MULTICS	`>udd>LispIO>format.fasl`
TENEX	`<LISPIO>FORMAT.FASL;13`
VAX/VMS	`[LISPIO]FORMAT.FAS;13`
UNIX	`/usr/lispio/format.fasl`

It would be impossible for each program that deals with file names to know about each different file name format that exists; a new COMMON LISP implementation might use a format different from any of its predecessors. Therefore, COMMON LISP provides *two* ways to represent file names: *namestrings*, which are strings in the implementation-dependent form customary for the file system, and *pathnames*, which are special abstract data objects that represent file names in an implementation-independent way. Functions are provided to convert between these two representations, and all manipulations of files can be expressed in machine-independent terms by using pathnames.

In order to allow COMMON LISP programs to operate in a network environment that may have more than one kind of file system, the pathname facility allows a file name to specify which file system is to be used. In this context, each file system is called a *host*, in keeping with the usual networking terminology.

23.1.1. Pathnames

All file systems dealt with by COMMON LISP are forced into a common framework, in which files are named by a LISP data object of type `pathname`.

A pathname always has six components, described below. These components are the common interface that allows programs to work the same way with different file systems; the mapping of the pathname components into the concepts peculiar to each file system is taken care of by the COMMON LISP implementation.

host

The name of the file system on which the file resides.

device

Corresponds to the "device" or "file structure" concept in many host file systems: the name of a (logical or physical) device containing files.

directory

Corresponds to the "directory" concept in many host file systems: the name of a group of related files (typically those belonging to a single user or project).

name

The name of a group of files that can be thought of as conceptually the "same" file.

type

Corresponds to the "filetype" or "extension" concept in many host file systems. This says what kind of file this is. Files with the same name but different type are usually related in some specific way, such as one being a source file, another the compiled form of that source, and a third the listing of error messages from the compiler.

version

Corresponds to the "version number" concept in many host file systems. Typically this is a number that is incremented every time the file is modified.

Note that a pathname is not necessarily the name of a specific file. Rather, it is a specification (possibly only a partial specification) of how to access a file. A pathname need not correspond to any file that actually exists, and more than one pathname can refer to the same file. For example, the pathname with a version of "newest" may refer to the same file as a pathname with the same components except a certain number as the version. Indeed, a pathname with version "newest" may refer to different files as time passes, because the meaning of such a pathname depends on the state of the file system. In file systems with such facilities as "links," multiple file names, logical devices, and so on, two pathnames that look quite different may turn out to address the same file. To access a file given a pathname, one must do a file system operation such as open.

Two important operations involving pathnames are *parsing* and *merging*. Parsing is the conversion of a namestring (which might be something supplied interactively by the user when asked to supply the name of a file) into a pathname object. This operation is implementation-dependent, because the format of namestrings is implementation-dependent. Merging takes a pathname with missing components and supplies values for those components from a source of defaults.

Not all of the components of a pathname need to be specified. If a component of a pathname is missing, its value is nil. Before the file system interface can do anything interesting with a file, such as opening the file, all the missing components of a pathname must be filled in (typically from a set of defaults). Pathnames with missing components may be used internally for various purposes; in particular, parsing a namestring that does not specify certain components will result in a pathname with missing components.

A component of a pathname can also be the keyword :wild. This is only useful when the pathname is being used with a directory-manipulating operation, where it means that the pathname component matches anything. The printed representation of a pathname typically designates :wild by an asterisk; however, this is host-dependent.

What values are allowed for components of a pathname depends, in general, on the pathname's host. However, in order for pathnames to be usable in a system-independent way, certain global conventions are adhered to. These conventions are stronger for the type and version than for the other components, since the type and version are explicitly manipulated by many programs, while the other components are usually treated as something supplied by the user that just needs to be remembered and copied from place to place.

The type is always a string or `nil` or `:wild`. It is expected that most programs that deal with files will supply a default type for each file.

The version is either a positive integer or a special symbol. The meanings of `nil` and `:wild` have been explained above. The keyword `:newest` refers to the largest version number that already exists in the file system when reading a file, or to a version number greater than any already existing in the file system when writing a new file. Some COMMON LISP implementors may choose to define other special version symbols. Some semi-standard names, suggested but not required to be supported by every COMMON LISP implementation, are `:oldest`, to refer to the smallest version number that exists in the file system; `:previous`, to refer to the version previous to the newest version; and `:installed`, to refer to a version that is officially installed for users (as opposed to a working or development version. Some COMMON LISP implementors may also choose to attach a meaning to non-positive version numbers (a typical convention is that `0` is synonymous with `:newest` and `-1` with `:previous`), but such interpretations are implementation-dependent.

The host may be a string, indicating a file system, or a list of strings, of which the first names the file system and the rest may be used for such a purpose as inter-network routing.

The device, directory, and name can each be a string (with host-dependent rules on allowed characters and length) or possibly some other COMMON LISP data structure (in which case such a component is said to be *structured* and has an implementation-dependent format). Structured components may be used to handle such file system features as hierarchical directories. COMMON LISP programs do not need to know about structured components unless they do host-dependent operations. Specifying a string as a pathname component for a host that requires a structured component will cause conversion of the string to the appropriate form.

The best way to compare two pathnames for equality is with `equal`, not `eql`. (On pathnames, `eql` is simply the same as `eq`.) Two pathname objects are `equal` if and only if all the corresponding components (host, device, and so on) are equivalent. (Whether or not uppercase and lowercase letters are considered equivalent in strings appearing in components depends on the file name conventions of the file system.) Pathnames that are `equal` should be functionally equivalent.

Some host file systems have features that do not fit into this pathname model. For instance, directories might be accessible as files; there might be complicated structure in the directories or names; or there might be a way to specify a directory relative to a "current" directory, such as the ‹ syntax in MULTICS or the special ". ." file name of UNIX. Such features are not allowed for by the standard COMMON LISP file system interface. An implementation is free to accommodate such features in its pathname representation and provide a parser that can process such specifications in namestrings; such features are then likely to work within that single implementation. However, note that once a program depends explicitly on any such features, it will not be portable.

23.1.2. Pathname Functions

These functions are what programs use to parse and default file names that have been typed in or otherwise supplied by the user.

Any argument called *pathname* in this manual may actually be a pathname, a string or symbol, or a stream. Any argument called *defaults* may likewise be a pathname, a string or symbol, or a stream.

In the examples, it is assumed that the host named CMUC runs the TOPS-20 operating system, and therefore uses TOPS-20 file system syntax; furthermore, an explicit host name is indicated by following the host name with a double colon. Remember, however, that namestring syntax is implementation-dependent, and this syntax is used here purely for the sake of examples.

pathname *pathname*   [*Function*]

The pathname function converts its argument to be a pathname. The argument may be a pathname, a string or symbol, or a stream; the result is always a pathname.

truename *pathname*   [*Function*]

The truename function endeavors to discover the "true name" of the file associated with the *pathname* within the file system. If the *pathname* is an open stream already associated with a file in the file system, that file is used. The "true name" is returned as a pathname. An error is signalled if an appropriate file cannot be located within the file system for the given *pathname*.

The truename function may be used to account for any file-name translations performed by the file system, for example.

For example, suppose that DOC: is a TOPS-20 logical device name that is translated by the TOPS-20 file system to be PS:<DOCUMENTATION>.

```
(setq file (open "CMUC::DOC:DUMPER.HLP"))
(namestring (pathname file)) ⇒ "CMUC::DOC:DUMPER.HLP"
(namestring (truename file))
   ⇒ "CMUC::PS:<DOCUMENTATION>DUMPER.HLP.13"
```

parse-namestring *thing* &optional *host defaults*   [*Function*]
               &key :start :end :junk-allowed

This turns *thing* into a pathname. The *thing* is usually a string (that is, a namestring), but it may be a symbol (in which case the print name is used) or a pathname or stream (in which case no parsing is needed, but an error check may be made for matching hosts).

This function does *not*, in general, do defaulting of pathname components, even though it has an argument named *defaults*; it only does parsing. The *host* and *defaults* arguments are present because in some implementations it may be that a namestring can only be parsed with reference to a particular file name syntax of several available in the implementation. If *host* is non-nil, it must be a host name that could appear in the host component of a pathname, or nil; if *host* is nil then the host name is extracted from the default pathname in *defaults* and used to determine the syntax convention. The *defaults* argument defaults to the value of *default-pathname-defaults*.

For a string (or symbol) argument, parse-namestring parses a file name within it in the range delimited by the :start and :end arguments (which are integer indices into *string*, defaulting to the beginning and end of the string).

If :junk-allowed is not nil, then the first value returned is the pathname parsed, or nil if no syntactically correct pathname was seen.

If :junk-allowed is nil (the default), then the entire substring is scanned. The returned value is the pathname parsed. An error is signalled if the substring does not consist entirely of the representation of a pathname, possibly surrounded on either side by whitespace characters if that is appropriate to the cultural conventions of the implementation.

In either case, the second value is the index into the string of the delimiter that terminated the parse, or the index beyond the substring if the parse terminated at the end of the substring (as will always be the case if :junk-allowed is false).

If *thing* is not a string or symbol, then *start* (which defaults to zero in any case) is always returned as the second value.

Parsing an empty string always succeeds, producing a pathname with all components (except the host) equal to nil.

Note that if *host* is specified and not nil, and *thing* contains a manifest host name, an error is signalled if the hosts do not match.

If *thing* contains an explicit host name and no explicit device name, then it may be appropriate, depending on the implementation environment, for parse-namestring to supply the standard default device for that host as the device component of the resulting pathname.

merge-pathnames *pathname* &optional *defaults default-version*   [*Function*]

This is the function that most programs should call to process a file name supplied by the user. It fills in unspecified components of *pathname* from the *defaults*, and returns a new pathname. The *pathname* and *defaults* arguments may each be a pathname, stream, string, or symbol. The returned value will always be a pathname.

defaults defaults to the value of *default-pathname-defaults*. *default-version* defaults to :newest.

Here is an example of the use of merge-pathnames:

```
(merge-pathnames "CMUC::FORMAT"
                 "CMUC::PS:<LISPIO>.FASL")
```
⇒ a pathname object that re-expressed as a namestring would be
   "CMUC::PS:<LISPIO>FORMAT.FASL.0"

Defaulting of pathname components is done by filling in components taken from another pathname. This is especially useful for cases such as a program that has an input file and an output file, and asks the user for the name of both, letting the unsupplied components of one name default from the other. Unspecified components of the output pathname will come from the input pathname, except that the type should default not to the type of the input but to the appropriate default type for output from this program.

The pathname merging operation takes as input a given pathname, a defaults pathname, and a default version, and returns a new pathname. Basically, the missing components in the given pathname are filled in from the defaults pathname, except that if no version is specified the default version is used. The default version is usually :newest; if no version is specified the newest version in existence should be used. The default version can be nil, to preserve the information that it was missing in the input pathname.

If the given pathname explicitly specifies a host and does not supply a device, then if the host component of the defaults matches the host component of the given pathname, then the device is taken from the defaults; otherwise the device will be the default file device for that host. Next, if the given pathname does not specify a host, device, directory, name, or type, each such component is copied from the defaults. The merging rules for the version are more complicated and depend on whether the pathname specifies a name. If the pathname doesn't specify a name, then the version, if not provided, will come from the defaults, just like the other components. However, if the pathname does specify a name, then the version is not affected by the defaults. The reason is that the version "belongs to" some other file name and is unlikely to have anything to do with the new one. Finally, if this process leaves the version missing, the default version is used.

The net effect is that if the user supplies just a name, then the host, device, directory, and type will come from the defaults, but the version will come from the default version argument to the merging operation. If the user supplies nothing, or just a directory, the name, type, and version will come over from the defaults together. If the host's file name syntax provides a way to input a version without a name or type, the user can let the name and type default but supply a version different from the one in the defaults.

`*default-pathname-defaults*`   [*Variable*]

This is the default pathname-defaults pathname; if any pathname primitive that needs a set of defaults is not given one, it uses this one. As a general rule, however, each program should have its own pathname defaults rather than using this one.

`make-pathname &key :host :device :directory :name`   [*Function*]
`            :type :version :defaults`

Given some components, `make-pathname` constructs and returns a pathname. After the components specified explicitly by the `:host`, `:device`, `:directory`, `:name`, `:type`, and `:version` arguments are filled in, the merging rules used by `merge-pathnames` are used to fill in any missing components from the defaults specified by the `:defaults` argument. The default value of the `:defaults` argument is a pathname whose host component is the same as the host component of the value of `*default-pathname-defaults*`, and whose other components are all `nil`.

Whenever a pathname is constructed, whether by `make-pathname` or some other function, the components may be canonicalized if appropriate. For example, if a file system is insensitive to case, then alphabetic characters may be forced to be all uppercase or all lowercase by the implementation.

`pathnamep` *object*   [*Function*]

This predicate is true if *object* is a pathname, and otherwise is false.

`(pathnamep x)` ≡ `(typep x 'pathname)`

```
pathname-host pathname                              [Function]
pathname-device pathname                            [Function]
pathname-directory pathname                         [Function]
pathname-name pathname                              [Function]
pathname-type pathname                              [Function]
pathname-version pathname                           [Function]
```

These return the components of the argument *pathname*, which may be a pathname, string or symbol, or stream. The returned values can be strings, special symbols, or some other object in the case of structured components. The type will always be a string or a symbol. The version will always be a number or a symbol.

```
namestring pathname                                 [Function]
file-namestring pathname                            [Function]
directory-namestring pathname                       [Function]
host-namestring pathname                            [Function]
enough-namestring pathname &optional defaults       [Function]
```

The *pathname* argument may be a pathname, a string or symbol, or a stream that is or was open to a file. The name represented by *pathname* is returned as a namelist in canonical form.

If *pathname* is a stream, the name returned represents the name used to *open* the file, which may not be the *actual* name of the file (see truename).

namestring returns the full form of the *pathname* as a string. file-namestring returns a string representing just the *name, type,* and *version* components of the *pathname*; the result of directory-namestring represents just the *directory-name* portion; and host-namestring returns a string for just the *host-name* portion. Note that a valid namestring cannot necessarily be constructed simply by concatenating some of the three shorter strings in some order.

enough-namestring takes another argument, *defaults*. It returns an abbreviated namestring that is just sufficient to identify the file named by *pathname* when considered relative to the *defaults* (which defaults to the value *default-pathname-defaults*). That is, it is required that

```
(merge-pathnames (enough-namestring pathname defaults)
                 defaults)
```

$\equiv$

```
(merge-pathnames (parse-namestring pathname nil defaults)
                 defaults)
```

in all cases; and the result of enough-namestring is, roughly speaking, the shortest reasonable string that will still satisfy this criterion.

user-homedir-pathname &optional *host*   [*Function*]

Returns a pathname for the user's "home directory" on *host*. The *host* argument defaults in some appropriate implementation-dependent manner. The concept of "home directory" is itself somewhat implementation-dependent, but from the point of view of COMMON LISP it is the directory where the user keeps personal files such as initialization files and mail. If it is impossible to determine this information, then nil is returned instead of a pathname; however, user-homedir-pathname never returns nil if the *host* argument is not specified. This function returns a pathname without any name, type, or version component (those components are all nil).

23.2. Opening and Closing Files

When a file is *opened*, a stream object is constructed to serve as the file system's ambassador to the LISP environment; operations on the stream are reflected by operations on the file in the file system. The act of *closing* the file (actually, the stream) ends the association; the transaction with the file system is terminated, and input/output may no longer be performed on the stream. The stream function close may be used to close a file; the functions described below may be used to open them. The basic operation is open, but with-open-file is usually more convenient for most applications.

open *filename* &key :direction :element-type   [*Function*]
                  :if-exists :if-does-not-exist

This returns a stream that is connected to the file specified by *filename*. The *filename* is the name of the file to be opened; it may be a string, a pathname, or a stream. (If the *filename* is a stream, then it is not closed first or otherwise affected; it is used merely to provide a file name for the opening of a new stream.)

The keyword arguments specify what kind of stream to produce and how to handle errors:

:direction
This argument specifies whether the stream should handle input, output, or both.

:input
The result will be an input stream. This is the default.

:output
The result will be an output stream.

:io

The result will be a bidirectional stream.

:probe

The result will be a no-directional stream (in effect, the stream is created and then closed). This is useful for determining whether a file exists without actually setting up a complete stream.

:element-type

This argument specifies the type of the unit of transaction for the stream. Anything that can be recognized as being a finite subtype of character or integer is acceptable. In particular, the following types are recognized:

string-char

The unit of transaction is a string-character. The functions read-char and/or write-char may be used on the stream. This is the default.

(unsigned-byte *n*)

The unit of transaction is an unsigned byte (a non-negative integer) of size *n*. The functions read-byte and/or write-byte may be used on the stream.

unsigned-byte

The unit of transaction is an unsigned byte (a non-negative integer); the size of the byte is determined by the file system. The functions read-byte and/or write-byte may be used on the stream.

(signed-byte *n*)

The unit of transaction is a signed byte of size *n*. The functions read-byte and/or write-byte may be used on the stream.

signed-byte

The unit of transaction is a signed byte; the size of the byte is determined by the file system. The functions read-byte and/or write-byte may be used on the stream.

character

The unit of transaction is any character, not just a string-character. The functions read-char and/or write-char may be used on the stream.

bit

The unit of transaction is a bit (values 0 and 1). The functions read-byte and/or write-byte may be used on the stream.

(mod *n*)

The unit of transaction is a non-negative integer less than *n*. The functions read-byte and/or write-byte may be used on the stream.

:default
The unit of transaction is to be determined by the file system, based on the file it finds. The type can be determined by using the function `stream-element-type`.

:if-exists
This argument specifies the action to be taken if the :direction is :output or :io and a file of the specified name already exists. If the direction is :input or :probe, this argument is ignored.

:error
Signal an error. This is the default when the version component of the *filename* is not :newest.

:new-version
Create a new file with the same file name, but with a larger version number. This is the default when the version component of the *filename* is :newest.

:rename
Rename the existing file to some other name, and then create a new file with the specified name.

:rename-and-delete
Rename the existing file to some other name and then delete it (but don't expunge it, on those systems that distinguish deletion from expunging). Then create a new file with the specified name.

:overwrite
The existing file is used, and output operations on the stream will destructively modify the file. If the :direction is :io, the file is opened in a bidirectional mode that allows both reading and writing. The file pointer is initially positioned at the beginning of the file; however, the file is not truncated back to length zero when it is opened. This mode is most useful when the `file-position` function can be used on the stream.

:append
The existing file is used, and output operations on the stream will destructively modify the file. The file pointer is initially positioned at the end of the file. If the :direction is :io, the file is opened in a bidirectional mode that allows both reading and writing.

`:supersede`

Supersede the existing file. If possible, the implementation should arrange not to destroy the old file until the new stream is closed, against the possibility that the stream will be closed in "abort" mode (see `close`). This differs from `:new-version` in that `:supersede` creates a new file with the same name as the old one, rather than a file name with a higher version number.

`nil`

Do not create a file or even a stream. Instead, simply return `nil` to indicate failure.

If the `:direction` is `:output` or `:io` and the value of `:if-exists` is `:new-version`, then the version of the (newly created) file that is opened will be a version greater than that of any other file in the file system whose other pathname components are the same as those of *filename*.

If the `:direction` is `:input` or `:probe` or the value of `:if-exists` is not `:new-version`, *and* the version component of the *filename* is `:newest`, then the file opened is that file already existing in the file system that has a version greater than that of any other file in the file system whose other pathname components are the same as those of *filename*.

Implementation note: The various file systems in existence today have widely differing capabilities. A given implementation may not be able to support all of these options in exactly the manner stated. An implementation is required to recognize all of these option keywords and to try to do something "reasonable" in the context of the host operating system. Implementors are encouraged to approximate the semantics specified here as closely as possible.

As an example, suppose that a file system does not support distinct file versions and does not distinguish the notions of deletion and expunging (in some file systems file deletion is reversible until an expunge operation is performed). Then `:new-version` might be treated the same as `:rename` or `:supersede`, and `:rename-and-delete` might be treated the same as `:supersede`.

If it is utterly impossible for an implementation to handle some option in a manner close to what is specified here, it may simply signal an error. The opening of files is an area where complete portability is too much to hope for; the intent here is simply to make things as portable as possible by providing specific names for a range of commonly supportable options.

`:if-does-not-exist`

This argument specifies the action to be taken if a file of the specified name does not already exist.

:error

Signal an error. This is the default if the :direction is :input, or if the :if-exists argument is :overwrite or :append.

:create

Create an empty file with the specified name, and then proceed as if it had already existed (but do not perform any processing directed by the :if-exists argument). This is the default if the :direction is :output or :io, and the :if-exists argument is anything but :overwrite or :append.

nil

Do not create a file or even a stream. Instead, simply return nil to indicate failure. This is the default if the :direction is :probe.

When the caller is finished with the stream, it should close the file by using the close function. The with-open-file form does this automatically, and so is preferred for most purposes. open should be used only when the control structure of the program necessitates opening and closing of a file in some way more complex than provided by with-open-file. It is suggested that any program that uses open directly should use the special form unwind-protect to close the file if an abnormal exit occurs.

---

with-open-file (*stream filename* {*options*}*)   [*Macro*]
         {*declaration*}* {*form*}*

---

with-open-file evaluates the *forms* of the body (an implicit progn) with the variable *stream* bound to a stream that reads or writes the file named by the value of *filename*. The *options* are evaluated and are used as keyword arguments to the function open.

When control leaves the body, either normally or abnormally (such as by use of throw), the file is automatically closed. If a new output file is being written, and control leaves abnormally, the file is aborted and the file system is left, so far as possible, as if the file had never been opened. Because with-open-file always closes the file, even when an error exit is taken, it is preferred over open for most applications.

filename is the name of the file to be opened; it may be a string, a pathname, or a stream. For example:

```
(with-open-file (ifile name :direction :input)
  (with-open-file (ofile (merge-pathname-defaults ifile
                                                  nil
                                                  "out")
                         :direction :output
                         :if-exists :supersede)
    (transduce-file ifile ofile)))
```

Implementation note: While `with-open-file` tries to automatically close the stream on exit from the construct, for robustness it is helpful if the garbage collector can detect discarded streams and automatically close them.

23.3. Renaming, Deleting, and Other File Operations

These functions provide a standard interface to operations provided in some form by most file systems. It may be that some implementations of COMMON LISP cannot support them all completely.

`rename-file` *file new-name*   [*Function*]

The specified *file* is renamed to *new-name* (which must be a filename). The *file* may be a string, a pathname, or a stream. If it is an open stream associated with a file, then the stream itself and the file associated with it are affected (if the file system permits).

`rename-file` returns three values if successful. The first value is the *new-name* with any missing components filled in by performing a `merge-pathnames` operation using *file* as the defaults. The second value is the `truename` of the file before it was renamed. The third value is the `truename` of the file after it was renamed.

If the renaming operation is not successful, an error is signalled.

It is an error to specify a filename containing a `:wild` component, for *file* to contain a `nil` component where the file system does not permit a `nil` component, or for the result of defaulting missing components of *new-name* from *file* to contain a `nil` component where the file system does not permit a `nil` component.

Compatibility note: This corresponds to the function called `renamef` in MACLISP and ZETALISP. The name `renamef` is not used in COMMON LISP because the convention that a trailing `f` means "file" conflicts with the use of a trailing `f` for forms related to `setf`.

`delete-file` *file*   [*Function*]

The specified *file* is deleted. The *file* may be a string, a pathname, or a stream. If it is an open stream associated with a file, then the stream itself and the file associated with it are affected (if the file system permits), in which case the stream may or may not be closed immediately, and the deletion may be immediate or delayed until the stream is explicitly closed, depending on the requirements of the file system.

`delete-file` returns a non-`nil` value if successful. It is left to the discretion of the implementation whether an attempt to delete a nonexistent file is considered to be successful. If the deleting operation is not successful, an error is signalled.

It is an error to specify a file name that contains a `:wild` component or one that contains a `nil` component where the file system does not permit a `nil` component.

Compatibility note: This corresponds to the function called `deletef` in MacLisp and ZetaLisp.

`probe-file` *file*   [*Function*]

This predicate is false if there is no file named *file*, and otherwise returns a pathname that is the true name of the file (which may be different from *file* because of file links, version numbers, or other artifacts of the file system). Note that if the *file* is an open stream associated with a file, then `probe-file` cannot return `nil` but will produce the true name of the associated file. See `truename` and the `:probe` value for the `:direction` argument to `open`.

Compatibility note: This corresponds to the function called `probef` in MacLisp and ZetaLisp.

`file-write-date` *file*   [*Function*]

file can be a filename or a stream that is open to a file. This returns the time at which the file was created or last written as an integer in universal time format (see section 25.4.1), or `nil` if this cannot be determined.

`file-author` *file*   [*Function*]

file can be a filename or a stream that is open to a file. This returns the name of the author of the file as a string, or `nil` if this cannot be determined.

file-position *file-stream* &optional *position*   [*Function*]

file-position returns or sets the current position within a random-access file.

(file-position *file-stream*) returns a non-negative integer indicating the current position within the *file-stream*, or nil if this cannot be determined. The file position at the start of a file will be zero. The value returned by file-position increases monotonically as input or output operations are performed. For a character file, performing a single read-char or write-char operation may cause the file position to be increased by more than 1 because of character-set translations (such as translating between the COMMON LISP #\Newline character and an external ASCII carriage-return/line-feed sequence) and other aspects of the implementation. For a binary file, every read-byte or write-byte operation increases the file position by 1.

(file-position *file-stream position*) sets the position within *file-stream* to be *position*. The *position* may be an integer, or :start for the beginning of the stream, or :end for the end of the stream. If the integer is too large or otherwise inappropriate, an error is signalled (the file-length function returns the length beyond which file-position may not access). An integer returned by file-position of one argument should, in general, be acceptable as a second argument for use with the same file. With two arguments, file-position returns t if the repositioning was performed successfully, or nil if it was not (for example, because the file was not random-access).

Implementation note: Implementations that have character files represented as a sequence of records of bounded size might choose to encode the file position as, for example, *record-number**256 + *character-within-record*. This is a valid encoding because it increases monotonically as each character is read or written, though not necessarily by 1 at each step. An integer might then be considered "inappropriate" as a second argument to file-position if, when decoded into record number and character number, it turned out that the specified record was too short for the specified character number.

Compatibility note: This corresponds to the function called filepos in MACLISP and ZETALISP.

---

file-length *file-stream*   [*Function*]

file-stream must be a stream that is open to a file. The length of the file is returned as a non-negative integer, or nil if the length cannot be determined. For a binary file, the length is specifically measured in units of the :element-type specified when the file was opened (see open).

Compatibility note: This corresponds to the function called `lengthf` in MacLisp and
ZetaLisp.

23.4. Loading Files

To *load* a file is to read through the file, evaluating each form in it. Programs are
typically stored in files; the expressions in the file are mostly special forms such
as `defun`, `defmacro`, and `defvar`, which define the functions and variables of the
program.

Loading a compiled ("fasload") file is similar, except that the file does not
contain text but rather pre-digested expressions created by the compiler that can
be loaded more quickly.

`load` *filename* `&key` `:verbose` `:print` `:if-does-not-exist`   *[Function]*

This function loads the file named by *filename* into the LISP environment. It is
assumed that a text (character file) can be automatically distinguished from an
object (binary) file by some appropriate implementation-dependent means, possibly
by the file type. The defaults for *filename* are taken from the variable `*default-
pathname-defaults*`. If the *filename* (after the merging in of the defaults) does
not explicitly specify a type, and both text and object types of the file are available
in the file system, `load` should try to select the more appropriate file by some
implementation-dependent means.

If the first argument is a stream rather than a pathname, then `load` determines
what kind of stream it is and loads directly from the stream.

The `:verbose` argument (which defaults to the value of `*load-verbose*`), if
true, permits `load` to print a message in the form of a comment (that is, with a
leading semicolon) to `*standard-output*` indicating what file is being loaded and
other useful information.

The `:print` argument (default `nil`), if true, causes the value of each expression
loaded to be printed to `*standard-output*`. If a binary file is being loaded, then
what is printed may not reflect precisely the contents of the source file, but nevertheless some information will be printed.

If a file is successfully loaded, `load` always returns a non-`nil` value. If
`:if-does-not-exist` is specified and is `nil`, `load` just returns `nil` rather than
signalling an error if the file does not exist.

`*load-verbose*`   *[Variable]*

This variable provides the default for the `:verbose` argument to `load`. Its initial
value is implementation-dependent.

23.5. Accessing Directories

The following function is a very simple portable primitive for examining a directory. Most file systems can support much more powerful directory-searching primitives, but no two are alike. It is expected that most implementations of COMMON LISP will extend the semantics of the `directory` function or provide more powerful primitives.

`directory` *pathname* &key   [*Function*]

A list of pathnames is returned, one for each file in the file system that matches the given *pathname*. (The *pathname* argument may be a pathname, a string, or a stream associated with a file.) For a file that matches, the `truename` appears in the result list. If no file matches the *pathname*, it is not an error; `directory` simply returns `nil`, the list of no results. Keywords such as `:wild` and `:newest` may be used in *pathname* to indicate the search space.

Implementation note: It is anticipated that an implementation may need to provide additional parameters to control the directory search. Therefore `directory` is specified to take additional keyword arguments so that implementations may experiment with extensions, even though no particular keywords are specified here.

As a simple example of such an extension, for a file system that supports the notion of cross-directory file links, a keyword argument `:links` might, if non-`nil`, specify that such links be included in the result list.

24

Errors

Errors may be signalled for a variety of reasons. Many built-in COMMON LISP functions may signal an error when given incorrect arguments. Other functions, described in this chapter, may be called by user programs for the purpose of signalling an error.

When an error is signalled, it is handled in an implementation-dependent way. It is expected that each implementation of COMMON LISP will provide an interactive debugger that prints the error message along with suitable contextual information such as which function detected the error. The user may interact with the debugger to examine or modify the state of the program in various ways, including abandoning the current computation ("aborting to top level") and continuing from the error. What "continuing" means depends on how the error is signalled; the details of this are specified below for each error signalling function.

An implementation may also choose to provide means (such as the errset special form in MACLISP) for a program to trap all errors and prevent the debugger from stepping in for certain errors.

Rationale: Error-handling of adequate flexibility and power for all systems written in COMMON LISP appears to require a complex error classification system. Experience with several error-handling systems in such dialects as MACLISP and ZETALISP indicates that further experimentation is needed in this area; it is too early to define a standard error-handling mechanism. Therefore COMMON LISP provides standard ways to *signal* errors, but no standard ways to *handle* errors. Of course a complete LISP system requires error-handling mechanisms, but many useful portable programs do not require them. It is expected that a future revision of COMMON LISP will address the problem of portable error-handling mechanisms.

Compatibility note: What is here called "continuing," ZETALISP calls "proceeding" from an error.

24.1. General Error-Signalling Functions

The functions in this section provide various mechanisms for signalling warnings, breaks, continuable errors, and fatal errors.

In each case, the caller specifies an error message (a string) that may be processed (and perhaps displayed to the user) by the error-handling mechanism. All messages are constructed by applying the function `format` to the quantities `nil`, *format-string*, and all the *args* to produce a string.

An error message string should not contain a newline character at either the beginning or end, and should not contain any sort of herald indicating that it is an error. The system will take care of these according to whatever its preferred style may be.

Conventionally, error messages are complete English sentences ending with a period. Newlines in the middle of long messages are acceptable. There should be no indentation after a newline in the middle of an error message. The error message need not mention the name of the function that signals the error; it is assumed that the debugger will make this information available.

Implementation note: If the debugger in a particular implementation displays error messages indented from the prevailing left margin (for example, indented by seven spaces because they are prefixed by the seven-character herald "`Error: `"), then the debugger should take care of inserting the appropriate indentation into a multi-line error message. Similarly, a debugger that prefixes error messages with semicolons so that they appear to be comments should take care of inserting a semicolon at the beginning of each line in a multi-line error message. These rules are suggested because, even within a single implementation, there may be more than one program that presents error messages to the user, and they may use different styles of presentation. The caller of `error` cannot anticipate all such possible styles, and so it is incumbent upon the presenter of the message to make any necessary adjustments.

COMMON LISP does not specify the manner in which error messages and other messages are displayed. For the purposes of exposition, a fairly simple style of textual presentation will be used in the examples in this chapter. The character › is used to represent the command prompt symbol for a debugger.

`error` *format-string* &rest *args*   [*Function*]

This function signals a fatal error. It is impossible to continue from this kind of error; thus `error` will never return to its caller.

The debugger printout in the following example is typical of what an implementation might print when `error` is called. Suppose that the (misspelled) symbol `emergnecy-shutdown` has no property named `command` (all too likely, as it is probably a typographical error for `emergency-shutdown`).

```
(defun command-dispatch (cmd)
  (let ((fn (get cmd 'command)))
    (if (not (null fn))
        (funcall fn))
        (error "The command ~S is unrecognized." cmd))))

(command-dispatch 'emergnecy-shutdown)
Error: The command EMERGNECY-SHUTDOWN is unrecognized.
Error signalled by function COMMAND-DISPATCH.
>
```

Compatibility note: ZETALISP calls this function `ferror`. MACLISP has a function named `error` that takes different arguments and can signal either a fatal or a continuable error.

`cerror` *continue-format-string error-format-string* &rest *args*   [*Function*]

`cerror` is used to signal continuable errors. Like `error`, it signals an error and enters the debugger. However, `cerror` allows the program to be continued from the debugger after resolving the error.

If the program is continued after encountering the error, `cerror` returns `nil`. The code that follows the call to `cerror` will then be executed. This code should correct the problem, perhaps by accepting a new value from the user if a variable was invalid.

If the code that corrects the problem interacts with the program's use and might possibly be misled, it should make sure the error has really been corrected before continuing. One way to do this is to put the call to `cerror` and the correction code in a loop, checking each time to see if the error has been corrected before terminating the loop.

The *continue-format-string* argument, like the *error-format-string* argument, is given as a control string to `format` along with the *args* to construct a message string. The error message string is used in the same way that `error` uses it. The continue message string should describe the effect of continuing. The intent is that this message can be displayed as an aid to the user in deciding whether and how to continue. For example, it might be used by an interactive debugger as part of the documentation of its "continue" command.

The content of the continue message should adhere to the rules of style for error messages. It should not include any statement of how the "continue" command is given, since this may be different for each debugger. (It is up to the debugger to supply this information according to its own particular style of presentation and user interaction.)

Here is an example where the caller of cerror, if continued, fixes the problem without any further user interaction:

```
(let ((nvals (list-length vals)))
  (unless (= nvals 3)
    (cond ((< nvals 3)
           (cerror "Assume missing values are zero."
                   "Too few values in ~S;~%~
                    three are required, ~
                    but ~R ~:[were~;was~] supplied."
                   nvals (= nvals 1))
           (setq vals (append vals (subseq '(0 0 0) nvals))))
          (t (cerror "Ignore all values after the first three."
                     "Too many values in ~S;~%~
                      three are required, ~
                      but ~R were supplied."
                     nvals)
             (setq vals (subseq vals 0 3)))))))
```

If vals were the list (-47), the interaction might look like this:

```
Error: Too few values in (-47);
         three are required, but one was supplied.
Error signalled by function EXAMPLE.
If continued: Assume missing values are zero.
>
```

In this example, a loop is used to ensure that a test is satisfied. (This example could be written more succinctly using assert or check-type, which indeed supply such loops.)

```
(do ()
    ((known-wordp word) word)
  (cerror "You will be prompted for a replacement word."
          "~S is an unknown word (possibly misspelled)."
          word)
  (format *query-io* "~&New word: ")
  (setq word (read *query-io*)))
```

In complex cases where the *error-format-string* uses some of the *args* and the *continue-format-string* uses others, it may be necessary to use the format directives

~* and ~@* to skip over unwanted arguments in one or both of the format control strings.

Compatibility note: The ZETALISP function fsignal is similar to this, but returns :no-action rather than nil, and fails to distinguish between the error message and the continue message.

---

warn *format-string* &rest *args*   [*Function*]

warn prints an error message, but normally doesn't go into the debugger. (However, this may be controlled by the variable *break-on-warnings*.) warn returns nil.

This function would be just the same as format with the output directed to the stream in *error-output*, except that warn may perform various implementation-dependent formatting and other actions. For example, an implementation of warn should take care of advancing to a fresh line before and after the error message and perhaps supplying the name of the function that called warn.

Compatibility note: The ZETALISP function compiler:warn is an approximate equivalent to this.

---

break-on-warnings   [*Variable*]

If *break-on-warnings* is not nil, then the function warn behaves like break. It prints its message and then goes to the debugger or break loop. Continuing causes warn to return nil. This flag is intended primarily for use when the user is debugging programs that issue warnings; in "production" use, the value of *break-on-warnings* should be nil.

break &optional *format-string* &rest *args*   [*Function*]

break prints the message and goes directly into the debugger, without allowing any possibility of interception by programmed error-handling facilities. (Right now, there aren't any error-handling facilities defined in COMMON LISP, but there might be in particular implementations, and there will be some defined by COMMON LISP in the future.) When continued, break returns nil. It is permissible to call break with no arguments; a suitable default message will be provided.

break is presumed to be used as a way of inserting temporary debugging "break-points" in a program, not as a way of signalling errors; it is expected that continuing from a break will not trigger any unusual recovery action. For this reason, break does not take the additional `format` control-string argument that `cerror` takes. This and the lack of any possibility of interception by programmed error-handling are the only program-visible differences between `break` and `cerror`. The interactive debugger may choose to display them differently; for instance, a `cerror` message might be prefixed with the herald "`Error:` " and a `break` message with "`Break:` ". This depends on the user-interface style of the particular implementation. A particular implementation may choose, according to its own style and needs, when `break` is called to go into a debugger different from the one used for handling errors. For example, it might go into an ordinary read-eval-print loop identical to the top-level one except for the provision of a "continue" command that causes `break` to return `nil`.

Compatibility note: In MacLisp, `break` is a special form (FEXPR) that takes two optional arguments. The first is a symbol (it would be a string if MacLisp had strings), which is not evaluated. The second is evaluated to produce a truth value specifying whether `break` should break (true) or return immediately (false). In COMMON LISP one makes a call to `break` conditional by putting it inside a conditional form such as `when` or `unless`.

24.2. Specialized Error-Signalling Forms and Macros

These facilities are designed to make it convenient for the user to insert error checks into his code.

`check-type` *place typespec* &optional *string*   [*Macro*]

`check-type` signals an error if the contents of *place* are not of the desired type. If the user continues from this error, he will be asked for a new value; `check-type` will store the new value in *place* and start over, checking the type of the new value and signalling another error if it is still not of the desired type. Subforms of *place* may be evaluated multiple times because of the implicit loop generated. `check-type` returns `nil`.

The *place* must be a generalized variable reference acceptable to `setf`. The *typespec* must be a type specifier; it is not evaluated. The *string* should be an English description of the type, starting with an indefinite article ("a" or "an"); it is evaluated. If *string* is not supplied, it is computed automatically from *typespec*. (The optional *string* argument is allowed because some applications of `check-type` may require a more specific description of what is wanted than can be generated automatically from the type specifier.)

The error message will mention *place*, its contents, and the desired type.

Implementation note: An implementation may choose to generate a somewhat differently worded error message if it recognizes that *place* is of a particular form, such as one of the arguments to the function that called check-type.

Examples:

```
(setq aardvarks '(sam harry fred))
(check-type aardvarks (vector integer))
Error: The value of AARDVARKS, (SAM HARRY FRED),
       is not a vector of integers.

(setq naards 'foo)
(check-type naards (integer 0 *) "a positive integer")
Error: The value of NAARDS, FOO, is not a positive integer.
```

Compatibility note: In ZETALISP the equivalent facility is called check-arg-type.

---

assert *test-form* [({*place*}*) [*string* {*arg*}*]]   [*Macro*]

assert signals an error if the value of *test-form* is nil. Continuing from this error will allow the user to alter the values of some variables, and assert will then start over, evaluating *test-form* again. assert returns nil.

test-form is any form. Each *place* (there may be any number of them, or none) must be a generalized-variable reference acceptable to setf. These should be variables on which *test-form* depends, whose values may sensibly be changed by the user in attempting to correct the error. Subforms of each *place* are only evaluated if an error is signalled, and may be re-evaluated if the error is re-signalled (after continuing without actually fixing the problem).

The *string* is an error message string, and the *args* are additional arguments; they are evaluated only if an error is signalled, and re-evaluated if the error is signalled again. The function format is applied in the usual way to *string* and *args* to produce the actual error message. If *string* is omitted (and therefore also the *args*), a default error message is used.

Implementation note: The debugger need not include the *test-form* in the error message, and the *places* should not be included in the message, but they should be made available for the user's perusal. If the user gives the "continue" command, he should be presented with the opportunity to alter the values of any or all of the references. The details of this depend on the implementation's style of user interface, of course.

Examples:

```
(assert (valve-closed-p vl))

(assert (valve-closed-p vl) () "Live steam is escaping!")

(assert (valve-closed-p vl)
        ((valve-manual-control vl))
        "Live steam is escaping!")
```

```
;; Note here that the user is invited to change BASE,
;; but not the bounds MINBASE and MAXBASE.
(assert (<= minbase base maxbase)
        (base)
        "Base ~D is not in the range [~D, ~D]"
        base minbase maxbase)
```

```
;; Note here that it is probably not desirable to include the
;; entire contents of the two matrices in the error message.
;; It is reasonable to assume that the debugger will give
;; the user access to the values of the places A and B.
(assert (= (array-dimension a 1)
           (array-dimension b 0))
        (a b)
        "Cannot multiply a ~D-by-~D matrix ~
         and a ~D-by-~D matrix."
        (array-dimension a 0)
        (array-dimension a 1)
        (array-dimension b 0)
        (array-dimension b 1))
```

24.3. Special Forms for Exhaustive Case Analysis

The syntax for etypecase and ctypecase is the same as for typecase, except that no otherwise clause is permitted. Similarly, the syntax for ecase and ccase is the same as for case except for the otherwise clause.

etypecase and ecase are similar to typecase and case, respectively, but signal a non-continuable error rather than returning nil if no clause is selected.

ctypecase and ccase are also similar to typecase and case, but signal a continuable error if no clause is selected.

etypecase *keyform* {(*type* {*form*}*)}*   [*Macro*]

This control construct is similar to typecase, but no explicit otherwise or t clause is permitted. If no clause is satisfied, `etypecase` signals an error with a message constructed from the clauses. It is not permissible to continue from this error. To supply his own error message, the user should use `typecase` with an `otherwise` clause containing a call to `error`. The name of this function stands for "exhaustive type case" or "error-checking type case." For example:

```
(setq x 1/3)
(etypecase x
  (integer x)
  (symbol (symbol-value x)))
Error: The value of X, 1/3, is neither
       an integer nor a symbol.
>
```

`ctypecase` *keyplace* {(*type* {*form*}*)}*   [*Macro*]

This control construct is similar to `typecase`, but no explicit `otherwise` or `t` clause is permitted. The *keyplace* must be a generalized variable reference acceptable to `setf`. If no clause is satisfied, `ctypecase` signals an error with a message constructed from the clauses. Continuing from this error causes `ctypecase` to accept a new value from the user, store it into *keyplace*, and start over, making the type tests again. Subforms of *keyplace* may be evaluated multiple times. The name of this function stands for "continuable exhaustive type case."

`ecase` *keyform* {({({key}*) | key} {*form*}*)}*   [*Macro*]

This control construct is similar to `case`, but no explicit `otherwise` or `t` clause is permitted. If no clause is satisfied, `ecase` signals an error with a message constructed from the clauses. It is not permissible to continue from this error. To supply an error message, the user should use `case` with an `otherwise` clause containing a call to `error`. The name of this function stands for "exhaustive case" or "error-checking case." For example:

```
(setq x 1/3)
(ecase x
  (alpha (foo))
  (omega (bar))
  ((zeta phi) (baz)))
Error: The value of X, 1/3, is not
       ALPHA, OMEGA, ZETA, or PHI.
```

`ccase` *keyform* {(({({key}* } | *key*} {*form*}*}}*   [*Macro*]

This control construct is similar to `case`, but no explicit `otherwise` or t clause is permitted. The *keyplace* must be a generalized variable reference acceptable to `setf`. If no clause is satisfied, `ccase` signals an error with a message constructed from the clauses. Continuing from this error causes `ccase` to accept a new value from the user, store it into *keyplace*, and start over, making the clause tests again. Subforms of keyplace may be evaluated multiple times. The name of this function stands for "continuable exhaustive case."

Rationale: The special forms `etypecase`, `ctypecase`, `ecase`, and `ccase` are included in COMMON LISP, even though a user could write them himself using the other standard facilities provided, because it is likely that many users will want these. COMMON LISP therefore provides a standard consistent set rather than allowing a variety of incompatible dialects to develop.

In addition, experience has shown that some LISP programmers are too lazy to put an appropriate `otherwise` clause into every `case` statement to check for cases they didn't anticipate, even if they would agree that it will probably hurt them later. If an `otherwise` clause can be included very easily by adding one character to the name of the construct, it is perhaps more likely that programmers will take the trouble to do it.

The e versions do nothing more than supply automatically generated `otherwise` clauses, but correct implementation of the c versions requires some care. It is therefore especially important that the c versions be provided by the system so users don't have to puzzle them out on their own. Individual implementations may be able to do a better job of supporting these special forms, using their own idiosyncratic facilities, than can be done using the error-signalling facilities defined by COMMON LISP.

Miscellaneous Features

In this chapter are described various things that don't seem to fit neatly anywhere else in this book: the compiler, the documentation function, debugging aids, environment inquiries (including facilities for calculating and measuring time), and the identity function.

25.1. The Compiler

The compiler is a program that may make code run faster by translating programs into an implementation-dependent form that can be executed more efficiently by the computer. Most of the time you can write programs without worrying about the compiler; compiling a file of code should produce an equivalent but more efficient program. When doing more esoteric things, you may need to think carefully about what happens at "compile time" and what happens at "load time." Then the difference between the syntaxes #. and #, becomes important, and the eval-when construct becomes particularly useful.

Most declarations are not used by the COMMON LISP interpreter; they may be used to give advice to the compiler. The compiler may attempt to check your advice and warn you if it is inconsistent.

Unlike most other LISP dialects, COMMON LISP recognizes special declarations in interpreted code as well as compiled code. This potential source of incompatibility between interpreted and compiled code is thereby *eliminated* in COMMON LISP.

The internal workings of a compiler will of course be highly implementation-dependent. The following functions provide a standard interface to the compiler, however.

compile *name* &optional *definition*   [*Function*]

If *definition* is supplied, it should be a lambda-expression, the interpreted function to be compiled. If it is not supplied, then *name* should be a symbol with a definition that is a lambda-expression; that definition is compiled and the resulting compiled code is put back into the symbol as its function definition.

The definition is compiled and a compiled-function object produced. If *name* is a non-`nil` symbol, then the compiled-function object is installed as the global function definition of the symbol and the symbol is returned. If *name* is `nil`, then the compiled-function object itself is returned. For example:

```
(defun foo ...) ⇒ foo                    ;A function definition.
(compile 'foo) ⇒ foo                     ;Compile it.
        ;Now foo runs faster.
(compile nil '(lambda (a b c) (- (* b b) (* 4 a c))))
    ⇒ a compiled function of three arguments that computes b² − 4ac
```

`compile-file` *input-pathname* &key `:output-file`   [*Function*]

The *input-pathname* must be a valid file specifier, such as a pathname. The defaults for *input-filename* are taken from the variable `*default-pathname-defaults*`. The file should be a LISP source file; its contents are compiled and written as a binary object file.

The `:output-file` argument may be used to specify an output pathname; it defaults in a manner appropriate to the implementation's file system conventions.

`disassemble` *name-or-compiled-function*   [*Function*]

The argument should be either a function object, a lambda-expression, or a symbol with a function definition. If the relevant function is not a compiled function, it is first compiled. In any case, the compiled code is then "reverse-assembled" and printed out in a symbolic format. This is primarily useful for debugging the compiler, but also often of use to the novice who wishes to understand the workings of compiled code.

Implementation note: Implementors are encouraged to make the output readable, preferably with helpful comments.

25.2. Documentation

A simple facility is provided for attaching strings to symbols for the purpose of on-line documentation. Rather than using the property list of the symbol, a separate function `documentation` is provided so that implementations can optimize the storage of documentation strings.

`documentation` *symbol doc-type*

This function returns the documentation string of type *doc-type* for the *symbol*, or `nil` if none exists. Both arguments must be symbols. Some kinds of documentation are provided automatically by certain COMMON LISP constructs if the user writes an optional documentation string within them:

Construct	Documentation Type
defvar	variable
defparameter	variable
defconstant	variable
defun	function
defmacro	function
defstruct	structure
deftype	type
defsetf	setf

In addition, names of special forms may also have `function` documentation. (Macros and special forms are not really functions, of course, but it is convenient to group them with functions for documentation purposes.)

`setf` may be used with `documentation` to update documentation information.

25.3. Debugging Tools

The utilities described in this section are sufficiently complex and sufficiently dependent on the host environment that their complete definition is beyond the scope of this manual. However, they are also sufficiently useful as to warrant mention here. It is expected every implementation will provide some version of these utilities, however clever or however simple.

`trace` *{function-name}* *   [Macro]*
`untrace` *{function-name}* *   [Macro]*

Invoking `trace` with one or more function names (symbols) causes the functions named to be traced. Henceforth, whenever such a function is invoked, information about the call, the arguments passed, and the eventually returned values, if any, will be printed to the stream that is the value of `*trace-output*`. For example:

```
(trace fft gcd string-upcase)
```

If a function call is open-coded (possibly as a result of an `inline` declaration), then such a call may not produce trace output.

Invoking `untrace` with one or more function names will cause those functions not to be traced any more.

Tracing an already traced function, or untracing a function not currently being traced, should produce no harmful effects, but may produce a warning message.

Calling `trace` with no argument forms will return a list of functions currently being traced.

Calling `untrace` with no argument forms will cause all currently traced functions to be no longer traced.

`trace` and `untrace` may also accept additional implementation-dependent argument formats. The format of the trace output is implementation-dependent.

`step` *form*   [*Macro*]

This evaluates *form* and returns what *form* returns. However, the user is allowed to interactively "single-step" through the evaluation of *form*, at least through those evaluation steps that are performed interpretively. The nature of the interaction is implementation-dependent. However, implementations are encouraged to respond to the typing of the character ? by providing help including a list of commands.

`time` *form*   [*Macro*]

This evaluates *form* and returns what *form* returns. However, as a side effect, various timing data and other information are printed to the stream that is the value of `*trace-output*`. The nature and format of the printed information is implementation-dependent. However, implementations are encouraged to provide such information as elapsed real time, machine run time, storage management statistics, and so on.

Compatibility note: This facility is inspired by the INTERLISP facility of the same name. Note that the MacLisp/ZetaLisp function `time` does something else entirely, namely return a quantity indicating relative elapsed real time.

`describe` *object*   [*Function*]

`describe` prints, to the stream in the variable `*standard-output*`, information about the *object*. Sometimes it will describe something that it finds inside something else; such recursive descriptions are indented appropriately. For instance, describe of a symbol will exhibit the symbol's value, its definition, and each of its properties. describe of a floating-point number will exhibit its internal representation in a way that is useful for tracking down round-off errors and the like. The nature and format of the output is implementation-dependent.

describe returns no values (that is, it returns what the expression (values) returns: zero values).

---

inspect *object*   [*Function*]

inspect is an interactive version of describe. The nature of the interaction is implementation-dependent, but the purpose of inspect is to make it easy to wander through a data structure, examining and modifying parts of it. Implementations are encouraged to respond to the typing of the character ? by providing help, including a list of commands.

---

room &optional *x*   [*Function*]

room prints, to the stream in the variable *standard-output*, information about the state of internal storage and its management. This might include descriptions of the amount of memory in use and the degree of memory compaction, possibly broken down by internal data type if that is appropriate. The nature and format of the printed information is implementation-dependent. The intent is to provide information that may help a user to tune his program to a particular implementation.

(room nil) prints out a minimal amount of information. (room t) prints out a maximal amount of information. Simply (room) prints out an intermediate amount of information that is likely to be useful.

---

ed &optional *x*   [*Function*]

If the implementation provides a resident editor, this function should invoke it.

(ed) or (ed nil) simply enters the editor, leaving you in the same state as the last time you were in the editor.

(ed *pathname*) edits the contents of the file specified by *pathname*. The *pathname* may be an actual pathname or a string.

(ed *symbol*) tries to let you edit the text for the function named *symbol*. The means by which the function text is obtained is implementation-dependent; it might involve searching the file system, or pretty-printing resident interpreted code, for example.

dribble &optional *pathname*   [*Function*]

(dribble *pathname*) rebinds *standard-input* and *standard-output*, and/or takes other appropriate action, so as to send a record of the input/output interaction to a file named by *pathname*. The primary purpose of this is to create a readable record of an interactive session.

(dribble) terminates the recording of input and output and closes the dribble file.

apropos *string* &optional *package*   [*Function*]
apropos-list *string* &optional *package*   [*Function*]

(apropos *string*) tries to find all available symbols whose print names contain *string* as a substring. (A symbol may be supplied for the *string*, in which case the print name of the symbol is used.) Whenever apropos finds a symbol, it prints out the symbol's name; in addition, information about the function definition and dynamic value of the symbol, if any, is printed. If *package* is specified and not nil, then only symbols available in that package are examined; otherwise "all" packages are searched, as if by do-all-symbols. Because a symbol may be available by way of more than one inheritance path, apropos may print information about the same symbol more than once. The information is printed to the stream that is the value of *standard-output*. apropos returns no values (that is, it returns what the expression (values) returns: zero values).

apropos-list performs the same search that apropos does, but prints nothing. It returns a list of the symbols whose print names contain *string* as a substring.

25.4. Environment Inquiries

Environment inquiry functions provide information about the environment in which a COMMON LISP program is being executed. They are described here in two categories: first, those dealing with determination and measurement of time, and second, all the others, most of which deal with identification of the computer hardware and software.

25.4.1. Time Functions

Time is represented in three different ways in COMMON LISP: Decoded Time, Universal Time, and Internal Time. The first two representations are used primarily to represent calendar time, and are precise only to one second. Internal Time is used primarily to represent measurements of computer time (such as run time) and is precise to some implementation-dependent fraction of a second, as specified by `internal-time-units-per-second`. Decoded Time format is used only for absolute time indications. Universal Time and Internal Time formats are used for both absolute and relative times.

Decoded Time format represents calendar time as a number of components:

- *Second*: an integer between 0 and 59, inclusive.
- *Minute*: an integer between 0 and 59, inclusive.
- *Hour*: an integer between 0 and 23, inclusive.
- *Date*: an integer between 1 and 31, inclusive (the upper limit actually depends on the month and year, of course).
- *Month*: an integer between 1 and 12, inclusive; 1 means January, 12 means December.
- *Year*: an integer indicating the year A.D. However, if this integer is between 0 and 99, the "obvious" year is used; more precisely, that year is assumed that is equal to the integer modulo 100 and within fifty years of the current year (inclusive backwards and exclusive forwards). Thus, in the year 1978, year 28 is 1928 but year 27 is 2027. (Functions that return time in this format always return a full year number.)

Compatibility note: This is incompatible with the ZETALISP definition in two ways. First, in ZETALISP a year between 0 and 99 always has 1900 added to it. Second, in ZETALISP time functions return the abbreviated year number between 0 and 99 rather than the full year number. The incompatibility is prompted by the imminent arrival of the twenty-first century. Note that (mod *year* 100) always reliably converts a year number to the abbreviated form, while the inverse conversion can be very difficult.

- *Day-of-week*: an integer between 0 and 6, inclusive; 0 means Monday, 1 means Tuesday, and so on; 6 means Sunday.
- *Daylight-saving-time-p*: a flag that, if not `nil`, indicates that daylight saving time is in effect.
- *Time-zone*: an integer specified as the number of hours west of GMT (Greenwich Mean Time). For example, in Massachusetts the time zone is 5, and in California it is 8. Any adjustment for daylight saving time is separate from this.

Universal Time represents time as a single non-negative integer. For relative time purposes, this is a number of seconds. For absolute time, this is the number of seconds since midnight, January 1, 1900 GMT. Thus the time 1 is 00:00:01

(that is, 12:00:01 A.M.) on January 1, 1900 GMT. Similarly, the time 2398291201 corresponds to time 00:00:01 on January 1, 1976 GMT. Recall that the year 1900 was *not* a leap year; for the purposes of COMMON LISP, a year is a leap year if and only if its number is divisible by 4, except that years divisible by 100 are *not* leap years, except that years divisible by 400 *are* leap years. Therefore the year 2000 will be a leap year. (Note that the "leap seconds" that are sporadically inserted by the world's official timekeepers as an additional correction are ignored; COMMON LISP assumes that every day is exactly 86400 seconds long.) Universal Time format is used as a standard time representation within the ARPANET; see reference [8]. Because the COMMON LISP Universal Time representation uses only non-negative integers, times before the base time of midnight, January 1, 1900 GMT cannot be processed by COMMON LISP.

Internal Time also represents time as a single integer, in terms of an implementation-dependent unit. Relative time is measured as a number of these units. Absolute time is relative to an arbitrary time base, typically the time at which the system began running.

get-decoded-time   [*Function*]

The current time is returned in Decoded Time format. Nine values are returned: *second, minute, hour, date, month, year, day-of-week, daylight-saving-time-p,* and *time-zone.*

Compatibility note: In ZETALISP the *time-zone* is not currently returned. Consider, however, the use of COMMON LISP in some mobile vehicle. It is entirely plausible that the time zone might change from time to time.

---

get-universal-time   [*Function*]

The current time of day is returned as a single integer in Universal Time format.

decode-universal-time *universal-time* &optional *time-zone*   [*Function*]

The time specified by *universal-time* in Universal Time format is converted to Decoded Time format. Nine values are returned: *second, minute, hour, date, month, year, day-of-week, daylight-saving-time-p,* and *time-zone.*

Compatibility note: In ZETALISP the *time-zone* is not currently returned. Consider, however, the use of COMMON LISP in some mobile vehicle. It is entirely plausible that the time-zone might change from time to time.

The *time-zone* argument defaults to the current time zone.

---

encode-universal-time *second minute hour date month year*   [*Function*]
                         &optional *time-zone*

The time specified by the given components of Decoded Time format is encoded
into Universal Time format and returned. If you don't specify *time-zone*, it defaults
to the current time zone adjusted for daylight saving time. If you provide *time-zone*
explicitly, no adjustment for daylight saving time is performed.

---

internal-time-units-per-second   [*Constant*]

This value is an integer, the implementation-dependent number of internal time
units in a second. (The internal time unit must be chosen so that one second is an
integral multiple of it.)

Rationale: The reason for allowing the internal time units to be implementation-dependent
is so that get-internal-run-time and get-internal-real-time can execute with minimum overhead. The idea is that it should be very likely that a fixnum will suffice as the
returned value from these functions. This probability can be tuned to the implementation by
trading off the speed of the machine against the word size. Any particular unit will be
inappropriate for some implementations: a microsecond is too long for a very fast machine,
while a much smaller unit would force many implementations to return bignums for most
calls to get-internal-time, rendering that function less useful for accurate timing
measurements.

---

get-internal-run-time   [*Function*]

The current run time is returned as a single integer in Internal Time format. The
precise meaning of this quantity is implementation-dependent; it may measure real
time, run time, CPU cycles, or some other quantity. The intent is that the difference
between the values of two calls to this function be the amount of time between the
two calls during which computational effort was expended on behalf of the executing
program.

---

get-internal-real-time   [*Function*]

The current time is returned as a single integer in Internal Time format. This time
is relative to an arbitrary time base, but the difference between the values of two
calls to this function will be the amount of elapsed real time between the two calls,
measured in the units defined by internal-time-units-per-second.

sleep *seconds*   [*Function*]

(sleep *n*) causes execution to cease and become dormant for approximately *n* seconds of real time, whereupon execution is resumed. The argument may be any non-negative non-complex number. sleep returns nil.

25.4.2. Other Environment Inquiries

For any of the following functions, if no appropriate and relevant result can be produced, nil is returned instead of a string.

Rationale: These inquiry facilities are functions rather than variables against the possibility that a COMMON LISP process might migrate from machine to machine. This need not happen in a distributed environment; consider, for example, dumping a core image file containing a compiler and then shipping it to another site.

---

lisp-implementation-type   [*Function*]

A string is returned that identifies the generic name of the particular COMMON LISP implementation. Examples: "Spice LISP", "Zetalisp".

lisp-implementation-version   [*Function*]

A string is returned that identifies the version of the particular COMMON LISP implementation; this information should be of use to maintainers of the implementation. Examples: "1192", "53.7 with complex numbers", "1746.9A, NEWIO 53, ETHER 5.3".

machine-type   [*Function*]

A string is returned that identifies the generic name of the computer hardware on which COMMON LISP is running. Examples: "DEC PDP-10", "DEC VAX-11/780".

machine-version   [*Function*]

A string is returned that identifies the version of the computer hardware on which COMMON LISP is running. Example: "KL10, microcode 9".

machine-instance   [*Function*]

A string is returned that identifies the particular instance of the computer hardware on which COMMON LISP is running; this might be a local nickname, for example, and/or a serial number. Examples: `"MIT-MC"`, `"CMU GP-VAX"`.

`software-type`   [*Function*]

A string is returned that identifies the generic name of any relevant supporting software. Examples: `"Spice"`, `"TOPS-20"`, `"ITS"`.

`software-version`   [*Function*]

A string is returned that identifies the version of any relevant supporting software; this information should be of use to maintainers of the implementation.

`short-site-name`   [*Function*]
`long-site-name`   [*Function*]

A string is returned that identifies the physical location of the computer hardware. Examples of short names: `"MIT AI Lab"`, `"CMU-CSD"`. Examples of long names:

```
"MIT Artificial Intelligence Laboratory"
"Massachusetts Institute of Technology
Artificial Intelligence Laboratory"
"Carnegie-Mellon University Computer Science Department"
```

See also `user-homedir-pathname`.

`*features*`   [*Variable*]

The value of the variable `*features*` should be a list of symbols that name "features" provided by the implementation. Most such names will be implementation-specific; typically a name for the implementation will be included. One standard feature name is `ieee-floating-point`, which should be present if and only if full IEEE proposed floating-point arithmetic [9] is supported.

The value of this variable is used by the `#+` and `#-` reader syntax.

25.5. Identity Function

This function is occasionally useful as an argument to other functions that require functions as arguments. (Got that?)

`identity` *object*   [*Function*]

The *object* is returned as the value of `identity`.

References

1. ANSI X3J3 Committee. "Draft Proposed American National Standard FORTRAN." *ACM SIGPLAN Notices* **11**, 3 (March 1976).

2. *American National Standard Programming Language FORTRAN*. ANSI X3.9-1978 edition. American National Standards Institute, Inc. (New York, New York, 1978).

3. Brooks, Rodney A.; Gabriel, Richard P.; and Steele, Guy L., Jr. "An Optimizing Compiler for Lexically Scoped LISP." *Proceedings of the 1982 Symposium on Compiler Construction*. ACM SIGPLAN (Boston, June 1982), 261-275. Proceedings published as *ACM SIGPLAN Notices* **17**, 6 (June 1982).

4. Cody, William J., Jr., and Waite, William. *Software Manual for the Elementary Functions*. Prentice-Hall (Englewood Cliffs, New Jersey, 1980).

5. Coonen, Jerome T. "An Implementation Guide to a Proposed Standard for Floating-Point Arithmetic." *Computer* **13**, 1 (Jan. 1980), 68-79. Errata for this paper appeared as [6].

6. Coonen, Jerome T. "Errata for 'An Implementation Guide to a Proposed Standard for Floating-Point Arithmetic'." *Computer* **14**, 3 (March 1981), 62. These are errata for [5].

7. Fateman, Richard J. "Reply to an Editorial." *ACM SIGSAM Bulletin* **25** (March 1973), 9-11.

8. Harrenstien, Kenneth L. *Time Server*. Request for Comments (RFC) 738 (NIC 42218), ARPANET Network Working Group (Oct. 1977). Available from the ARPANET Network Information Center.

9. IEEE Computer Society Standard Committee, Microprocessor Standards Subcommittee, Floating-Point Working Group. "A Proposed Standard for Binary Floating-Point Arithmetic." *Computer* **14**, 3 (March 1981), 51-62.

10. Knuth, Donald E. *The Art of Computer Programming*. Volume 2: *Seminumerical Algorithms*. Addison-Wesley (Reading, Massachusetts, 1969).

11. Marti, J.; Hearn, A.C.; Griss, M.L.; and Griss, C. "Standard LISP Report." *SIGPLAN Notices* **14**, 10 (Oct. 1979), 48-68.

12. Moon, David. *MacLISP Reference Manual, Revision 0*. M.I.T. Project MAC (Cambridge, Massachusetts, April 1974).

13. Moon, David; Stallman, Richard; and Weinreb, Daniel. *LISP Machine Manual, Fifth Edition*. MIT Artificial Intelligence Lab. (Cambridge, Massachusetts, January 1983).

14. Penfield, Paul, Jr. "Principal Values and Branch Cuts in Complex APL." *APL 81 Conference Proceedings*. ACM SIGAPL (San Francisco, Sept. 1981), 248-256. Proceedings published as *APL Quote Quad* **12**, 1 (September 1981).

15. Pitman, Kent M. *The Revised MacLISP Manual*. MIT/LCR/TR 295, MIT Lab. for Computer Science (Cambridge, Massachusetts, May 1983).

16. The Utah Symbolic Computation Group. *The Portable Standard LISP Users Manual*. Tech. Rept. TR-10, Department of Computer Science, University of Utah (Salt Lake City, Jan. 1982).

17. Reiser, John F. *Analysis of Additive Random Number Generators*. Tech. Rept. STAN-CS-77-601, Stanford University Computer Science Department (March 1977).

18. Steele, Guy Lewis Jr., and Sussman, Gerald Jay. *The Revised Report on SCHEME: A Dialect of LISP*. AI Memo 452, MIT Artificial Intelligence Lab. (Cambridge, Massachusetts, Jan. 1978).

19. Suzuki, Norihisa. "Analysis of Pointer 'Rotation'." *Comm. ACM* **25**, 5 (May 1982), 330-335.

20. Teitelman, Warren, et al. *InterLISP Reference Manual*. Xerox Palo Alto Research Center (Palo Alto, California, 1978). Third revision.

21. Weinreb, Daniel, and Moon, David. *LISP Machine Manual, Fourth Edition*. MIT Artificial Intelligence Lab. (Cambridge, Massachusetts, July 1981).

22. White, Jon L. "NIL: A Perspective." *Proceedings of the 1979 MACSYMA Users' Conference*. MIT Laboratory for Computer Science (Cambridge, Massachusetts, June 1979).

Index

ORDERING INFORMATION

To order additional copies of this book, fill in and mail this form or call the toll-free telephone number below. Orders under $50 must be prepaid by check or charge card; postage and handling are free on prepaid orders. There is a 10 percent discount on orders of two or more copies.

Digital Press/Order Processing
Digital Equipment Corporation
12A Esquire Road
Billerica, MA 01862

QTY.	TITLE	ORDER NO.	PRICE*	TOTAL
	Steele, COMMON LISP	EY-00031-DP	$30.00	

Total	
Discount	
Add state sales tax	
Total remitted	

METHOD OF PAYMENT

_____ Check included (Make checks   _____ MasterCard/Visa

payable to Digital Equipment   Charge Card Acc't No. _____

Corporation)   Expiration Date _____

_____ Purchase order (Please attach)   Authorized Signature _____

Name _____   Phone _____

Address _____

City _____ State _____ Zip _____

TOLL-FREE ORDER NUMBER

To order books by MasterCard or VISA, call 1-800-343-8321. In Massachusetts, call 1-617-663-4152. Phone lines are open from 8:00 A.M. to 4:00 P.M., Eastern time.

*Price and terms quoted are U.S. only and are subject to change without notice. For prices outside the U.S., contact the nearest office of Educational Services, Digital Equipment Corporation.